ESSENTIAL BUSINESS LAW

Paul Hilder

Collins Educational

An imprint of HarperCollinsPublishers

Also in the HarperCollins Essential Series

Essential Accountancy and Finance, Bijon Kar

Essential Business Studies, Stephen Barnes

Essential GCSE Business Studies, Renée Huggett

Essential Government and Politics, Jim Cordell

Essential Information Technology, Tony Berk

Essential Marketing, Tony Proctor

Essential Practical Psychology, Keith Maglennon

Essential Psychology, G.C. Davenport

Essential Research Skills, Val Bailey *et al.*

Published in 1995 by Collins Educational
An imprint of HarperCollins*Publishers*
77–85 Fulham Palace Road
Hammersmith
London W6 8JB

ISBN 0-00-322369-8

British Library Cataloguing-in-publication data
A catalogue record for this book is available from the British Library

Cover design Ridgeway Associates
Printed in Great Britain by Scotprint, Musselburgh

Contents

Acknowledgements

I would like to thank Helen, Stefan and Dominic for their support, love and encouragement. Thanks also to Amanda Binnersley for her endless dedication and knowledge, and to Dave Gair for his talented input.

The publishers and author would like to thank Pitman Publishing for permission to reproduce Figure 10.4 from D. Keenan and S. Riches, *Business Law*, 2nd edition, 1990, on page 261.

① How to use this book

This aim of this book is to enable you to learn the practical skills necessary to understand, and to be able to apply, the law relating to business. It is written in simple English with you, the student, in mind. It is laid out clearly, and uses visual aids to help you assimilate and retain information.

Illustrations

The study of law involves learning, understanding and remembering many cases, so any technique that makes this easier will be valuable. The old saying 'a picture is worth a thousand words' has been given educational credibility by the use of word/picture association, particularly in language teaching. I believe that this method is particularly applicable to the learning of law cases. So, where a case, through its name or by its circumstances, lends itself to graphical representation, a picture is often included. Here is an example.

***Everet v. Williams* (1725)**

Two highwaymen formed a partnership to commit crime. A dispute arose about the division of the spoils and a court action was commenced.

 COURT HELD
The claim was dismissed because the partnership was illegal. The partners were sentenced to be hanged!

Signs are also used to help you find different features that occur frequently throughout the book.

 This sign will indicate an activity for you to do. This might be some research, a set of questions, a review process or some other activity that will help you better absorb the material.

 This sign (VC = vital case) will appear next to any case that it is vital that you both know and understand in order to appreciate a particular piece or rule of law. I recommend that you take notes on these cases and index them in a way that makes it easy for you to find them when you need them.

 This sign will be used where the result of a case includes an equitable remedy. It is very important that you

► **Equitable remedies** are remedies that a court may grant to a person bringing a court action. Equity has evolved to make the law more fair and reasonable, and people who seek an equitable remedy must have acted fairly themselves. See Chapter 9 for examples of equitable remedies.

► **Prima facie** – at first appearance.

► **Simple contract** – an informal contract that can be made orally, in writing, or can be implied by conduct, for example, bidding at an auction.

appreciate, learn and remember the different **equitable remedies**, so look out for this sign to help you to do just that.

 This sign will apear wherever the result of a court case is given.

The aims and objectives of each chapter will be specified at the beginning of the chapter. At the end of the chapter, the main points that you should have learnt will be restated in a chapter summary box.

Terminology

When studying law, we must use and understand the meaning of some Latin phrases. In this book I have only used Latin where it is absolutely necessary. Where a Latin term is first used a translation will be given.

Other legal terminology will also be explained in a similar way. Where sections are quoted from an Act they will appear in a headed box. For example:

Sale of Goods Act 1979, s. 3

(2) Where necessaries are sold and delivered to a person who by reason of mental incapacity or drunkenness is incompetent to contract, he must pay a reasonable price for them.
(3) ... necessaries means goods suitable to the condition in life of the person concerned and to his actual requirements at the time of sale and delivery.

The appendices contain a guide on how to find fuller reports of cases, for students who have access to a law library. However, most of the cases in this book have been reported fully enough to satisfy the needs of all students at this level.

Note that any case that is quoted in this book has been subject to the jurisdiction of the British courts. They may involve foreign companies or individuals but the court action has taken place here.

THE STUDY OF LAW

Traditionally, law has been an extremely difficult subject to study. The use of Latin, coupled with the closed nature of the legal professions, has meant that traditional legal text books were often aimed at those with some prior knowledge or understanding of the subject. Those who had neither simply had to get on with it. Further, there has been a vested interest, on the part of those who have written the material (who are invariably members of the legal profession) in maintaining the status quo. After all, they themselves have been a product of the system!

Reform

You have chosen a good time to begin (or continue) your legal studies. The law is now evolving to become much more user-friendly. Reform, following a difficult decade, has been forced upon the English legal system. Several recent serious **miscarriages of justice**, including the Guildford Four, the Birmingham Six, the Taylor sisters and the Eddy Browning case, have all 'coloured' the public's view of the English legal system. Further, the government has decided to cut the amount of money made available to citizens to obtain legal support and legal representation in court. These and other factors have led the Law Society to realize that the profession must evolve and reforms are planned.

One likely outcome is a new legal qualification, set below that of a solicitor, and probably to be called a para-legal. The development of the position of para-legal is evidenced by the new level of higher education courses, the HND Legal Studies. These courses are essentially 'skills' based and are a real departure from the traditional, totally academic law degree courses. At the end of an HND course a diplomate should be able to undertake all the routine tasks normally completed by a solicitor, for example, drafting contracts and wills, attending minor court cases, advising clients at police stations and conveyancing.

▶ A miscarriage of justice may be said to have taken place when someone who is charged with an offence is either innocent of the offence but found guilty or guilty but found innocent. In a recent notorious case, Eddy Browning was released after a successful appeal to the Court of Appeal. He had spent six years in prison after being convicted of murdering Mrs Wilkes, a pregnant mother, on the hard shoulder of a motorway.

▶ The Law Society is the professional body for solicitors in England and Wales. It was founded in 1831 and is responsible for the admission, training, examination, conduct and discipline of solicitors. (See Chapter 5 for other suggested reforms of the legal system.)

Outside college

The 'great debate' about the reform of the legal system has led to a proliferation of media coverage in both the television and newspapers. Many of the programmes and articles have been of great interest to the student of law. Watch out in the listings for any legal issues relevant to your studies in the following television and radio programmes.

Street Legal
Nation
Newsnight
World in Action
First Tuesday
Cutting Edge
Rough Justice
Trial and Error
Law in Action (Radio 4)

Remember that the law, especially that relating to the business environment, can change daily. The result of a court judgment can affect the way contracts will be interpreted from that day forward. Therefore, it is vital that you keep a watch on the legal news. It is expensive and hard to find the time to take and read a broadsheet daily paper. It is far better to read a serious Sunday paper, which will have a résumé of all the important legal rulings that have occurred in the previous week.

Assignments

Most courses with an element of law in them will place the student in the position of legal adviser. In order to pass a course you must normally have acquired enough legal knowledge, in a given area, to be able to solve a contractual problem, or to act as an adviser to a fictional managing director, who requires information about a specific legal problem.

The art of writing good legal reports, assignments or essays is to try and spot the legal case or piece of legislation that has been the basis for the setting of the assignment. The great thing about law is that your lecturer or tutor cannot make up the rules or cases. He or she must work with the set of rules and laws that already exist.

Each aspect of an assignment should be divided into separate problem areas. Normally an assignment might contain a series of events, which should be split up and taken one at a time. Each separate problem must be addressed individually and then the whole picture should be drawn together at the conclusion of the assignment.

Do I need to remember every case?

Nobody can be expected to remember the details of every case. The most important thing to remember from each case is the principle of law that the case established. In order to do well in an examination you must be able to name the main cases and legislation that apply to a particular topic. Where there is a choice of cases stating the same legal point, use the one that you will remember best. Try using word/picture association. Either use the illustrations in the book or think up a visual image of your own that will help you to remember the name or circumstances of a case.

Note-taking

If your course involves attending lectures and taking notes, then make sure that you are prepared beforehand. Do not try to write down every word that the lecturer says. Just try to get down the sense of what is being said in a clear and concise manner. Make a separate alphabetical index of all the cases that are mentioned in your notes. You must review your notes. If you just attend a lecture and pay no attention to your notes until three months later, when you come to look at them again they will make no sense to you.

After each lecture, review your notes the same day, preferably with a colleague. A good method of review to use is the 'traffic light' method. Make sure that you understand what you have written down. Add things if it helps to make your notes clearer. Use a red (or pink) highlighter pen to mark anything that doesn't make sense, or where you have missed some information, suspect that you have got it wrong or you just don't understand the topic. At the next lecture or seminar you can ask your tutor for clarification or you can discuss the problem with your fellow students. Mark items in amber (or yellow) that you feel you understand, but where you need to look up further information or cases. Use green to highlight the areas that you are particularly comfortable with, so you will be able to comment on these when called upon to speak in a workshop or seminar.

A planned and prepared attitude to lectures is absolutely necessary. Educationalists now accept that lectures play a minor role in the acquisition of information. It is widely agreed that the attention span of an average student, in a lecture, is twenty minutes. Therefore you must get as much information as you can while you are concentrating on the subject.

The graph in the margin shows that you are far more likely to acquire knowledge by taking part in an active learning exercise. This is based on the simple principle of: **I hear, I forget; I see, I remember; I do, I understand**.

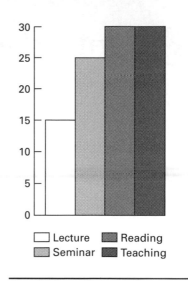

Acquisition of knowledge

Other methods of study

Where once students were encouraged to compete against each other, now the approach is for students to work together. Try to find a few fellow students with whom you can work throughout the course. I am not suggesting that you copy somebody else or that you all submit the same answers or assignments, but that you should discuss the legal problem together and agree on what you feel the correct solution is. It is very easy to think that you are the only person who doesn't understand a particular topic. What you will find is that there will be some areas that you understand and others don't understand, and vice versa.

On the BTEC BND/C GNVQ Level 3 and HND/C (soon to be the GNVQ Level 4) courses, many assignments are group based, and you will be required to work together to produce an assignment or a presentation. This is aimed at developing problem-solving people, who can work with others and who possess good communication skills. The legal profession has recognized that it needs more people who can work together to produce solutions, as opposed to the traditional law graduate who may have been given a thorough academic grounding, but has no real practical skills.

Retrieving information

This book features four ways to retrieve information: through the contents page, the table of statutes, the table of cases and the index. In the table of statutes, all Acts are listed alphabetically, and sections listed numerically below the main Act headings, with the page numbers of where they appear in the book. The table of cases lists all cases alphabetically, with page numbers. Through the index you can locate all the sections and subsections of the book, together with key topics and definitions of the important terms. The contents page lists all major sections.

② Introduction to law

Chapter objectives

By the end of this chapter you should be able to:

▌ define criminal law and understand the classification of crimes

▌ recognize the level of proof required to convict in a criminal case

▌ appreciate the relationship between the state and the citizen

▌ define civil law

▌ identify the areas of law covered in contract, i.e. trusts, property, family and succession law

▌ define the torts of negligence, nuisance and trespass

▌ recognize the overlap between civil and criminal law

▌ define public law, including constitutional and administrative law.

DEFINITIONS

This chapter is designed to help you towards a clear definition of the law. We would all probably know if we had broken a law, yet most of us would struggle to arrive at a satisfactory explanation of what a law is. A useful starting point is to understand the distinction between two major branches of the law relating to England and Wales: criminal law and civil law.

▶ The law in Scotland is different from that in England and Wales. For example, a Scottish criminal court can return a verdict of 'not proven', which rests between 'guilty' and 'not guilty'. Many independent observers feel that Scottish law is better and more efficient.

CRIMINAL LAW

Criminal law affects and governs us all. We have no choice about whether we agree to abide by or to reject a criminal law: it applies to us whether we choose to obey it or not. Criminal law controls the relationship between the state and the citizen. As a society evolves, the state tends to play a greater role in the lives of its citizens. It will make certain actions criminal – which actions these are will vary over time and will be different for different states. If a citizen breaks a criminal law he or she (if caught) can expect to be punished by the state after appearing and being convicted in a court.

Clearly, in England and Wales we consider the right to life to be very important. Therefore murder is, and probably always has been, the most serious offence under our criminal law (apart from **treason**, which is not a common offence). We hold the right to life so dear that even when a police officer shoots and kills an armed robber, in order to save his or her own or another's life, the officer is generally forced to stand trial in order to satisfy the state that the act was within the law.

In some other countries, the state uses murder and execution as a political weapon. For instance, President Galtieri, of Argentina, used his police force to murder thousands of people who were against his policies. What he did was probably against Argentinian law, but, because he was acting as the state, the law wasn't enforced. Comparing England and Wales with Galtieri's Argentina might give us reason to suggest that a society cannot be considered to be developed and democratic if it doesn't have a system of rules and regulations that apply to every citizen, regardless of status. The principle behind this system is known as the '**rule of law**'.

As our society has developed so either the criminal law has been added to or acts that were previously considered criminal have become **decriminalized**. For example, throughout the twentieth century there have been many Acts that have regulated the employment of children, culminating in the Children Act 1989. These Acts have, among other things, made it criminal to breach the employment regulations relating to children, to sell tobacco to children and to mistreat children. Yet in the nineteenth century the Industrial Revolution was fuelled by a large child labour force. This is a clear indication of how the criminal law consists only of the actions that are prohibited by a state at any one given time.

Prior to the Suicide Act 1961, it was a criminal offence to attempt to commit suicide. Now it is not an offence and the state attempts to help where previously it sought to punish.

All of the following are currently criminal offences:

- soliciting in a public place for the purposes of prostitution
- possession of cocaine
- supplying arms to Iraq
- insider dealing

This list illustrates the problems that face the lawmakers of any society. Members of the British government have recently been brought before the Scott Inquiry to explain their decision to prosecute the directors of an engineering company for supplying arms to Iraq. Previously, firms had been encouraged to supply arms to Iraq when Iraq was at war with the much-hated Iran. Today's friend may be tomorrow's enemy.

Currently, euthanasia and the possession of certain controlled drugs are criminal offences in England and Wales. The Netherlands, however, has decriminalized euthanasia and the possession of so-called soft drugs, such as cannabis. It has been suggested that in the future English law may follow a similar route.

The British government, in the Criminal Justice and Public Order

► **Treason** – conduct comprising a breach of allegiance owed to the sovereign or the state. This is a very old offence, dating back to before the Treason Act 1351. It includes: plotting the death or serious injury of the sovereign, or his or her spouse or heir; waging war against the sovereign in his or her realm; and giving aid to the sovereign's enemies.

► **Rule of law** – every citizen is equal under the law and all will have the same access to and treatment by the courts.

► **Decriminalize** – to remove an action from the legal category of criminal offence. This is normally achieved by the introduction of a new Act of Parliament, which amends or repeals a previous Act.

► You could probably list ten offences that you would expect all developed societies to consider criminal. These might include murder, rape, robbery, burglary, theft and arson.

Act 1994 (CJAPOA94), has recently created criminal offences to deal with the perceived problems of 'raves' and 'hunt saboteurs'. Prior to this Act, it was considered the right of every citizen to enter upon any land to demonstrate, or to gather to play music. Now, provided the provisions of the Act are satisfied, any person who fails to leave the scene of a rave when required to do so by the police, or returns to the place within seven days, will be liable to three months imprisonment or a fine, or both (CJAPOA94, Section 63(6)). A 'hunt saboteur' or other person who trespasses on to any land, in the open air, with the intention of intimidating, disrupting or obstructing any lawful activity will commit the offence of aggravated trespass (Section 68(1)). Aggravated trespass attracts the same penalties as Section 63(6).

Terminology of criminal law

In the criminal justice system, the terminology used in the courts reflects the nature of the court action. In England and Wales the case is brought on behalf of the state, represented by the Crown Prosecution Service, against the accused, who may be convicted or acquitted. If the state convinces a court **beyond all reasonable doubt** that a person has committed a crime, then that person will be convicted of that offence and will be punished by the court. The court could impose a sentence ranging from a conditional discharge to life imprisonment, depending upon the nature of the crime committed.

▶ **Beyond all reasonable doubt** – the prosecution must prove this in order to secure a conviction.

(ACT) Criminal case study

Search through a daily newspaper and select a crime that is currently in the news. Establish the facts of the case and research in a criminal law book (*Moriarty's Police Law* is an excellent reference text) the exact wording of the charge. Which law has been broken? Which Act of Parliament prohibited the particular action? Follow the case until it finishes and record the details of the sentence or acquittal. Why was that particular sentence given or why was the accused not convicted? What was the maximum sentence that could have been given? In what type of court did the hearing take place? Complete your case study in a report format, filling no more than two sides of A4 paper, with sections corresponding to each question asked above.

CIVIL LAW

If criminal law is concerned with the relationship between the state and the individual, then civil law is concerned with relationships between individuals. These relationships are generally entered into freely, though some are imposed by law. An agreement to purchase a car is a good example of an agreement freely entered into, while the duty not to annoy a neighbour by making lots of noise is imposed by civil law. Traditionally, the role of the state was to ensure that there was a mechanism in place for settling disputes, if people could not reach agreement. This mechanism has been the courts.

Under the classification of civil law we must include the law of **tort**, contract, trusts, property, succession, mercantile law and the majority of family law. We shall meet certain torts later on in this book, but to give an idea of the workings of the different types of torts I have included some simple outline examples here.

Tort of negligence

Negligence is an expanding area of the law of tort concerned with imposing a standard of behaviour upon all citizens. When one person fails to maintain those standards and another person is injured or suffers loss because of this, the second person may be successful in obtaining damages under the tort of negligence. However, they must prove the following three factors:

1 that the person who was allegedly negligent owed the other a 'duty of care';
2 that the duty of care was breached;
3 that the plaintiff suffered as a result of the breach.

A duty of care will exist where a **plaintiff** is able to prove that a **defendant** should have had the plaintiff in his or her contemplation, when committing the act in question. Therefore, the defendant should have realized that there was a possibility of harm being caused to the plaintiff.

(ACT) Investigate a driver's duty of care with regard to the passengers in his or her car. If the driver drives recklessly or negligently, causing an accident in which a passenger in the car is injured, will the passenger be able to establish a duty of care? You will find Chapter 19 helpful in answering this question.

Tort of nuisance

Private nuisance

This tort concerns interference with your right to enjoy your land. It has two elements: public and private. Private nuisance is concerned with one person making a complaint about another person's activities, where those activities are unreasonably affecting the first person's reasonable use or enjoyment of his or her land. The activity complained of must be a regular occurrence.

A one-off event, such as a party, would not normally constitute a nuisance (in law!). Normally the activities must be an associated and continuing state of affairs. However, a temporary interference can be actionable if it is sufficiently grave and serious. The following case is a good example of private nuisance.

▶ **Tort** – from the French, meaning 'wrong', is the area of law that covers a breach of a right or duty imposed by the law. A wronged person can obtain damages in a civil court for an act or omission that has caused him or her damage.

▶ For example, a person who had been wrongly administered drugs in a hospital could sue the doctor or health authority, in the tort of negligence, for damages to compensate for any injury sustained. In some medical negligence cases, awards of damages have amounted to millions of pounds.

▶ **Plaintiff** – the person who sues or commences an action in a civil court.
▶ **Defendant** – the person alleged to be at fault in a civil trial or the person being prosecuted in a criminal trial.

▶ See Chapter 19 for more on the duty of care.

▶ Land, in this context, includes water. An action was brought under private nuisance against the South West Water Company by the owner of a West Country beach, who claimed damages for the depositing of raw sewage at sea, close enough to the beach to affect the quality of the bathing water.

► In *Mantana v. National Provincial Bank Ltd* (1936) 2 All ER 633, the defendants were held to be liable for the noise, dust and disruption caused by their temporary building work to the plaintiff's business.

► **Injunction** – an order of the court, addressed to a named person, prohibiting that person from continuing to perform a certain act (prohibitory injunction) or ordering that person to carry out a certain act (mandatory injunction).

► Historically, the tort of public nuisance covered four categories: public decency, public health, public safety and public convenience. Public health is now largely covered by legislation.

Christie v. Davey (1893) 1 Ch 316 High Court

 The plaintiff and the defendant lived next door to each other. The plaintiff gave music lessons in her house, the noise of which annoyed the defendant. The defendant wrote abusive letters to the plaintiff, asking for the lessons to be stopped. When the lessons continued, he started banging on a party wall, beating trays and shouting on each occasion that the lessons were in progress, solely to annoy the plaintiff.

COURT HELD
*The giving of music lessons was not an unreasonable use of the house, but the noise wilfully created by the defendant constituted a nuisance. The plaintiff obtained an **injunction** to restrain the defendant from making any further noise.*

Public nuisance

This tort is concerned with any acts or omissions that materially affect the reasonable comfort and convenience of life, either of the public as a whole, or a particular section of it, as well as the general health, safety and well-being of the public.

Normally public nuisance is a criminal offence, an example being a quarry company blasting stones and debris all over a particular neighbourhood. However, an individual can take legal action if he or she suffers special damage, over and above the damage suffered by the rest of the population. The following case is a good example.

Castle v. St Augustine's Links (1922) 38 TLR 615

The defendant was a taxi driver who had the misfortune to be driving his car along a road adjacent to a golf course when a golfer drove off the thirteenth tee. The shot was wayward and it smashed the taxi windscreen, causing the plaintiff to lose an eye. There was evidence to show that balls frequently landed in the road from the thirteenth tee.

 COURT HELD
The situation of the tee made it a public nuisance, so the plaintiff was able to recover for his special damages.

Tort of trespass

The tort of trespass is concerned with the direct infringement of an individual's rights. Where this direct infringement occurs, a person can commence an action *per se*, without proof of any damage. For example, wandering in a farmer's field (where there is no public right of way) is an act of trespass, for which a farmer could sue.

► *Per se* – in itself.

Trespass to land

This tort involves direct interference with a person's possession and enjoyment of his or her land. This could be a trespass on to land; a refusal to leave after initially being invited on to land; the placing of items on land; tunnelling underneath land; or flying over it so as to interfere with the buildings or structures on it.

Trespass to the person

This is where the term 'assault and battery' originates. Trespass to the person can be split into three different parts – assault, battery and **false imprisonment**. Assault is the putting of another in fear of the imminent application of force upon his or her person. The person threatening the assault must be capable of immediately carrying out the threat. Any qualification of the threat will render the tort invalid. Battery is the actual application of force to another. This is shown in the following case.

► **False imprisonment** occurs when a person is deprived of his or her total freedom of movement. The restraint may be actual or may be caused by someone using threats of force to restrict another's freedom of movement.

Tuberville v. Savage (1669) 1 Mod Rep. 3

This case concerned a dispute between two individuals. One said to the other, putting his hand on his sword, 'If it were not **Assize** time, I would not take such language from you.' The defendant brought an action claiming assault.

COURT HELD
As it was Assize time there was no imminent threat of force, therefore there was no assault.

► **Assize** Courts – prior to the Courts Act 1971, England and Wales were divided into six circuits, which were toured by visiting judges from the Queen's Bench Division three or four times a year. The period of each visit was known as 'Assize time'. The courts had the power to judge both civil and criminal cases. (For an explanation of the different courts and their structure, see Chapter 4.)

Trespass to goods

This tort involves the intentional, direct and unlawful interference with goods in the possession of another. Generally the interference must be direct and forcible, but a mere touching has been held to be enough. The tort of trespass can include theft, criminal damage, or even just the moving or hiding of another's goods. The associated tort of conversion deals with a person who has obtained possession of goods, which is totally inconsistent with the rights of the actual owner of the goods. Probably the best example of this tort is where a person has bought stolen goods, knowing or suspecting them to be stolen. However, it is possible to be in breach of this tort, even when the goods have been innocently obtained. The original owner can sue under this tort and if successful the court can order the return of the goods.

 With three or four of your colleagues discuss an incident that has happened to you or to someone that you know. Use the text so far in this chapter to establish what kind of law might have been broken. It could have been a tort, a crime or a motoring offence, or even all three at the same time.

Law of contract

This will be dealt with in detail in Chapters 9 to 14 of this book. The law of contract is concerned with legally enforceable agreements made between two or more persons. The role of the courts is to **arbitrate** when disputes arise between contracting parties.

▶ **Arbitrate** – help to settle.

Law of trusts

A trust describes a relationship whereby a trustee is given the power to hold property in trust on behalf of another, called a beneficiary. The trustee is considered to be the legal owner of the property. There may be several trustees and several beneficiaries in any one trust. The law of trusts regulates the behaviour of the respective parties in a trust.

Law of property

This section of law relates to the different rights arising out of the ownership or possession of property. Property can be defined as anything that can be owned. The following fall into this category:

- land
- goods
- **intellectual property**
- **goodwill**
- debts

▶ **Intellectual property** – a creative work, such as a computer program, to which the owner or maker has legal rights.

▶ **Goodwill** – the established customer base and reputation of a business.

The ownership and possession of property belonging to a company will be discussed in Chapter 8. However, at this introductory stage, it is useful to draw the distinction between possession and ownership. A person who has ownership of an item of property has the greatest rights possible to that property in law. If I decided to set fire to my car and I was the sole owner, and no other person would be put in danger, or suffer any loss by my actions, then I would be free to do so. However, if I caused any injury or damage by my actions I would be liable for my actions. If the car had been lent to me and I had possession of it but not ownership, then I would not be free to burn it.

Family law

Family law is concerned, naturally enough, with all matters relating to the family. This includes, among other areas, marriage, divorce and the custody, maintenance and welfare of children.

Law of succession

The law of succession deals with all matters relating to the distribution of property after death. Succession is more commonly known as 'probate', and includes all the laws governing the interpretation of wills and legislating for when people die **intestate**.

► **Intestate** – describing a person who dies without making a will.

Terminology of civil law

In a civil court the person who is seeking the help of the court is called the plaintiff. The process is called commencing an action or suing. The other party is called the defendant. If the plaintiff is successful in proving, on a **balance of probabilities**, that he or she has a valid claim then the court will award judgment in the plaintiff's favour. The court will then aim to compensate the plaintiff by awarding any one of a number of remedies from damages to an injunction.

► **Balance of probabilities** – the burden of proof is less demanding in a civil action than in a criminal action. It merely has to be proved that it was probably as the plaintiff stated.

FURTHER CLASSIFICATION

This simple distinction between civil and criminal law has merely been used to try to illustrate the major differences. The reality is that many wrongful acts will, of course, be criminal acts and **tortious acts** at one and the same time.

Whether an act is criminal or tortious often depends on the viewpoint from which you are looking at an action. If Smith was punched in the eye by Jones, causing Smith to have a black eye, Jones would have committed the offence of assault, occasioning actual bodily harm, contrary to Offences against the Person Act 1861, s. 47. The state would seek to punish Jones by having him convicted in court and he would receive a suitable sentence. The courts have limited powers to award compensation to Smith under the Powers of the Criminal Courts Act 1973, s. 35. A court is under a statutory duty to give reasons for not making such an award in an appropriate case. Such an award can be imposed as a sentence in its own right.

► **Tortious act** – a wrongful act, constituting or amounting to the breach of a specific tort.

► The Courts and Legal Services Act 1990 imposes an award limit of £5,000 for any one offence, for cases tried in a magistrates' court. The Crown Court has no limit.

To obtain proper damages to compensate for the injuries suffered and any other financial loss, Smith would have to sue Jones in the tort of trespass to the person. The conviction in the criminal court would be excellent evidence for the action in the civil court.

Having outlined criminal law and the major areas of civil law, we shall now look to see how they fit into the wider picture of our legal system. The legal system is generally split into two sections. Civil law is one of them; the other is public law. As we saw above, civil law deals with such aspects of relationships between individuals that are of no direct concern to the state. Public law contains those areas of law that govern the relationship between the state and its citizens. It includes criminal law (discussed above), constitutional law and administrative law.

► Civil law is also described as private law.

Constitutional law

Constitutional law is concerned with the relationships between the different players in our system of government – the monarch, parliament and its make-up and procedures, the composition of local government, and the rights and duties of citizens. This area of law has been much discussed in recent years, with issues such as reform of the House of Lords and the Maastricht Treaty featuring greatly in political discussion.

Administrative law

The growth of the welfare state, coupled with an increase in the numbers of unemployed people, has ensured that this area of law has grown steadily since the Second World War. Because of these factors, more citizens have become directly involved with the government agencies, notably the Department of Social Security (DSS). Administrative law has grown to provide a method of dispute settlement between aggrieved citizens and government agencies.

 Now that you have completed this chapter look back at the chapter objectives set out at the beginning. Can you now do all the things that these objectives suggest? If not, look again at the relevant sections of the chapter.

CHAPTER SUMMARY

1 Criminal law governs the relationship between the state and the citizen. The state determines which acts to prohibit, and at any time an act may be criminalized or decriminalized.
2 In order to secure a criminal conviction the prosecution must prove beyond all reasonable doubt that the defendant has committed the offence. The state seeks to punish a person who commits a crime by imposing one of a range of sentences.
3 Civil law is concerned with relationships between individuals, most of which are entered into freely, though some are imposed by law. The courts seek to compensate an injured party, not to punish the party at fault, by awarding damages.
4 Civil law includes the following areas of law: tort, contract, trusts, property, succession, mercantile law and family law.
5 Different torts exist to enable people to recover damages for different wrongs that they have suffered. These torts include negligence, nuisance and trespass.
6 In a civil court the plaintiff must prove, on a balance of probabilities, that the facts were as the plaintiff presented them and, therefore, that he or she has a valid claim.
7 Public law covers the whole relationship between a state and its citizens. It includes criminal law, constitutional law and administrative law.

3 Sources of law

Chapter objectives

By the end of this chapter you should be able to:

▌ understand the reasons for the historical development of the British legal system and recognize the beginnings of our present legal system

▌ recognize the integral parts of the British political system

▌ define equity, and understand the reasons for its growth and development

▌ understand the following terms: simple majority; bi-cameral; convention; public Bills; private members' Bills; standing committees; delegated legislation; judicial review; statutory interpretation

▌ explain the passage of a Bill through the Houses of Parliament

▌ appreciate the role of the judiciary in the interpretation of statutes and understand the different rules applied by them

▌ understand judicial precedent and appreciate the difference between *ratio decidendi* and *obiter dicta*. Acknowledge the role of the European Community in the British legal system.

A HISTORY OF THE LEGAL SYSTEM

In order to understand the complexities of the modern English legal system all students must have a basic knowledge of its historical development. I propose to deal with around 900 years of development in a few paragraphs. A business law student does not need to get bogged down in Latin and history, but he or she must know enough to understand 'common law' and 'equity'.

1066 and all that

Prior to the Norman Conquest, the English system of justice was essentially local, administered by the local landowners. The Normans brought with them the first centralized, national government and out of this came a national system of justice. The Domesday Book was a record made of the conquered country. It was an amazing achievement that is without parallel in European

▶ EEC, EC or EU? There is no simple answer to this question. The European Economic Community (EEC) came into being on 1 January 1958. Britain joined the EEC on 22 January 1972. The Treaty on European Union was signed at Maastricht on 7 February 1992 and from that time onwards the EEC was to become known as the European Community (EC), a term that was already in wide use. The Treaty on European Unity, which has become known as the Maastricht Treaty, also established the European Union (EU). The EU consists of the EC; the European Coal and Steel Community; the European Atomic Energy Community; the Common Foreign and Security Policy; the Co-operation on Justice and Home Affairs. We are now all citizens of the EU, despite the fact that it is not yet fully in existence. For legal purposes all three titles may be used. This is because it is possible that the law or directive being quoted could have come from any one of the three different groupings, EEC, EC or EU. While it may seem confusing, be prepared to see all three titles used in this and other text books.

history. One of the aims of this exercise was to enable the rulers of England to set up a system of courts to administer the same laws throughout the country. This is the origin of the term common law, i.e. law that is common to the whole country.

First, the **Curia Regis** was formed. It had both lawmaking and judicial powers. The *Curia Regis* is the forerunner of parliament and our modern system of courts. It was composed of the king, major landowners and officials. It met in full only once a year, but lesser groupings met regularly to solve disputes, generally over questions of land.

► *Curia Regis* – King's Council, the first royal court.

From the *Curia Regis*, judges were dispatched to all parts of the country to try cases originally relating to land, but later relating to crime as well. These were the forerunners of the Assize judges mentioned in Chapter 2. Upon returning to London, where they were based, the judges discussed their cases and began to establish a uniform pattern of law throughout the country, by selecting the best of the customary laws they had encountered. Out of this practice evolved the basis of the common law.

In order to commence an action in the common law courts a person had to obtain a writ. This was basically a letter addressed, on behalf of the monarch, to a sheriff ordering the sheriff to ensure that procedures were carried out to resolve the dispute. Originally the monarch may have signed these writs, but soon the Chancery writ department, under the control of the Lord Chancellor (whose modern role is described in Chapter 4), evolved to issue writs, of which there was a standard range. If a particular problem was not covered by an existing writ, one could be commissioned from the Lord Chancellor's department. This system allowed for the growth and spread of the common law. However, in the Provisions of Oxford (1258) the issue of further different types of writ was prohibited.

► The barons were upset at the loss of revenue from their own courts, caused by the growth of the common law. They forced Henry III to pass the Provisions of Oxford in 1258, in order to curb the growth of the common law.

This action was partially invalidated by the new king, Edward I, who enacted the Statute of Westminster II in 1285. This enabled further writs to be issued to cover different areas, provided that they were similar to those that had been issued prior to 1258. This was an important development for two reasons. First, it allowed the continued growth of the common law. Second, it meant that any growth would have to be cautious, because of the restrictions placed upon it by the pre-1258 writs.

Medieval period

Common law continued to grow, and the law of contract and the law of torts evolved out of the pre-1258 writ of trespass. The Curia Regis gradually surrendered its judicial powers to a range of ancillary courts (described more fully in their modern context in Chapter 4).

- **The Courts of Assize** had mainly criminal jurisdiction, administered by judges touring the country on a circuit.

- **The Court of the King's** (later **Queen's**) **Bench** had wide **appellate** jurisdiction, mainly criminal, though it was later extended to cover all types of civil actions.
- **The Court of Common Pleas** heard all civil actions between citizens, specializing in cases concerning land.
- **The Court of Exchequer** was concerned mainly with revenue, though it also had a limited civil jurisdiction.
- **The Court of Exchequer Chamber** was an appellate court.

► **Appellate** – able to hear appeals from lower courts.

Origins of equity

Under the Normans, the route of appeal against the decision of a royal judge was to **petition** the king, as the figurehead of the judicial system. As the number of petitions grew the king began to pass them on to his Lord Chancellor, who quickly became the person deputed to deal with these petitions.

► **Petition** – to make an appeal.

The Lord Chancellor tended to determine cases on the basis of common sense and fairness, not being bound by the strict guidelines laid down by common law and the writ system. The Lord Chancellor's court became extremely popular and it grew into a permanent Chancery Court. Thus evolved a system of law that became known as equity.

Equity evolved as a complementary branch of law to challenge and work in competition against common law, with judges from the different branches giving different judgments. This continued until James I ordered that where equity and common law conflicted, equity should prevail.

However, equity became a victim of its own qualities. It was flexible (not being bound by the pre-1258 position), informal and recognized new actions, for example, trusts. Further, it provided new remedies. This flexibility led one seventeenth-century scholar to write 'Equity varies with the length of the Chancellor's foot', implying that there was no uniformity of decision in the Court of Chancery. Equity evolved to meet this challenge and, by the middle of the nineteenth century, had itself become regulated into a set of uniform rules. These included the new remedies of injunction and **specific performance**.

The position of equity and common law was finally resolved by the Judicature Acts 1873–5. The whole of the judicial system was undergoing reform at that time, and this included the decision that equity and common law were to be administered from the same court. The court system was also reformed and the majority of those reforms are still present in our current court system. The court system will be covered in more detail in Chapter 4.

► **Specific performance** – an order of the court addressed to a named person, directing that the person performs his or her part of a contract.

 Write a report, explaining the reasons for the growth of equity. Remember to be concise, accurate and interesting. Use no more than one page of A4 paper.

In this chapter we shall be examining the sources of British law. The major lawmaking bodies are Parliament and the judges, and, more recently, the European Community, but there are other lesser sources of law, including custom.

PARLIAMENT

The British system of government is based on the **sovereignty** of parliament. This means that the courts, judges and all other bodies are subservient to Parliament. Historically, Parliament was not very interested in the making of law, but throughout the last two centuries it has come to play a pre-eminent role in lawmaking. Since the joining of the European Community, enacted by the European Communities Act 1972, a degree of British sovereignty has been relinquished to the European Community. However, theoretically, absolute sovereignty remains with Britain because at any time Britain could decide to leave the European Community. As we shall see a little later on in this chapter, regulations from the European Community are immediately binding and take precedence over laws made by Parliament.

The modern British political system

In order to understand the parliamentary lawmaking process, a basic knowledge of the British political system is required. The British parliamentary system is **bi-cameral**. It has an electoral system based on a **simple majority system**. After a general election, by **convention** held at least every five years, the leader of the party with a majority of the 651 parliamentary seats is invited by the monarch to form a government. The British electoral system has traditionally produced governments with a large majority over the other parties in the House of Commons.

A majority can probably be described as large where one party has an overall majority of 60 to 70 seats. This type of majority allows a government to carry through its programme, even when some of its own MPs refuse to support it.

The voting system, as used in the UK, has consistently produced a party with an overall majority after a general election. The year 1974 represents the exception that proves the rule. In that year the Labour party were returned as the largest party in Parliament, but they were 34 seats short of an overall majority. Harold Wilson formed a government, as leader of the largest party, but he quickly held another general election, in which he achieved an overall majority, only a few months later.

Many people have called for reform of the voting system used in the UK. Most commentators would like to see a form of proportional representation (PR) used, where seats are allocated more fairly in accordance with the amount of votes cast. The Liberal Democrats suffer the most under our present system, regularly

▶ **Sovereignty** – ultimate source of power and authority in a state or political system.

▶ **Bi-cameral** – having two chambers: the House of Commons and the House of Lords. Members are elected to the House of Commons, while entrance to the House of Lords is gained by birth, via a hereditary peerage; a life peerage; as a Law Lord (Lords of Appeal in Ordinary, see Chapter 4); as one of roughly 25 high-ranking clergy.

▶ **Simple majority system** – commonly known as a 'first past the post' system. Britain is divided into 651 constituencies, each of which is represented by one member of parliament (MP). To gain his or her seat the MP has obtained more of the votes cast in a general election than any other candidate in that constituency.

▶ **Convention** – a rule that has existed for a long time and has no legal backing, though it is still considered to be binding. For example, it is a convention that when a party is defeated in a general election and another party has an overall majority, the losing prime minister resigns.

polling 20 per cent of the votes cast, yet only receiving around 20 seats. If a form of PR were used, they could expect to achieve around 110 seats.

Constituency of Huntingdon

Smith (Labour)	15946	
Jones (Lib Dem)	16042	Jones is elected
Thatcher (Communist)	13987	
Benn (Conservative)	16008	

Prior to a general election, all the political parties publish their proposed legislative programmes in their manifestos. Once elected the government then maps out a programme of legislation and commences to implement its policies. In the 1992 election the Conservatives were returned with an overall majority of 21 seats.

(ACT) If you don't already know, find out who your local MP is. This information will be in your local library, in *Keesing's Archives* or in any other political reference book. *Hansard*, the word-for-word report of all debates in parliament, will contain details of every word that your MP has said in the House. Check in the index to find when your MP has spoken and what he or she has said.

Establish the result of the 1992 election and compare it to the results of all of the post-war elections in your constituency. Has the constituency always been held by the same party? If so, why? If not, what caused the seat to change hands? What has your MP done since entering Parliament? Has he or she enacted any legislation? Write a short historical report on your constituency, followed by a short critical report on your MP.

Legislation

Bills

A draft of a proposed Act of Parliament is called a Bill. The procedure governing the passing of a Bill by Parliament depends basically on whether it is a 'public' or a 'private' Bill. In order to become law a public Bill must pass through a set process in both the House of Commons and the House of Lords (see below). The vast majority of public Bills are introduced by the government, while others are introduced by MPs as **private members' Bills**. Public Bills can be introduced in either House, the less controversial tending to begin the process in the House of Lords.

While public Bills generally affect the whole of the country, private Bills affect a certain section of the country or particular bodies, for example, the British Railways Board. Private Bills are often introduced by the organization seeking to vary the law or by

▶ **Private members' Bills** – a public Bill introduced in the House of Commons by a private member, i.e. an MP who doesn't have an appointment in the government. A certain amount of parliamentary time is allocated for members to introduce legislation. Each parliamentary year all MPs enter their Bills into a ballot. The first six private members' Bills to be drawn from the ballot stand a fair chance of getting passed, especially if they are non-contentious or have government support. A private members' Bill is a public Bill. A successful private members' Bill will become law across the whole country.

► As it passes through the House of Commons each Bill is allocated a **standing committee** to examine it. Between twenty and fifty members sit on the committee, reflecting the differing party strengths in the House. When the Bill completes its passage through Parliament the committee finishes.

a local authority. Public Bills that also affect private interests are sometimes termed hybrid Bills.

First Reading	Merely an introductory stage with no debate.
Second Reading	The principle of the Bill is debated, after it has been introduced by the Government Minister responsible for the Department from which the Bill has originated. Generally, a vote is taken at this stage.
Committee Stage	The Bill is examined clause by clause in a **standing committee,** or, for constitutional Bill,s a committee of the whole house. Amendments are proposed at this stage.
Report Stage	Amendments are considered by the whole house, where the government majority normally allows it to reject or accept any amendments passed in the previous stage.
Third Reading	Short debate on the Bill followed by a vote before it passes to the House of Lords.
House of Lords	The same procedure is followed.
House of Commons	Any Lords' Amendments are considered and may be either accepted or rejected.
Royal Assent	The Bill becomes an Act of Parliament when signed by a Royal Commissioner on behalf of the monarch

An Act becomes law on the day that it receives the Royal Assent, unless otherwise specified. Provision may be made for the Act to come into force on a later date, on the direction of a statutory instrument or a minister of the crown. Once an Act becomes law it is supreme. If it affects any previously determined case law, then from that day forward the provisions of the Act overrule the case law. It is the duty of the judiciary to implement and, where the wording of an Act is unclear, to interpret the meaning of an Act. Judges have no power of review over an Act of Parliament.

► If an Act were passed that banned the use of motor vehicles in England and Wales, it would be the job of the judges to apply that legislation, however silly or unfair it might be.

Delegated legislation

The growth of the welfare state and the increased involvement of the government in all aspects of its citizens' lives has led to a growth in the use of delegated legislation. As the name suggests, the power to make legislation is passed from Parliament to other bodies. Normally an enabling Act will be passed by Parliament, specifying the guidelines within which others may draw up specific rules. The increasing pace of change of technology has been a major factor in the growth of delegated legislation. In fact an Act could even be obsolete by the time it came into being, so a quicker process for making legislation is required.

Gestation period of an Act of Parliament

It normally takes a long time to pass an Act of Parliament. First, there is the need for general consultation with all interested parties and, if it is a particularly important or controversial matter, there might even be a **Royal Commission**. For example, the Royal Commission on Criminal Justice was set up in March 1991 to investigate the mechanisms of the criminal justice system, after a series of miscarriages of justice, culminating in the release of the **Birmingham Six**. When it reported in July 1993, it made 352 recommendations. The most drastic of these recommendations were:

- ending the right to trial by jury for minor cases;
- the setting up of an independent review body to investigate miscarriages;
- a formal system of plea bargaining;
- the replacement of committal proceedings;
- the continuation of the right to silence.

The government accepted certain of the recommendations and totally rejected others. The Criminal Justice and Public Order Act 1994 (CJAPOA94) enacted some of the recommendations, for example, the replacement of committal proceedings and the creation of offences aimed at protecting jurors. However, the Act went totally against the advice of the RC and introduced, under strictly controlled circumstances, the right of the prosecution or the judge to invite the jury to draw adverse inferences where the accused has failed to respond to police questioning. This is the removal of the so-called 'right to silence'.

There are three main types of delegated legislation:

1 orders in Council;
2 statutory instruments;
3 bylaws.

Orders in Council

These are made under the authority of an enabling Act, by the Queen on the advice of her Privy Councillors. This is another tradition, because the Privy Council is in reality the Cabinet, since all Cabinet ministers are honorary members of the Privy Council. As with so many of the roles that the Queen plays within our constitution, her part is merely a formality.

Statutory instruments

Each departmental minister makes rules and orders relating to his or her area of government. For example, the Minister for the Environment makes compulsory purchase orders on land or houses that, for whatever reason, are required by the government. Collectively, these orders are known as statutory instruments. A proportion of statutory instruments need to be confirmed by Parliament, prior to their implementation. Confirmation involves the statutory instrument being put before Parliament, where a vote is taken to either accept or reject it.

▶ A **Royal Commission** (RC) is an advisory body set up to investigate a particular topic or area of the law. RCs are appointed by the Crown using its prerogative powers. It is therefore the government that decides to appoint an RC on behalf of the Crown. An RC will be headed by one person and will consist of leading authorities in the particular area being studied. The RC will examine evidence from government departments, witnesses and interested groups. A report listing recommendations will then be made. A government is free either to accept or to reject the findings of an RC. The Royal Commission on Criminal Justice, headed by Viscount Runciman, reported in July 1993, making over 350 recommendations.

▶ **Birmingham Six** – In 1975 six people were convicted of carrying out two pub bombings in Birmingham. The evidence against them consisted of alleged confessions, and circumstantial and forensic evidence. The confessions were allegedly obtained after the six were systematically beaten by their interrogators. The forensic evidence subsequently became discredited and the other evidence remained circumstantial, having no real substance. Leave to appeal against the convictions was refused in 1976. The six then started a civil action against the police and prison warders for assault. The House of Lords blocked the progress of the action on the grounds that it would undermine the criminal conviction. The Court of Appeal again refused an appeal in 1988, but in 1991 the six were acquitted after further doubts were raised about the police evidence.

▶ *Intra vires* – within the limit of their powers.

▶ The High Court, Queen's Bench Division, has the power of **judicial review**. A person may apply to the High Court for judicial review where they consider that an inferior court, an administrative authority or a tribunal has acted either incorrectly or *ultra vires* (beyond the limit of their powers). The High Court may grant the remedy of *certiorari* (to be informed), whereby the decision of the inferior court or other body is quashed; *mandamus* (we command), an order from the High Court to another body to complete a specific public duty relating to its responsibilities, for example, an order to an inferior court to hear a specific case; or **prohibition**, an order of the High Court to an inferior court, administrative authority or tribunal not to carry out an *ultra vires* act.

▶ Remember, statute law is law made by the passing of an Act of Parliament. Case law is made by judges giving judgment on the circumstances of a particular case. Statute law will always overrule case law.

Bylaws

Bylaws are restricted in their operation to a particular area, normally a local authority or city. For example, in London there are special regulations relating to gatherings and demonstrations, which affect the free movement of MPs close to Parliament, when Parliament is sitting. Bylaws must be *intra vires* and reasonable. They are normally confirmed by a minister on behalf of Parliament.

The courts have no power of **judicial review** in relation to Acts of Parliament. However, judges can review delegated legislation to ensure that a body has not acted *ultra vires* and can challenge bylaws on the grounds of unreasonableness. This has been a somewhat controversial area, because the courts have shown themselves willing to rule the actions of ministers *ultra vires*, where a minister has acted beyond the powers given by the Act under which a direction has been made. An interesting modern example was when Michael Heseltine, as Minister for Trade and Industry, announced the closure of a number of coal pits. The National Union of Mineworkers (NUM) sought a ruling from the High Court that he had exceeded his powers. The court confirmed the NUM view, stating that he had failed to follow the procedures laid down in the Pits Act 1964, in that he had not undertaken a consultation procedure before announcing the closures.

A further recent example comes from the days of the Greater London Council (GLC). In 1984 the Transport Secretary, Nicholas Ridley, required the GLC to contribute £50 million towards the new London Transport Authority. The High Court ruled that Nicholas Ridley was acting *ultra vires*. The government, instead of accepting defeat, merely moved the goal posts. They introduced new legislation to force the GLC to pay the money. This is a classic example of the sovereignty of Parliament, where, if the courts rule that the government has acted beyond its powers, the government, by making new legislation, simply changes the rules.

Statutory interpretation

It has been stated that the courts have no power of judicial review of an Act of Parliament, but the courts are charged with applying and interpreting legislation. It is difficult for a drafter to cover every eventuality when drafting a Bill that becomes an Act. There will always be problems of interpretation; problems with the meaning of a word; or the way in which a particular phrase has been worded. These issues often only arise when a case comes before a court. The guidelines used by judges when faced with the task of interpretation can be split into two areas: statutory and common-law rules.

Statutory rules

1 Parliament recognized the difficulties faced by judges and, in order to aid interpretation, passed the Interpretation Act 1978.

This Act went some way to clearing up minor points, such as where 'he' is written, it should also be taken, unless otherwise stated, to include 'she'. A similar provision was also made in relation to the singular and plural.

2 Most modern Acts include sections to assist in the interpretation of the wording of the Act. In the Theft Act 1968, s. 10, on aggravated burglary, a 'weapon of offence' is defined as 'any article made or adapted for use for causing injury to or incapacitating a person, or intended by the person having it with him for such use'.

3 Where further clarification is sought the courts may look at the Act itself, as a whole, and take into account any notes, headings or punctuation in order to try and interpret any ambiguous words.

ACT In order to help you understand the difficulties of drafting rules try the following activity in a group. Choose some area of activity known to you and try to draft a set of rules for it – you will be acting very much like a parliamentary drafter. Then act rather like the court in interpreting the rules. Test the rules by asking: 'Suppose this happened. How would the rules apply in this case?'

Common-law rules

The common-law rules used by judges in interpretation are as follows:

1 literal rule
2 golden rule
3 mischief rule
4 *ejusdem generis* rule
5 *ut res magis valeat quam pereat*
6 *expressio unius est exclusio alterius*
7 presumption rule
8 other sources.

Literal rule

On the basis of the literal rule, the courts take the view that, where the wording of an Act is absolutely clear, that wording must be applied literally, even if it defeats the object of the legislation. The following case is a good example of this.

Fisher v. Bell (1961) 1 QB 394

A shopkeeper had a display of flick-knives in his shop window. He was charged with contravening the Restriction of Offensive Weapons Act 1959. The Act stated that it was an offence to offer flick-knives for sale.

▶ The Restriction of Offensive Weapons Act 1961 was passed to close the loophole exploited in *Fisher*.

COURT HELD

The law of contract has established that goods on display are not 'on offer for sale', they are 'an invitation to treat', that is an invitation for the purchaser to make an offer, the seller having the option to accept or reject the offer. Therefore, although the purpose of the Act was defeated by the literal interpretation of the wording, the shopkeeper was acquitted of the offence.

► See also *Whiteley v. Chappell* (1868/9) 4 LRQB 147.

Golden rule

Following the golden rule, where there is ambiguity in the meaning of a word or phrase, the court adopts the interpretation that produces the most sensible result. The following case illustrates an instance where the court used this rule to obtain the result that the legislation was originally intended to produce.

R v. Callan (1872) LR 1 CCR 367

Callan was charged with bigamy, contrary to s. 57 of the Offences Against the Person Act 1861.

> Whosoever being married shall marry any other person during the life of the former husband or wife shall be guilty of an offence.

The word marry at that time had two alternative meanings: first to go through a ceremony of marriage; second to contract a valid marriage. The defence suggested that the defendant was married and that once married, which involved a change in the legal status of the person, it was not possible to marry again, because the person's legal status would remain the same.

► See also *Re Sigsworth* (1935) Ch 89 and *Adler v. George* (1964) 2 QB 7.

COURT HELD

Using the 'golden rule', the court interpreted the words 'to marry' to mean 'go through a marriage ceremony'.
Therefore, they were able to convict the defendant and achieve the original purpose of the legislation.

Mischief rule

The mischief rule was established in *Heydon's Case* in 1584. The literal meaning of the words of the Act is forsaken and the words are interpreted to match the original purpose of the Act. The following is an example of this principle.

Smith v. Hughes (1960) 1 WLR 830

Under s. 1 of the Street Offences Act 1959, it is an offence to 'loiter or solicit in a street or public place for the purposes of prostitution'. This case rested upon whether a person was contravening the Act by soliciting for business from an upstairs window, by tapping on the glass and beckoning to potential clients. Clearly the room was not a public place, therefore the literal interpretation would have to find that no offence was being committed.

COURT HELD

The original intention of the legislation was to prevent prostitutes from soliciting in public places. It was not important that, in this case, the soliciting was being done from private premises. The actions of the prostitute were visible to the general public in the street, therefore an offence was being committed.

▶ See also *Jones v. Wrotham Park Settled Estates* (1980) AC 74.

Ejusdem generis *rule*

Where specific words of the same class are mentioned in an Act, and these are followed by general words, the general words should be interpreted to be persons or things of the same or similar kind. This is known as the *ejusdem generis* rule. For example, if an Act refers to 'dogs, cats and other animals', then the 'other animals' could only include other domestic pets, not wild animals.

▶ *Ejusdem generis* – of the same kind.

Expressio unius est exclusio alterius

Under the rule of *expressio unius est exclusio alterius*, if specific words are used with no other qualification, then all other things are excluded. If an Act stated 'cats and dogs', without adding 'and other animals', then all other animals would be excluded.

▶ *Expressio unius est exclusio alterius* – The inclusion of the one is the exclusion of the other.

Presumption rule

The main tenets of the presumption rule are that, unless stated otherwise, the court will infer the following: the Act will apply to the UK; it will not create strict liability offences; it will not be **retrospective**; it will not repeal earlier legislation.

▶ **Retrospective** – backdated.

Other sources

In interpreting an Act the court may make reference to the materials that were used in the creation of the Act. Prior to forming legislation the government may have produced a '**white**' or '**green**' **paper**. An Act may follow on from the report of a Royal Commission. In those cases a court may refer to the documentation in order to ascertain the actual intention of the legislation. However, the use of this method of interpretation is severely restricted.

▶ In *Pepper v. Hart* (1993) 1 All ER 42, the House of Lords decided that judges could refer to *Hansard*, the official record of parliamentary proceedings, if the legislation is ambiguous or obscure, or leads to absurdity, and the statements relied on in *Hansard* are clear and made by a Minister or other promoter of the Bill.

 In as few words as possible, write down definitions of the following: 1 literal rule; 2 golden rule; 3 mischief rule; 4 *ejusdem generis* rule; 5 *ut res magis valeat quam pereat*; 6 *expressio unius, exclusio alterius*; 7 presumption rule.

▶ **White paper** – a paper outlining proposed government legislation.
▶ **Green paper** – a paper setting out government policy options for discussion.

JUDICIAL PRECEDENT – CASE LAW

We now turn our attention to the second major lawmaking body,

► ***Stare decisis et non quieta movere*** – stick to what is decided so as to not unsettle what is already established.

the judges and judge-made law. The principle of judicial precedent is quite simple. It is based upon the rule of ***stare decisis et non quieta movere***. Where a case that has been decided is followed by a similar case, the same decision should and must be made if the first court was a higher court than the second, and sometimes even if it was a court on the same level. This practice began, as we learned in Chapter 2, with the Norman itinerant judges.

► The principal of judicial precedent is known as the **doctrine of judicial precedent**.

Two important historical developments have made the modern system of judicial precedent possible. The first is the creation of a comprehensive and reliable method of recording court decisions. In 1865 the Incorporated Council of Law Reporting was formed, in order to provide a reliable means of publishing law reports. Since that time it has published the *Law Reports* and, since 1953, the *Weekly Law Reports*. These are accepted as being authoritative and are checked by the relevant judges prior to publication. The second is the reform of the courts system, under the Judicature Acts of 1873–5, which gave us our present court structure.

The hierarchy of precedent

European Court of Justice	Since the joining of the EC in 1973, decisions by the ECJ, on matters relating to EC law, are binding on all English Courts. Under Sec. 177 of the Treaty of Rome, ECJ decisions are not binding on the ECJ itself, though it does tend to follow previous decisions.
Superior Courts House of Lords	Final court of appeal in the English Legal System. Its decisions on non-EC matters are binding on all other courts. Since the Practice Statement 1966, the Lords is no longer bound by its previous decisions, though it rarely overturns them.
Court of Appeal (civil division)	Bound by the House of Lords and normally also by its own decisions. In *Young v. Bristol Aeroplane Co.* (1944) KB 718, it was established that it could depart from previous decisions in the following circumstances: (1) where two previous conflicting decisions exist, the Court of Appeal can choose which to follow; (2) if a previous decision is in conflict with a subsequent decision of the House of Lords; (3) where a previous decision has been made *per incuriam*, i.e. where a statute or House of Lords decision has been ignored.
Court of Appeal (criminal division)	Bound by the House of Lords, and by its own decisions, though it has greater flexibility than the civil division because it is dealing with the liberty of an individual.
High Court – divisional courts	Bound by the House of Lords, the Court of Appeal and by its own decisions, with the same *Young v. Bristol Aeroplane* qualification. Each divisional court will also be bound by its own previous decisions.
High Court – ordinary courts	Bound by the House of Lords, Court of Appeal, and the divisional courts. However, where civil cases are tried at first instance, the decisions do not normally bind other High Court judges, though they are a strong persuasive authority and are usually followed unless the judge in the later case feels that it is wrong to do so. In such a case a judge must give clear reasons for not following the original decision.
Inferior courts Crown Court Magistrates' court Youth court County court	These courts do not normally create any binding precedents. They are bound by all of the above superior courts. However, where a High Court judge presides in the Crown Court it is likely that the Court decision would create a binding precedent on the inferior courts.

In order to understand how judicial precedent works we must first investigate which decisions bind which court and who has the final say. In Chapter 4 we shall examine the structure of the court system in detail, but here it will be useful to explain how precedent functions. Precedent starts at the top and works down the structure. In simple terms the decisions of the top court, the European Court of Justice, bind all of the other courts.

 Drawing on the information given above, create a chart showing the operation of judicial precedent.

Formulation and use of precedent

When delivering or passing judgment in a case the judge makes a speech. A speech may run to thousands of words in a complicated case or it may be relatively short in a simple case. In the speech the judge will outline the facts of the case, the law relating to those facts and the reason for his or her decision. This latter part includes the legal reasons used as the basis for the decision and becomes the *ratio decidendi* of the case. The *ratio decidendi* forms the precedent for other similar cases. Other comments by the judge that are not directly related to the reasons that have influenced his or her decision are known as *obiter dicta*. These are not binding, though they should be treated as a strong persuasive authority. A later and possibly inferior court can only refuse to follow *obiter dicta* where it is convinced that it is wrong, giving a clear statement of reasons for not doing so. This point is especially valid where a judge, in his or her speech, has described an artificial situation in the *obiter dicta*, and stated what the law would be if that situation arose.

> ► **Ratio decidendi** – reason for the decision.

> ► **Obiter dicta** – words spoken by the way.

Strangely, it is the judge hearing a later case who decides what the *ratio decidendi* of a previous case was, and of course he or she is generally not the judge who made the original decision. Where no precedent exists, i.e. where the circumstances of a case are totally new, then a judge must decide the case based on the general principles of English law. Where precedent is claimed it is for **counsel** to suggest to the judge that it should apply to the case in hand.

> ► **Counsel** is the term used to describe a barrister, or barristers collectively.

Dividing the *obiter* from the *ratio* is by no means a simple matter. The only sure conclusion is that whatever is *ratio* isn't *obiter* and vice versa. What the *ratio* should be is the point of law on which the judge based his or her decision in a particular case. However, it is possible for a judge in a later case to **distinguish** this case from an earlier similar case by pointing to or finding some material difference in the facts of the two cases. In this way, a judge is able to avoid a binding precedent.

> ► **Distinguish** – to provide reasons to show that a case currently under consideration is different from a previous case.

Upon appeal on a point of law a precedent may be reversed, where that appeal is successful. A precedent may be overruled, when in a subsequent case a higher court decides a similar case differently, though any previous decisions remain unaffected, under the maxim *res judicata pro veritae accipitur*.

To illustrate precedent in action we shall compare two cases, one

> ► **Res judicata pro veritae accipitur** – A thing once decided should be regarded as the truth. Once a case has been heard and decided, the same matter cannot be taken before the courts again, even if the law has subsequently changed.

a celebrated case and the other an excellent example of how precedent can be applied to extend the law.

Donoghue v. Stevenson (1932) AC 562

 In this case a woman was bought a glass of ginger beer in a café by a friend. The beer was in an opaque bottle. After drinking some of the beer she poured more into a glass and out fell the remains of a decomposed snail. The plaintiff sued the manufacturer of the ginger beer under the tort of negligence, under which it had to be proved that the manufacturer owed a duty of care to the plaintiff. She could not sue the café owner or the manufacturer in contract because she, herself, had not bought the drink.

► The implications of this case are examined in more detail in Chapter 19, p. 352.

 COURT HELD
The plaintiff could succeed. A manufacturer of a product owes a duty to the consumer to take reasonable care to ensure that the product does not injure the consumer in any way.

Stennet v. Hancock and Peters (1939) 2 All ER 578

The plaintiff was walking on a pavement when she was hit by part of a wheel that had come off a passing lorry. The lorry had recently been faultily repaired. She claimed damages from the garage owner, under the rule established in *Donoghue*.

 COURT HELD
The plaintiff succeeded, based on the rule established by the case of Donoghue.

(ACT) In one paragraph, record the rule established in the case of *Donoghue*.

EUROPEAN COMMUNITY LEGISLATION

The UK effectively joined the European Community (EC) under the European Communities Act 1972. From that time on the various legislative authorities of the EC have had the power to make legislation for the UK. The Act of Accession brought with it certain obligations agreed under the original requirements of the Treaty of Rome and the Treaty of Accession. These obligations are considered to be the primary source of EC Law. Secondary EC legislation comes in three main forms: regulations, directives and decisions.

Regulations

These are most similar to an Act of Parliament and become law in all member states when they are enacted.

Directives

These are given to member states, with a time limit within which the directive must be implemented. However, it is left to individual member states to create legislation to enforce the directive. The European Directive on Product Liability was adopted in 1985 and contained a directive for implementation by 1988. This was implemented in the UK by the Consumer Protection Act 1987. Where member states have been slow, or have failed to implement a directive, the European Court has intervened to enforce the directive, as if it were a regulation. **Directive 93/13/EC**, which limits the use of exclusion clauses, has been adopted and recently implemented in the UK (see Chapter 14, page 257). It is left to the member states to choose the methods by which the changes are brought about, though this is usually done by passing an Act of Parliament.

Decisions

These are addressed to particular states, bodies or individuals and bind those people or bodies to whom they are addressed.

Both the House of Commons and the House of Lords have select committees that monitor EC legislation.

 In three paragraphs, outline the different types of EC legislation.

▶ **Directive 93/13/EC** – The EC Directive on Unfair Contract Terms was implemented by Statutory Instrument (SI) 1994, Number 3159. The SI states that the new Regulations are to be known as the Unfair Terms in Consumer Contracts Regulations 1994 (UTCR94).

CUSTOM

Where once custom was an important source of law, most customs have now been assimilated into the legal system, either by case law or by legislation. For a custom to have the force of law it must have been in existence since 1189; must be clear and reasonable; and must have been in operation without interruption.

OTHER LESSER SOURCES

The law of the trading merchants, ecclesiastical law and the texts of learned writers added to the development of law. Many of their practices and customs have been absorbed into the legal system. Out of the practice of the merchants has evolved the law relating to cheques, international money orders, insurance and partnership legislation. The role of the ecclesiastical courts has been taken over by the Family Division of the High Court, though an ecclesiastical court still exists to deal with ecclesiastical matters. Where further information on an ancient law is sought, then very, very rarely the writings of a learned author may be consulted by a court.

 Now that you have completed this chapter look back at the objectives listed at the beginning. Can you do all the things that they suggest? If not, look again at the relevant sections of the chapter.

 Take a sheet of paper and write 'The law' in the middle of it. Then use the text in this chapter to show where it comes from by writing the sources of law around the outside and drawing arrows to the centre. For example, one source of law is parliamentary legislation.

CHAPTER SUMMARY

1 The present legal system has developed from the structure that the Normans created after 1066. Equity evolved out of the Chancery Court to represent fairness and justice, a role it still enjoys today.

2 The British political system is almost unique in the Western world in operating a 'first past the post' electoral system. This has had a major effect on the post-war legal system. Our simple majority system has produced strong, powerful governments, who have been able to legislate freely, being under no real pressure from the opposition. This led, until 1977, to a series of policy 'U-turns' being made by the different parties. As soon as a new government was elected they repealed the major legislation that had been formulated by the previous government.

3 Entry into the EC has undermined the sovereignty of Parliament in the sense that EC law overrides law passed by Parliament. But parliamentary sovereignty remains in that Parliament has the power to take Britain out of the EC.

4 The judiciary plays a major role in the creation of law via judicial precedent.

 The court system

Chapter objectives

By the end of this chapter you should be able to:

▮ describe the structure of the civil courts of England and Wales, including jurisdiction and routes of appeal

▮ describe the structure of the criminal courts, including jurisdiction and routes of appeal

▮ understand the roles of the main legal personnel who can be found in the courts

▮ appreciate the role of the European Court of Justice in the court system

▮ identify the courts classified as being superior or inferior

▮ recognize the different roles of barristers and solicitors; appreciate the moves that are currently being taken to reform/merge the two professions and identify other areas that are in need of reform.

The system of courts in England and Wales is extremely complex. The present system was created by the Judicature Acts 1873–5. The only significant changes since that time have been the advent of the European Court of Justice and the creation of the Court of Appeal, Criminal Division in 1966, under the 1966 Criminal Appeal Act. Civil procedure was also changed by the Lord Chancellor in July 1991, after recommendations made in the Civil Justice Review. The reforms, detailed later in this chapter, altered the jurisdiction of the county courts and High Court, giving the county courts a much larger jurisdiction. Students (and lecturers) tend to get very confused by this structure and by the appeals procedure. What I have attempted to do here is to simplify the system, avoiding unnecessary detail.

The courts can be classified a number of ways. Normally they are split into those with criminal and those with civil jurisdiction. As we shall see, this is not a perfect classification because many of the courts have both criminal and civil jurisdiction. However, in our complex system this distinction is perhaps the most useful.

► At all times I am referring to the legal system in England and Wales. Scotland and Northern Ireland have their own systems, with different laws, courts and administrative systems, though the House of Lords acts as the final court of appeal for Scotland and Northern Ireland.

▶ **Jurisdiction** – the power of a court to hear a case.

CIVIL COURTS

The structure of the civil courts is shown in the following chart. It is best to look at the chart as a whole first and then to refer back to it when looking in detail at the workings, composition and **jurisdiction** of a particular court. A useful way of trying to remember the structure and workings of the civil court is to compare the system to a shopping expedition. On the high street you will find a number of different shops. They will vary in size, they will sell different things, some will be more expensive than others, some will be sole outlets and others will be part of a national or international chain. When you wish to purchase a small item, you would probably pop into the corner shop. If you are contemplating buying furniture or another major item for the home, then you might visit a department store. In order to purchase a new car you would visit a high street main dealer garage.

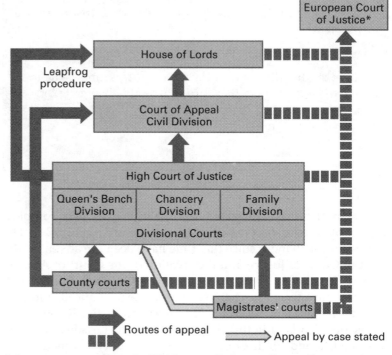

The civil court structure

* Any court may refer to the ECJ for a preliminary ruling on European law

Magistrates' courts

The magistrates' court has a predominantly criminal jurisdiction. However, it has the power to deal with the following civil matters: local function in regard to the sale of alcohol on licensed premises; betting and gaming licensing; certain matrimonial matters (when known as the family proceedings court), including the granting of injunctions and maintenance orders; affiliation orders; welfare of children, including care orders, adoption, custody and guardianship; enforcement of debts owed to the public utilities, gas, water and electricity companies; and enforcement of local community charges.

County courts

The county court has traditionally been the corner shop of the legal system. The changes to the jurisdiction of the county court, introduced in the Lord Chancellor's reforms of July 1991, have greatly expanded the role of the county court to the detriment of the High Court. A county court now has unlimited jurisdiction for all **general list** county court cases. The allocation of the case list is now determined by the following guidelines, illustrated below.

> ► **General list** cases are the types of cases that may be heard in a court: for example, tort, contract and negligence.

Cases will be allocated for trial at either a High Court or a county court, according to the criteria of substance, importance and complexity, together with judicial availability.

- Cases involving amounts below £25,000 will be tried in a county court, unless they are of particular importance or complexity, but in case of contract or tort there is now no upper limit on the amount involved. All personal injury cases below £50,000 should begin in a county court.
- Cases involving amounts above £50,000 will be tried in the High Court, unless they are straightforward and, if so, they will be allocated to the county court.
- Cases involving amounts between £25,000 and £50,000 will be allocated on the basis of the above-mentioned criteria.

The reforms of 1991 further increased the jurisdiction of a district judge (formerly known as a registrar) to £5,000 and increased the limit for automatic **reference to arbitration** to £1,000.

> ► **Reference to arbitration** – this means that the case will be heard informally, in a room at the court, without a full court hearing.

There are around 300 county courts in England and Wales, presided over by a circuit judge, who normally sits alone. A district judge can also be found in the county court, hearing actions where the amount contested is less than £5,000. Actions, in some circumstances, are limited to geographical jurisdiction, i.e. the defendant attends the court local to the area in which the issue arose or where he or she lives or works. About 180 courts are designated divorce courts. These courts have jurisdiction over undefended divorces and other related matters, such as guardianship and adoption. For those matters there is no geographical restriction. Most consumer complaints, small business debts and so on are dealt with here. We shall look in more detail at the 'small claims procedure' in Chapter 5.

> ► In 1992 the county courts disposed of 26,722 cases by trial and 80,332 by means of arbitration.

The High Court of Justice

The High Court of Justice can be viewed as the department store of the courts system. It is split into three separate courts or divisions, each of which has a different area of jurisdiction and specialization:

the Queen's Bench Division, the Chancery Division and the Family Division.

Queen's Bench Division

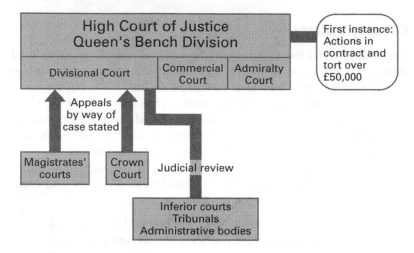

Headed by the Lord Chief Justice, this is the busiest of the courts within the High Court, with around fifty High Court judges. In the ordinary court you will normally find one High Court judge in residence, hearing cases on contract and tort. In the divisional court it is more normal to find three judges, presiding over appeals, **by way of case stated**, from magistrates' courts and from the Crown Court.

The court also exercises a supervisory jurisdiction. It has the power of judicial review over the actions of inferior courts, tribunals and administrative bodies, and may make orders of *certiorari*, *mandamus* and prohibition. It may also issue writs of **habeas corpus**.

Within the division there are two specialist courts, one dealing with admiralty matters (shipping disputes, losses at sea, etc.) and the other with commercial matters (insurance, banking, etc.).

Chancery Division

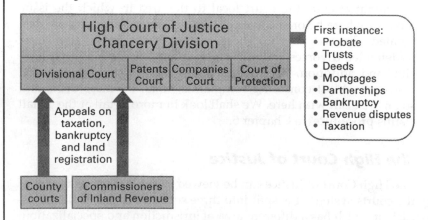

▶ **By way of case stated** – where an appellant alleges that a case has not been properly decided according to the rules of judicial precedent, i.e. on a point of law.

▶ Remember from Chapter 3 that a person may apply to the High Court for judicial review where they consider that an inferior court, tribunal or administrative body has acted either incorrectly or *ultra vires*. See also Chapter 3, p. 22, for explanations of *certiorari*, *mandamus*, and prohibition.

▶ **Habeas corpus** is a writ that may be brought before the divisional court of the Queen's Bench Division (or, out of hours, any High Court judge), questioning the validity of the detention of a particular person. If the High Court feels that the detention is unlawful it will order that the person be released.

The Court of Chancery sits in eight provincial centres throughout England and Wales, though a large percentage of cases are heard in the divisional courts in London. The majority of cases concern contentious probate, bankruptcy and revenue disputes. There are three specialist courts in the division, one dealing with patent disputes, one with the winding up of companies, and the third, a Court of Protection, with the affairs of mental patients. Headed by the Lord Chancellor, though presided over by the Vice Chancellor, the Court of Chancery consists of around twelve High Court judges.

Family Division

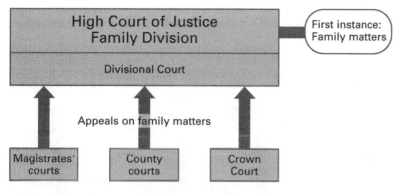

The Family Division is headed by a president and has around sixteen High Court judges. The jurisdiction of the Family Division covers all of the contentious and problem areas that can be found within the area of the family. These include defended divorces, matrimonial property matters, guardianship, wardship, adoption, legitimacy and decrees of presumption of death. Its appellate role is carried out by the divisional courts in matters relating to guardianship, adoption and affiliation proceedings. It hears appeals, by way of case stated, from magistrates' and county courts, and from the Crown Court, on matrimonial proceedings and other family matters.

Court of Appeal, Civil Division

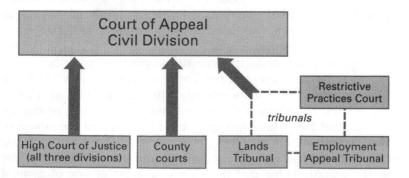

The court consists of twenty-eight **Lord Justices of Appeal**, between one and five of which will preside over a case, depending

► The **Lord Justices of Appeal** preside in the Court of Appeal and are normally promoted from the High Court. To become eligible to become a Lord Justice of Appeal, a person must have had a right of audience in relation to all proceedings in the High Court for at least ten years, or must be or have been a puisne judge (Courts and Legal Services Act 1990, s. 71).

► **Ex officio** – by virtue of holding an office.

► The **Lord Chief Justice** heads the Criminal Division of the Court of Appeal and he or she also presides over the Queen's Bench Division of the High Court.

► The **Master of the Rolls** is the head of the Civil Division of the Court of Appeal, and is and remains a judge who sits in the Court of Appeal. The Master of the Rolls is responsible for the admission of solicitors to the Rolls of the Supreme Court.

► The **Lord Chancellor** is appointed by the Prime Minister, normally from the House of Commons and a member of the government with a place in the Cabinet. The Lord Chancellor is the Speaker of the House of Lords, head of the legal profession and judiciary, chair of the Judicial Committee of the Privy Council and head of the Chancery Division. The Lord Chancellor effectively appoints all judges, though in the case of the appellate court judges the Prime Minister makes the actual appointment, after taking advice from the Lord Chancellor, on behalf of the Queen. The Lord Chancellor is the keeper of the Great Seal of the Realm. Because it is a political appointment, should the government be defeated, then the current Lord Chancellor would be replaced.

► The **Lords of Appeal in Ordinary** are commonly known as the Law Lords, and are mostly chosen from judges who have presided in the Court of Appeal. To be eligible to become a Lord of Appeal, a person must have had a right of audience in relation to all proceedings in the High Court for at least fifteen years, or to have held high judicial office for two years (Courts and Legal Services Act 1990, s. 71). (This is known as a fifteen year Supreme Court qualification.) When appointed, Law Lords are automatically made life peers. They also preside in the Judicial Committee of the Privy Council.

upon its complexity. Normally, either two or three judges will preside. Certain high ranking judges are **ex officio** members of the Court of Appeal, including the **Lord Chief Justice**, the **Master of the Rolls**, the Lords of Appeal in Ordinary (see below), the **Lord Chancellor** and the President of the Family Division. The Master of the Rolls is the head of the division and is the only person who regularly presides in the Court of Appeal. An appeal constitutes a rehearing of the case, by way of reviewing the documentary evidence and listening to arguments from counsel. Normally, no fresh evidence is allowed to be submitted, neither are witnesses heard. The court may uphold or reverse the whole or any part of the decision of the lower court, alter the damages awarded, or make a different order concerning costs. If new evidence is discovered it may order a new trial.

House of Lords

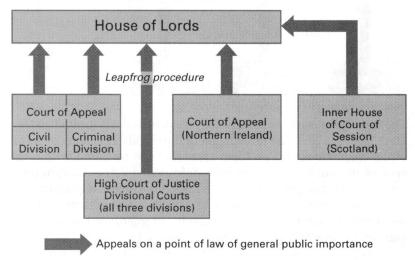

Appeals on a point of law of general public importance

The House of Lords has judicial as well as parliamentary functions. It is the final court of appeal for all domestic matters, acting for Northern Ireland and Scotland as well as for England and Wales. The court is presided over by up to eleven **Lords of Appeal in Ordinary**, of whom two are normally Scottish and one Irish. Almost entirely appellate, there is no right of appeal to the House, as an appeal can only be made with the permission of the House itself or with the consent of the Court of Appeal, on a matter of public interest. The Administration of Justice Act 1969, ss. 12 and 13, provides that where both parties consent, a leapfrog procedure may be available, whereby a case could be heard in the House of Lords on appeal from the High Court. For this to happen the House of Lords or the trial judge must consent, and it must be certified by the High Court judge that it concerns a point of law of general public importance, and either that the decision is bound by a previous Court of Appeal or House decision or it concerns the interpretation of a statute. The House of Lords hears some seventy cases a year. A minimum of three Lords of Appeal will preside, but as many as seven have presided. The decision reached is based on a majority view.

European Court of Justice

ANY DOMESTIC COURT OR TRIBUNAL MAY APPLY FOR A HEARING

This is the final court of appeal on all matters relating to the interpretation of European Community (EC) law. Under Article 177 of the European Economic Community Treaty, the final court of appeal in a member state must refer a case that concerns any matter relating to EC law to the European Court of Justice (ECJ). Any domestic court may refer a case concerning a point of EC law to the ECJ for a ruling, which will then be used by a domestic court to reach the correct decision in a case. A ruling can take between eight and eighteen months to be given. A right of appeal to the ECJ exists on a matter of law.

The court is composed of thirteen judges, assisted by five advocates general. Normally seven judges will preside, aided by one advocate general. The judges elect one of their number to be president of the court. The judges are chosen from high judicial positions within the member states. The advocates general are of similar pedigree. Article 166 describes the role of the advocates general as being to make 'reasoned submissions on cases brought before the court, in order to assist the court'. The court ruling or judgment is then left to the national court of the member state to enforce.

In the 1980s the UK government was frequently the subject of rulings from the ECJ. For example, the government sought to exempt spectacles from VAT. In the case of the *EC Commission v. UK* (Case 353/85, reported in *The Times*, 24 February 1988), the ECJ upheld the view of the Commission that spectacles were subject to VAT. Spectacles were not, as the UK government argued, a medical service, which would have exempted them from VAT.

To facilitate the speeding up of obtaining a ruling from the ECJ, a Court of First Instance was inaugurated in 1989, sitting in Luxembourg. It has twelve judges, one representing each member state. Its purpose is to reduce the workload of the ECJ by conclusively determining the facts of a case, enabling the ECJ to rule exclusively on points of law. The Court of First Instance hears cases brought by persons, not by member states or institutions.

CRIMINAL COURTS

The structure of the criminal courts is shown in the following chart. A business organization involved in legal proceedings is more likely to find itself in the civil courts that the criminal courts. It is useful to have a basic understanding, however, of the procedures for the trial of criminal cases.

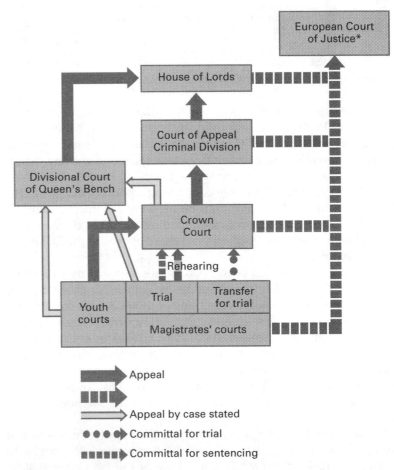

The criminal court structure

Magistrates' courts

As the county courts are to the civil courts system, the magistrates' courts are to the criminal court system. I suspect that many of us, myself included, have fallen foul of the law for one reason or another in a minor way. In our society, there must be very few people who drive a car who haven't contravened some law or regulation that could have landed them before the magistrates. For most of us this will be our only contact with the criminal court system, unless we are called upon to act as a juror.

There is one very important difference between the role of county courts and that of magistrates' courts. The county court can be bypassed in the civil system, by an action commencing in the High Court. However, the magistrates' court is the court of first instance for all criminal cases. This means that, on a typical morning at a busy magistrates' court, there could be people appearing on charges ranging from being drunk to having committed murder. It is not possible to bypass the magistrates' court. Having said that, the role of the magistrates' court has recently been drastically changed. Historically, the magistrates had the power to review a case, where the offence was indictable (see below), to ensure that there was sufficient evidence to commit the case to the Crown Court. Therefore, their role was twofold: that of hearing summary cases and those indictable cases that they felt capable of dealing with, given the consent of the accused, and that of examining justices. The second role was abolished by the Criminal Justice and Public Order Act 1994 (CJAPOA94).

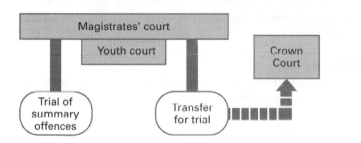

The CJAPOA94 responded to the recommendations of the Runciman Royal Commission (see Chapter 3, p. 21), which had highlighted the failings of the existing committal system. The magistrates now have a new role, that of transferring to the Crown Court any cases that are:

1 triable on indictment only;
2 triable either way, where the court has decided that the case is more suited to being heard on indictment, or the accused has not consented to be tried summarily.

Indictable offences

Indictable offences are offences that may be tried on **indictment**, before a judge and jury at the Crown Court. Most serious offences, including murder, rape and burglary, are indictable. An attempt to commit an indictable offence is itself indictable. Some less serious indictable offences may be tried either by magistrates or on indictment, and are known as offences triable either way (see below).

▶ **Indictment** – a formal document upon which the charge(s) are written, which is read out to the accused at the trial.

Summary offences

Summary offences are offences that can only be tried 'summarily', that is, before magistrates, and not before a judge and jury. These include minor motoring offences, and being drunk and disorderly. Juveniles must always be tried summarily in the separate youth courts that have replaced the former juvenile courts, regardless of the offence, with the exceptions of murder, or where charged jointly with an adult, or where the youth is aged between 14 and 17 and is charged with an offence punishable with fourteen or more years' imprisonment, or where the court feels that it is likely that the youth will be sentenced to a long period of imprisonment.

Offences triable either way

Certain indictable offences can be tried either at the magistrates' court or the Crown Court. When considering whether to accept an indictable offence for trial at a magistrates' court, the magistrates must consider the seriousness of the offence and whether it is suitable for trial at the magistrates' court. Where magistrates consider that an indictable case is suitable for them to hear they must offer the accused the option of trial at the Crown Court. The accused must be informed that, if he or she opts for trial at the magistrates' court, he or she might, if convicted, still be sent to the Crown Court for sentencing. Currently, the maximum penalties that magistrates can impose are six months' imprisonment and/or a fine of £5,000 per offence.

Magistrates

There are two types of magistrate: stipendiary magistrates and justices of the peace (JPs). Stipendiary magistrates are found in major inner-city areas. They are professionals and are paid. In order to become a stipendiary magistrate a person must have spent at least seven years as a barrister or a solicitor. They are selected by the Lord Chancellor. Justices of the peace are also appointed by the Lord Chancellor, on the recommendation of local Magistrates' Courts Advisory Committees, but they are lay persons and generally have no legal qualifications. Stipendiary magistrates may preside singly, while there must be a minimum of two and a maximum of seven JPs. The only qualification for becoming a JP is residential: a JP must reside within 15 miles of the court at which he or she sits.

 Either alone or in a group visit your local magistrates' court for the morning. A magistrates' court can be found in most towns, but they normally only sit on certain days of the week. Ensure that you attend on the right day by telephoning the court (see *Yellow Pages* under 'Courts'). Take down details of the cases that are dealt with, including the offence or other matter and the court action. Try to identify the roles of the different people who work in the court. When you get back, review what you have seen and reconcile it against your notes and the text in this chapter. Could you identify the different roles of the magistrates, between that of trying cases and that of transferring them?

Crown Court

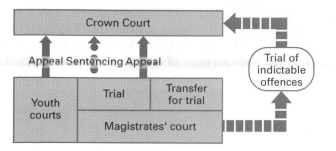

The Crown Court has an unlimited jurisdiction over all criminal cases tried on indictment, and acts as a court for the hearing of appeals from magistrates' courts. The Crown Court system was created by the Courts Act 1971, and replaced the system of Assize courts described in Chapter 3. The Crown Court retained a **circuit system** and introduced a three-tier system. In each of the circuits there are towns designated as first-, second- and third-tier centres. The three-tier system is used to allocate cases between the Crown Court centres.

The Old Bailey is the Central Criminal Court and the principal Crown Court for Central London.

First-tier centres deal with both criminal and High Court civil cases. They are presided over by **puisne judges**, **circuit judges** and **recorders**.

Second-tier centres deal with only criminal cases and are also presided over by puisne judges, circuit judges and recorders.

Third-tier centres also deal only with criminal cases but are presided over by circuit judges and recorders only.

The type of case to be heard will determine which category of judge will preside and at which type of centre it will be held. There are four categories of crimes:

Class 1 The most serious offences, for example, murder. These offences must be tried by a High Court judge.
Theoretically, the death penalty has been retained for the following, and some other rare and uncommon offences: genocide, treason and any attempts or conspiracy to commit either of these offences. However, it is unlikely that the death penalty will ever again be passed in England and Wales.

Class 2 Offences that are slightly less serious than murder, including rape, incest (with a girl under the age of 13), manslaughter, illegal abortion, infanticide, sedition and mutiny, and attempts to commit, incite or conspire to commit such offences. These offences will normally be

▶ **Circuit system** – a system of dividing England and Wales into regional *circuits* for the purpose of court administration. The system now comprises the circuits of South-eastern, North-eastern, Midland and Oxford, Northern, Western, and Wales and Chester.

▶ **Puisne** (pronounced puny) **judges** are ordinary judges of the High Court. To qualify for appointment as a puisne judge, a person must have had a right of audience in relation to all proceedings in the High Court for at least ten years, or he or she must have been a circuit judge for at least two years (Courts and Legal Services Act 1990, s. 71). **Circuit judges** must have a ten-year Crown Court or ten-year county court qualification (CLSA90, s. 71), or they could be a recorder, or have held a full-time appointment for at least three years in one of the offices listed in the CLSA90 – e.g. as a stipendary or as a district judge. Circuit judges preside in the county courts and Crown Courts and, on invitation, in the High Court. **Recorders** must have a ten-year Crown Court or ten-year county court qualification (CLSA90, s. 71). Recorders act as part-time judges, sitting normally in the Crown Courts and occasionally in a county court or High Court.

tried by a High Court judge, but may be tried by a circuit judge.

Class 3 All indictable offences that are not Class 1 or 2 offences, including robbery, wounding or grievous bodily harm with intent. Any of the aforementioned judges may try such a case.

Class 4 Cases that may be tried either at a Magistrates' Court or at a Crown Court, including causing death by reckless driving, burglary and other offences not covered by classes 1–3, and appeals from magistrates and juvenile courts. Cases submitted for sentencing after conviction from magistrates' courts. Normally a circuit judge or a recorder will preside, but on occasion it can be a High Court judge.

Court of Appeal, Criminal Division

This court was created by the Criminal Appeal Act 1966. Because it is a divisional court, the major details are the same as described in the civil section. This division is headed by the Lord Chief Justice. Between three and five judges will preside over appeals against sentencing and appeals on points of law from the Crown Courts. The Criminal Justice Act 1988 gave the court the power to increase sentences if they thought it suitable on cases referred to them by the **Attorney General**.

House of Lords

The House of Lords plays the same role in both the civil and criminal systems, though the vast majority of its work rests with the civil law (see p. 36 above). It hears criminal appeals from the Court of Appeal, Criminal Division, and from the Divisional Court of the Queen's Bench Division. Either the prosecution or defence may appeal in both cases, with leave, provided a point of law of general public importance is involved.

European Court of Justice

The European Court of Justice plays the same role in both the civil and criminal systems (see p. 37 above).

OTHER COURTS

Restrictive Practices Court

This court was established by the Restrictive Trade Practices Acts 1956–76 and the Restrictive Practices Courts Act 1976. Its role is to supervise the enforcement of actions brought before it by the Monopolies and Mergers Commission and the Director General of Fair Trading. These two institutions were created by the Fair

► The **Attorney General** is normally a member of the House of Commons and is a political appointee. The Attorney General is the legal adviser to the government, is a practising barrister and is head of the English Bar. It is the Attorney General who prosecutes in important criminal cases and who represents the Crown in civil matters. Prosecutions are also brought in the name of the Attorney General in certain matters, for example, public nuisance.

Trading Act 1973. Where the Director General feels that a business is acting in a manner that is prejudicial to the interests of consumers, he or she can require it to stop. If a business fails to desist or breaks a requirement to stop, then the Director General can proceed against that business in the Restrictive Practices Court. The court also determines which contractual conditions agreed by suppliers to establish minimum retail price levels are exempted from the Resale Prices Acts 1964–76.

The Restrictive Practices Court consists of five High Court judges and ten **lay persons**. Normally one judge will sit with two lay persons. Appeals can be made from this court to the Court of Appeal (Civil) on any question of law in England and Wales; to the Court of Session in Scotland or the Court of Appeal in Northern Ireland.

► A **lay person** is a non-professional person. Lay persons may be found in two different places within the legal system: as magistrates and as members of a jury.

Employment Appeal Tribunal

While it is called a tribunal, the Employment Appeal Tribunal (EAT) is generally thought of as a court. It is staffed by judges from the High Court and the Court of Appeal, and lay persons with appropriate specialist knowledge. The lay persons are representatives of employers and representatives of workers, normally trade unionists. Its main jurisdiction lies in hearing appeals from industrial tribunals, on points of law from the following legislation:

Equal Pay Act 1970
Sex Discrimination Acts 1975 and 1986
Employment Protection Act 1975
Race Relations Act 1976
Employment Protection (Consolidation) Act 1978.

Normally one judge and either two or four lay persons preside, with an equal number of lay persons being drawn from employers' and workers' representatives. Procedure in the EAT is relatively informal. Appeals can be made from this court to the Court of Appeal (Civil) on any question of law in England and Wales, to the Court of Session in Scotland or the Court of Appeal in Northern Ireland.

Coroners' courts

The office of coroner is one of the oldest in our legal system, dating back to the twelfth century. Currently, a coroner's duties are governed by the Coroners' Acts 1887–1980 and the Administration of Justice Act 1982. A coroner must be a barrister, solicitor or medical practitioner of at least five years' standing. The jurisdiction of the court is geographical, and concerns two main areas: deaths and treasure trove. Where a person dies a sudden, unnatural or violent death, or dies in prison, a coroner will hold an inquest to establish the cause of death. A coroner may, however, hold an inquest into any death.

A coroner may summon a jury of between seven and eleven persons to assist in deciding the cause of death. A coroner must do this if he or she suspects that a death is due to murder, manslaughter, infanticide, a road accident, poisoning or a notifiable disease. In court, a coroner conducts the proceedings in an inquisitorial manner, calling and questioning witnesses. Where a person has been charged over the killing of another, a coroner will open the proceedings and then adjourn them until the trial of that person has taken place.

Judicial Committee of the Privy Council

This Judicial Committee is a throwback to the days of the *Curia Regis*. It is staffed by the Law Lords, all former Lord Chancellors and the current Lord Chancellor, and, on occasion, when hearing a matter concerning their particular country, by high-ranking judges from the Commonwealth. Its appellate jurisdiction remains in the following areas:

- ecclesiastical courts;
- admiralty court;
- medical and dental professions, and opticians' tribunals;
- colonies, protectorates and those Commonwealth countries that have not abolished the Privy Council as their final court of appeal.

▶ **Quorum** – the minimum number of judges that must be present in order for the court to be able to sit.

The **quorum** of the Privy Council is three, though five judges will sit in an important case. Procedure is informal. The court sits as an advisory board, not delivering a judgment but giving advice to the Queen upon which an Order in Council (see Chapter 3 for a definition) is made.

Minor courts

Other minor, specialist civil courts also exist: namely the ecclesiastical courts, Court of Chivalry, naval courts and the courts martial. Such courts are of little interest to a mainstream law student.

OTHER METHODS OF CLASSIFYING COURTS

At the beginning of this chapter I said that to classify courts as being either of criminal or civil jurisdiction would be to give an incomplete picture. As we have seen, several of the courts have jurisdiction over both types of case. There are other methods used to classify courts and I will briefly detail these below.

Supreme Court

The Supreme Court of Judicature was the title given to the Court of Appeal and the High Court by the Judicature Acts (1873–5); and it was extended to include the Crown Court by the Courts Act 1971. It excludes the House of Lords because, at the time of its creation, the Liberal government of the day fully intended to abolish the House of Lords as the final court of appeal. However, they lost power at the vital moment and failed to complete the job.

Inferior and superior courts

The magistrates' and county courts are described as inferior courts, while all other courts are known as **superior courts**. These terms reflect the different powers that reside with the different courts. Inferior courts are limited in the cases they can try and also have a limited geographical jurisdiction.

► **Superior courts** – House of Lords, the Court of Appeal, High Court and the Crown Court.

The inferior courts may also be known as 'courts of first instance', i.e. they have no power to hear a case on appeal. Therefore, all other courts can be termed 'appeal courts'.

 Examine the list of following cases and determine which court they would first appear in and which court they would be likely to finish up in, should the accused or defendant contest the case:

1 drunkenness;
2 incest;
3 divorce;
4 maintenance orders;
5 the winding up of a company;
6 murder;
7 probate;
8 the loss of a ship at sea.

THE PERSONNEL OF THE LEGAL WORLD

Where possible I have noted the duties, origins and roles of the different players in the legal system, where we have first come across them in the text. I now plan to acquaint you with the other major players from the Civil Division, whom I haven't yet had the chance to introduce. I will start with the legal profession, which is divided into barristers and solicitors.

Barristers

The recruitment, training, control and appointment of barristers is overseen by the Senate of the Inns of Court and the Bar. There are four Inns of Court, all situated in central London. They are Lincoln's Inn, Gray's Inn, Inner Temple and Middle Temple.

In order to become a barrister a person must first obtain at least a second-class honours degree in law, passing the seven qualifying subjects. Non-law graduates and mature students may complete a

► The Senate of the Inns of Court and the Bar is also known as the Bar Council.

one-year full-time or two-year part-time Common Professional Examination (CPE). A candidate must then gain admittance to one of the Inns before commencing the second section of the training supervised by the Council of Legal Education. This second stage is a one-year vocational Bar finals course, at the end of which exams must be passed. There is also an eating qualification to be satisfied, whereby a student must dine at least twenty-four times in the Hall of their particular Inn! Upon completing these two stages a student may be 'called to the bar', but in order to become qualified to practise in their own right, a prospective barrister must spend a year of pupillage (further training) in a barristers' chambers.

▶ See below for full details of the changes to the rights of audience.

Barristers have recently lost their exclusive right to be heard (have rights of audience) in the House of Lords, the Privy Council, the Court of Appeal, the High Court, the Crown Court and the Employment Appeal Tribunal. Solicitors, in private practice, can now speak in all of the superior courts.

Barristers have no contractual relationship with their clients and cannot sue for their fees; neither can they be sued in negligence if they lose a case, with regard to their performance in court or in preparation of court work. A solicitor selects a barrister for his or her client and a solicitor will always be present at any meeting between the barrister and the client. Simply put, a solicitor will then do all of the background work, such as interviewing witnesses and obtaining evidence, while a barrister will 'perform' on behalf of the client in court.

In chambers, barristers advise solicitors and others on legal matters, for which they can be sued in negligence, should they provide wrong advice. Barristers of some standing, normally fifteen years, can apply to the Lord Chancellor to become a Queen's Counsel (QC). This process is commonly known as 'taking silk', because the robe worn in court by a QC is made of silk.

Solicitors

The Law Society, which was created by the Solicitors Act 1974, controls the admission, training and recruitment of solicitors. A potential solicitor must first obtain a law degree. Non-law graduates or mature students must complete a Common Professional Exam (CPE), which is a one-year full-time course (two years part-time) leading to a diploma in law. After that the new Legal Practice Course (LPC) must be completed, either one year full-time, or two years part-time. Finally, the trainee solicitor must spend a training period of two years as an articled clerk in a legal environment, normally a solicitors' practice, having signed a training contract. All trainees must also complete a Professional Skills Course prior to being admitted as a solicitor. There is now a requirement for all solicitors to undertake continuing education courses.

A school leaver may now qualify as a solicitor. To do so he or she must first pass the Solicitors' First Examination, which is organized by the Law Society. Next the LPC must be passed, followed by four years as an articled clerk. Such trainees are then in the same position as students who have followed the law degree route.

At the end of the training period a solicitor may have his or her name placed on the Roll of Solicitors. However, in order to practise, a solicitor must obtain a practising certificate from the Law Society. This certificate is renewable annually.

As detailed below, solicitors in private practice who have obtained a certificate of advocacy have unlimited rights of audience in all courts. A certificate of advocacy is not required for the inferior courts, where all solicitors have rights of audience.

The workload of a solicitor includes conveyancing, probate, advising clients on their legal rights, both criminal and civil, the representation of clients in both the magistrates' and county courts, and matrimonial work. In more recent times solicitors have also taken advantage of the relaxation in the financial services sector and are now recommending mortgages, insurance, investment and other policies. This, coupled with the breaking of the tradition that solicitors may not advertise, has led to a major change for solicitors, who are having to become increasingly marketing orientated.

Complaints

There exist complaints procedures against both barristers and solicitors. Barristers are dealt with by the Professional Conduct Committee, which refers suitable cases to the Senate Disciplinary Tribunal. As stated above, barristers are not liable in negligence to clients in respect of work performed in court or closely connected with it.

Complaints against solicitors are made to the Solicitors' Complaints Bureau, who may refer serious complaints of misconduct to the Solicitors' Disciplinary Tribunal, which was created by the Solicitors Act 1974 and has the power to suspend a solicitor or strike him or her off the roll. There is also a **Legal Services Ombudsman** who handles complaints that are not dealt with to the satisfaction of the complainant by the Solicitors' Complaints Bureau. In 1989 around 20,000 complaints were made, with roughly 10 per cent giving rise to disciplinary action. A solicitor has a right of appeal against a disciplinary decision to the Master of the Rolls and/or to the High Court. In 1989 nearly £15 million was paid out of the Solicitors' Compensation Fund. This fund, to which all solicitors contribute, compensates clients whose solicitors have misappropriated their funds.

Criticisms of restrictive practices among the legal profession

The legal world has been one of the great bastions of restrictive practices. When the various constituent parts of the legal professions are examined – namely solicitors, barristers and judges – it is evident that their members are dominated by male, white, public-school-educated people. The following figures, taken from the Law Society's 1990 annual statistical report, illustrate the under-representation of women and ethnic minorities.

Gender

Female law graduates and new trainee solicitors number 50 per cent of the total, and 47 per cent of newly admitted solicitors are female. However, only 23 per cent of solicitors who hold a certificate to practise are female. Indeed, of those who have held a certificate for more than fifteen years, only 6 per cent are female, while 87 per cent of all partners are male.

Race

Of all solicitors and barristers only 1 per cent are 'non-white' (the term used by the Law Society). An applicant from an ethnic minority may have to make twice as many applications as a white applicant to obtain a place as a trainee solicitor. This has encouraged the formation of firms of non-white solicitors which are sought out by ethnic minority clients. This is a clear indication that many people from ethnic minorities feel that the legal system is prejudiced against them, and that their interests are better protected by solicitors or barristers from similar backgrounds.

The Bar established a Race Relations Committee in 1983, followed by the Law Society in 1986, to examine ways of addressing the problem of the lack of representation of ethnic minorities in the legal professions. The Courts and Legal Services Act 1990, s. 64, made it illegal to discriminate against the recruitment of barristers on the grounds of sex or race. However, while rules exist to prevent discrimination, the statistics illustrate that the legal profession continues to appoint people in its own familiar image.

The under-representation of members of ethnic minorities and women in the two sections of the legal profession is continued and compounded among judges, who are, as we have learned, appointed from the ranks of barristers and solicitors.

The Courts and Legal Services Act 1990

This Act followed on from a government white paper on the reform of the legal system, but the restrictive practices of both barristers and solicitors have been largely retained. To most observers, it has been another whitewash. The rights of audience, without which the profession of barrister would probably disappear, have been kept, with the proviso that those rights may be extended by the Lord Chancellor (a former barrister) and the Lord Chancellor's four senior judges (all barristers). They will be advised as to the suitability of this action by the Advisory Committee on Legal Education and Conduct. This committee consists of two practising barristers, two practising solicitors, two law teachers and eight lay members. It is chaired by a senior judge. It shouldn't be too difficult to reach a conclusion about the independence of this committee!

▶ Defenders of the present system would point out that a recent Director of Public Prosecutions is female and that some leading members of the judiciary are female.

Extension of rights of audience

In December 1993 the Lord Chancellor's Department announced the end of the barristers' historic monopoly of appearance in the superior courts. The Lord Chancellor, Lord Mackay of Clashfern, in committee with four other senior judges, approved an application made by the Law Society to allow their members in private practice to appear in the superior courts. The application was made possible by the Courts and Legal Services Act 1990.

From March 1994 a small group of solicitors, including those who have previously qualified as barristers, those who currently sit as part-time judges and those who have obtained a certificate of advocacy, will be able to appear in the higher courts. Other solicitors who wish to gain rights of audience in the superior courts will have to undergo training, leading to a certificate in advocacy. The first batch of solicitors who have completed this training are to appear in the superior courts in late 1994. This will end the need to appoint both a solicitor and a barrister to present or defend a case in the superior courts.

Solicitors who wish to obtain the right to appear in the superior courts will be able to apply for higher court qualifications, in either criminal or civil proceedings, or both. Solicitors who obtain the civil higher court qualification will obtain rights of audience in the High Court in all proceedings and in all other courts in civil proceedings. Solicitors who obtain the criminal higher court qualification will obtain rights of audience in the Crown Court in all proceedings and in all other courts for criminal proceedings. A solicitor who obtains the all-proceedings qualification (both criminal and civil) will be able to appear in all courts.

To be eligible to apply for a higher courts qualification, a solicitor must have practised for a minimum of three years. The Law Society has constructed a series of training packages and tests that solicitors must successfully complete before they will be awarded any of the higher court qualifications. The final section of the training will lead to the award of a certificate of advocacy.

Only those solicitors in private practice will be able to take advantage of the new rules relating to appearance in the superior courts. Those who work in the public sector, for example the Crown Prosecution Service, will not be able to appear in the superior courts. This restriction must now only be temporary; indeed it seems to be an unreasonable restraint of trade to prevent those in the public sector from enjoying the same benefits as those employed in the private sector.

Other 'tinkerings' instituted by the Courts and Legal Services Act 1990 included:

- a Legal Services Ombudsman, with no powers of enforcement, to monitor the way in which complaints are dealt with – the ombudsman merely has a power to recommend compensation;
- the extension of the right to conduct conveyancing to other

▶ **Inquisitorial** describes a system whereby the court, through a judge, attempts to establish the truth in a case by asking questions of witnesses, experts and lawyers. All evidence that has been collected must be made known to the court and to all interested parties.

▶ The *Juge d'instruction* is the French equivalent of our Crown Court judge. *Juges d'instruction* perform an inquisitorial role, questioning witnesses and the accused in court, attempting to ascertain the truth.

▶ **Adversarial** describes a system whereby the prosecution must prove that the defendant has committed the offence with which he or she has been charged. The court is merely the arena for the opposing parties to fight in, with the judge playing no part other than to act as a referee.

▶ Under the **legal aid** system the state provides help to persons who are involved in court action or who wish to seek the advice of a solicitor. The criteria for qualifying for legal aid have become more and more dependent upon the income of the applicant, and now only the very poorest qualify for legal aid in civil cases. The government is proposing that in the future only certain franchised solicitors will be able to offer legal aid. Currently pilot schemes are in operation, testing the feasibility of this proposal.

authorized bodies;

- the extension of the rights of others to prepare applications for probate; and
- a review to be instituted into the criteria to be used in the selection and appointment of judges.

The question of reform has not been fully answered by this Act. It would appear that no one is prepared to consider the wholesale reforms necessary to give us a modern judicial system. Our system is constantly producing miscarriages of justice – the Guildford Four, the Birmingham Six, etc. I would not lay the blame on any one section of the system for producing these results. The whole system is in dire need of reform. The following radical changes, which I suspect will find few supporters among the ranks of the judiciary or other legal professionals, could bring our system into the twentieth century.

1 Solicitors and barristers should be merged into one profession. This would cut costs dramatically, end the 'rights of audience' restrictive practice and go some way to stopping the practice whereby barristers may pick up a brief for the first time on the morning of a criminal trial.
2 Judges should be replaced with trained elected professionals. The current system consists largely of elderly, rich, white former public schoolboys, who appoint clones of themselves, and so the system continues.
3 Judges should further take an **inquisitorial** role, based on the French *juge d'instruction*. Coupled with this, the court system should change from being an **adversarial** to an inquisitorial one. This would involve all the evidence in the case being brought into open court, not just the evidence that the prosecution seek to present to prove their case.

The Royal Commission on Criminal Justice, which reported in July 1993, has yet again missed the chance to recommend wholesale reform. This is probably tied into a question of political will, as well as those within the system protecting themselves. Perhaps the greatest threat to the present system is economic. In 1993, wholesale changes to the **legal aid** system were announced, introducing a system of franchising legal aid work to legal practices. In order to reduce the legal aid bill, it would now appear that the government has decided to target the legal professions as well as disfranchising the vast majority of the population from the right to legal aid.

The Law Society appears to recognize this threat and is in the process of creating a lower-level qualification, which will probably be called a para-legal. A para-legal will undertake all of the solicitor's routine work, such as conveyancing, probate and the giving of advice to persons detained at police stations. While this will cut costs, it will inevitably lead to unemployment for numbers of solicitors. Currently, there are thousands of law graduates who are struggling to obtain articles in solicitors' offices. The creation of the post of para-legal will probably necessitate a review and change in the way that solicitors are recruited and trained. This could have a knock-on effect for barristers, whose rights of audience will be further threatened by frustrated solicitors, because their bread-and-butter work will have been taken over by para-legals.

Legal executives

This title covers people who work in solicitors' offices, but who either cannot or do not wish to become solicitors. The Institute of Legal Executives has its own examination and qualification structure. Indeed, the County Courts Act 1984 enabled the Lord Chancellor to give legal executives limited rights of audience in the county court.

Solicitor General

The Solicitor General is the deputy to the Attorney General and, when deputizing or when authorized, has the same powers as the Attorney General.

Director of Public Prosecutions

The Director of Public Prosecutions (DPP), unlike the Lord Chancellor, Attorney General and Solicitor General, is not a political appointee. He or she is appointed by the Home Secretary, and must be a barrister or solicitor of at least ten years' standing. Because the DPP is appointed as a civil servant, and is therefore impartial, when a government changes the DPP does not. Governed by the Prosecution of Offences Act 1985, the duties of the DPP are exclusively related to the criminal law. He or she is responsible for overseeing the vast majority of all criminal proceedings and is the head of the **Crown Prosecution Service**.

Clerk of the court

The clerk of the court plays an important role in the administration of justice in the magistrates' courts. A clerk is a paid official who will normally be a qualified solicitor or barrister. The clerk is in charge of the court, playing a pivotal role between the justices and persons appearing in the court. A clerk should not normally retire with the justices when they consider their verdict, though he or she may do so where clarification is required on a point of law. A clerk also helps in the training of justices.

(ACT) Now you have completed this chapter look back at the chapter objectives at the beginning. Can you do all the things that they suggest? If not, look again at the relevant sections of the chapter.

▶ The **Crown Prosecution Service** (CPS) was established by statute in 1985. The DPP is responsible for the CPS, which is split into twenty-nine different regions, each headed by a Chief Crown Prosecutor. The CPS is responsible for the actual prosecution of alleged offenders in the courts, employing solicitors and barristers to work as prosecutors. Some questions have been raised about the quality of the CPS prosecutors. The recent changes to the rights of audience, announced by the Lord Chancellor, specifically excluded CPS solicitors from being able to speak in the superior courts.

CHAPTER SUMMARY

1 The present court system in England and Wales has remained largely unchanged since its creation by the Judicature Acts 1873–5.

2 The majority of courts have either a criminal or a civil jurisdiction, though some – for example, magistrates' courts – have both criminal and civil jurisdiction in certain matters.

3 The major courts having civil jurisdiction are magistrates' courts, county courts, the High Court (divided into the Queen's Bench, Chancery and Family Divisions), Court of Appeal (Civil Division) and the House of Lords.

4 The major courts having criminal jurisdiction are magistrates' courts, the Crown Court, Court of Appeal (Criminal Division) and the House of Lords.

5 The European Court of Justice is the final court of appeal on all matters relating to the interpretation of European Community law. Under Article 177 of the European Economic Community Treaty, the final court of appeal in a member state must refer a case, which concerns any matter relating to EC law, to the European Court of Justice.

6 The courts may also be classified as being either superior or inferior. The magistrates' and county courts are classified as inferior, while all other courts are superior. The Court of Appeal, the High Court and the Crown Court may also be classified together as the Supreme Court of Judicature.

7 The legal profession is divided into two branches: barristers and solicitors. Barristers appear recently to have lost their traditional advantages over solicitors, namely the sole rights of audience in the superior courts. However, only time will tell if the changes detailed in this chapter will cause the legal professions to merge.

8 Recent miscarriages of justice have forced the government to review the workings of the criminal and civil justice system. The Courts and Legal Services Act 1990 and the Royal Commission on Criminal Justice 1993 introduced and advised limited reforms, but both fell short of a wholesale reform of the legal system.

Court procedures

In this chapter we shall look at the way a trial is conducted in the High Court and county courts, together with a detailed picture of the way that a small claim is followed and the role that the different legal players take.

PRE-TRIAL HIGH COURT ACTION

We can identify seven steps in the pre-trial procedure for a High Court action:

1 commencing the action, for example by writ;
2 acknowledgement of service;
3 pleadings;
4 discovery and inspection of documents;
5 summons for directions;
6 setting down the action for trial;
7 High Court hearing.

All or some of these steps will take place, depending on the complexities and nature of the case in question. The procedure outlined in the following summary would apply, for example, to a contractual dispute being heard in the Queen's Bench Division.

Commencing the action

High Court proceedings are normally initiated by the issuing of a writ. Indeed, a writ must be used when the action is one in tort (other than trespass to land), one in which a claim made by the plaintiff is based upon an allegation of fraud, an action in probate or one in which damages are claimed in respect of personal injuries, death or the infringement of a patent. For the student of business law, the writ is by far the most important method of commencing a High Court action.

► **Originating summons** – the Rules of the Supreme Court state that proceedings should be instituted by originating summons where the question is one of interpretation of an Act or of particular documents, or where there is unlikely to be any substantial dispute of fact. Certain Acts, such as the Landlord and Tenant Act 1954, require that in certain circumstances an originating summons be used to commence an action. Actions commenced by originating summons will normally be heard in the Chancery Division. Evidence is normally presented in the form of an affadavit.

► **Central Office** – the administrative organization of the Supreme Court in London (see Chapter 4, p. 44).

► **District registry** – an office of the High Court outside London, corresponding in function to the Central Office. There are district registries in all major towns and cities in England and Wales.

An action commenced by writ will normally be very expensive for all parties. In situations where the material facts of the dispute are not in question, but the interpretation of a particular Act or of documents are disputed, it is more normal and less expensive to seek the ruling of the court via an **originating summons**. There are also other less important methods of beginning an action, for example, originating petition and originating notice of motion, which are of little importance to this text.

Serving of the writ

The first stage in commencing a High Court action by writ involves the plaintiff, normally through his or her solicitor, obtaining the necessary forms from the **Central Office** of the Supreme Court or from a **district registry**. The plaintiff must then complete the forms outlining the claim in general terms, but stating the remedy that he or she seeks. In order for these forms to become a writ, two copies must be registered with the Supreme Court and a fee paid. A signed copy is retained by the court, while the second copy is sealed and returned to the plaintiff. This copy becomes the writ in action, which must then be served on the defendant or, if acceptable, on the defendant's solicitor. A writ must be served within four months of issue.

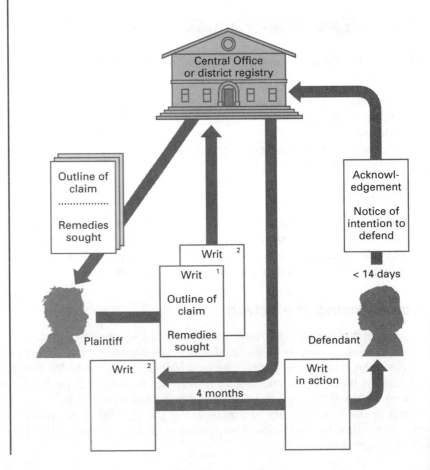

Service of the writ and acknowledgement of service

Acknowledgement of service

The second stage involves the defendant acknowledging receipt of the writ to the issuing court and either notifying that he or she intends to defend the action or accepting liability (very unlikely). A defendant has fourteen days from receipt of the writ to reply to the court. If a reply is not made within fourteen days, then a plaintiff can ask for judgment to be brought against the defendant anyway. Further, should the defendant fail to reply, the defendant would not be able to deny liability at a later stage and he or she would have to agree to the amount of damages fixed by the court.

If, after the defendant acknowledges service and defence of the claim, the plaintiff considers that there is no valid defence, the plaintiff may apply to a Master for **summary judgment**, under Order 14 of the **Rules of the Supreme Court**.

Pleadings

The pleadings are part of the interlocutory stage of the trial, whereby all matters of contention that can be resolved, prior to a trial, are resolved. The interlocutory stage may include all or some of the following: pleadings, discovery of documents, summons for directions, interrogatories and setting down for trial.

(a) The first pleading is the **statement of claim**, which is sent by the plaintiff to the defendant. It must be sent within fourteen days of receiving notice that the defendant intends to defend the case. It will detail the material facts of the case and outline any alleged injuries or losses sustained and the remedies sought. While the plaintiff need not at this stage detail what evidence he or she has, all other details of the claim must be included. This is because, should the case reach a trial, the plaintiff will not be able to make any allegation of which the defendant has not been given prior notice.

(b) The defendant must submit a **defence** of the plaintiff's statement of claim, repudiating each allegation made. Should the defendant fail to deny any allegation, then the court will accept that allegation as being proven.

(c) This stage is also used for the plaintiff to **reply** to any new matters brought up in the defendant's defence. It is not always used because there may be nothing new in the defence. Only in exceptional circumstances, with the leave of the Court, may a defendant reply with a further pleading – known as a **subsequent pleading**. However, in some cases he or she could seek to 'muddy the waters' further by submitting a counterclaim. A plaintiff must reply to this with a defence.

Should either side feel that the pleadings are vaguely worded and that they would like further clarification, they can apply for further and better particulars from the opposition. Particulars are details of allegations of fact, and do not relate to evidence. Where either party

▶ **Summary judgment** – Order 14 of the Rules of the Supreme Court allows a plaintiff, in an action for debt or damages in the High Court, to have judgment awarded against the defendant, without the defendant being allowed to contest the case.

▶ The **Rules of the Supreme Court** govern practice and procedure in the High Court and in the Court of Appeal. The rules are made by the Supreme Court Rule Committee, which comprises the Lord Chancellor, the Master of the Rolls, four legal practitioners, and the heads of the Chancery, Queen's Bench and Family Divisions of the High Court.

▶ **Subsequent pleadings** – a defendant may answer a plaintiff's reply with a rejoinder, to which the plaintiff may reply with a surrejoinder, which may be answered with a rebutter, which in turn may be replied to with a surrebutter. All subsequent pleadings can only be served with the leave of the Court. Surrejoinders, rebutters and surrebutters are rarely used.

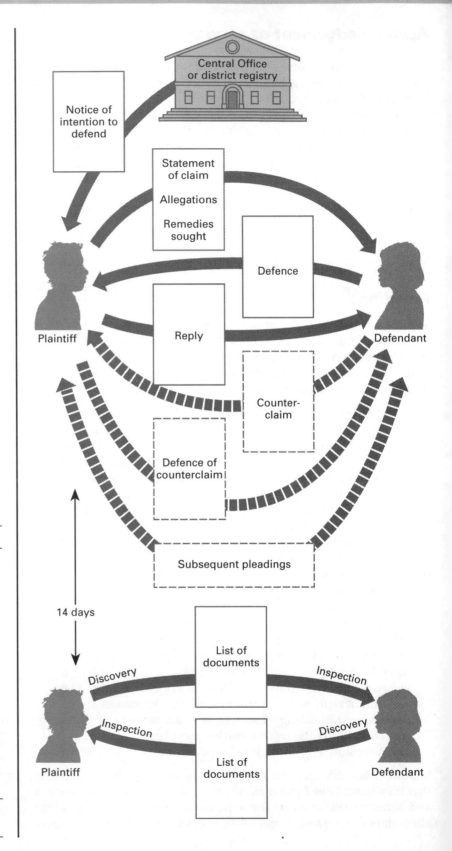

Pleadings

Discovery and inspection of documents

makes reference to a document in the pleadings, the other party can request to see it (see below, under discovery of documents). At this stage, both sides will be playing 'cat and mouse' with each other. If the defendant expects to lose a case, he or she will want to know what evidence the plaintiff has in order to try to minimize any damages that may have to be paid

The final stage is the close of pleadings, which occurs fourteen days after service of the reply, if there is one, or, if not, fourteen days after service of the defence to counterclaim, if there is one, or, if not, fourteen days after service of the defence.

Discovery and inspection of documents

Discovery commences fourteen days after the final pleading. It involves each party providing the other with a full list of the documents that each holds relating to the case. Both parties can then inspect the other party's documents, other than those marked 'without prejudice'. It used to be common practice to mark the majority of documents – or certainly any that would help the opposition – 'without prejudice'. Now, expert reports that are going to be produced at the trial must be made available to the opposition within ten weeks of the end of pleadings.

Summons for directions

The plaintiff must take out a summons for directions within one month of the close of pleadings. At the hearing of the summons, the solicitors of both parties will appear before a **Queen's Bench Master**, who will direct on the following:

(a) the adequacy of, or the need for, further pleadings;
(b) whether there is to be a **jury**;
(c) if the parties have not undergone discovery of documents, then the Master can order either or both parties to swear an **affidavit** disclosing all relevant documents in their possession;
(d) whether the Master feels that either party should answer **interrogatories**;
(e) the time for the setting down of trial.

Either of the parties to an action may make application to a Master for guidance, but should a plaintiff fail to take out a summons for directions, then a defendant can ask for the case to be dismissed, 'for want of prosecution'.

Setting down the action for trial

A plaintiff must 'set down' the action at the Central Office of the Supreme Court, in order for the trial to take place. This involves the plaintiff filing two sets of documents with the court, including the writ, the pleadings, all orders made on the summons for directions, and certain legal aid documents (if any). The case is then entered in

► A **Queen's Bench Master** is a junior judicial officer of the Queen's Bench Division, whose job it is to supervise the interlocutory proceedings. Conventionally, a Master must have held a general advocacy qualification for at least seven years.

► A **jury** is very rare in civil trials, only appearing in about 1 per cent of cases. Juries only preside over cases concerning fraud, malicious prosecution, defamation and false imprisonment, and even in these cases the right can be denied by a judge.

► An **affidavit** is a sworn written statement, made before a person authorized to take oaths, in this case, the Queen's Bench Master.

► **Interrogatories** are formal written questions submitted by one party to another, required to be answered on oath. Such questions must relate to some aspect of the case, which may help in either saving costs or disposing fairly of the case.

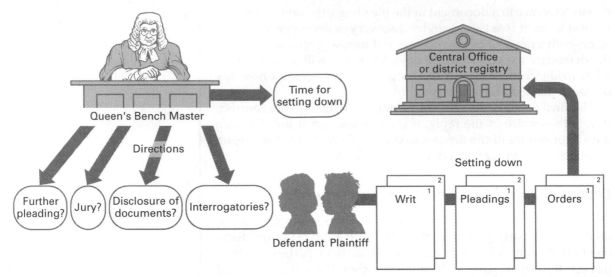

Summons for directions and setting down for trial

the appropriate list of cases awaiting trial. Should the plaintiff fail to do so then the defendant can either 'set down' the action himself or herself or apply to have the action dismissed.

High Court hearing

Once the setting down stage has been completed, the parties must wait for the case to be listed in the **Day's List**, when they and their legal representatives must attend court for the hearing.

You will probably have understood by now why it is said that only the very rich or the very poor (with legal aid) can afford to sue in the High Court. It may seem that the only people to gain from a High Court action are the solicitors and barristers. A substantial percentage of cases are settled out of court, at some stage between the serving of the writ and the morning of the court action. On average, there are about 35,000 High Court actions each year, of which around 10,000 get to the 'setting down' stage. Out of the 10,000, only about 2,500 actually get to trial. The process can take between one to five years, even more in personal injury cases. During the pre-trial stage the defence may make an offer 'without prejudice' to settle the claim. This means that the defence is not admitting the claim but is prepared to offer a sum in settlement of the case. This may be accepted or rejected by the plaintiff. Several of these offers may be made prior to the plaintiff's accepting what he or she feels is a satisfactory amount.

There is a Supreme Court rule that where a defendant offers an amount for settlement by making a payment into court, and the plaintiff rejects that amount, then, should the plaintiff subsequently be awarded less than that amount at the trial, he or she will be liable for the costs of both parties from the date of refusal of the payment into court. When it is considered that a trial adds between 50 and 75 per cent to the total legal costs, it is no surprise that many cases are settled prior to trial. Indeed, Prime Minister John Major's legal advisers advised him to settle at this stage, after a payment into court had been made, in his recent libel action against one of the major newspapers.

 Watch the news or read a serious newspaper to find a controversial case that is currently going through the High Court. Why has the action been brought? Follow the case to its conclusion. What was the result? Why was that the result? What remedy was awarded? If damages were awarded, how much were they and how were the costs of the case allocated?

HIGH COURT PROCEDURE

The court action commences with the plaintiff's counsel outlining the case, using the pleadings. Counsel will then call and examine any witnesses, and submit any documents in evidence. The defence counsel may cross-examine the plaintiff's witnesses, if desired. The procedure is then reversed, with the defence calling its witnesses and submitting documents. If the defendant is not considering using witnesses or documents, then the defence counsel will simply **address** the court. The plaintiff may also be given the chance to further address the court at the end of the defendant's case, where the defence counsel has raised a matter that appears to negate the case. This is known as 'rebutting' evidence.

▶ **Address** – speak to the court, outlining a particular side's case.

Once the preliminary stage has been completed, it is then time for the counsels to outline their arguments to the court again. The defence counsel goes first this time, followed by the counsel for the plaintiff. During these addresses a judge may comment on the questionable aspects of the respective arguments.

A judge will then deliver a judgment, in a simple case, at the end of the counsels' addresses, stating the law and the reasons why he or she has reached a particular decision. These are the *obiter dicta* and *ratio decidendi* of the case. If the judge accepts that his or her decision is bound by precedent, reference will be made to the precedent in the judgment. A judge may 'reserve' judgment, if he or she considers that the issues raised in the case require further consideration before the judge can make a decision. The case will then be adjourned for a period of time determined by the judge, for the judge to contemplate his or her judgement.

▶ *Obiter dicta* and *ratio decidendi* are explained in detail in Chapter 3, p. 27.

If there is a jury in the case then a judge will 'sum up', outlining the matters of fact that the jury must decide upon and directing the jury on the points of law. When the jury returns with a verdict, the judge will then deliver his or her judgment.

After the judgment has been delivered the winning counsel will ask for costs. It is a golden rule that costs follow judgment. Where either party considers that they wish to appeal, they can ask for a **stay of execution** at this stage.

▶ **Stay of execution** – an order suspending the execution of an order of the court.

Draw a simple chart outlining the different stages of a pre-trial action. In two paragraphs explain why you think that the system is in need of reform.

COUNTY COURT ACTION

The procedure for a typical county court action is as follows:

1 summons request;
2 defendant's response;
3 pre-trial review;
4 trial.

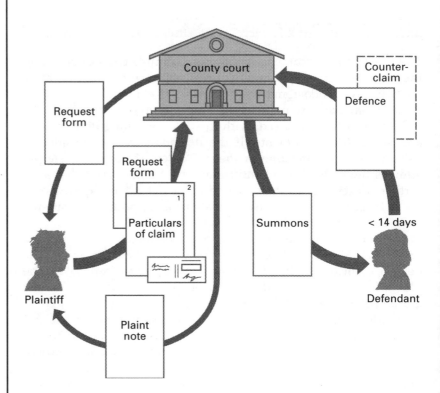

Summons request and defendant's response

Summons request

The plaintiff must first obtain from a county court a 'request form'. This must then be completed, together with two copies of **particulars of claim** and, with the appropriate fee, be returned to the court.

The court will then register the claim, issue the plaintiff with a plaint note bearing the court reference number for the action, and issue a **summons** to the defendant.

Accompanying the summons will be particulars of claim, and an admission, defence and counterclaim form.

▶ **Particulars of claim** – an outline of the claim, giving the facts on which the claim is based.

▶ **Summons** – a written order of the court, requiring a person to appear in a specified court at a specified time.

Defendant's response

A defendant, upon receipt of the summons, will have fourteen days within which either to admit the claim, or submit a defence or a counterclaim against the plaintiff to the court. Any defence must be specific, outlining the grounds and basis for the defence.

Pre-trial review

A fixed date will be given by the court for a pre-trial review. On this date both parties will appear before a district judge, who will conduct a review of the case. Any matters that can be settled prior to trial will be agreed and a date will be fixed for the trial.

Trial

It is important to note that, depending upon the complexity of a case and the financial circumstances of the parties involved, either or neither party may choose not be represented by a solicitor in a county court action. Indeed, many people choose to represent themselves in county court actions.

The procedure is very similar to that in the High Court: first, the plaintiff makes an opening speech, followed by any witnesses or documents that he or she wishes to produce, and the defendant may cross-examine; next the procedure is reversed with the defence producing its evidence; then the defence makes a final speech, which is followed by a final reply from the plaintiff. The judge will then enter a judgment. The winning party is known as the judgment creditor and the losing party as the judgment debtor.

► Remember, the **plaintiff** is the person who is owed the money or who has the complaint. The **defendant** is the person who is being taken to court because the plaintiff has some complaint against him or her.

SMALL CLAIMS PROCEDURE

The county courts operate a small claims system with a special arbitration procedure for claims under £1,000. If the defendant has a defence, the case is referred to a district judge at a county court for arbitration. Difficult cases of law may be referred back to the county court for trial before a circuit judge. Arbitration involves a case being heard by the judge in an informal situation, where the judge is enabled to allow the proceedings to follow a pattern that best suits the case. Judges are encouraged to take an inquisitorial role by asking questions of both parties to ascertain the facts of the case. He or she tries to point the parties towards the most sensible settlement, after hearing both sides of the story.

A district judge's award is binding. It may be set aside only on the grounds that the judge acted contrary to the rules of natural justice in not granting the parties a fair hearing, or that the records of the procedures show that he or she made an error of law. Records of arbitration are brief and often do not state the reason for the award, so proceedings rarely go any further.

A small claim

In order to apply for a summons, a plaintiff must obtain three copies of form N1 from any county court. These must be completed with the name and address of the plaintiff, the details of the claim and the details of the person whom the claim is against. Upon registration of the three sets of forms and the payment of a fee to the court, a plaintiff will be issued with a form N205A. This acts as a receipt and bears the case reference number. It is known as a 'notice of issue'.

The court will then post a copy of the summons to the defendant, together with a reply form N9A and N9B. The defendant then has fourteen days to reply to the summons, commencing the day after the summons is received. When the summons is served upon the defendant, the court will inform the plaintiff by forwarding a form N222. A summons must normally be served within four months of issue. Where a prospective defendant cannot be found, a court, upon application, will allow further time.

Upon receipt of the summons a defendant has the following options:

1 ignore the summons;
2 pay the amount claimed;
3 send a copy of form N9A to the plaintiff agreeing that they owe the money;
4 return N9B to the court, disputing the claim entirely or agreeing that they owe some of the amount claimed.

Defendant ignores a summons

If a plaintiff fails to receive any response from the defendant, they can ask the court to enter **judgment by default**.

To obtain judgment by default, the bottom section of form N205A must be completed, by ticking box A stating that the defendant has failed to reply to the summons. The details of the claim, including the amount claimed and the preferred method of payment, must also be written on the form, which must then be returned to the court.

The court will use the form N205A to complete a judgment form N30. The N30 informs the defendant how much he or she has to pay, how it is to be paid, when it has to be paid and to whom it must be paid. Copies will be sent to the defendant and the plaintiff.

Defendant admits the claim

A defendant may admit liability by completing form N9A and returning it to the plaintiff within fourteen days of receiving the summons. On this form a defendant can detail his or her financial commitments, and offer to pay the claim either in instalments or by a given future date. Obviously, if a defendant has little or no income, then the most sensible (or only) solution is to accept payment by instalments. If a plaintiff accepts the offer of payment

► **Judgment by default** – a decision of the court in favour of the plaintiff.

made by the defendant on the form, the plaintiff must complete the bottom section of form 205A, ticking box B and giving details of the accepted offer of payment. The completed form, upon being returned to the court, will be used to complete a judgment order form N30(1). This is known as 'entering judgment by acceptance'. The N30(1) details the amount to be paid, when it must be paid and the address to which payment should be sent. Copies of the form are sent to both the plaintiff and the defendant.

Plaintiff refuses the defendant's offer

A plaintiff is not bound to accept an offer of payment made in the manner described above. If a plaintiff feels that a defendant ought to pay the money sooner, or in larger amounts, he or she can ask the court to arbitrate to set a higher rate. However, a court will not set a rate of repayment that would be difficult for a defendant to maintain. In order to dispute the offer, a plaintiff must complete form N205A, ticking box B. A reason for the non-acceptance of the offer must be given, together with the preferred payments detailed in section C. Forms N205A and the N9A must then be returned to the court. The same process should be used where the defendant admits the claim, but makes no suggestions as to how to pay.

A court officer will then look at the forms N9A and N205A, and decide what they feel is the most 'just' rate of payment. The court will then complete a form N30(2), thereby entering 'judgment by determination'. Copies of this form will then be sent to both the defendant and the plaintiff. If a plaintiff is unhappy with the decision reached by the court officer, he or she can appeal on a form N244. This must be returned to the court within fourteen days of receiving the form N30(2). The N244 is an application for a district judge to review the case, hear the arguments about payment and arrive at a decision. The plaintiff and defendant will be given a date to attend court to meet with the district judge. It will be an informal meeting, with the **unrobed** judge, the defendant and the plaintiff. The judge will adopt an inquisitorial role, asking questions of both sides, in order to determine the most 'just' rate of payment. The judge will then inform both sides of his or her decision. If the judge decides to alter the rate of payment, the court will issue a form N30(3) to both parties, detailing the new amounts and times of payment.

▶ **Unrobed** – the judge will be in normal everyday clothes, and will not be wearing a wig or anything else that would make him or her look different from an ordinary member of the public.

Defendant admits part of the claim

A defendant may admit liability for part of the claim by completing forms N9A and N9B, and sending them to the court. Copies of those forms, together with a form N225A, will be sent to the plaintiff. If the offer of part payment is accepted then parts B and C of N225A must be completed and returned to the court. Then the court will 'enter judgment on acceptance', completing form N30(1) detailing the means, method and address of payment to both parties. Should the plaintiff accept the offer of part payment, but not the means or time by which payment is made, the plaintiff can detail his or her objections on form N225A.

The same procedure outlined above, under 'Plaintiff refuses the defendant's offer', again becomes applicable.

Defendant disputes the claim

If a defendant disputes all or some of the claim he or she will return the form N9B to the court, stating the reasons. If the defendant replies that the debt has previously been settled (a 'states paid' defence) the court will forward the plaintiff the N9B and a form N236. The plaintiff should complete form N236, stating whether he or she has been paid, also stating that the plaintiff wants the action to continue, and return it to the court.

Where a plaintiff doesn't accept the part admission, part A of form N225A should be completed and returned to the court. The district judge will examine the case and decide either:

1 to arrange for a 'preliminary appointment' to see both parties;
2 to set a date for an 'arbitration' hearing;
3 to decide that the case is too difficult to be dealt with under the small claims procedure and order a trial in open court. (This decision can be made at any one of these three stages. There is a right of appeal against the decision.)

At any meeting with the arbitrator (the judge arbitrating in the case) either or both parties may be accompanied by a 'friend'. The friend may ask questions or speak on behalf of either party. Where possible the friend should not be a witness in the case. The 'friend' is known as a lay representative. Where a lay representative is going to attend, form Ex83 should be completed and handed to the judge at the meeting.

Where a judge decides to hold a preliminary appointment both parties will be sent a form N18. This will state the date, time and place of the hearing, which will take place in private, in the judge's chambers. At the hearing the judge will read the case, ask questions and endeavour to resolve the dispute. If the judge cannot resolve the dispute he or she will decide the next course of action, advise on how to prepare for the arbitration hearing and decide how long the hearing will take. Both parties will be sent form N18A, giving the date of the arbitration hearing, and the details of any other things that need to be done prior to the hearing.

The arbitration hearing

At the hearing the arbitrator will listen to the evidence from both sides, which may be given either orally or in writing. Witnesses may be called, both expert and non-expert, to give evidence. Should either party wish to force a witness to attend to give evidence, a witness summons may be obtained from the court. After hearing the evidence and questioning the witnesses, an arbitrator will reach a decision. This decision is known as an award.

Setting aside an award

There are only limited grounds for appealing against an award made by an arbitrator. The first is that the hearing was not conducted properly; the second is that the law was applied incorrectly. If a plaintiff feels that either of these conditions is satisfied then he or she can appeal on form N244. Both parties will then receive an appointment with a circuit judge, who will decide the merits of the appeal. Where this course is taken, the appellant may become liable for the costs of the other party.

ACT Imagine that you want to use the small claims court to recover £350 from a trader who has failed to complete some work for you. Draw up a list showing what you would have to do, in the order in which you would do it. Next put yourself in the position of the trader and draw up a list illustrating what you would do to defend the action.

Improvements to the small claims system

The Civil Justice Review, which precipitated the changes introduced to the court system in 1991, recognized the value of the small claims system and recommended changes to improve it. Acting upon the proposals, the Lord Chancellor introduced the following changes in July 1991:

- all personal injury cases below £25,000 will normally be tried in a county court;
- all personal injury cases below £50,000 will begin in a county court;
- all cases involving amounts below £25,000 will normally be tried in a county court;
- cases involving amounts above £50,000 will normally be tried in the High Court;

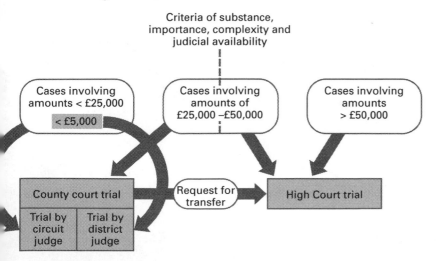

► The changes to the jurisdiction of the county court were introduced by the Lord Chancellor, under the High Court and County Courts Jurisdiction Order 1991, SI 1991/724.

- cases involving amounts between £25,000–£50,000 will be allocated either to the High Court or county court, depending upon the criteria of substance, importance and complexity, and judicial availability;
- a district judge's trial jurisdiction is increased to £5,000;
- the limit for automatic reference to arbitration is increased to £5,000.

The main aim of the Civil Justice Review was to ensure that civil business was dealt with at the appropriate level. Therefore, many of the minor functions performed by district judges have now been devolved to court administrative staff, thus freeing district judges' time to deal with the new work released to the county courts.

 Now that you have completed this chapter look back at the chapter objectives at the beginning. Can you do all the things that these suggest? If not, look again at the relevant sections of the chapter.

CHAPTER SUMMARY

1 The pre-trial period of a High Court action is extremely important, with the vast majority of cases being settled prior to trial.
2 The small claims procedure has been made much more 'user-friendly', simplifying claims, allowing 'friends' in court and raising the threshold of automatic arbitration to £1,000.
3 The July 1991 changes have increased the power and relevance of the county court to the detriment of the High Court.

(6) *Sole traders*

Chapter objectives

By the end of this chapter you should be able to:

■ recognize the differences between a public sector and a private sector organization

■ know the characteristics of sole traders and the obligations imposed on them by the Business Names Act 1985

■ recognize the tort of passing off and the circumstances under which it may apply

■ know the circumstances under which an individual may be made bankrupt

■ understand the procedures by which bankruptcy may be avoided under the Deeds of Arrangement Act 1914 or the Insolvency Act 1986

■ describe the role of a trustee in bankruptcy proceedings

■ appreciate the advantages and disadvantages of being in business as a sole trader.

Business organizations belong to either the **private sector** or the **public sector**. While private sector organizations are obviously the focus of a business law book, we should, for balance, examine the public sector.

PUBLIC SECTOR

The public sector consists of organizations that are owned and managed, wholly or partly, by the government. Public sector organizations can be grouped into four main areas.

1. Some public sector organizations are controlled by central government, i.e. by Parliament, under the direction of a Minister of the Crown: for example, the armed forces.
2. Some are created by central government, and are known as quasi-autonomous non-governmental organizations (quangos). These are funded by central government but have considerable autonomy in the running of their own particular enterprise. The Welsh Development Agency (WDA), set up to control the industrial development of Wales, is a good example

▶ **Private sector** – the part of a country's economy that consists of privately owned enterprises.

▶ **Public sector** – the part of a country's economy that consists of state-owned institutions, including nationalized industries and services provided by local authorities.

of a quango.

3 Some are local government organizations that are partly funded by central government: for example, county councils.

4 Nationalized industries are public sector organizations, though these are now few and far between. In 1994, British Rail was privatized by the Conservative government. A back-bench revolt in the Conservative party prevented the planned privatization of the Post Office, also in 1994. The Conservatives had previously denationalized gas, water and telecommunications. In a nationalized industry the minister responsible for the particular area of operation – for British Rail it was the Minister of Transport – will appoint a Board to run the operation.

PRIVATE SECTOR

The private business sector contains all those organizations that are owned and managed by private citizens rather than by the state. These include people like Tom the carpenter, working for himself, local solicitors or GPs, who are likely to be a few professionals in partnership, and companies as large as Marks & Spencer and ICI.

In the private sector there are three main types of business organization: sole traders, partnerships and companies. In this chapter we shall be concentrating on company law as it relates to sole traders.

Contractual capacity

First, however, it will be helpful to outline the contractual capacity of the three different categories of player – that is, their ability to enter into contracts – and the extent of the liability that each player has.

Sole traders

Sole traders enter into contracts, and can sue and be sued, as individuals, with unlimited liability.

Partnerships

► For a full discussion of partnerships, see Chapter 7.

Partnerships enter into contracts as partners, and can sue and be sued, as partners or as a partnership. All partners are liable for each other's business actions and business debts. Most partnerships are normally of unlimited liability, that is all partners will be individually liable for the liabilities of the partnership. It is possible, though not the norm, to be able to limit the liability of a partner, though all partnerships must have at least one partner whose liability is unlimited.

Companies

An incorporated company is known as a juristic person or corporate entity. The process of incorporation creates a 'legal' person in its own right and the company obtains a separate legal identity from its members. A company will be liable without limit for any debts, but the members of the company will, unless it is a company with unlimited liability, have their liability limited to any amount outstanding to be paid on their shares.

▶ For a full discussion of companies, see Chapter 8.

THE GROWTH OF THE SOLE TRADER

The sole trader is the simplest form of business organization. In the 1980s there was an enthusiasm for entrepreneurship that fostered the idea that anyone could go into business and make a fortune. There was a massive growth in the number of sole traders, fuelled by the Enterprise Allowance Scheme (EAS), which enabled anyone who had been unemployed for a short period of time, and who was in receipt of benefit at the time of application, to start his or her own business. The state would pay people who qualified for the scheme £40 per week, for a period of 52 weeks, to help them get their business off the ground.

The statistics indicate that the EAS was something of a disaster. Although business advice was offered, the viability of the enterprises being set up was not adequately checked, and over 90 per cent of those enterprises subsequently failed. However, there were some notable successes (for example, the comedian Harry Enfield). It was alleged that the EAS was used by some unemployed people as a way of having to avoid signing on, and just claiming the allowance instead of benefit. The system still exists, but now the criteria for acceptance are much more stringent.

STARTING UP

To become a sole trader you merely have to start trading. There are no other legal restrictions. Many types of business are run by sole traders, from shopkeepers, carpenters, car mechanics and electricians to chimney sweeps. The sole trader is by far the most prevalent type of business organization. Depending upon the turnover of a business it may well be worth while registering for value added tax (VAT). Indeed, at a certain turnover a business must register for VAT, but under that figure it is voluntary.

When a business registers for VAT, it must account for all the VAT that it pays on the purchase of goods and it must collect VAT on all of its sales (apart from a specified list of goods that are not liable to VAT, such as children's shoes). It must pay the collected VAT to the Customs and Excise Department, after deducting the VAT that has been paid out. There are different levels of VAT and not all items are liable. There is no VAT payable on newspapers,

► There is currently great controversy over alleged government proposals to extend VAT to products that are either exempt or zero rated. The existing rules are extremely complex with similar products being either exempt, zero rated or subject to VAT. Cakes are zero rated while biscuits are subject to VAT. Customs and Excise officers have determined, probably after a long tasting session, that Jaffa Cakes are cakes, not biscuits, and are therefore zero rated. Other similar products have been found to be biscuits and subject to VAT.

food or children's clothes, though the government has recently added VAT to domestic fuel.

Any premises used by a sole trader must comply with any laws or regulations relating to the control of business premises, for example the Health and Safety at Work Act 1974 and the Shops Act 1950. Where a sole trader uses his or her own residential premises for the purposes of business, he or she will have to apply to the local council for permission. A sole trader will also be liable for any visitors to the premises under the Occupiers Liability Act 1957. It is absolutely necessary, though not strictly compulsory, for sole traders to take out insurance to cover any liability in tort to anyone who is damaged by their products, premises, or by any of their acts or omissions.

(ACT) What is the difference between a private and a public sector organization? List three examples of each type, of which you have personal experience or knowledge.

BUSINESS NAMES

A sole trader starting up a business in his or her own name – for example, Ray Plug, Electrician – will not be subject to the Business Names Act 1985 (BNA85). The BNA85 aims to prevent people from giving names to their businesses that suggest that they:

- are part of another company;
- have the same name as another company;
- are by 'royal' appointment;
- are a society, institute or charity, have some type of international connection or are some type of financial organization;
- have some connection with a government department.

Disclosure under the BNA85

Under the provisions of the BNA85, a person trading under a business name must declare his or her real name and an address at which he or she can be contacted in the UK. This is to enable the serving of writs or summonses against him or her. The required details must be included upon all the business stationery used by a business, for example, letters, bills, invoices and receipts, and must be supplied if they are requested by anyone dealing with the sole trader. Failure to comply with the above provisions is a criminal offence.

Contractual effects of non-compliance

Where traders fail to comply with the above provisions, in certain circumstances, a court may prevent them from claiming successfully against another party, where they have defaulted upon their contractual obligations. For example, suppose Jim Brown, trading as Cheap Washing Machine Parts, supplies parts to Ian Stuart, a washing machine repairer, who subsequently fails to pay for the goods. Jim refuses to pay for the goods because they were faulty and he wishes to return them, but is unable to do so because he cannot trace Jim Brown. Then Jim sues Ian for non-payment of the goods and the court refuses to enforce the obligation because Jim has failed to comply with the provisions of the BNA85.

Tort of passing off

A trader may also be liable under the tort of passing off, i.e. trading under a business name that is liable to be confused with that of another existing business. An example might be a shop called Mark & Spencer, which could obviously be confused with the famous high street chain. This will only apply where the two businesses trade in the same area of business; for example, Marks & Spencer – Coal Merchants, would probably not breach this tort. However, should a trader commence business in his or her own name – for example, F.W. Woolworth – then this tort would not be infringed, so long as the trader doesn't pretend, by way of advertisement or other means, that there is any association with the famous company that bears the same name. A party injured under this tort may apply to a court for an injunction to stop the other party from continuing to use the name.

SOLE TRADER ORGANIZATION

Despite the name, sole traders need not work alone. They may employ people and, where they do so, they will be bound to comply with all laws and regulations governing employment, taxation and other matters. A typical sole trader, such as a carpenter, may work alone for a few years to establish the business, after which time he or she might have built up enough work, or customers, to warrant employing another carpenter. Growth might continue until the business employs a considerable number of people. At that stage the carpenter would need to consider either setting up a partnership or becoming a limited liability company.

 Which of the following would constitute an offence under the BNA85?

1 Joan Williams trading as Joan's Fashions, failing to indicate her full name on an order form.
2 Joan Williams trading as Joan's Fashions, failing to indicate the full details of ownership on the outside of her trading premises.
3 Henry Boots trading as a chemist, indicating in his

advertising that he has a nationwide chain of shops, when he only has one.

4 Frederick Smythe, trading as a cobbler by royal appointment, because he once fixed the heel of Princess Anne's shoe.

CAPITAL

For the purposes of examining the law relating to sole traders, I will take the case of Tom Saw, the carpenter, as our example. When Tom commences his business he will undoubtedly take money or property, such as his van or tools, into the business with him. Further, he may borrow money from a bank or other lending institution in order to buy a van, tools or materials. Lenders will rarely lend money unless they are guaranteed that, where a business fails, they will get their money back. This is known as a secured loan. For a sole trader a lender will normally require that a **charge** is placed on the family home, against which a loan will be advanced.

Tom Saw will be able to take all the profits from his business. That is one of the major advantages of being a sole trader. When he has paid off all his debts and taxes, he has no one else to answer to or divide the profits with. However, the downside of this type of enterprise is that Tom will be liable for all the debts that the business incurs. This liability for debt will spread to Tom's possessions as well, including his house, if he cannot satisfy his creditors. Even if there is no charge on his house, he may still have to sell it if there is no other way of meeting the debts.

► A **charge** is a legal interest in land, which is granted to secure a loan of money. In the example of Tom Saw the charge is placed on his house, giving the chargee (the person in whose favour the charge has been made) the right to be repaid from the proceeds of the sale of the property, in priority to any other claims. The bank or other lender will normally be a chargee.

THE BANKRUPTCY OF A SOLE TRADER

If Tom Saw is unable to pay his debts, a court may decide that he is insolvent. In other words, he may be declared bankrupt. In order to understand the process of bankruptcy, we need to look at the main procedures of the Insolvency Act 1986 (IA86) and the Deeds of Arrangement Act 1914 (DAA14).

Petition for bankruptcy

For a person to be made bankrupt, an application, known as a petition for bankruptcy, must be made to the High Court or a county court. This petition can be made by one or more of the person's creditors or by the debtor himself or herself.

Petition by a creditor

To bring a petition for bankruptcy a creditor, or two or more creditors who are together owed £750 or more, must have obtained judgment for a debt of £750 or more, or have served a statutory demand for payment on the debtor. Under a statutory demand a debtor must pay the debt within three weeks. If the debtor fails to do so a creditor may petition for bankruptcy.

A court may either grant the bankruptcy order or dismiss the petition where the court feels that the debtor:

- has made an **offer of security** to secure the debt; or
- has entered into a voluntary arrangement (see below) to repay the debt, which the creditor has refused.

Petition by a debtor

It is possible for a person to ask a court to make him or her bankrupt. Where a person is in a hopeless position, e.g. with debts of £80,000 and no real assets, it may be the best thing for everyone, including the person and his or her family, to go bankrupt. A debtor may only petition for bankruptcy when unable to pay his or her debts. That is the only time that a court will grant the order.

When applying for bankruptcy a debtor must take details of his or her circumstances to the court. This is known as a statement of affairs. In the statement the assets and liabilities of the debtor must be listed. If the debts are £2,000 or less and the assets are £2,000 or more, and the person has not been previously declared bankrupt in the preceding five years, a court will appoint an **insolvency practitioner** to investigate the possibility of the debtor making a voluntary agreement with his or her creditors.

Methods of avoiding bankruptcy

If Tom is facing bankruptcy, he may be able to avoid being made bankrupt by one of the three following main methods:

1 entering into a voluntary arrangement with the creditors;
2 agreeing to place the business in the hands of a trustee in order to benefit the creditors;
3 obtaining an interim order.

Voluntary arrangement

Under the DAA14, Tom could come to an arrangement with his creditors whereby he agrees to pay them a certain amount in the pound for each pound that he owes. For example, if Tom owes £600 to Angela, and Tom agrees to pay his creditors 75p in the pound, he would pay Angela £450.

Since the more recent legislation (IA86), voluntary arrangements are not so widely used. They have the advantage that the arrangement can be made outside court, but they have a major disadvantage for the debtor, in that if a creditor is unhappy with the arrangement the creditor can petition the court to have the debtor made bankrupt. In any case a majority of creditors, who are owed a majority of the debt, must agree to the arrangement.

► **Offer of security** – the pledging of some assets, for example, a house or other property, to be used as security against a debt. In the example of a house, the deeds of the house would be lodged with the creditor or a charge would be placed on the property. If the debt were not paid the creditor would be able to sell off the asset to satisfy the debt.

► **Insolvency practitioner** – a person, normally an accountant, who investigates and reports on the affairs of a bankrupt. Insolvency practice has been one of the real growth industries of the late 1980s and early 1990s.

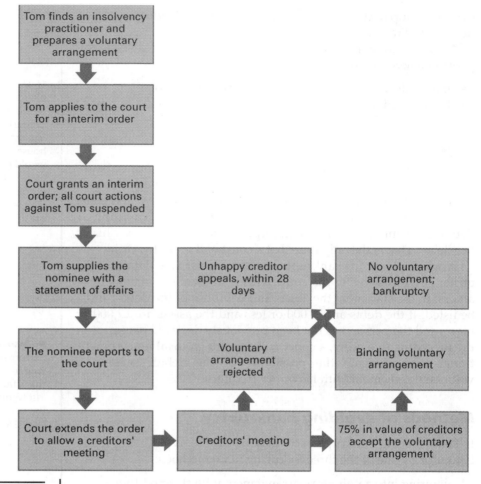

Tom finds an insolvency practitioner and prepares a voluntary arrangement

↓

Tom applies to the court for an interim order

↓

Court grants an interim order; all court actions against Tom suspended

↓

Tom supplies the nominee with a statement of affairs

↓

The nominee reports to the court

↓

Court extends the order to allow a creditors' meeting → Creditors' meeting → 75% in value of creditors accept the voluntary arrangement

Unhappy creditor appeals, within 28 days → No voluntary arrangement; bankruptcy

Voluntary arrangement rejected

Binding voluntary arrangement

Tom makes an application for a voluntary arrangement under the Insolvency Act 1986

Trustee

Tom may offer to put the running of his business into the hands of a trustee, normally an accountant, who will either manage or attempt to sell the business, to pay off the creditors. The creditors must agree to the handing over to a trustee on the same basis as above.

Interim order

An interim order may be granted to Tom upon application to a court, provided that he has not made an application in the preceding twelve months, either when a bankruptcy petition has been tendered against him or when Tom has himself petitioned for bankruptcy. An interim order is superior to a voluntary arrangement obtained under the DAA14 because it can be easier to obtain.

The granting of an interim order will stop any bankruptcy proceedings, normally for a period of fourteen days, so any secured creditor will not be able to force the sale of a property upon which a charge has been made. However, the rights of a secured creditor will not be affected. The secured creditor will retain the right to be paid before any of the unsecured creditors.

Under an interim order a debtor must consult with a Department of Trade and Industry (DTI) registered insolvency practitioner. The insolvency practitioner becomes the 'nominee' and is then responsible for the drawing up and presentation of the arrangement to the creditors. Should the arrangement be accepted by the creditors, the nominee then becomes responsible for the supervision and implementation of the arrangement.

During the fourteen-day period the nominee will report back to the court on the viability of the debtor's proposal. If the report is favourable then a court may extend the interim order to enable a meeting of creditors to take place, to determine the arrangement. Where the arrangement is accepted by 75 per cent of the creditors in value, i.e. the amount of creditors who are owed 75 per cent of the total money, the order would then become binding upon all the creditors and any creditor unhappy with the order could not then petition for bankruptcy. The nominee will then supervise the arrangement, normally taking legal possession of the debtor's property in order to comply with the arrangement.

An unhappy creditor must apply within twenty-eight days to have the agreement set aside. This application can only be made on the grounds that there was some irregularity in the calling or conduct of the creditors' meeting, or that the agreement was prejudicial to the applicant.

 What are the three main ways that a person unable to pay business debts may be able to settle matters without being made bankrupt by the courts? What are the advantages and disadvantages of each? Look in your local papers to find a court report of a local bankruptcy. How had the person been made bankrupt?

Procedure in bankruptcy

Where Tom is unable to fend off his creditors, or where he chooses himself to go bankrupt, then upon his bankruptcy the following proceedings will take place.

Property

Tom's property will automatically pass into the hands of a civil servant called the Official Receiver, except for any tools, vehicles or other equipment necessary for him to continue in his job as a carpenter. It is not in a bankrupt's, nor a creditor's, interest to deprive a bankrupt of the means of earning his living.

Tom will also be able to retain the basic necessary domestic items to enable him and his family to live. For example, bedding, ordinary domestic furniture, provisions and other household appliances will be left with Tom, unless it is possible to sell them off and replace them with cheaper alternatives. In reality these circumstances rarely arise, since second-hand household goods do not

► Don't forget that any secured creditor will be able to force the sale of the asset on which he or she has taken a charge, to recover a debt. If the sale of the asset does not fully satisfy the debt, then the creditor will become an unsecured creditor for the remainder of the debt. Any surplus after the sale of the asset will become part of the bankrupt's assets, so it will be available for distribution to the creditors.

usually achieve a premium price, so most household goods would remain with Tom.

Statement of affairs

Within twenty-one days of the bankruptcy order being made, Tom must furnish the court with a statement of affairs containing the following information:

(a) assets and liabilities;
(b) details of all of his known creditors;
(c) details of any securities held by his creditors, if any.

This will enable the Official Receiver to analyse Tom's position. While this procedure appears clear and precise, in reality it is normally extremely messy. People who are threatened with bankruptcy can take the ostrich principle, ignoring their financial position and continuing to trade, hoping that something will turn up. During this period they tend not to answer the telephone, nor to read mail because they know that it will probably be creditors demanding money. By the time bankruptcy arrives, people who have taken the ostrich approach rarely have any idea of their true financial situation.

For example, I know of someone who was unfortunately declared bankrupt after having had his own thriving business. Towards the end of his business he used to put all his letters, and there were lots of them, in a carrier bag and then burn them on the fire without opening them. My friend's landlord repossessed his shop and the financial records of the business became lost. His true financial position was never fully established.

▶ **Trustee in bankruptcy** – a person who is entrusted with the property of a bankrupt to sell and distribute the proceeds to the creditors, in accordance with the provisions of the IA86.

It is possible that some other qualified person will be given charge of Tom's affairs. In any case, the Official Receiver or the other qualified person will become Tom's **trustee in bankruptcy**. Tom's creditors may, in certain circumstances, create a committee of creditors to oversee the dispersal of the assets.

A trustee may apply to the court for a public examination of Tom, in order to try to discover why Tom's business has failed, and to establish if there had been any fraud or underhand dealings in the management of the business. Alternatively, 50 per cent of the creditors in value may require the Official Receiver to apply for a public examination.

The role of a trustee

Collection of monies due

A trustee in bankruptcy will chase any money that is owed to Tom. This may include, with the agreement of Tom's creditors, carrying on Tom's business for a period, if that would enable him to collect more money. Where Tom has a debtor who is also a creditor, i.e. someone who owes Tom money and to whom Tom owes money, then the debt may be set off. For example, if Jim owes Tom £3,000 and Tom owes Jim £2,500, then Jim may merely pay £500 to the trustee.

Under the provisions of the IA86 the trustee may examine any transactions that Tom may have carried out prior to going bankrupt, to establish if Tom has made any transactions at undervalue or any preference payments. A **transaction at undervalue** may be recovered at any time in the five years following the bankruptcy petition, while a **preference payment** may be recovered either in the six months following a petition or in two years where the payment was made to a close associate.

Establishing creditors

All persons who claim that they are creditors of Tom will be invited to state their claim to the trustee. The trustee will normally accept what appear to be genuine valid claims, though where there is any doubt about the viability of a claim, a creditor will be asked to make a sworn statement in front of a solicitor.

Disposal of assets

A trustee must sell off all Tom's assets to distribute them among his creditors. This will include the family home, regardless of the fact that Tom and his family will be made homeless, although there are rules governing this unfortunate but frequently occurring situation. The house will probably be held in joint names between Tom and his wife. However, even if it is solely owned by Tom, his wife will have a right of occupation in the house under the Matrimonial Homes Act 1983. If the house is solely owned by Tom and he has children under the age of 18, he will also have a right of occupation. Where a right of occupation is in existence, on application to the court, the sale of the matrimonial home may be postponed for a year to allow Tom and his family to find somewhere else to live. After the period of postponement has elapsed, a trustee will normally be able to sell the property, after obtaining an order of sale from the court.

Dispersal of assets

A trustee must pay creditors in the order specified in the IA86. The Act identifies preferential creditors, unsecured creditors and deferred creditors.

Preferential creditors

The Act seeks to look after the state and the employee, in preference to anyone else. The first to be paid will be the trustee (surprise, surprise), then any remaining assets will be used to go towards paying debts to the preferential creditors, in the following order:

- Inland Revenue – income tax contributions that ought to have been collected, or that were deducted and not paid to the Inland Revenue, in the twelve months prior to bankruptcy;
- Customs and Excise – sums due from VAT (six months prior to

▶ **Transaction at undervalue** – the transfer of property or assets at below their true value, made in anticipation of insolvency. A sole trader may sell property cheaply to a relative or friend, for example, to avoid its being sold to benefit his or her creditors.

▶ To see how a transaction at undervalue is affected when made by a company, see Chapter 8, p. 122.

▶ **Preference payment** – a payment made in full to one of the creditors to the detriment of the other creditors.

▶ If a sole trader holds the leasehold of any property, for example, if he or she is renting a shop, then the trustee will inform the landlord of the situation and any further liability under the lease will end. The landlord will become an unsecured creditor.

bankruptcy) and car tax (twelve months);

- betting and gaming duty, due to the Betting and Gaming Board;
- employees – wages and other benefits due;
- Social Security – contributions not paid, including National Insurance and State Pension, in the twelve months prior to bankruptcy.

 Look at the figure on page 74, showing the stages of reaching a voluntary agreement through an interim order. Try to draw a similar figure to show the stages of bankruptcy proceedings.

If Tom owed a total of £10,000 to his preferential creditors and had assets of £2,500, each creditor would then be paid a quarter of what they were owed, leaving no money at all for anyone else.

Employees are protected under these circumstances by the Employment Protection (Consolidation) Act 1978. The Act enables them to claim for lost wages and other statutory entitlements from the DSS, leaving the Department to try to recover from Tom as a preferential creditor.

Unsecured creditors

If there is any money left in the kitty after the preferential creditors have been paid, and there generally isn't, then any unsecured creditors will be paid. The majority of these will be trade creditors, i.e. people who have supplied goods to Tom but have not received payment for them. The same rules apply as above: where £1,000 is left in the kitty and debts total £5,000, each creditor will get one-fifth of what he or she is owed.

Deferred creditors

These are the last to be paid and consequently they usually get nothing. A deferred creditor is someone who is linked to the bankrupt, normally by marriage, and they will receive no payment until all other creditors have been paid in full.

 1 What are the four main roles of a trustee in bankruptcy?
2 Under which circumstances may a bankrupt be able to retain temporary possession of the family home?

Duration of bankruptcy

Once a bankruptcy order is made, all debts owed by Tom will cease to be due, except those owed to the Crown – for example, tax owed to the Inland Revenue. Any enquiries relating to non-payment, etc. must be directed through the Official Receiver. As this is Tom's first bankruptcy he would automatically be discharged after three years. If he had owed less than £20,000 at the time of the bankruptcy, and if the assets amounted to £2,000 or more, then discharge would take

► Employees are limited to what they will be able to claim as preferential creditors. Only sums due for the four months before bankruptcy, up to £800 per employee, can be claimed. Similar limits apply to claiming from the DSS.

place after two years. This short period is known as summary administration. However, where a bankrupt seeks to obstruct the court, or to fail to comply with any statutory obligation, a court may refuse to discharge him or her, prolonging the time limits. If Tom had been bankrupted in the preceding fifteen years, he would have to wait five years before he could apply to be discharged.

During the period of undischarged bankruptcy a person is not prevented from continuing in business, but he or she is prevented from obtaining credit of more than £250. If a bankrupt breaches the credit limit, he or she commits a criminal offence. An undischarged bankrupt cannot become a Member of Parliament, a councillor, a lay magistrate or a director of a company, or be concerned in the management of a company.

When a bankrupt is discharged by a court, his or her liability for any civil debts incurred in the course of his or her business will normally be terminated. However, where a fine has been imposed for a criminal offence, such as an offence under the Trades Description Act, the debt will remain. The discharged bankrupt will then be free to start up in business again, though it will probably be difficult for him or her to find any means of borrowing money or a source of credit.

 Tom Saw has been made bankrupt with the following debts and liabilities:

Mrs Saw	Wife	£10,000
Ron Smith	Employee (Wages)	£1,000
Henry's Supplies	Trade creditor	£5,000
Inland Revenue	Unpaid income tax	£7,500
VAT	Unpaid VAT	£2,500
Trustee	Costs of the proceedings	£12,500
Wood Supplies UK	Trade creditor	£22,500
Pins and Nails	Trade creditor	£12,500

Tom, feeling that he was in danger of being made bankrupt, made a gift of his house, valued at £10,000, to his wife, eight months prior to the actual bankruptcy. At the same time Tom also paid off Joe Davis, a supplier who was also a close friend, a sum of £12,500.

Tom's assets at the time of the bankruptcy amounted to £5,000, not including the house. How would the trustee, using all of his or her powers, collect and distribute Tom's assets? In other words, who would get what?

ADVANTAGES AND DISADVANTAGES OF BEING A SOLE TRADER

	Advantages	*Disadvantages*
1 Commencement	Simple, just find your first customer.	Too simple, perhaps people commence without knowing or considering the implications of going into business.
2 Legal requirements	Generally none, depending upon the nature of the business.	Name must comply with the BNA85.
3 Raising of capital		Not easy, normally must be a secured loan on a property.
4 Management	Hands-on, sole control of the business with no one to answer to.	Very difficult to run a business, working in it and providing objective management. Professional advice does not come cheap.
5 Profits	All profits will stay with the sole trader. In the good times this is great.	When business is poor there may be few (or no) profits.
6 Accounting	Very simple to account for a small business. Rarely is there a need to employ an accountant. There is no requirement to publish details. The tax collector has become very friendly to the small enterprise.	Most sole traders do not seek professional advice, which could mean that they are not obtaining the benefits (grants, tax allowances and reliefs, etc.) that they may be able to claim.
7 Liability		A sole trader will be liable for all his or her debts, this means the family home could be lost in order to pay creditors.

CHAPTER SUMMARY

1. The public sector is made up of organizations that are owned and managed by the government, while the private sector is made up of privately owned organizations.
2. A sole trader is the simplest and most common form of business organization, common examples being a window cleaner, a carpenter and a person offering secretarial services.
3. The Business Names Act 1985 controls business names and requires persons to register the name of their business when they trade in a name different from their own. Non-compliance with the Act may prevent a person from being able to sue another party successfully.
4. The tort of passing off occurs when a person chooses a name for their business that is the same as, or similar to, another business. Passing off does not occur where a person trades under his or her own name, provided that he or she does not suggest, by any means, association with another famous company.

5   A person may petition for bankruptcy when he or she has insufficient income to pay his or her debts. Creditors may petition where they are owed £750 or more.

6   A potential bankrupt may be able to avoid bankruptcy by entering into a voluntary arrangement, putting the business into the hands of a trustee, or obtaining an interim order.

7   Upon bankruptcy a trustee, normally the Official Receiver, will be appointed to: (a) collect any monies due; (b) establish and identify all creditors; (c) dispose of a bankrupt's assets; (d) pay creditors in accordance with the provisions of the IA86.

8   An undischarged bankrupt cannot become a Member of Parliament, a councillor, a lay magistrate or a director of a company, or be concerned in the management of a company.

Partnership

Chapter objectives

By the end of this chapter you should be able to:

▌ understand the definition of a partnership, as outlined in the Partnership Act 1890

▌ know the rules to be used in determining the existence of a partnership provided by s. 2 of the Partnership Act 1890

▌ recognize the relationship that the law demands between partners and the circumstances under which a sleeping partner may be created

▌ understand the apparent authority of a partner to bind a firm, the rights and duties of partners, the method of excluding a partner and the rules relating to the ownership of partnership property

▌ appreciate the ways in which a partnership may be dissolved, and the effects upon the partnership property and assets of dissolution

▌ know how a limited partnership may be created under the Limited Partnership Act 1907

▌ appreciate the effects of insolvency upon a partnership

▌ know the advantages and disadvantages of partnership as a form of business enterprise.

Starting up a partnership

In the previous chapter we saw how easy it is to commence your own business as a sole trader. We shall now turn our attention to the next type of business organization: partnership. Perhaps surprisingly, it is simple to commence business as a partnership. You merely start trading and no formal agreement is required, since in such a case the Partnership Act of 1890 (PA1890) lays down clearly the relationship between the partners.

However, partnership is often fraught with difficulty, so it is advisable to have a written partnership agreement governing the relationship. When business is going well, all will be fine in a partnership, but in times of crisis partners tend to fall out. The first thing to remember about partnership is that all partners to a business will be jointly and severally liable (see definition on page 89) for the debts of the business. Should the business go bankrupt, all the partners are liable to lose their homes to settle any debts.

Partners are free to form an agreement between themselves, normally in the form of a partnership deed, which will specify the basis upon which the partners have agreed to work. However, the PA1890 will govern the relationship between the partnership and third parties.

Partnership organization and names

A partnership may not contain more than twenty partners (Companies Act 1985), though solicitors and certain other professions are exempted from this provision, and may have more partners. A partnership must conform to the provisions of the Business Names Act 1985, as detailed in Chapter 6. However, a partnership need not list all partners on business stationery or in the trading name. It will be sufficient for the name(s) of certain of the partners to be followed by 'and Co.'. For example, where Williams, Simmons, Crockett, Jones and Wilson are in business, they could trade under the name of 'Williams, Simmons and Co.'. A full list of partners must be prominently displayed at the principal place of business. A firm of partners can contract, sue and be sued under the shortened version of the partnership name.

DEFINITION OF PARTNERSHIP

> **PA1890, s. 1**
>
> Partnership is the relation that subsists between persons carrying on a business in common with a view of profit.

This means that persons who carry out business together with a view to making a profit will be partners whether they wish to be or not. For example, if two people set up a market stall together, they will be partners for the purposes of the Act, even though they may not have considered partnership.

The partnership will only commence when the 'carrying on' has begun. This means that preparation to 'carry on' will not constitute partnership. Should goods be ordered to stock a shop by a partner, when the business has yet to start trading, then the partnership will not be bound by the order. The partner who had placed the order would be singly liable for the order. This point is illustrated in the following case.

Spicer (Keith) Ltd v. Mansell **(1970) 1 WLR 333**

In this case two people were intending to form a limited company to start a restaurant. They had opened a bank account and ordered goods but had not yet started trading. The plaintiff supplied goods, upon receiving an order from one of the persons, who subsequently went bankrupt before the bill was paid. The plaintiff then brought an action against the other person, alleging that the two were in partnership and, therefore, that he could recover from the other person.

COURT HELD
There was no partnership. The two people had not commenced trading.

Nature of business

Section 45 of the PA1890 states that a business can be any trade, profession or occupation, though there are certain exceptions: for example, barristers cannot be partners. Where people come together to run a friendly society or where the making of a profit is not the motive for the venture, then a partnership will probably not exist.

Rules for determining existence of partnership

Section 2 of the PA1890 provides guidelines that a court may use to determine whether a partnership is in existence. In the following circumstances partnership will not exist.

PA1890, s. 2

(3) (a) where a person receives payment of a debt out of the profits of a business, whether by instalment or not;
   (b) where a servant or agent of the business is paid out of the profits of a business;
   (c) where a widow or child of a deceased partner receives an annual annuity from a business;
   (d) where money is lent to a partner(s) who is in business, or about to start up in business, and interest on the money is to be repaid out of the net profits of the business, provided that the agreement has been formed in a written contract, signed by all parties to the agreement;
   (e) where a person receives payment from the profits of a business in consideration for him selling the **goodwill** of the business.

▶ Remember **goodwill**, defined in Chapter 2, p. 12.

Under s. 3 those listed under s. 2(3)(d) and (e) above will become deferred creditors in the event of bankruptcy.

Section 2 also states that joint ownership of a property will not itself give rise to a partnership, even where profits are shared from the use of the land.

PA1890, s. 2(2)

The sharing of gross returns does not of itself create a partnership, whether or not the persons sharing such returns have a joint or common right or interest in any property from which or from the use of which the returns are derived.

 Jean and Sharon formed a knitting circle to knit socks to send to Bosnian children suffering in the war in the former Yugoslavia. Could they be considered to be partners under either of the following circumstances?

1 The circle grew to include 100 knitters and money was raised by holding jumble sales. This was put into the buying of wool to knit more socks.
2 The circle grew to 100 knitters. Jean and Sharon saw the potential of a business and started to pay themselves a salary out of the money raised by the circle.

Section 2 of the PA1890 is best illustrated by the following classic case.

Cox v. Coulson (1916) 2 KB 177

In this comical and painful case the plaintiff (Cox) was a theatregoer who was shot by an actor when, during the course of the play, the actor fired a gun that had been negligently loaded with a defective round. The play had been put on by the defendant (Coulson), who leased the theatre, in conjunction with a Mr Mills who oversaw the production of the play, including the hiring of actors. The agreement between Coulson and Mills was that Coulson was to receive 60 per cent of the play's receipts, the other 40 per cent going to Mr Mills, who had to pay for the actors out of his share. Mr Mills was vicariously liable for the negligence, but the plaintiff sought to sue Coulson because he had more money, alleging that the two men were in a partnership and, therefore, they were both liable.

 COURT HELD

The two men were not in a relationship of partnership; they were merely sharing the gross receipts from the venture. There was no stated intention that they wanted to be partners. If they had stipulated, either orally or in writing, that they were in partnership then the plaintiff could have succeeded. In the absence of any such intention, under PA1890, s. 2, it was not possible to infer a relationship of partnership from the sharing of gross receipts.

► **Prima facie** – at first appearance.

► In *Pooley v. Driver* (1876) 7 Ch 458, third parties who lent money to a partnership were held to be partners. The terms of the loan gave them rights that would not have been afforded to an ordinary lender, notwithstanding that the written agreement specifically stated that they were not to become partners.

► A **fiduciary** relationship – where a person is in a position of trust in relation to another. The person is under a duty to disclose all information to the other and to act in the other's best interests.

► *Uberrimae fidei* – a contract of utmost good faith.

> **PA1890, s. 2(3)**
>
> The receipt by a person of a share of the profits of a business is **prima facie** evidence that he is a partner in the business, but the receipt of such a share, or of a payment contingent on or varying with the profits of a business, does not of itself make him a partner in a business.

Despite the findings in the case of *Cox v. Coulson*, s. 2(3) states that in normal circumstances, where a person receives a share of the profits, he or she will be considered to be a partner.

RELATIONSHIPS AND TYPES OF PARTNERS

The relationship between partners is **fiduciary** and there is a presumption of *uberrimae fidei*; therefore, a partner must disclose to all other partners anything that he or she knows that is material to the business.

All partners must have complete and absolute faith in each other. This is because any partner will be able to make contracts that will bind the whole of the partnership, known under the PA1890 as a firm. If the partnership becomes insolvent, the assets of all of the partners, subject to limited exceptions, may be sold to settle the debts.

The pitfalls of insolvency and partnership can be illustrated in this example. Simon had three shops and was trading quite successfully. He wished to open a fourth shop but he was unable to persuade anyone to lend him the money, his house already having been remortgaged to the full value of the house. Simon persuaded his friend, Robert, to remortgage his house for £10,000 to allow them to open the fourth shop together. The shop was opened with Robert taking no active role in the business. The shop failed, leaving debts of £38,000. Simon went bankrupt, having no assets to speak of. Robert then remained liable for the repayment of his personal debt to his mortgage company of £10,000 that he borrowed on his house to start the business, plus the £38,000 that the business ended up owing to its creditors. This sad tale demonstrates that you really need to be sure of a partner before going into business with him or her.

Sleeping partners

Where a partner takes no active role in the management of a firm, merely providing capital and drawing profit, he or she will generally have limited liability for the debts of the firm, under the Limited Partnerships Act 1907.

General partners

This is the normal type of partner who takes an active part in the running of the business. See PA1890, s. 24(1), below.

> **PA1890, s. 24(1)**
>
> All the partners are entitled to share equally in the capital and profits of the business, and must contribute equally towards the losses whether of capital or otherwise sustained by the firm.

Where a partnership agreement is in existence, it is free to limit the activities of certain of the parties in the business, for example, limiting their capacity to enter into contractual relationships on behalf of the firm. However, this will merely be an internal arrangement. Where the partner enters into a contract with a third party, the whole of the firm will be bound. The value of this limitation to the other partners is that a breach of the agreement by one of the partners could enable the dissolution of the firm and the exclusion of the partner who has breached the partnership agreement.

POWER OF A PARTNER TO BIND THE FIRM

> **PA1890, s. 5**
>
> Every partner is an agent of the firm and his other partners for the purpose of the business of the partnership; and the acts of every partner who does any act for carrying on in the usual way business of the kind carried on by the firm of which he is a member bind the firm and his partners, unless the partner so acting has in fact no authority to act for the firm in the particular matter, and the person with whom he is dealing either knows that he has no authority, or does not know or believe him to be a partner.

Section 5 of the PA1890 dictates that where a partner is acting in the normal course of the business, any contract that the partner makes will bind the firm. Only where he or she is not acting in the course of the business, or has no authority to so act and the other party is aware of the lack of authority, will the firm not be bound. This power to bind the firm is based on the law of agency.

Agency

A partner will be an agent of the firm and will have the power to bind the firm by his or her **actual authority**, that is the authority that the partners have agreed, either expressly or by implication. The actual authority of a partner could be specified in the deed of partnership. In dealings with third parties, an act carried out in breach of actual authority will not bind the firm where the third

▶ **Actual authority** is also known as express authority;

party knows of the breach, or where the partner specifically states that the partner is acting on his or her own behalf and does not intend to bind the firm, or where the third party doesn't know that the person is a partner.

Apparent authority

► **Apparent authority** is also called ostensible authority.

A partner will also bind the firm by any act that is carried out under his or her **apparent authority**, provided that the act is one normally carried out by that type of business. The following case is the one most often used to illustrate whether or not an act is committed in the 'normal type of business'.

Mercantile Credit Co. v. Garrod (1962) 3 All ER 1103

 The defendant (Garrod) was in partnership with Parkin, trading as car repairers and agents for lock-up garages. The partnership agreement forbade the buying and selling of cars. Parkin, without the knowledge or authority of Garrod, bought a car that he resold to the plaintiffs. It transpired that the contract between Parkin and the plaintiffs was void and the original owner repossessed the car from the plaintiffs, leaving them £700 out of pocket. The plaintiffs sued Garrod to recover the £700. The question that the court had to answer was whether the buying and selling of the car constituted a normal act for persons carrying out that type of business.

COURT HELD
The plaintiffs could succeed. Car sales were considered to be normal transactions for a business of that type, therefore Parkin had apparent authority to make the transaction.

The apparent authority of a partner will depend upon the type of business that the partnership is conducting. In all types of partnership the following will normally be within the apparent authority of a partner:

1 to sell any goods or property belonging to the firm (not land);
2 to purchase goods that would normally or necessarily be used in the firm's business;
3 to receive payments from third parties on behalf of the firm;
4 to hire staff to work for the firm;
5 to engage a solicitor to act for the firm in defence of any claim against the firm.

A commercial partnership, i.e. one that buys and sells goods, will have the following additional apparent authority:

► **Negotiable instrument** – a written document that constitutes an obligation to pay a sum of money, for example, a cheque, a bill of exchange or promissory note (a signed note promising to pay a certain amount of money, either on demand or at a determinable future time).

1 to borrow money on behalf of the firm and, for that purpose, to pledge as security goods or chattels of the firm;
2 to sanction payments in and out of the firm, whether they be by **negotiable instrument** or not.

The following will always be outside the apparent authority of a partner, unless they have been agreed upon by all of the partners of a firm:

1. entering the firm into arbitration when it is in dispute with a third party;
2. accepting shares in lieu of payment from another party;
3. entering into a deed in favour of another party, for example, a deed of a gift;
4. entering into a guarantee on behalf of the partnership, unless that is normal practice for the trade or business that the firm is in.

 Outline the rule of agency as it applies to partnership. What is the difference between actual and apparent authority?

LIABILITY OF THE FIRM FOR WRONGS

PA1890, s. 10

Where, by any wrongful act or omission of any partner acting in the ordinary course of the business of the firm, or with the authority of his co-partners, loss or injury is caused to any person not being a partner in the firm, or any penalty is incurred, the firm is liable therefore to the same extent as the partner so acting or omitting to act.

Section 10 of the PA1890 makes all partners liable for any wrongful act or omission of one of the partners when it is carried out in the normal course of business, or if the other partners agree to the act. This could include bribery, industrial espionage or some other act. 'Wrongful' will cover any torts committed by a partner but generally not criminal acts, unless they are committed vicariously, or perhaps where an offence is committed by a partner under consumer legislation, for example, the Consumer Protection Act 1987 (CPA87). The CPA87 makes it a criminal offence to supply consumer goods that are not reasonably safe, or to offer, agree to supply or expose for supply such goods.

Misapplication of property

Section 11 of the PA1890 deals with situations where a partner obtains, under his or her apparent authority, property from a third party that the partner then subsequently misapplies. If the third party suffers any loss then the firm will be liable to make good that loss. Liability under PA1890, ss. 10 and 11 is **joint** and **several**.

▶ See Chapter 18 for full details of offences under consumer legislation.

▶ **Joint and several liability** – A legal action by a creditor can be brought against any one or more of a firm's partners, in other words he, she or they can be severed from the firm and sued individually. If the judgment against one partner is not satisfied – for example, if the partner does not have enough assets to satisfy the debt – then the creditor will not be able to sue the other partners for the remaining debt. This established rule has been varied by the Civil Liability (Contribution) Act 1978. In certain circumstances this allows for a right of action against any other person who is jointly liable where an original action has not been satisfied (paid). It is better to sue in the name of the partnership. This automatically joins all partners to the debt. The debt will be met first by the assets of the partnership, then by the individual assets of all the partners.

Persons liable by 'holding out'

> **PA1890, s. 14(1)**
>
> Every person who by words spoken or written or by conduct represents himself, or who knowingly suffers himself to be represented, as a partner in a particular firm, is liable as a partner to one who has on the faith of any such representation given credit to the firm.

Where a person represents him or herself as being a partner of a firm in order to obtain benefit, that person will be liable for any benefit gained, as if that person were a partner. This is more often committed unintentionally, in circumstances where a partner has retired from the partnership but his or her name continues to be shown on letterheads or at the place of business under the requirements of the Business Names Act 1985.

To be liable under this section the 'partner' must know and consent to the 'holding out'. Section 36 of the PA1890 states that, where a deceased partner's name is used, his or her estate will not be liable for any claims against it.

The following case illustrates the application of PA1890, s. 14(1), to an instance of partnership debts.

Tower Cabinet Co. Ltd v. Ingram (1949) 1 All ER 1033

VC Two persons called Christmas and Ingram commenced a partnership in 1946, as household furnishers, trading under the name of Merry's. The partnership was dissolved in 1947 with the agreement of both partners. Christmas continued to trade, using new letterheads from which Ingram's name had been removed in accordance with an agreement made between the two partners. Christmas subsequently ordered some furniture from the plaintiff, using the old notepaper with Ingram's name upon it. When the bill for the furniture was not paid, the plaintiff obtained judgment against Merry's, which they then sought to enforce against Ingram.

 COURT HELD
Ingram was not liable. The notepaper with his name on had been accidentally used. He did not consent to the holding out, nor was he was aware of it.

---

 1 What will be the normal apparent authority of a partner to bind a firm?

2 What extra powers will the partner of a commercial firm have?

3 What will normally be outside the apparent authority of a partner?

New partners

Section 17 of the PA1890 provides that a new partner will not be liable for any debts or obligations incurred prior to his or her joining the partnership, unless the partner expressly or impliedly agrees to assume liability for the debts or obligations (as under **novation**, see below). A retired partner will continue to be liable for any debts incurred while he or she was a partner, or any debts subsequently incurred by any arrangements made before the partner retired, unless the creditors and partners have agreed to release the partner from his or her liabilities upon retirement.

The required agreement is called a novation and all three parties must agree to it: namely the retiring partner, the creditors and the existing partners. In effect a novation substitutes a new agreement, under which the existing partners, and possibly any new ones, take over the liability of the old partnership, accepting the liability under the new formation of the firm.

If a creditor does not agree to the novation, he or she may still claim against the retired partner. In such circumstances the retiring partner should seek an **indemnity** from the partnership, whereby the partnership would pay any amount that the retired party might have to pay. Indemnities are much more widely used than novations and they may be catered for by the insertion of a clause in a partnership agreement.

► An **indemnity** is an agreement by one party to pay the costs or debts incurred by another party.

Notification of retirement

Section 36 of the PA1890 states the rules to be followed when a partner retires. The partner must advertise his or retirement in the *London Gazette*, but may still be liable under this section for debts incurred after the retirement, unless a creditor receives adequate notice of his or her retirement. The Act identifies three different groups of creditors who will be affected differently by the retirement of a partner. Where a party deals with a firm after a change in its constitution – for example, the retirement of a partner – that party will be entitled to treat the firm as being unchanged until the party receives adequate notice of the change. In the following example, which explains the provisions, the retiring partner is called Cole.

► *London Gazette* – a daily journal published in London by Her Majesty's Stationery Office (HMSO), containing news and notices relating to the business world.

Creditors who have previously dealt with the partnership and knew Cole to be a partner
In these circumstances the creditor will need actual notice of the retirement of the partner, for example, by receiving a letter from the partnership with Cole's name removed or crossed out. The publishing of Cole's retirement in the *London Gazette* will only be adequate notice of his retirement if the creditor actually reads the announcement. If any of these methods are used then Cole will not be liable for any debts incurred after his retirement.

Creditors who had only dealt with the partnership after the retirement of Cole, but knew him to be a partner before his retirement

This type of creditor will not be able to make Cole liable for any post-retirement debts, if notice of retirement has been published in the *London Gazette*, regardless of whether they have read it or not.

Creditors who had no dealings with the partnership prior to Cole's retirement and did not know Cole as a partner of the firm

Cole will not be liable to this type of creditor, even where notification of retirement has not been placed in the *London Gazette*.

GENERAL RIGHTS AND DUTIES OF PARTNERS

As we have seen, a partnership is based on a relationship of *uberrimae fidei* and we shall shortly discover that the law expects high standards of behaviour from partners. However, most partnerships should also be founded on a partnership agreement, also known as a partnership deed, which should cover the following points:

(a) date of commencement;
(b) length of time that the partnership is to last;
(c) the identity of the partners;
(d) the type and name of business;
(e) location of the business;
(f) duties of the partners, for example, hours to be committed to the business;
(g) the partnership bankers and the arrangements for signing cheques, for example, the placing of a limit on the amount of one cheque without the signature of two of the partners;
(h) entitlement to holiday and the arrangements for determining holiday periods;
(i) actual authority of each partner;
(j) payment of salaries to partners, how much and when;
(k) admittance of new partners;
(l) retirement of partners;
(m) payment of tax;
(n) payment of profit, including the time, method and allocation;
(o) method of accounting;
(p) termination;
(q) method of arbitration in case of dispute.

Relations between the partners

Relations between the partners are covered in PA1890, ss. 19–31. In the partnership agreement the partners may vary the terms implied by the Act that relate to their internal relationships, but they cannot vary relationships between the partnership and third parties. For example, s. 19 allows partners to vary the business that the partnership is involved in, though s. 24 states that all partners must be in agreement with the change. Other minor changes only require the agreement of the majority of the partners.

 Alone, or in a group of three or four, draft an agreement to cover a partnership trading as a commercial organization, with four partners. The agreement should cater for all of the foreseeable events that may befall a partnership, including death, retirement and recruitment of new partners.

Section 24 of the PA1890 provides a series of rules relating to the interests and duties of partners:

1 all partners are entitled to an equal share in the profits and must bear an equal share of the losses;
2 the firm must indemnify a partner against any payment he or she makes and any liability incurred in the course of the business;
3 where a partner makes a payment into the firm above his or her prescribed amount he or she will be entitled to 5 per cent interest per annum;
4 a partner will not be entitled, before the ascertainment of profits, to interest on the capital subscribed by him or her;
5 every partner may take part in the management of the business;
6 no partner shall be entitled to remuneration for his or her part in the business;
7 all existing partners must agree to the introduction of a new partner;
8 ordinary matters may be determined by a majority of the partners;
9 the partnership books should be kept at the place of business and all partners should have access to them.

Where any of these terms are broken the other partner(s) will have a right of action for damages or an injunction to prevent the breach recurring.

Expulsion of a partner

> **PA1890, s. 25**
>
> No majority of the partners can expel any partner unless a power to do so has been conferred by express agreement between the parties.

Where such an expulsion clause exists it will still need to be proved that the clause covers the reason for which the partner was being expelled; that the expelled partner knew why he or she was being expelled and that the expellers were acting in good faith. If all of the above three factors are covered then the expulsion will generally be enforced by a court.

The duties of partners towards each other

The duties of partners towards each other are covered in PA1890, ss. 28–31.

Duty of partners to render accounts etc.

> **PA1890, s. 28**
>
> Partners are bound to render true accounts and full information of all things affecting the partnership to any partner or his legal representatives.

Under *uberrimae fidei* this becomes a positive duty to tell all of the partners of anything material to the partnership. To remain silent on any material issue would constitute a breach of this section. The case of *Law v. Law* illustrates the application of this principle.

Law v. Law (1905) 1 Ch 140

This case concerned two brothers trading as a partnership, one of whom bought the other out for an agreed price. The retiring partner then found out that the selling partner had known that the partnership had other assets that he had failed to disclose and the retiring partner then brought an action for misrepresentation.

 COURT HELD
The retiring partner could succeed, as the selling brother was under a duty to disclose all material information. He was forced to make a further payment to his brother.

Accountability of partners for private profits
Section 29 of the PA1890 states that a partner must account to the other partners for any benefit he or she obtains without the consent of the other parties, from any transaction concerning the partnership, or from any use by the partner of the partnership property, name or business connection. An example of this might be a partner buying goods at a discount, then reselling them to his or her firm, retaining the profit.

Duty of partner not to compete with firm
Section 30 of the PA1890 allows a partner to be involved in a competing business, but the partner must hand to the partnership any profit that he or she makes from the competing business.

Rights of assignee of share in partnership
Section 31 of the PA1890 allows a partner to assign his or her share in the partnership, for example, to raise money to use as capital.

The assignee will have no right to interfere with the management of the partnership, nor to challenge the accounts. He or she will merely have the right to receive any profits due to the assignor. Where the partnership is dissolved the assignee will have the right to receive the assignor's share of the assets and a statement of accounts.

PARTNERSHIP PROPERTY

It is important to establish whether property is owned individually by one partner, or jointly by the partnership, for a number of reasons.

(a) Should the partnership become insolvent, creditors may wish to claim the property.
(b) Should the property increase or decrease in value, the profit or loss will be attributed to the owner of the property, i.e. either to the individual partner or to the firm.
(c) Partnership property can only be used according to the Act, or as detailed in the partnership agreement. A partner's individual property may be used as he or she so wishes, unless its use has been contracted into the partnership.

Even though property has been used by the partnership, it may still belong to an individual partner. It does not necessarily belong to the partnership. This point is illustrated in the following case.

Miles v. Clarke **(1953) 1 All ER 779**

The defendant set up in business as a photographer, obtaining the lease of a premises and various items of photographic equipment. Business did not go well and he was joined by the plaintiff, a freelance photographer, who had considerable business contacts. The two then traded as a partnership, each of them taking equal profits from the business. For personal reasons it became necessary to dissolve the business. The plaintiff claimed a half share of all the assets of the business.

 COURT HELD
The plaintiff could not succeed. He had no right to the property bought before he entered the partnership. He was granted half of the stock in trade that had been purchased in the normal course of the business.

The Act recognizes two main categories of property relating to partnerships: property brought into the partnership by one of the partners and property bought with partnership money.

Deciding who owns the property of the partnership

> **PA1890, s. 21**
>
> Unless the contrary intention appears, property bought with money belonging to the firm is deemed to have been bought on behalf of the firm.

Where property is bought with partnership money it will be difficult to disprove that it has been bought on behalf of the firm.

Section 20 of the PA1890 is much less clear. It states that property brought into the firm, or bought on account of the firm, or for the purposes and in the course of the partnership business, is to be called partnership property. Such property must only be used for the purposes of the partnership in accordance with the partnership agreement.

No guidance is given on how to identify partnership property from individually owned property. The clearest guidance may be found in the partnership agreement, which should state what property is considered to be partnership and what property is individual. In the absence of any direction in the partnership agreement, a court will normally rule that property is partnership property under the following circumstances:

(a) where it is brought into the partnership and its value is credited to the capital account of one of the partners, i.e. it forms part of his or her capital contribution to the partnership;

(b) where the property is treated by the partners as partnership property.

The following case illustrates point (b) above.

Pilling v. Pilling (1865) 3 De G.J. & S. 162

VC A father went into partnership with his two sons. The rights and duties of each partner were detailed in a partnership agreement, which stated that the assets of the partnership should rest with the father. Each partner was to receive a third share of the profits, the father paying an extra £150 a year to each of the sons out of his profits. The assets of the business, mainly buildings and machinery, were to be depreciated before profit was calculated. The father was also to receive an extra 4 per cent a year interest on his capital contribution.

The partnership continued for around ten years but it was not run as prescribed in the agreement. All of the partners received a return on the capital investment, the extra £150 was paid out of profits and no depreciation was charged. The court was asked to judge whether the assets of the business had become partnership property.

COURT HELD

The way that the partners had conducted the business implied that they had substituted a new partnership agreement in place of the original. The fact that all three partners had enjoyed a return on the capital persuaded the court that the property now belonged to the partnership, despite the original intentions of the father.

Section 20(2) of the PA1890 states that any land, or interest in land, that a partnership acquires must be held in a trust for the benefit of all partners. Other property owned by the partnership, such as office equipment, is jointly owned by the partners. It is possible for a partner to steal jointly owned property, where, for example, the partner sells it, intending permanently to deprive the other partners of it, and keeps all the proceeds.

DISSOLUTION OF THE PARTNERSHIP

The dissolution of the partnership is covered by ss. 32–44 of the PA1890.

PA1890, s. 32

Subject to any agreement between the partners a partnership is dissolved:

(a) if entered into for a fixed term, by the expiration of that term;
(b) if entered into for a single adventure or undertaking, by the termination of that adventure or undertaking;
(c) if entered into for an undefined time, by any partner giving notice to the other or others of his intention to dissolve the partnership.

This section provides clear rules for the dissolution of a partnership. The subsections are explained in simpler terms below.

(a) A fixed term could be a number of years, for example, five, at the end of which time the partnership would automatically dissolve, or it could be for the lifetime of the partners, being ended by the death of one of the partners.
(b) A single undertaking could be, for example, the building of the Channel Tunnel. At the opening of the tunnel the partnership would dissolve.
(c) Any partner may serve notice on all the other partners of his or her intention to dissolve the partnership. This will be effective from the time of receipt or from any later time given in the notice of dissolution. Where the partnership has been created by deed, written notice of dissolution must be given, otherwise it may be made by word of mouth. The partnership agreement may specify the method of dissolution to be used. If it does so, it must be followed. Where partners seek to dissolve a

▶ **Partnership at will** – a partnership that has had no time set for its duration. Any partner may dissolve the partnership by giving notice to the other partner(s).

partnership to fraudulently exclude other partner(s) from future business, a court will probably refuse to dissolve the partnership.

In examples (a) and (b) above, should the partnership continue after the specified time, it will be inferred that the partners have entered into a new agreement to continue on the same terms as the original partnership. Any such new agreement will be a **partnership at will**.

Dissolution by bankruptcy, death or charge

PA1890, s. 33

(1) Subject to any agreement between the partners, every partnership is dissolved as regards all partners by the death or bankruptcy of any partner.
(2) A partnership may, at the option of other partners, be dissolved if any partner suffers his share of the partnership property to be charged under this Act for his separate debt.

▶ See below for details of the statutory rules on the dissolution of partnerships.

Section 33 can be examined under the three headings of death, bankruptcy and charge.

Death
In a two-partner partnership, the death of one partner will dissolve the agreement (you cannot be a partner on your own). In other cases the partnership agreement will normally state the procedure to be followed upon the death of a partner. The deceased partner's partnership assets will pass to his or her estate, being paid out in accordance with the partnership agreement or according to the statutory provisions.

Bankruptcy
The procedure followed on bankruptcy is similar to that for the death of a partner. The partnership is dissolved but the existing partners can agree before the dissolution to continue without the bankrupt partner, his or her share of the partnership assets being paid out to the bankrupt partner's trustee in bankruptcy.

Charge
A creditor may have a charge placed on the assets of a partner in a judgment for debt. This is made available under s. 23, which gives a creditor the right to apply to a court for a charging order against a partner's assets and share of profits. A receiver may be appointed to collect the assets and profits. The other partners are given power under this section to buy off the creditor, and where an order of sale is obtained by the creditor, to purchase the partner's share. In such circumstances, the partners will have the option to dissolve the partnership.

Dissolution by illegality of partnership

> **PA1890, s. 34**
>
> A partnership is in every case dissolved by the happening of any event that makes it unlawful for the business of the firm to be carried on or for the members of the firm to carry it on in partnership.

This section cannot be varied by any express clause in the partnership agreement. All illegal partnerships will be dissolved.

The next case concerned two highwaymen who were in dispute over the sharing out of the proceeds of their robberies.

Everet v. Williams (1725)

Two highwaymen formed a partnership to commit crime. A dispute arose about the division of the spoils and a court action was commenced.

 COURT HELD
The claim was dismissed because the partnership was illegal. The partners were sentenced to be hanged!

A partnership will also be dissolved where the purpose of the contract becomes illegal. For example, in the case of a partnership formed to provide boat trips, should the partners then decide to switch to the transportation of illegal immigrants, the partnership would be dissolved because of its illegal purpose.

In certain partnerships, for example, solicitors, it is a requirement that all parties are in possession of an annual practising certificate. Should a partner fail to obtain his or her annual certificate, or be struck off for disciplinary reasons, the partnership may be technically dissolved because of its inability to comply with the law.

 Outline five ways in which a partnership may be dissolved, other than by a court order.

Dissolution by the court

> **PA1890, s. 35(b)**
>
> On application by a partner the court may decree a dissolution of the partnership in any of the following cases. ...
>
> (b) When a partner, other than the partner suing, becomes in any other way permanently incapable of performing his part of the partnership contract.

The permanently incapacitated partner may not apply, but any of the other partners can. The incapacity must be permanent or be prescribed to be permanent after a fixed time, as detailed in the partnership agreement; for example, after six months of incapacity a partner will be deemed to be permanently incapacitated.

> **PA1890, s. 35(c)**
>
> (c) When a partner, other than the partner suing, has been guilty of such conduct as, in the opinion of the court, regard being had to the nature of the business, is calculated to prejudicially affect the carrying on of the business.

This may occur where a partner commits an act that, though not being prohibited in the partnership agreement, brings discredit or bad publicity to the firm. An example of this might be a criminal offence or serious immoral behaviour that might prejudice the general public's feelings towards the partnership. Again, the guilty partner cannot sue for the dissolution.

> **PA1890, s. 35(d)**
>
> (d) Wilful or persistent breaches of the partnership agreement.

In these circumstances the relationship will probably have broken down between the partners. One of the partners may fail to attend for work, fail to account for money in the prescribed manner or be acting in such a way that it is impossible for the other partner(s) to work with him or her. The party in default may not sue for dissolution.

> **PA1890, s. 35(e)**
>
> (e) When the business or the partnership can only be carried on at a loss.

Clearly, there is no point in being in business together if it is making a loss.

> **PA1890, s. 35(f)**
>
> (f) Whenever in any case circumstances have arisen that, in the opinion of the Court, render it just and equitable that the partnership be dissolved.

This is a 'catch all' section that allows for a partner to sue for the dissolution of a partnership, in circumstances other than those outlined above.

Mental incapacity

Section 35(a) of the PA1890 was repealed by the Mental Health Act 1983, s. 96. This allows for the dissolution of a partnership, on the grounds that a partner has become so mentally ill as to no longer be capable of managing his or her own affairs.

Effects of dissolution

The PA1890 supplies a series of rules to be followed covering the actual break-up of the partnership, relating to the advertising of the dissolution, the winding up, the allocation of partnership resources and the apportionment of post-partnership profits.

Section 37 of the PA1890 gives the right, upon dissolution or upon retirement of a partner, to advertise the event, making provision, where necessary, for the requirement of the other partners to agree. Details of the dissolution will normally be placed in the *London Gazette*.

Section 38 of the PA1890 allows for the powers of the partners to bind the firm to continue after the dissolution, for the purposes of the winding up of the company. Transactions that were begun prior to dissolution may be finished. The partners may conduct the winding up of the firm themselves; they need not appoint a **liquidator**. A firm will not be bound after dissolution by the acts of a bankrupt partner, except where a solvent partner has 'held out' or allowed others to represent him or her as still being a partner of the bankrupt.

▶ **Liquidator** – under the Companies Act 1985, a liquidator must be a qualified insolvency practitioner, normally a solicitor or an accountant. It is the liquidator's job to collect all monies owed to the company, realize all other assets and pay off the creditors in accordance with the rules laid down in the Act.

Rule for distribution of assets on final settlement of accounts

> **PA1890, s. 37**
>
> In settling accounts between the partners after a dissolution of partnership, the following rules shall, subject to any agreement, be observed.
>
> (a) Losses, including losses and deficiencies of capital, shall be paid first out of profits, next out of capital, and lastly, if necessary, by the partners individually in the proportion in which they were entitled to share profits.
> (b) The assets of the firm including the sums, if any, contributed by the partners to make up losses or deficiencies of capital, shall be applied in the following manner and order:
>   (1) in paying the debts and liabilities of the firm to persons who are not partners therein;
>   (2) in paying to each partner rateably what is due from the firm to him for advances as distinguished from capital;
>   (3) in paying to each partner rateably what is due from the firm to him in respect of capital;
>   (4) the ultimate residue, if any, shall be divided among the partners in the proportion in which the profits are divisible.

The first part of this section provides the rules for the paying out of losses and it is important to remember that in recent times this has become more important than the distribution of profit. The costs of the winding up will also have to be paid out of the assets, as at s. 44(3) (see below).

(ACT) Outline three sets of circumstances where a court may order the dissolution of a partnership. Then take the partnership deed you drew up earlier in the chapter and see how well it would specify what ought to be done on the dissolution of the partnership.

Section 39 of the PA1890 states that all partners have the right to use the assets of the partnership to pay the partnership creditors. Therefore, the personal representatives of any deceased partner, or an assignee, will not be able to withdraw any capital prior to the partnership debts being paid. Each partner is given a **lien** over the assets of the partnership, which becomes effective on the dissolution of the firm. A partner may apply to a court for the appointment of a receiver to supervise the distribution of the assets.

Under PA1890, s. 44, payments will be paid out of the assets in the following order:

1. to partnership creditors;
2. repayment of monies lent by partners to the partnership (over and above initial capital);
3. the costs of the winding up;
4. capital repayments to the partners;
5. any remaining profits to be repaid according to the profit-sharing ratios, i.e. split equally, unless the partnership agreement states otherwise.

Section 42 of the PA1890 allows for the distribution of profits made during the process of winding up, or after a dissolution, where there is an outgoing partner. Any profits made must be shared equally between all partners. The outgoing partner, or the partner's representatives, will have the option of accepting 5 per cent per annum interest on capital employed, or such figure as a court may attribute to the use of his or her assets. Any partner who continues to manage the business after dissolution will be able to claim a managerial allowance.

Goodwill

Goodwill is an asset belonging to the partnership and, upon dissolution, unless otherwise provided for in the partnership agreement, must be sold, the proceeds being dispersed as if they were capital. Should the goodwill not be sold, a partner may continue to trade using the goodwill, provided that by his or her trading the partner does not make any of the previous partners liable for any of debts or acts.

Where the goodwill is assigned, the other partners will be prevented from trading in the company name, or soliciting previous customers or clients of the firm, though not from commencing a new business in competition. A purchaser of goodwill will have the right to continue trading in the name of the partnership, though it must not be suggested that the original partners are still in the firm,

▶ **Lien** – the right of a seller to retain property until his or her claim on it is satisfied, for example, in the case of an unpaid seller, until the goods have been paid for.

▶ For definition of **goodwill**, see marginal note on p. 12.

and the purchaser will have the right to solicit former customers. A seller will normally be prevented from opening up in business in competition with a purchaser, by a restriction in the agreement of sale.

LIMITED PARTNERSHIPS

It is possible for a partner to have limited liability under the Limited Partnership Act 1907. The limited partner may be a **corporate body** or a sleeping partner. A limited partnership must be constituted in the following manner, with not more than twenty partners (although solicitors and certain other professions may have more than twenty partners):

▶ A **corporate body** is a body that has a separate legal existence: for example, a limited company.

1 one or more general partners, who will manage the partnership and be liable for partnership debts as in a normal partnership;
2 one or more limited partners, who have made a contribution to the assets of the limited partnership, their liability being limited to the amount that they contribute.

A limited partner cannot take any role in the management of the limited partnership. A partner who does this will become fully liable for all partnership debts and not benefit from limited liability. Once a limited partner has made his or her capital contribution, the capital cannot be withdrawn without the partner remaining liable to the limited partnership for the amount withdrawn. A limited partner has the right to inspect the firm's accounts. However, a limited partner does not have any power to bind the limited partnership, nor can he or she call for its dissolution in any of the following circumstances:

- by the giving of notice (s. 32(c));
- in the case of death or bankruptcy of a limited partner (s. 33(1));
- where a charge is placed on the assets of a limited partner (s. 33(2));
- in the case of the mental disorder of a limited partner (the Mental Health Act 1983, s. 96).

A limited partnership must be registered with the Registrar of Companies, by the submission of a signed statement containing the following details:

(a) the firm's name;
(b) the type of business;
(c) the location of the business;
(d) details of all partners;
(e) the date of commencement of the partnership;
(f) the duration of the partnership (if any);
(g) a statement that the partnership is to be limited;

(h) details of each limited partner, including the amount invested, and the nature of the investment, for example, money or property.

Should the above statement not be registered then the limited partner will be treated as a general partner, with unlimited liability. Where any changes are made in the constitution of the limited partnership – for example, a general partner becoming a limited partner – the Registrar of Companies must be informed within seven days. If they are not so registered, the partner will continue to have unlimited liability, until the Registrar is satisfied that all requirements have been complied with. To be valid, the change from general to limited partner must be advertised in the *London Gazette*.

The following table illustrates the different powers available to limited and general partners.

		Limited partners	General partners
1	Can take part in the management of the partnership	No (but may give advice)	Yes
2	Can dissolve the partnership by notice	No	Yes
3	Have unlimited liability	No	Yes
4	Can bind the partnership to a contract	No	Yes
5	Death, bankruptcy or mental disorder may dissolve the firm	No	Yes
6	Have limited liability	Yes	No
7	Can inspect the partnership books	Yes	Yes

EFFECT OF INSOLVENCY ON THE PARTNERSHIP

The law relating to the insolvency of partnerships is contained in the Insolvency Act 1986. The Act applies different rules according to the partnership's age and number of partners.

The first category is partnerships that have been in existence for more than three years, having eight or more partners.

These partnerships are treated as 'unregistered companies' and are wound up in the same way as a company (see procedure on page 122).

The second and third categories are partnerships with eight or more partners that have been in existence for less than three years, and partnerships with fewer than eight partners that have been in business for more than three years.

The second two categories may be wound up in the same way as the first category, though the partners may seek to avoid the penalties of being wound up, for example, being banned from holding a directorship (Directors Disqualification Act 1986) and being made bankrupt, by entering into voluntary arrangements with their creditors. The procedure is the same as detailed in Chapter 6, including reaching agreement with 75 per cent of their creditors and obtaining an interim order with the help of an insolvency practitioner.

The following case illustrates the procedure to be followed where certain members of the partnership are forced into bankruptcy. Unless otherwise agreed in the partnership agreement, the deficit must be calculated in the same way that the partners contributed capital, not in the proportion that profits and losses are apportioned.

Garner v. Murray (1904) 1 Ch 57

In this case the partnership was dissolved with one of the partners being insolvent. After the first payments had been made – for example, the payments to outside creditors – the balance sheet was left as below:

Liabilities	£	Assets	£	£
Garner (capital)	2,500	Cash		1,891
Murray (capital)	314	Wilkins (owes)	263	
		Deficit	660	
				923
	2,814			2,814

Wilkins owed the partnership £263, plus a third share of the deficit £220 (£263 + £220 = £483). His insolvency meant that the debt was passed on to the other two partners, who had to make good the deficit on the ratio of their initial capital investment. Garner had invested £2,500, while Murray had invested £314, so Garner had to pay the larger percentage of the debt, as he had invested almost eight times more than Murray.

It must be remembered that partners' debts are unlimited, joint and several. A creditor may choose to pursue one partner, where the creditor feels that the partner has more assets than the partnership, i.e. the family home, before he or she sues the partnership. Where this happens the pursued partner will be able to claim from the other partners, for a contribution towards anything that the pursued partner has paid to the creditor.

ACT Maya has entered into a business venture with her two brothers. She now wants to take no further role in the business, merely wishing to leave her initial investment of £10,000 in the partnership, in return for a share of the profits. Examine whether it is possible for Maya to retire from the partnership, thus ending her liability to any creditor, while continuing to receive profits from the partnership.

PARTNERSHIP ADVANTAGES AND DISADVANTAGES

	Advantages	Disadvantages
1 Commencement	Simple, just find your first customer.	Too simple, it is possible to be in a partnership without even knowing it.
2 Legal Requirements		Generally none, but a limited partnership must be registered with the Registrar of Companies. Name must comply with the BNA85.
3 Raising of Capital	Easier to raise than as a sole trader. The bigger the partnership the easier it is to raise capital.	Will still probably need to be a secured loan on a property.
4 Management	All general partners have the right to take part in the management of the business. Limited partners are forbidden to take part in the management of the business.	Management by a group of people can be difficult when they all have an equal say. When times are hard, problems invariably arise.
5 Profits	Profits will be shared equally between the partners, unless specified differently in the partnership agreement.	In hard times the profits have to be shared around the partners.
6 Accounting	The partnership will (it is hoped) be able to afford professional advice. This should enable it to obtain valuable advice concerning grants, loans, tax allowances, etc.	A partnership will normally have to keep a quite sophisticated set of accounts to allow for the requirements of the Inland Revenue.
7 Liability	Liability is spread among all the general partners. A limited partner's liability will be set by the amount registered on the limited partnership agreement.	Liability is unlimited, joint and several. All partners will be personally liable for the debts of the partnership. It is even possible to pursue a single partner for the debts of the whole partnership. The family home could be lost! All partners will be bound by each other's acts; should a partner enter into a disastrous contract, the partnership will be bound.

CHAPTER SUMMARY

1 Section 1 of the PA1890 defines partnership as a relationship that exists between persons carrying on a business with a view of profit.
2 The relationship between partners is considered to be one of *uberrimae fidei,* i.e. one of absolute good faith.
3 A partner is considered to be an agent of the firm with the apparent authority to bind the firm to the following: sell goods or property belonging to the firm; purchase goods normally used by the firm; accept payment; hire staff and employ a

solicitor on behalf of the firm. A commercial partner will also have the power to borrow money on behalf of the firm and to sanction payments out of the firm.

4   The apparent authority of a partner will not normally stretch to the following: entering the firm into arbitration in case of dispute; accepting shares in lieu of payment; entering into a deed in favour of another party; entering into a contract of guarantee, unless that is normal practice for the firm.

5   Section 17 of the PA1890 provides that a new partner will not be liable for any debts incurred prior to his or her joining the partnership, unless the new partner agrees to them. A retiring partner will only be able to avoid liability incurred when he or she was a partner if the retiring partner follows the rules prescribed in s. 36.

6   Where partners fail to enter into a partnership agreement, or fail to cater for an eventuality in an agreement, it will normally be ascertained that a partnership exists and the terms of the Act will be applied.

7   A partnership will be dissolved, unless previously agreed, by death, bankruptcy or the placing of a charge on the assets of a partner.

8   The PA1890 provides rules to be followed in the dissolution of a partnership relating to payment of creditors, payment of other monies, goodwill and other matters.

9   The Limited Partnership Act 1907 provides the rules for the formation of a partnership with limited liability.

10   The insolvency of partnerships is dealt with under the Insolvency Act 1986.

Companies

Chapter objectives

By the end of this chapter you should be able to:

▌ understand the differences between the public and the private sector, including the different nature of the types of business found in each

▌ recognize the different types of companies, including registered companies, both public limited and private limited, chartered companies and statutory companies

▌ appreciate the importance of the juristic person

▌ understand the process of registration of a company, including the memorandum of association, articles of association, and Forms G10 and G12

▌ recognize the ways in which a company may avoid being put into liquidation

▌ know the procedure of the winding-up of a company, and its effects on the creditors, debtors and members of the company

▌ understand the role of the Official Receiver and the implications of the Insolvency Act 1986.

In this chapter we shall examine the most common form of business organization in the UK: the limited company. There are various types of company, which we shall detail, but they all share a vital difference from both sole traders and partnerships, and this is that they are a **separate entity** in law. We shall start by looking at the different types of company.

► See *Salomon v. Salomon*, p. 112 below.

SOLE AND AGGREGATE CORPORATE BODIES

Corporations sole

A corporation sole is in constant existence. It is an institution that enjoys perpetual succession. For example, certain Anglican bishops exist as a corporation sole. When a bishop dies or is replaced, the corporation sole continues regardless of the change. If property is held by a corporation sole, there are no problems with transferring property between an office holder and his or her successor. Corporations sole are not generally suited to the commercial environment and they are not of serious interest to a student of business law.

Corporations aggregate

Corporations aggregate include the major commercial business organizations. The three main types are:

1 registered companies;
2 chartered companies;
3 statutory companies.

Registered companies

This is the most common type of company and there are around 750,000 registered in the UK. The formation of a registered company is governed by the Companies Act 1985 (as amended by the Companies Act 1989). Once the **promoters** of a company have complied with the stated formalities, i.e. have registered with Companies House, the company's details will be available for public inspection. A registered company may be either a public limited company or a private limited company (see below).

> ► The **promoters** are the persons who are setting up the company.

Chartered companies

A company may be created by Royal Charter, a historical method of creation that has fallen into disuse. The first companies to be created in this way were the great international trading companies, such as the Hudson's Bay Company and the East India Company. Now chartered companies are generally non-commercial organizations, such as the Institute of Chartered Surveyors and the British Broadcasting Corporation (BBC).

Statutory companies

Statutory companies, which are created by Act of Parliament, are normally used to create nationalized industries. However, statutory companies have now virtually disappeared, mainly because of the Conservative government's opposition to nationalized industries. The government has denationalized a whole series of industries, including water, gas, electricity and, most recently, British Rail. The Labour party appears to have accepted the decline of public ownership. An example of a remaining statutory company is British Coal.

► See also Chapter 6, p. 68.

Corporations aggregate

Unincorporated	Incorporated

1 Sole traders	1 Registered company
	(a) Private limited company (Ltd),
	    e.g. Tom's Carpentry Ltd
	(b) Public limited company (plc),
	    e.g. Lloyds Bank plc

2 Partnerships	2 Chartered company, e.g. Institute of Chartered Surveyors 3 Statutory company, e.g. British Coal

TYPES OF LIMITATION

In this book we are going to concentrate on companies registered under the Companies Act 1985 (CA85). Registered companies may be limited by shares or by guarantee, or may have unlimited liability. Under the CA85, s. 1, a company may be limited or unlimited in the following ways.

(a) It may be limited by shares, meaning that the liability of the members of the company will be limited to any amount that remains outstanding on their shares. An example of this could be one of the denationalized industries, where a deposit had to be sent with the application for shares. The shares were then allocated and the balance had to be paid at a given future date. This system was used in the privatization of British Telecom. If the industry had gone into liquidation before the date of payment for the balance of the shares, the applicant would be liable to pay the balance outstanding on the shares and nothing else.

(b) It may be limited by guarantee, in which case the members will have guaranteed an amount of money to be paid into the business in case of liquidation. For example, each member may have agreed to pay £10,000 should the company be put into liquidation and with ten members that would total £100,000. If the company were liquidated with debts of £250,000, then each member's liability would end with the payment of the agreed £10,000. The outstanding £150,000 would not be recoverable.

(c) It may be unlimited, in which case the members of the company will be liable for all of the debts of the company, should it go into liquidation.

 What is the difference between a public and a private sector organization? List three examples of each that you have personal knowledge or experience of. If you are unsure refer back to the beginning of Chapter 6.

► **Liquidation** – the process of terminating a company's affairs by realizing its assets to discharge its liabilities. The liquidation procedure is also referred to as **winding-up**.

PUBLIC AND PRIVATE COMPANIES

Under the CA85, s. 1, a company may be registered as being either public or private. A public company is one that has been registered as a public company under the provisions of the CA85. It may offer shares and **debentures** for sale to the public, which may then be traded on the stock market. A private limited company is one that, under the Act, is not a public company. It is a criminal offence for a private limited company to offer its shares for sale to the general public (Financial Services Act 1986, s. 170).

A public limited company must have a minimum authorized share capital of £50,000, of which a quarter must be paid up. For example, if the authorized share capital is £50,000, then £12,500

► **Debenture** – a loan made to a company, normally secured on a company's assets. It may take the form of a loan from a single institution, such as a bank, or an issue of debentures may be made available to the public, by a debenture trust deed. The holder of the debenture obtains certain rights that are guarded. A trustee will be appointed to protect the interest of the debenture holders, and may take action to do so where he or she thinks fit.

must be paid up; if the authorized share capital is £100,000, then £25,000 must be paid up. No such restrictions are placed on a private limited company. Indeed, one member could legitimately commence a private limited company with £1, there being no minimum requirement.

A public limited company must register a **memorandum of association** that states that it is a public limited company, complying with Table F of the Companies Regulations 1985. It must also have at least two directors and two members. A private limited company need only have two members and one director. Single member private companies, limited by shares or guarantee, are allowed by the Companies Single Members Private Limited Companies Regulations 1992 (15/07/92).

A public limited company must produce a set of audited accounts within seven months of the end of its financial year, while a private limited company has ten months. A private limited company may be able, depending upon its size and turnover, to avoid certain of the regulations relating to the preparation and publication of accounts.

A public limited company must end its business name with the suffix Public Limited Company (plc). A private limited company is required to contain the word Limited (Ltd) in its title. Both are required to obtain a certificate of incorporation before trading, while a public limited company also has to obtain a certificate to trade from the Registrar of Companies, prior to commencing trading. In a public limited company the company secretary must be qualified, as demanded by the CA85, s. 286. There is no such requirement for a private limited company.

The following table illustrates the differences between a public limited company and a private limited company.

> ▶ The **memorandum of association** contains a clause that states how much a company may raise by the issuing of shares. This is called the nominal share capital or authorized share capital.

	Private limited company	*Public limited company*
1 Name	Must contain Ltd	Must end plc
2 Certificate of incorporation	Must obtain prior to trading	Must obtain prior to trading
3 Certificate to trade	Doesn't need one	Must obtain prior to trading
4 Initial capital	No minimum requirement	Minimum of £50,000
5 Accounts	Within 10 months after end of its financial year	Within 7 months after end of its financial year
6 Shares	Forbidden to sell to the public	May sell shares and debentures to the public
7 Membership	Must have at least one member and one director	Must have at least two members and two directors

CHARACTERISTICS OF AN INCORPORATED BODY

An incorporated company is known as a **juristic person**. The process of incorporation creates a 'legal' person in its own right and the company obtains a legal identity separate from its members. A company will be liable without limit for any debts, but the

> ▶ **Juristic person** – an entity, such as a corporation, recognized as having legal personality, i.e. capable of enjoying and being subject to legal rights and duties. Also known as an 'artificial person', in contrast with a human being, who is referred to as a 'natural person'.

members of the company will (unless it is a company with unlimited liability) have their liability limited to any amount outstanding to be paid on their shares.

The following (fictional) example illustrates how limited liability works. Patrick was keen to invest in the privatization of the BBC. The government invited applications for shares in the BBC, priced at £1.50, requiring the payment of the shares to be made in three equal instalments, the first being required at the time of application. Patrick applied for 1,000 shares, sending a payment of £500. The government accepted Patrick's offer and he was allocated 1,000 shares. Unfortunately, the BBC became insolvent and Patrick had to pay the balance outstanding on his shares, two instalments at £500 each, making £1,000. The limit of Patrick's liability was £1,000 and, if his shares had been fully paid up, he would not have had to pay any more money. However, he would still have lost money because the share value would probably have dropped to virtually nothing.

 1 What are the three different types of corporations aggregate?
2 How may each different type be created?
3 List three examples of each, different from the examples given in the text.

The members of a company may change without affecting the company itself. This is known as perpetual succession. Shares, which represent the ownership of the company, may be transferred and members may die, but the company will carry on. This is in stark contrast to a partnership and to a sole trader, which would both normally be ended or seriously affected by death. All assets of a company are owned by the company, not the members.

This separation of the members from the company itself, recognizing the creation of a separate legal entity, was established in the following landmark case.

Salomon v. Salomon Ltd (1897) AC 22

(VC) Aron Salomon was a cobbler, in business as a sole trader. He turned his business into a limited company in 1892. The purchase price of the business was set at £38,782: Aron took 20,000 shares valued at £1 each, while six other members of the family took one share each. Aron was paid £8,782 and the remaining £10,000 balance of the purchase price was lent to the company by Aron, as a secured loan. A charge was placed on the assets of the company to secure the loan.

The company then experienced difficulty and was wound up, a liquidator being appointed. The company's liabilities, including the £10,000 loan to Aron, were £7,733 more than the company's assets. The question arose as to whether the secured loan should be paid to Aron. The creditors claimed that he had merely lent the money to himself, therefore the remainder of the assets should be paid to them, not to him.

COURT HELD

The House of Lords ruled that the company was a distinct and separate entity, so the secured loan made by Aron Salomon to Salomon Ltd was valid. Because it was secured it had to be repaid before any other debts. This meant that all other creditors, apart from Aron, got nothing.

Veil of incorporation

The principle of a company having a separate identity from its members is known as the veil of incorporation. In certain circumstances the veil of incorporation may be lifted to enable any person, normally the company directors, to be prosecuted where they have acted fraudulently or failed to comply with any of the regulations. When the veil is lifted the directors will generally be made personally liable for the debts of the company, if they have been party to fraudulent trading, or continuing to trade, knowing that the company was insolvent.

Civil and criminal liability

A company may be liable for the criminal and civil actions of its employees, through the principle of **vicarious liability**.

THE PROCESS OF REGISTRATION

The process of registering a company is the same for a public limited company or a private limited company. The relevant forms can be obtained from the Registrar of Companies, Company House, Cardiff CF4 3TT. The required details are listed below:

(a) memorandum of association;
(b) articles of association;
(c) Form G10;
(d) Form G12.

Memorandum of association

The memorandum must be constructed in the form prescribed in the Act, containing the following details:

1 the name of the company;
2 the address of the registered office of the company;
3 the company objectives;
4 the amount of liability of the members;
5 the authorized capital.

The name of the company

The company name must conform to the Business Names Act 1985

► In November 1993, Roger Levitt pleaded guilty to fraudulent trading, after his financial services company had collapsed with debts of £34 million. The offence carried a maximum sentence of seven years' imprisonment: Levitt received 180 hours' community service.

► **Vicarious liability** – a legal liability imposed on one person for the crimes or torts committed by another. An employer will normally be vicariously liable for acts committed in the course of his or her work by an employee.

and the provisions in the CA85. The name must end in plc or Ltd, unless the company is a private company limited by guarantee and is a charity or other organization with non-commercial objectives, in which case it may omit Ltd from the name (CA85, s. 30).

A register of names is maintained by the Registrar, who will not register a company name that is the same as one already on the register, though the Registrar will register a similar name. A company may apply, within twelve months, to the Department of Trade and Industry (DTI), for the removal of a similar name from the register (CA85, s. 28). For example, a company could register as the Red Balloon Company, when there was already a company called the Red and Green Balloon Company. It would be for the Red and Green Balloon Company to object to the name of the Red Balloon Company. Where an objection is made, a company may be ordered to change its name by the DTI. A company may also change its name voluntarily, on a **special resolution**.

An offensive or criminal name will not be registered: for example, Racists Against Immigrants Ltd. Names suggesting the provision of sexual services or prostitutes will not be registered.

The company name must comply with the Business Names Act 1985, as described in Chapter 6. Points covered by the BNA85 include: not using names that suggest links with government departments; furnishing full details upon application; and displaying the full name on stationery and at business premises. This last point is also covered under the CA85, ss. 348 and 349. A company must display its full name outside any place of business and outside the registered office. The full name must also be contained in any business stationery. Failure to comply may result in the commission of an offence and the directors becoming personally liable, for example, where a contract is signed in anything less than the full name of the company.

The address of the registered office of the company
The details of the registered office must be provided on Form G10 (see p. 117). The country of registration – for example, England – is included in the memorandum. The directors may change the location of a registered office after the passing of an **ordinary resolution** or where they have been empowered to do so in the articles.

The company objectives
In this section the company must state its general trading objectives. For the Ford Motor Company, for instance, this would be the manufacture and sale of motor vehicles. Historically, this has been a problem area. If a company stated, for example, that the manufacture and sale of washing machines was its company objective, then any act taken outside that area, such as the manufacture and sale of vacuum cleaners, could be ruled *ultra vires* and void at common law.

▶ **Special resolution** – a motion passed by 75 per cent of those voting at a general meeting, where notice had been given that the motion would be proposed as a special resolution. The notice must have been given twenty-one days prior to the meeting, unless there are exceptional circumstances, in which case 95 per cent in value of share capital or 95 per cent in voting rights must agree to the meeting.

▶ **Ordinary resolution** – a decision reached by a simple majority (i.e. more than 50 per cent) of those voting.
Extraordinary resolution – a decision reached by a majority of not less than 75 per cent of those voting at a general meeting, of which fourteen days' notice (seven for an unlimited company) that the resolution will be proposed has been given.

▶ *Ultra vires* – beyond the limit of their powers.

The following case illustrates the application of the *ultra vires* principle.

Ashbury Railway Carriage Co. Ltd v. Riche (1875) LR 7

The company's objectives stated that it manufactured and sold railway rolling stock, and that its business was mechanical engineering and general contracting. The company entered into a contract to build a railway in Belgium, but the directors later changed their minds and repudiated the contract. Riche, who had been subcontracted by Ashbury, sued Ashbury for breach of contract.

COURT HELD
The plaintiff could not succeed, because the contract was ultra vires, not being the type of business that the company had included in its objectives; therefore, it was void.

 If you were the Registrar of Companies, which of the following names would you refuse to register as new companies? Give reasons for your answers.

1 Tesco Ltd
2 Madame Fifi's Brothel Ltd
3 Assassins Ltd
4 Fiord Motor Company plc

Companies Act 1985, s. 35
Section 9(1) of the European Communities Act 1972 addressed the problem of the capacity of companies and the *ultra vires* rule. The act provided the following:

European Communities Act 1972, s. 9(1)

Acts done by the organs of the company shall be binding upon it even if those acts are not within the objectives of the company, unless such acts exceed the powers that the law confers or allows to be conferred on those organs.

The provisions later became incorporated into CA85, s. 35. This section allows that a company may make a general statement as to its objectives, for example, to trade as a general commercial business, so it will now be rare that the *ultra vires* rule would be applicable. It will not be possible to question the validity of an act carried out by a company on the basis of anything contained in its memorandum.

Section 35 and the retention of ultra vires
Section 35 retains the right of any member to have a contract ruled *ultra vires*. They may apply to a court for an injunction to prevent

► **Written resolution** – a resolution signed by all company members and treated as effective, even though it is not passed as a properly convened company meeting. Under the CA85, private companies can pass resolutions in this way in certain circumstances.

► **Holding company** – a company that controls a subsidiary company. A company will be a holding company:

1 if it holds a majority of the voting rights in a subsidiary company;
2 if it is a member of the subsidiary company, having the right to remove the majority of the board of the subsidiary company;
3 if it is a member of the subsidiary company and together with other members has control of the subsidiary company;
4 if it is itself a subsidiary of a holding company.

the directors entering into a contract, unless the contract has been ratified by a special resolution or, in the case of a private company, a **written resolution**. In deciding whether to grant the injunction a court will make reference to the objectives of the company. Where the contract has been entered into, the option to have it stopped will no longer be available.

Section 35 and the power of directors

The directors of a company must still act within the limitations placed upon them by the articles of association (see below, p. 117). Where a director acts in excess of his or her powers, the director's action may be ratified by a special resolution. A further special resolution may be passed where a director has become liable when acting outside his or her powers, to relieve the director of any liability. The company will be able to avoid contracts made between its own directors and the directors of its **holding company**, when they have been made *ultra vires*, where not ratified as above.

Capacity summed up

To a third party, such as a supplier of goods to a company, who acts in good faith, i.e. not fraudulently, there is now no problem in obtaining enforcement of a contract against a company, where that contract has been entered into by an authorized officer of the company, such as the branch manager of a shop. Where such an officer has entered into a contract it will still be valid. The officer's unauthorized action will be a matter to be dealt with inside the company.

The idea of 'constructive notice' of a company's objectives now no longer applies. Even where a third party is aware of the objectives of a company and enters into a contract with the company that falls outside the company's objectives, the third party will still be able to enforce the contract.

Charities

Special provisions are made for charities. Because of their nature they are normally bound to work within their stated objectives. Section 35 will not apply to charities unless a third party has supplied consideration to a charity, either not knowing that the contract was *ultra vires* to the charity or not knowing that the company was a charity.

Changing the company objectives

The company objectives may be changed by virtue of a special resolution. The change will be valid provided that no application to cancel the change is made to a court within twenty-one days of the special resolution. Such an application may be made by the holders of at least 15 per cent of the issued share capital. The company must send a copy of the altered memorandum to the Registrar of Companies.

The amount of liability of the members

Where the company has limited liability this will simply be stated in the memorandum.

The authorized capital

The amount of authorized capital must be stated, including the method of division into shares: for example, £75,000 divided into 75,000 shares, valued at £1 each. The share price is known as the nominal value.

The memorandum will be concluded with a statement made by the members that states that they wish to form a company and that they agree to take the shares as detailed in the document.

 What are the differences between ordinary, special, extraordinary and written resolutions?

Articles of association

The articles govern the internal administration of the company. The promoters of the company determine the rules to be put in the articles, covering matters such as meetings, categories of shares, appointment of directors and other such matters. The CA85 provides a set of model articles that may be used by the promoters. Where no articles are provided the model articles will be automatically applied. (Note that Table A may only be used by a company limited by shares.)

Form G10

This form is entitled 'The statement of the first directors and secretary and intended situation of registered office'. The details of the director(s) and the company secretary, together with the location of the registered office, are recorded on this form. Their appointment as the directors and company secretary of the company will then be confirmed.

Form G12

This form is entitled 'The statutory declaration of compliance with requirements on application for registration of a company'. The declaration may be made by one of the named directors, the proposed company secretary or a solicitor who has been involved in the formation of the company. The declaration must normally be made in the presence of a **commissioner of oaths**. Should a false declaration be made, the proposer could be prosecuted for the criminal offence of perjury.

When all these forms have been completed and registered to the satisfaction of the Registrar of Companies, the Registrar will issue a certificate of incorporation. A private company may then com-

▶ A **commissioner of oaths** is a solicitor, or other person appointed by the Lord Chancellor, who takes statements from people under oath. Such statements are called affidavits. A person who makes an untruthful affidavit may be prosecuted for the criminal offence of perjury.

mence trading as a private limited company, while a public limited company must also obtain a certificate to trade, from the Registrar, after satisfying the minimum requirements relating to the issue of shares.

COMPANY MEETINGS

A company is bound to hold certain meetings throughout the year. These are known as general meetings, and are meetings of company members whose decisions can bind the company. However, a private limited company may vote unanimously not to hold them.

The Companies Act 1985 specifies certain reserved powers that can only be exercised by a general meeting. These include altering the memorandum and articles of association; removing a director before his or her term of office has expired; and putting the company into voluntary liquidation (or voluntary winding-up).

TYPES OF CHARGE

► Refer back to Chapter 6, p. 72, if you cannot remember what a charge is.

There are two ways in which a charge may be placed on the assets of a company. First, a fixed charge may be placed on the fixed assets of a company, such as buildings. Second, a floating charge may be taken over the total assets of a company. This will only be realized in the event of certain circumstances, such as the liquidation of the company. A charge must normally be registered with the Registrar of Companies to be valid. Where the charge is removed, that must also be registered by the submission of a memorandum of discharge.

COMPANY DISSOLUTION

There is more than one way to dissolve a company. We generally think of companies going into liquidation but they may just cease to exist. The different forms of dissolution are discussed below.

1   A company may go into compulsory liquidation because it cannot meet its debts. Company insolvency is governed by the Insolvency Act 1986 (IA86). Alternatively, as may happen in a partnership, the members of the company may simply feel that they no longer wish to work together and they may decide to go into voluntary liquidation.

2   The Attorney General may institute proceedings to dissolve a company where the objectives of a company are found to be offensive or illegal, for example, breeding Pit Bull Terriers.

3   The Registrar of Companies may dissolve a company that has ceased to trade, under the CA85, s. 652.

4 A company may be dissolved by a court order where its undertakings are transferred to another company by the IA86, s. 84(1–4).

1 Outline the process for registering a limited liability company.
2 What effect has the European Communities Act 1972, s. 9(1), had on the *ultra vires* rule?

We are concerned here with what happens when a company goes bust and we shall now examine the detailed process by which a company may be wound up or may seek to avoid winding-up by entering into an arrangement with its creditors.

Voluntary winding-up

The winding-up of a company may be agreed at any time by the shareholders of a company. A special resolution may be passed to effect the winding-up where the company is solvent or, where insolvent, by an extraordinary resolution, which states that the company cannot meet its liabilities. An ordinary resolution may be utilized where a company has accomplished the purpose of its existence, as detailed in the company articles. The resolution must be published in the *London Gazette*, within fourteen days of its being passed.

A majority of the directors of the company may publish a statutory declaration, within five weeks of the resolution, stating that the company will be able to satisfy all creditors, in full, within twelve months – in other words, a declaration that the company is solvent.

Where a declaration of solvency is made, the members of the company will be in control of the winding-up. Where no such declaration is made, the company will be insolvent and the creditors will control the winding-up.

In a solvent winding-up the members will appoint a **liquidator** to implement and control the procedure. In an insolvent winding-up the creditors will meet to appoint a liquidator. They also have the power to appoint a liquidation committee of up to five creditors, to supervise the procedure and work with the liquidator.

► See Chapter 7, p.101, for a definition of **liquidator**.

Effect of the passing of a winding-up resolution

The company does not cease to exist upon the passing of a resolution, but it may not continue to trade other than for the purposes of enabling it to be wound up. The liquidator will take charge of the assets of the company and any transfers of shares or changes in the members' rights must be approved by the liquidator. The directors of the company lose their powers upon the appointment of a liquidator. However, they may be kept on by the liquidator, or by the creditors, in the case of a voluntary creditors' winding-up. In an insolvent winding-up the employees will be dismissed, but they may be re-employed by the liquidator under a new contract.

The liquidator may allow the company to continue to trade if he or she considers that it will be beneficial to the winding-up procedure, for example, where it is in the process of completing a major contract. The liquidator is invested with all the powers of the company and may enter into or defend court actions, accept or collect monies and act in all instances on behalf of the company.

In a voluntary members' winding-up a liquidator may, when backed by an extraordinary resolution, pay off all, or certain classes of, creditors, or enter into any arrangements with the company's creditors. In a creditors' voluntary winding-up, the liquidator will need the approval of the court, the liquidation committee or the creditors.

Liquidation of assets

► To remind yourself of the different types of creditors, see Chapter 6.

The first people to obtain payment will be any secured creditors, who will receive payment when the asset upon which they have a charge is sold. Schedule 6 of the IA86 determines the order in which a liquidator must pay off a company's creditors and, after paying for the services of the liquidator, the liquidator must begin with the preferential creditors, who are paid as follows:

1 income tax not paid in the twelve months prior to liquidation;
2 VAT that had been due in the six months prior to liquidation;
3 car tax due in the twelve-month period prior to liquidation;
4 betting and gaming duty due in the twelve-month period prior to liquidation;
5 National Insurance contributions due in the twelve-month period prior to liquidation;
6 any sums owed to state or occupational pension schemes;
7 any wages owed to employees, up to a maximum of £800, due in the four-month period prior to liquidation;
8 holiday pay owed to employees.

After the preferential creditors have been paid, the liquidator will then pay off any creditors who have a floating charge over the assets of the company. The trade or unsecured creditors will be the next to be paid off, followed lastly by the deferred creditors.

Compulsory winding-up

We have seen that a company may be voluntarily wound up by its members or its creditors. Now we must examine the ways in which a company may be compulsorily wound up, which are covered by the IA86, s. 122.

Insolvency Act 1986, s. 122(1)
A company may be wound up by the court if:
(a) the company has by special resolution resolved that the company be wound up by the court;
(b) being a public company that was registered as such on its original incorporation, the company has not been issued with a certificate under section 117 of the Companies Act 1985 and

more than a year has expired since it was so registered;

(c) it is an old public company, within the meaning of the Companies Consolidation (Consequential Provisions) Act 1985;

(d) the company does not commence its business within a year from its incorporation or suspends its business for a whole year;

(e) the number of members is reduced to below two;

(f) the company is unable to pay its debts;

(g) the court is of the opinion that it is just and equitable that the company should be wound up.

Insolvency

We shall now examine what happens when a company is unable to pay its debts. Section 123 of the IA86 determines that a company is unable to pay its debts when:

- a creditor, who is owed £750 or more, has served a demand for payment on the company at its registered address, which the company has failed to pay within three weeks;
- **execution** has been issued on a judgment, which has been returned unpaid, either fully or in part;
- it is proved to the satisfaction of the court that the company is unable to pay its debts as they fall due;
- its assets are proved to be less than its liabilities, consideration having been given to its prospects.

► **Execution** – the court has issued a warrant to enable bailiffs to seize goods belonging to the judgment debtor, to sell them to recover the money owed.

 How might a company be wound up voluntarily?

Application for compulsory liquidation

A **petition** must be made for the compulsory liquidation of a company. It must be presented to the Chancery Division of the High Court or, where the paid-up share capital does not exceed £120,000, to the county court having jurisdiction for the area where the company's registered office is situated.

► **Petition** – application.

The petition may be presented by any, or all, of the following persons:

1 a creditor;
2 the directors of the company, on behalf of the company itself;
3 a **contributory**;

or it may be presented by

4 the Secretary of State, normally after an investigation into the company that has established fraudulent trading or some other contravention of the Act.

► **Contributory** – a past or present member of a company, who may be liable to contribute to the company's assets in the case of the liquidation of the company.

The court will fix the date and time of the hearing, which must be advertised in the *London Gazette* at least seven working days beforehand. The advertisement must be made in a form prescribed under the Act. If it is not then the petitioner may become liable for the costs of the court hearing. The advertisement is intended to warn any creditors, contributories or other interested parties, and to invite them to support or oppose the petition. Any parties who wish to appear at the hearing must give notice of their intention to the petitioner.

A court may, or may not, grant a winding-up order, depending upon the circumstances outlined above. Where an order is granted, a provisional liquidator will be appointed by the court, or the Official Receiver may be immediately appointed. In any case, once the order comes into effect, which may be some time after the court hearing, the Official Receiver will be appointed as the liquidator.

The actual liquidation of the company will be deemed to date back to the original petition, not the date of the court order by the IA86, s. 86. This has several important consequences:

> ► **Transaction at undervalue** – where the directors know that the company cannot pay its debts and make a gift of or sell a company asset at less than its value. See also Chapter 6, p. 77.

> ► **Preference payment** – a payment that has been made to a particular creditor, when the directors knew that the company was insolvent, to the detriment of other creditors. See also Chapter 6, p. 77.

1 the liquidator will have the power to set aside any transactions made at **undervalue**, in the two years prior to liquidation;
2 the liquidator will have the power to set aside any **preference payment** made to a creditor in the six months prior to liquidation or to a connected person, such as a director, in the two years prior to liquidation;
3 the liquidator will be able to avoid any floating charges made in the year before liquidation by an unconnected chargee or in the two years before by a connected chargee, such as a director.

 What are liquidators and what is their role in the winding-up of a company?

Procedures of liquidation

When an order is granted the Official Receiver becomes the liquidator, all staff are sacked, all legal actions against the company are suspended and the transfer of any shares or property becomes void. One or more directors, together with the company secretary, must submit a statement of affairs, outlining the financial position of the company, within twenty-one days of the making of the order. The dissolution of a company is usually automatic three months after the final report has been filed with the Registrar.

The Official Receiver will decide within twelve weeks whether to call separate meetings of contributaries and creditors. Should the Receiver decide not to, owing to a lack of interest, the Receiver must inform all concerned parties of his or her intention. Should 25 per cent of the creditors in value object to the decision not to hold a meeting, then the liquidator must convene a meeting. At a meeting the creditors may vote to appoint their own liquidator or appoint a liquidation committee to work with the liquidator.

When the liquidator has realized the assets of the company and paid off the creditors in the prescribed manner, he or she reports to the DTI. After that time the liquidator may apply to the court for the company to be dissolved; the order of dissolution is sent to the

Registrar of Companies, who dissolves the company and advertises the dissolution in the *London Gazette*.

Alternatives to liquidation

Just as a sole trader and a partnership can make an arrangement with their creditors to avoid going bankrupt, so can a company make an arrangement to avoid going into liquidation. A company may either go into administration or enter into a voluntary arrangement with its creditors. We shall examine both of these options.

Voluntary arrangement

The procedure for entering into a voluntary arrangement is detailed in the IA86, ss. 1–7. A company that is in trouble reaching an agreement with its creditors makes a voluntary arrangement either to pay a **composition** or to rearrange the payment of its debts. The latter might mean, for example, gaining the agreement of creditors for a longer period of repayment.

▶ **Composition** – an agreement made between a debtor and a creditor to accept part payment of a debt in full settlement: for example, a payment of 60 pence for every pound owed would fully discharge the debt.

In order to obtain a voluntary arrangement, a director, or the liquidator where the company is being wound up, must appoint a nominee, who must be a qualified insolvency practitioner. The nominee, with the assistance of the company directors, will produce a proposal to save the company. The details of the proposal will be presented to both the court and the creditors. Separate meetings of both creditors and shareholders are called to examine the proposals. If both of them agree to accept the proposals, then the agreement will become binding upon all parties, except a secured or preferential creditor, neither of whom is bound unless they have specifically agreed to the proposals.

Section 6 of the IA86 gives the grounds under which a creditor or shareholder may object to an agreed voluntary arrangement:

(a) when the arrangement is prejudicial to a particular creditor;
(b) where the proper procedure has not been followed in relation to the holding of any meeting under Part 1 of the IA68, ss. 1–7.

Any objection must be made within twenty-eight days of the report of the acceptance of a voluntary arrangement to the court. If a court accepts an application made under this section, it may either revoke or suspend the arrangement to allow further proposals to be made. Where the company is in liquidation or is the subject of an administration order (see below), at the time of the agreement of an arrangement, the court will have the power to suspend or terminate any proceedings currently being pursued against the company.

Section 7 details that the arrangement will be supervised by an insolvency practitioner, not necessarily the nominee, who shall be called the supervisor. This section also allows persons to make complaints to the court regarding the conduct of a supervisor, also stating the powers available to a supervisor.

Administration orders

Sections 8–27 of the IA86 contain the law relating to the issue and conduct of administration orders. An administration order may be sought by the company, its directors, or any member or creditor, where they feel that a company may become insolvent. An applicant must petition the court for an order of administration. An order may be granted where a court feels that it may enable:

(a) a company to realize its assets more profitably than in a liquidation;
(b) to be sold as a going concern;
(c) approval of a voluntary arrangement;
(d) approval of a scheme of arrangement.

Effect of a petition for an administration order

A petition will freeze most of a company's actions. Its assets will become frozen, so any judgments made against it cannot be enforced and any other property in its possession, such as hire purchase goods, cannot be recovered. The majority of legal actions concerning the company will also be suspended, for example, any new legal proceedings against the company or a petition for voluntary liquidation. However, a petition will not affect the appointment of a receiver or an application for the compulsory liquidation of the company.

 Wembley Widgets is going through a tough trading period. The finance director, Shirley Borrow, has approached you for advice: she wishes to stop the company from being put into liquidation by its creditors. Advise her what she would have to do to enter into a voluntary arrangement.

Granting of an administration order

When an order is granted, the effects started by the petition – i.e. the freezing of assets – will continue, though it will no longer be possible for the company to be compulsorily wound up. The court will appoint an administrator who will be responsible for the management of the company, including control and transfer of assets, removal of directors, calling of meetings, borrowing in the name of the company and the general management of the company, all in furtherance of the details in the order.

The administrator is bound to produce a proposal for the implementation of the goals outlined in the order, normally within three months of the granting of the order. The proposals must be notified to the members and creditors, and a meeting must be called to approve the proposals. Where the proposals are accepted the order will normally be extended to allow the implementation of the report. Should the proposals be rejected then the order will probably be withdrawn by the court.

CHAPTER SUMMARY

1 The most common type of incorporated business organization in the UK is the registered company, which may be a private limited company, a public limited company or an unlimited company. A company may be limited by shares or by guarantee.

2 A registered company will become a juristic person. That means that it will have its own legal existence, be able to own property and be legally liable for the actions of its employees.

3 The registration process requires the submission of a memorandum of association, articles of association, and Forms G10 and G12 to the Registrar of Companies.

4 A company may be dissolved voluntarily or compulsorily. A court will wind up a company in the following circumstances:

   (a) when a company has passed a special resolution to effect the winding-up;

   (b). being a public company that was registered as such on its original incorporation, the company has not been issued with a certificate under the CA85, s. 117, and more than a year has expired since it was so registered;

   (c) it is an old public company, within the meaning of the Companies Consolidation (Consequential Provisions) Act 1985;

   (d) the company does not commence its business within a year from its incorporation or suspends its business for a whole year;

   (e) the number of members is reduced to below two;

   (f) the company is unable to pay its debts;

   (g) the court is of the opinion that it is just and equitable that the company should be wound up.

Introduction to contract and agreement

DEFINITION OF CONTRACT

Contract – An agreement between two or more parties, to do or to abstain from doing an act or certain acts. At the outset the parties have the intention that the contract will be enforceable in a court of law.

Throughout the course of a day most of us enter into many contracts. We do this without thinking and generally without any problems. These might include boarding a bus, buying a sandwich and making a public phone call. It is only when problems occur that we begin to understand the need for a complex set of legal rules to govern all of these seemingly simple transactions.

First, we shall look at one **simple contract** that a person might enter into and examine how the contract is formed. The purchase of a newspaper will illustrate how a simple contract is really quite a complex business transaction. We shall place the purchaser in the shop with the shopkeeper waiting to serve him or her. The purchaser selects a newspaper, hands the money to the shopkeeper, receives the change and leaves the shop with a purchase.

That simple transaction includes the seven essential elements of the formation of a simple contract:

1 agreement;
2 consideration;
3 intention to create legal relation;
4 form;
5 capacity;
6 legal purpose;
7 reality of consent.

► **Simple contract** – an informal contract that can be made orally or in writing, or can be implied by conduct: for example, bidding at an auction.

Agreement

Agreement between two parties occurs when one party makes an offer that the other accepts. Surprisingly, in the case of our newspaper purchase it is the purchaser who makes the offer to purchase and the shopkeeper who accepts the offer. This will be explained fully later (see p. 130).

Consideration

Consideration is a legal term that in a contract can represent either the money exchanged, the act performed or the goods bought. There must be consideration on both sides. In the sale of a car, on one side the consideration would be the car and on the other the money paid for it. No valid contract exists if either side fails to provide consideration. A contract to make a gift of an item is invalid, unless it is made in the from of a **deed**. A deed releases the receiving party from providing any consideration.

► Consideration will be examined in detail in Chapter 10.

► **Deed** – a written document that must make it clear that it is intended to be a deed, and must be signed, witnessed and delivered.

Intention to create legal relations

We do not intend all the arrangements that we make to become fully legally enforceable contracts. The law takes the view that generally speaking domestic arrangements, such as those between a husband and wife or within a family, are not legally enforceable. However, there are exceptions, as we shall see in Chapter 10.

► Intention to create legal relations will be examined in detail in Chapter 10.

Form

In some cases, such as the sale of land, a contract must be in the form of a deed. The vast majority of everyday contracts can be made orally, while nearly all business contracts are written down. It is much easier to bring or defend an action in court with the evidence of a written contract.

Capacity

Both parties (sides or people) to the contract must be legally capable of entering into a contract. The law recognizes that some people may not have the necessary mental ability to appreciate the consequences of their actions. Therefore they should not be held liable for their actions. These people could include children, i.e. people under the age of 18 (legally known as minors), drunks or the **mentally disordered**.

Legal purpose

A valid contract cannot be made for an illegal purpose, such as to commit a murder, or to let a house as a brothel, or to trade with the enemy in time of war.

Reality of consent

A contract must be entered into freely. A person must not be forced into consenting to enter a contract. If force is used, this would be a contract entered into under duress and such contracts are not binding. Further the law looks for a 'meeting of the minds'. Where a party consents to a contract that that party thought was for one thing, while the other party consented to the same contract but thought it was for a different thing, that contract may be invalid.

If we now return to our newspaper purchase we can identify the different elements of the contract.

1 **Agreement:** The purchaser offered to purchase the newspaper from the shopkeeper, who accepted the offer, i.e. there was offer and acceptance.
2 **Consideration:** This was represented by the money on one side and by the newspaper on the other side.
3 **Intention to create legal relations:** We can assume that there was an intention to create legal relations because this was a business transaction. The law assumes that in all business transactions there is an intention to create legal relations.
4 **Form:** An oral contract is fine in the circumstances of this case.
5 **Capacity:** In the absence of other information, we can assume that both parties are adults with no mental health problems

▶ Form, capacity and the illegality of contracts will be examined in detail in Chapter 11.

▶ **Mentally disordered** – for the purposes of the Mental Health Act 1983, those suffering from mental illness, arrested or incomplete development of mind, psychopathic disorder, and any other disorder or disability of the mind.

▶ Reality of consent will be examined in detail in Chapter 12.

and, therefore, both have the capacity to enter into this contract.

6 **Legal purpose:** The purpose of the transaction – reading a newspaper – is legal.

7 **Reality of consent:** This simple transaction has obviously been entered into freely by both parties.

VALIDITY OF CONTRACTS

Only when all seven of these essential elements are present is there what is legally known as a valid contract, i.e. one that could be enforced by law. If one of the parties fails to complete his or her part of the contract, he or she could be sued for breach of contract.

 In a group of three or four, analyse the last major contract entered into by one of the group. Establish the seven essential elements of the contract. At what time was the contract made? Who was the offeree? What constituted consideration in the contract?

If one or more of the seven essential elements is missing from a contract, it can be deemed invalid. An invalid contract may be either void or voidable.

Void contract

A void contract is one that has no legal force from the moment of its making: its provisions should be treated as null and void. A contract may be void, for example, if there is no capacity to contract, or if the purpose of the contract is illegal. Any property passed or any monies paid under a void contract must be returned to the original owners. Where goods have been sold on to a third party, these may be recovered by the original owner.

► A contract may also be void by mistake (see Chapter 12 (p. 189) for an explanation of mistake). For an example of such a contract, see *Cundy v. Lindsay* (1878) (Chapter 12, p. 194).

Voidable contract

The voidable contract operates as a valid contract until one of the parties takes steps to end or avoid the contract. Any property passed or monies paid should be returned. However, where this is not possible, such as when the goods have been sold on to a third party, they will not be recoverable by the original owner. Examples of contracts that may be voidable include those founded on a misrepresentation and certain contracts entered into by a minor.

► For an example of a voidable contract entered into by a minor, see *Nash v. Inman* (Chapter 11, p. 173).

Unenforceable contract

A third category of contract is the unenforceable contract. This is a valid contract but it is one that cannot be enforced in a court of law if either of the parties fails, or refuses, to carry out the terms of the

► A contract of guarantee will contain a debtor, a creditor and a guarantor. Where Susan sells goods to Andrew, Mike could guarantee that Andrew will pay for the goods, thus making himself secondarily liable for the debt. If Andrew fails to pay for the goods, then Mike is contractually bound to pay Jane. A guarantor plays no other part in the contract.

contract. A contract of guarantee is an unenforceable contract unless it is evidenced in writing.

 Give a definition of the following types of contract: void, voidable and unenforceable.

In this chapter and in the chapters that follow, we shall be examining the seven essential elements of a contract in detail. Agreement will be covered in this chapter; consideration and intention to create legal relations in Chapter 10; form, capacity and legal purpose in Chapter 11; and reality of consent in Chapter 12.

AGREEMENT

As we stated earlier, agreement between two parties occurs when one party makes an offer that the other accepts. In order to understand agreement, therefore, we need to look at the rules of offer and acceptance.

OFFER

> **Offer** – a statement of the terms on which the offeror (the party making the offer) is willing to be bound, should the offer be accepted by the offeree (a party who is capable of accepting the offer).

An offer may be made to one person, to a group of persons or to the whole world. Only a person to whom an offer is made is capable of accepting (can accept) an offer. If Asif offered to sell his car for £500 to Peter Jones and Peter refused the offer, Peter's twin brother Paul would not be capable of accepting the offer.

If Asif had offered to sell the car to anyone in the Jones family, then Paul could be capable of accepting the offer. Further examples of an offer being made to a group of persons could be where an offer is made to the members of a club, to the residents of a particular area or to the employees of a company.

An offer that is made to the whole world can only be made where the contract will be a **unilateral** (as opposed to a **bilateral**) **contract**: for example, an advert placed offering a reward for the return of a lost item.

We shall now examine how the courts have interpreted the application of an offer, starting with one of the most famous cases in English law, to which we shall return later in the book.

► **Unilateral contract** – a contract where there is a promise made by one party to perform a certain act in return for the action of another party.

► **Bilateral contract** – a contract where promises are made by both parties to perform or not to perform an act or future acts. Most business contracts are bilateral.

Carlill v. Carbolic Smoke Ball Company (1893) 1 QB 256

(VC) In this case the defendants were the manufacturers of the 'Carbolic Smoke Ball'. The invention was supposed to protect users of the product from contracting influenza. They advertised the product with a £100 payment to be made to any person who used the preparation three times daily for two weeks and who then later contracted influenza. They further stated that a sum of £1,000 had been deposited in a bank for the purpose of showing the sincerity of the advertisement.

Mrs Carlill bought a smoke ball and during the course of the treatment she contracted a severe bout of influenza. The company refused to pay the promised £100, so she sued for breach of contract.

The defendants raised a number of points in their defence:

1 the advert constituted an attempt to contract with the whole world which was not possible in English law;
2 there was no consideration on the part of Mrs Carlill;
3 the vagueness of the offer, since the relationship between the using of the preparation and the contracting of influenza was given no specific time limit;
4 Mrs Carlill failed to communicate her acceptance of the offer;
5 plaintiffs had no intention to create legal relations and the offer was in fact a traders' puff.

(ACT) Review the defences raised in this case and compare them with the criteria for a binding contract given in this chapter. Are any of the defences valid? Do you agree with the findings of the court below?

COURT HELD

1 The advert was not an attempt to contract with the whole world, but an offer to contract with those persons who bought the product and complied with the conditions in good faith, believing the advert to be genuine.
2 Mrs Carlill supplied consideration by using the preparation for the specified time.
3 Despite no time limit being stated, the court took the view that it must have been the intention of the defendants to protect the purchaser throughout the recommended course of treatment.
4 The nature of the offer made the communication of acceptance unnecessary. The mere act of purchase and application of the treatment was sufficient.
5 The court felt that the depositing of the sum of money in the bank account for the settlement of claims negated the defendants' claim that it was merely a traders' puff.

The Court of Appeal, therefore, rejected all of the defendant's defences and found in favour of Mrs Carlill. Because of the varied nature of the

► **Traders' puff** – a statement that means nothing: for example, 'we sell the best cars'. It is immeasurable and therefore meaningless, carrying no validity in law.

► In *Wood v. Lectrik Ltd* (1932), a company offered an electric comb that would remove grey hair with ten days' use, offering a £500 guarantee. Defendant complied with the conditions of use to no good effect and claimed the £500. The court held that it was a valid contract.

defendant's defences, this very important case will feature in other areas of the formation of simple contracts.

Has an offer been made?

It is sometimes difficult to establish whether or not an offer has actually been made. The following cases illustrate the difficulty where one party attempts to accept an offer that the other party states has not been made.

Gibson v. Manchester City Council (1979) 1 All ER 972

 The council had undertaken a policy of selling its council houses to its tenants. Gibson applied on a council form for details of the sale price and mortgage arrangements. The city treasurer replied giving the details of the terms that the council 'may be prepared to sell at'. Gibson was invited to make an application to purchase the property on an enclosed application form.

In between Gibson's submitting the form and contracts being exchanged, the political control of the council changed. The policy of selling council houses ceased, the council deciding only to proceed with those in which contracts had been exchanged. Gibson then proceeded to sue the council for **specific performance**, forcing it to complete the sale of the house.

> *COURT HELD*
> *The House of Lords decided that the council at no stage made a formal offer to Gibson. The documentation that Gibson received was merely illustrating the financial arrangements that the council might be prepared to accept. The phrases 'may be prepared to sell' and 'make a formal application to buy' were obviously an **invitation to treat**, not an offer, and therefore could not be accepted.*

It is interesting to contrast the previous case with the following one, which deals with the same purchase, with slightly different details and a very different result.

Storer v. Manchester City Council (1974) 3 All ER 824 (CA)

This case was also to do with the sale of a council house. The town clerk was instructed to devise a simpler system for the sale, so he constructed an agreement for sale. This agreement was dispatched to the plaintiff (Storer) in response to an enquiry about the possibility of buying his house. The town clerk advised the plaintiff that if he wished to go ahead with the sale he should sign the agreement and return it, whereupon the clerk would sign the agreement on behalf of the council. Before dispatching the form, the clerk had completed all

► **Specific performance** – an equitable and, therefore, discretionary remedy, that a court may grant, ordering the party in breach of a contract to complete the contract.

► **Invitation to treat** – a legal term that can best be described as an invitation for others to make offers. Examples of this are goods in a shop, items in a catalogue and cars in a car showroom. It is the potential purchaser who makes the offer to purchase an item in a shop. The shopkeeper may accept or refuse the offer.

details, apart from the date of cessation of tenancy. The plaintiff then signed and returned the form. However, before the clerk signed the form, political control of the council changed hands and the policy was reversed. Only those cases in which contracts had been exchanged were authorized to proceed. The plaintiff sued for specific performance of the contract.

COURT HELD

The agreement of sale constituted an offer. The nature of the document was to dispense with legal formalities, therefore a further exchange of contracts was unnecessary. The contract was completed when the plaintiff signed the agreement. The clerk was bound to sign the agreement on behalf of the council. An order of specific performance was granted.

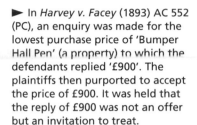

► In *Harvey v. Facey* (1893) AC 552 (PC), an enquiry was made for the lowest purchase price of 'Bumper Hall Pen' (a property) to which the defendants replied '£900'. The plaintiffs then purported to accept the price of £900. It was held that the reply of £900 was not an offer but an invitation to treat.

(ACT) Outline the rules relating to the making of an offer. Why were there different results in the two *Manchester City Council* cases?

INVITATION TO TREAT

Having defined an offer and examined how the law interprets it, we must now examine how the law has interpreted the difference between offer and invitation to treat. In order to do so we should examine the concept of invitation to treat.

The law has tended to recognize five different areas where an invitation to treat may be found:

1   goods on display in shops;
2   advertisements;
3   catalogues, price lists and brochures, and prospectuses;
4   tenders;
5   auctions.

The following cases illustrate how this principle is applied.

Goods on display in shops

***Pharmaceutical Society of Great Britain v. Boots Cash Chemists (Southern) Ltd* (1953) 1 QB 401**

 Boots had converted its Edgware branch into a self-service supermarket, the type that currently we are all quite used to. Customers selected their purchases and took them to a checkout to pay for them. In one section of the shop there were poisons displayed which were controlled by the Poisons and Pharmacy Act 1933. The Act made it an offence to sell the poisons other than under the supervision of a qualified pharmacist. There was a qualified pharmacist at the checkout

who could prevent the sale of the poisons if it was deemed necessary. Boots was prosecuted for contravening the Act.

COURT HELD

The goods in the shop were not an offer but merely an invitation to treat. The customer selected items and took them to the checkout where they made an offer to purchase them. The contract was made when the cashier accepted the offer. Prior to the acceptance, the pharmacist at the checkout could refuse any offer to purchase any restricted items. Boots was cleared of committing the offence.

At first this may seem unusual, because we are used to thinking that goods in supermarkets are offers, which we accept by putting into a basket or a trolley. Indeed, supermarkets use language that confuses the issue, for example, 'this week's special offer'. However, if we think about this in practical terms, defining goods on the shelf legally as invitations to treat, rather than as offers, this is the only real way in which the system can work. The following example should convince you.

A car is displayed on a garage forecourt bearing a price of £15,000. If one of the zeros was to fall off in the heat of the midday sun, the car would then bear a price of £1,500. If the display of the car constituted an offer then a potential purchaser could accept the offer at £1,500 and probably cause the garage to go bankrupt. Therefore, in all cases it is the purchaser who makes the offer and the vendor (seller) who accepts the offer to complete the contract.

Advertisements

Partridge v. Crittenden **(1968) 2 All ER 421**

In this case the defendant placed an advertisement in a magazine stating 'Bramble finch cocks, Bramble finch hens, 25 shillings each'. The defendant was charged under the Protection of Birds Act 1954 with offering wild birds for sale.

COURT HELD

The advertisement constituted an invitation to treat, not an offer, therefore the defendant had not committed the offence.

Catalogues, price lists and brochures, and prospectuses
Anything advertised in any publications of this sort will be an invitation to treat. For example, with the nationalization of British Telecom, the government invited people to apply for shares in the company at a given price. The government then allocated the shares to whomever they decided they wanted to.

The provisions of *Carlill* (see page 131 above) must be consid-

▶ In *Fisher v. Bell* (1961) 1 QB 394, a shopkeeper was prosecuted for offering flick-knives for sale in a shop window. Court held there was no offence; knives were an invitation to treat. The Restriction of Offensive Weapons Act 1961 was passed to close the loophole in this case. See Chapter 3, pp. 23–4, for more on this case.

ered, because the nature of an offer may make it available to everyone who satisfies the conditions of the offer. For example, in 1992 Hoover issued an advertised promotion that offered free international travel to anyone who bought certain of their products. The nature of the promotion meant that the advertisement could be considered to be an offer. Hoover found itself with a very large bill to pay as a result of the success (or failure!) of the promotion.

Tenders

A tender is an offer to contract made by a supplier or purchaser in response to an invitation to tender, which is made by a party seeking supplies or the selling of certain goods. Once accepted, a tender is a valid contract and therefore works in the opposite way to an ordinary contract. There are two forms of tender.

1 **A tender for specific items.** 'The County Council of Gwent invites tenders for the supply of six Mini Metro vans.' Where a party responds to a call for tenders by putting in a tender and Gwent accepts that tender, that becomes a valid contract.
2 **A tender for goods to be supplied, as and when required.** 'The County Council of Gwent invites tenders for the supply of heating oil, as and when required during the period January–December 1994.' Where a party tenders for this and is accepted, a contract exists each time Gwent orders oil from them. Gwent County Council is not contractually bound to order any oil. The supplier is in the condition of having made a 'standing offer' and they may withdraw that offer at any time prior to Gwent making an order. Once Gwent makes an order, then the supplier is contractually bound to supply that amount.

Great Northern Railway v. Witham **(1873) LR 9 CP 16**

The railway company invited tenders for the supply of goods over the period of one year, to be supplied as and when required. The defendant successfully tendered for the order, which operated smoothly for a period of time. The defendant then declined to supply an order and was sued for breach of contract.

COURT HELD

This type of tender was a series of contracts. The defendant could therefore choose to withdraw the standing offer prior to an order being made. Once an order was placed, a binding contract was formed. The defendants were found to be in breach of contract.

Auctions

The advertisement advertising an auction is an invitation to treat and therefore if the auction fails to take place the auctioneer is not liable.

▶ In *Percival Ltd v. London County Council* (1918) 87 LJKB 677, the successful tenderer sued because no goods were ordered. The court held that no contract existed until goods were ordered, and therefore it was not a breach of contract not to order any goods.

▶ In *Harris v. Nickerson* (1873) LR 8 QB 286, an auctioneer was held not liable for the travelling expenses of a person who attended an auction to bid for lots that had been withdrawn.

When an auctioneer invites bids at an auction, he or she is asking for invitations to treat. A contract is made when the auctioneer closes the bidding by banging the auctioneer's hammer. Where goods are being auctioned with a **reserve price**, an auctioneer may withdraw the goods from the sale after the hammer has fallen and no contract will exist. If goods are being sold 'without reserve', then the auctioneer must sell the goods to the highest bidder and a contract is formed on the fall of the auctioneer's hammer. This is now stated in legislation (see Chapter 16, page 309).

> **Sale of Goods Act 1979, s. 57(2)**
>
> A sale by auction is complete when the auctioneer announces its completion by the fall of the hammer, or in other customary manner; and until the announcement is made any bidder may retract his bid.

► **Reserve price** – a price below which a seller is not prepared to sell the goods.

 Making reference to relevant cases, explain the differences between an offer and an invitation to treat. Under what circumstances, and in which type of case, may an offer be made to the whole world?

REQUIREMENTS OF AN OFFER

There are five requirements that must be satisfied for an offer to be valid.

1 It must be solid and determinable, and not an invitation to treat.
2 It must be made in certain terms.
3 It must be communicated to the offeree.
4 It must not have been revoked.
5 It must not have lapsed.

We identified the first of these when we established the difference between an offer and an invitation to treat. We shall now examine the other four requirements.

Certain terms

► **Inchoate** – incomplete.

► **Construct** – to rewrite a contract in order to make it clear.

If an offer is vague or cannot be determined, then the acceptance of that offer may not constitute a valid contract. This is known as an **inchoate** contract. The courts have adopted the view that they will not **construct** a contract for the parties, but where a vague clause can be struck out of the contract to make a satisfactory contract, that will be done.

Nicolene Ltd v. Simmonds (1953) 1 All ER 822 (CA)

 This case rested on the wording of a contract between the two parties, for the sale of 3,000 tons of steel reinforcement bars. The vendor broke the contract and the buyer claimed damages. The defendant vendor alleged that there was no valid contract because the following sentence in the contract rendered it indeterminable: 'We are in agreement that the usual conditions of acceptance apply.'

COURT HELD

Because there were no usual conditions of acceptance, the court ignored the sentence because it was meaningless. The court considered that its removal left a valid contract, therefore, it found for the plaintiff buyer.

Where the parties have previously transacted with each other, a court may make reference to their previous dealings, or to normal trade customs, in determining whether there is a valid contract in existence. In certain industries there are customary ways of purchasing, describing, delivering and paying for goods, which to outsiders might seem vague. Where a person operates in a particular industry, a court may imply that the person knew of all the particular customs when entering into the contract, regardless of whether he or she did or not.

Should a contract appear to be vague, but contain a term making reference to arbitration in case of dispute, then a court will generally enforce the contract.

Foley v. Classique Coaches Ltd (1934) 2 KB 1

 Foley was a landowner who sold part of his land to Classique Coaches on the understanding that they purchased petrol from him, 'at a price to be agreed between the parties from time to time'. This contract was performed for a period of time until Classique wished to purchase their petrol from a cheaper supplier. They then sought to **repudiate** the contract, relying on the vagueness of the arrangements in the contract. Foley sought an injunction to enforce the contract. In the contract there was a clause stating that, in case of dispute, reference would be made to the Arbitration Act 1889, for arbitration.

COURT HELD

While the arrangements for the future purchase price of petrol were not fixed, there was a contract for supply at a reasonable price. Further, there was in existence a clause whereby in case of dispute the two parties would refer to arbitration. The court felt that this was a valid mechanism for ascertaining a price, therefore the injunction was granted.

▶ See also Chapter 14, p. 244, on irrelevant and meaningless terms.

▶ In *Winn v. Bull* (1877) 7 ChD 29, written agreement for the lease of a house, made 'subject to the preparation and approval of a formal contract', was held not to be a binding contract. The decision formed the basis of the modern house purchase agreement. A house is not bought or sold until the contracts are signed and exchanged. All negotiations prior to exchange are made 'subject to contract' and they may be changed right up until the contracts are actually signed and exchanged.

▶ *Scammel v. Ouston* (1941) AC 251 concerned an agreement for the purchase of a van on hire purchase terms that were never determined. The defendant declined to supply the van. The plaintiff sued to enforce the contract. The court held that there was no contract because the hire purchase arrangements had never been agreed.

▶ **Repudiate** – to indicate, by words or deeds, that a contract will not be completed. (See **Anticipatory breach**, Chapter 13, p. 230.)

▶ See also *Hillas and Co. Ltd v. Arcos Ltd* (1932) 1 All ER Rep 494 (Chapter 14, p. 244), where defendants contracted with plaintiffs to supply wood in 1930, with an option to supply further in 1931. The contract was vaguely worded but operated throughout 1930. Defendants tried to avoid the 1931 part of the contract because it was vague. Court made reference to the earlier dealings and found a valid contract.

▶ In *British Steel Corporation v. Cleveland Bridge and Engineering Co. Ltd* (1984) 1 All ER 504, the two parties had been unable to reach agreement on the terms of the contract, despite the fact that the contract had largely been completed and the vast majority of the goods had been manufactured, delivered and accepted. The court held that there was no binding contract, though the plaintiffs (British Steel) were entitled to payment on a quantum meruit basis, because they had done work at the request of the defendant who had then accepted the work.

▶ Remember, an offer is a statement of the terms on which the offeror (the party making the offer) is willing to be bound, should the offer be accepted by the offeree (a party who is capable of accepting the offer).

▶ **Revoked** – withdrawn.

▶ Remember, consideration is the benefit that both sides to a contract must obtain. In the sale of a car, on one side the car would be the consideration, while on the other side it would be the money.

Communication to the offeree

In order for a person to be able to accept an offer, he or she must be aware of the existence of the offer. An offer may be communicated by word, written, implied or made by conduct, or a mixture of any method. If somebody offered £1,000 reward for the return of a lost cat, and the cat was returned by a finder who had no knowledge of the reward, the finder would not be able to claim the prize. This is illustrated in *Dickinson v. Dodds* (see below), where an offer was made that the offeree had no real chance to accept or reject.

Revocation of an offer

An offer may be **revoked** at any time prior to the offer being accepted, provided that the offeree is notified of the revocation. The communication of the revocation can be made by any means and can also be carried out by a third party.

Dickinson v. Dodds (1876) 2 ChD 463

 This case involved the sale of houses between the two parties. Dodds offered the houses to Dickinson, offering to keep the offer open until Friday, 9 a.m. On the Thursday afternoon, Dickinson was told by a third party that Dodds had agreed to sell the houses to another party. Despite this, Dickinson attempted to accept the offer by delivering an acceptance within the original time limit.

COURT HELD
Dodds's revocation of the offer had been communicated to Dickinson by the third party, prior to his attempting to accept. Therefore, there was not a valid contract between Dickinson and Dodds. Further, Dickinson had not supplied any consideration for the option to purchase.

Where an offer is made and the offeree is given fourteen days to accept the offer, the offer can still be withdrawn without legal penalty (as in Dickinson). This is because the offeree is giving no consideration for the option to purchase. As you will remember, in order for a valid contract to exist there must be consideration on both sides. If a purchaser were to put a deposit on an offer with an option to purchase in fourteen days, then that would constitute 'consideration'. Should the offer then be revoked within the fourteen days, the offeree would be able to sue for damages for breach of contract.

Postal rules
There are special rules relating to the revocation of an offer where the 'post' has been the method used for communication. It must

first be stated that 'It must have been in the contemplation of both parties that the post was to be used'. This means that both parties must have thought that communicating by letter was the way in which the contractual negotiations were to be carried out. When the postal rules apply then the following points must be remembered.

A letter in acceptance of an offer becomes valid at the time of posting. A valid contract exists from the moment the letter is posted, meaning that even if the letter never arrives, there could still be a valid contract. For this to apply, the letter must be correctly stamped and addressed. If it is not, the rule is invalid. It is for the party who is alleging that they have posted the acceptance to provide evidence of posting and correct addressing of the letter. This could be in the form of a statement from the person who posted and addressed the letter, or other documentary evidence, such as a copy of the letter.

Household Fire Insurance v. Grant (1879) 4 Ex.D. 216 (CA)

 The defendant applied for shares in the company, via an agent. He paid a deposit of £5 and requested the allotment of 100 shares, the balance to be paid within twelve months. The company accepted the application and a letter of allotment was posted to Grant, but it never arrived. The insurance company then went into liquidation and the liquidator sought the balance from Grant, who refused to pay on the basis that there was no valid contract.

COURT HELD
The contract was completed at the moment the letter was posted, regardless of the fact that it never arrived. Grant was liable to pay the balance.

A letter of acceptance must be contrasted with a letter of revocation, which only becomes valid upon receipt by the offeree. This raises the question of what happens when a letter of acceptance crosses with a letter of revocation in the post? That question was answered in the following case.

Byrne v. Van Tienhoven and Co. (1880) 5 CPD 344

 This case concerned an international contract for the supply of tin plate. The defendants, who were based in Wales, offered by letter to sell tin plate to the plaintiffs, who were in New York. The offer was posted on 1 October and was followed by a letter of revocation on 8 October. Meanwhile, the plaintiffs accepted the offer by telegraph on 11 October, confirming by letter on 15 October. The letter of revocation arrived on 20 October. The different letters had crossed in the post.

COURT HELD

The contract came into being on 11 October when the plaintiffs accepted the offer. The letter of acceptance concluded the contract, while the letter of revocation was invalid because it arrived after the contract had been accepted.

▶ In *Holwell Securities Ltd v. Hughes* (1973) 1 All ER 161, an option to purchase land was given subject to written receipt of acceptance. The letter of acceptance never arrived and the court held that no contract existed. See also Chapter 10, p. 150, on method of acceptance.

An offeror can exclude this rule by stating in the terms of the offer that written acceptance must be received. This has the effect of placing an offeree in the position of having to deliver a written acceptance. If the acceptance is lost in the post then there exists no valid contract. Where no method of acceptance is stipulated, a court would probably conclude that any of the normal methods of communication would suffice.

 John offered to sell his car to Ruth, giving her fourteen days to decide. The same day, Caroline, a friend of Ruth, met John and agreed to pay the asking price, and John sold her the car. Three days later Ruth saw Caroline driving the car, she then decided to buy it from John but it had been sold. Is there any breach of contract between (a) John and Ruth; (b) Ruth and Caroline; (c) John and Caroline, if Caroline refuses to pay for the car? Give reasons for your answers.

Electronic communication

▶ **Electronic mail** – messages sent from one computer to another, appearing on the screen of a computer and not in any paper form.

While the rules governing postal negotiation are relatively clear, the case with instantaneous, electronic messages is not as clear, since it takes the law a while to catch up with technology. In the future we shall see cases concerning **electronic mail** before the courts. The present position, however, is stated in the following case.

Entores Ltd v. Miles Far Eastern Corporation (1955) 2 QB 327

▶ In *Brinkibon Ltd v. Stahag Stahl und Stahlwarenhandels Gmbh* (1983) 2 AC 34, the House of Lords commented on the problem of an acceptance being received by a machine and not being immediately read. The House indicated that when the acceptance was communicated would depend upon the intention of the parties and sound business practice.

The plaintiffs, who were based in London, offered goods to the Dutch agents of the defendants, via a telex message. The defendants accepted via a telex message. Later the plaintiffs wished to sue for breach of contract. To do so under English law they had to prove that the contract was made in England.

COURT HELD

The contract was made in England when the telex message was received by the plaintiff. This established that a telex is only valid when it is received by the person to whom it is addressed.

This rule can, it appears, be used to govern telephone messages. Where an acceptance by telephone is not received by the offeror, then no valid contract exists.

Lapse of an offer

An offer may lapse and therefore become incapable of acceptance. There are three main ways in which an offer may lapse:

1 death of either party;
2 where an offer is conditional and that condition is not satisfied;
3 expiry of time.

Death of either party

This area of law is unclear. Common sense suggests that the death of either party should terminate the offer. However, the courts have made a distinction as to whether acceptance was made prior to death. It appears that if an offer is made and the offeree dies prior to acceptance, then the offer lapses. If, in a **personal service contract**, the offeror dies before or after acceptance, then the offer lapses. In a non-personal service contract, it appears that the offer can be accepted until the offeree is notified of the death of the offeror.

> ► **Personal service contract** – a contract to perform an act or service: for example, playing a harp in a concert.

After acceptance, the death of either party has no effect on the contract unless it is a personal service contract, in which case it is discharged. This means that where Liz enters into a contract to buy a washing machine from Sarah, and Sarah dies prior to the delivery of the washing machine to Liz, Liz could sue Sarah's **personal representatives** for breach of contract, should they fail to honour the contract.

> ► **Personal representative** – a person appointed to dispose of the assets of someone who dies. When people make a will they normally name the persons whom they wish to be their personal representatives. Such persons are generally known as executors. If someone dies leaving no will, administrators are appointed to administer the estate.

Unsatisfied condition

Where an offeror makes a condition to his or her offer that must be satisfied, and where that is subsequently not satisfied, then an offer will lapse.

Financings Ltd v. Stimson (1962) 3 All ER 386

Stimson agreed to acquire a car from a dealer, signing a hire purchase agreement that stated that the agreement would only become valid upon acceptance by the finance company. The dealer was acting as an agent of the finance company. He paid the first instalment and took possession of the car on 18 March. He returned the car to the dealers on 20 March, being unhappy with the condition of the car. The finance company were not informed of the return. The car was subsequently stolen from the dealer and recovered in poor condition, prior to the finance company signing the acceptance on 25 March. The car was sold by the finance company who then sued Stimson for breach of contract, because he refused to pay any further instalments.

COURT HELD
No breach of contract had occurred, and Stimson was not bound by the agreement. The offer contained an implied

*condition that the goods would be in substantially the same condition
at the time the offer was accepted as they were when it was made.
Further, the offer had been revoked prior to acceptance by the
returning of the car to the company's agent.*

Expiry of time

Where an offer contains a time limit within which it must be
accepted, then the offer lapses if it is not accepted inside the set
time. If no time limit is set, the offer will lapse after a 'reasonable'
time. The 'reasonableness' is a matter to be determined by a court,
in case of dispute.

***Ramsgate Victoria Hotel Co. v. Montefiore* (1866) LR 1 Exch 109**

The defendant applied to take shares in the hotel company on 8 June
1864, by letter. On 23 November 1864, shares were allotted to the
defendant. There had been no interim communication between the hotel
and the defendant. The defendant refused the shares, leaving the plaintiffs to sue for breach of contract.

  COURT HELD

*The defendant's refusal of the shares was justified, therefore
no contract existed. The failure of the plaintiffs to notify their
acceptance in a reasonable time caused the offer to lapse.*

REJECTION

The rejection of an offer will have the effect of terminating it. It will
not then be possible to accept an offer after a rejection has been
made.

There are many rules relating to what might have seemed a
simple enough matter, the making of an offer. Now we shall turn
our attention to the acceptance of that offer.

ACCEPTANCE

Acceptance in the law of contract means an unequivocal
acceptance to the terms of an offer.

The following points must be considered when testing the validity
of an acceptance:

1 acceptance must be absolute and unqualified;
2 acceptance must be communicated;
3 the acceptor must be aware of the existence of an offer;

4 acceptance must follow a prescribed method;

5 the motive of the acceptor is irrelevant.

Absolute and unqualified

When an acceptance is made it must not introduce any new terms to the contract. If new conditions are added to the acceptance, then it becomes a counter-offer and has the effect of destroying the original offer. Once an offeree has made a counter-offer, the offeree cannot then make a further acceptance purporting to accept the original offer, even if he or she is seeking to pay the original asking price. In the situation described above, it is the offeree who then becomes the offeror, by making a counter-offer that the original offeror may accept and turn into a valid contract. The following example should make the position clear.

If Steve offers to sell his car to Daniel for £500, and Daniel offers £450, then that becomes a counter-offer that destroys the original offer. Steve then becomes the offeree and can accept Daniel's offer of £450. However, if Steve rejects it, and Daniel then says 'OK, I want the car, I'll give you £500', Steve is not bound to accept that offer.

The following case illustrates this point.

Hyde v. Wrench (1840) 3 Beav 334

This case concerned the sale of a farm. The plaintiff was offered the farm for £1,000. He made an offer of £950 that the defendant asked for time to consider. The defendant then turned down the offer. The plaintiff then purported to accept the original offer of £1,000, which the defendant declined to accept. The plaintiff then sought to enforce the contract, seeking an order of specific performance.

COURT HELD

The first purported acceptance was, in fact, a counter-offer that destroyed the original offer. Therefore the plaintiff could not later accept the original offer. There was no binding contract.

 List the circumstances under which an offer can lapse.

Where a party seeks more information about an offer, but does not seek to offer less money or alter the conditions or terms of payment, then that will not constitute a counter-offer and the offer will remain open. This is really a matter of common sense, as it is natural enough to want to know as many details as possible about a purchase. If you were offered a Ford Capri for £2,000, you might ask what the mileage was or how many previous owners it had

had. These sorts of questions are requests for further information and are not counter-offers.

The following case illustrates where an enquiry is considered to be a request for further information and not a counter-offer.

Stevenson, Jacques and Co. v. McLean (1880) 5 QBD 346

 The plaintiff was offered an option to buy steel at £2.00 per ton and was given until Monday to accept the offer. On the Monday the plaintiff telegraphed to ascertain whether the defendant would accept £2.00 per ton and delivery over two months. The defendant received the telegraph at 10.00 a.m., made no reply and sold the steel elsewhere, telegraphing the withdrawal of the offer, which the plaintiffs received at 1.46 p.m. Meanwhile, the plaintiff telegraphed at 1.34 p.m., purporting to accept the original offer. The court had to decide whether the first enquiry was a counter-offer and, if it was not, whether there was a valid contract or whether the offer had been revoked.

 COURT HELD
The first enquiry was a request for further information and not a counter-offer. The offer remained open and capable of being accepted; the second telegraph concluded the contract before the revocation was received by the plaintiffs.

▶ In *Alpenstow Ltd v. Regalian Properties plc* (1985) 2 All ER 545, the court found that the phrase 'subject to contract' appeared so late on in the negotiations that it was after agreement had been reached and therefore after the contract had been formed.

Generally speaking, any acceptance that is made 'subject to contract' will not constitute an absolute acceptance. Where a party clearly has intended that there should be a valid contract and both parties have been working as if that contract existed, then exceptionally a court may not interpret 'subject to contract' as meaning that no contract existed.

Standard form contracts

Where businesses contract with each other, problems arise when each wishes to conclude a contract using its own preprinted, pre-designed contractual forms, many of which will contain clauses that are contrary to the terms of the original offer. This has become known as the 'battle of the forms'. The following case illustrates how the courts have interpreted this battle.

Butler Machine Tool Company Ltd v. Ex-Cell-O Corporation Ltd (1979) 1 All ER 965

 Butler quoted for the supply of a machine, delivery to be made within ten months of order. The quotation contained a clause that stated that 'in case of costs increasing the quoted cost would be increased to Ex-Cell-O'. Ex-Cell-O ordered the machine using their own form, which varied the conditions, asking for installation and delivery within eleven months. There was a tear-off slip on the bottom of the acceptance form. It said: 'Please sign and return to Ex Cell, we accept your order on the terms and conditions stated therein and undertake to deliver by ...'.

The form was signed on behalf of Butler and returned to Ex-Cell-O. A dispute arose when, by the time the machine was delivered, costs had increased and Butler sought to invoke the price-variation clause to claim a further £2,892. Ex-Cell-O refused the increase, stating that they had contracted on their own terms. The court had to choose on what terms the parties had contracted.

COURT HELD

The acceptance from Ex-Cell-O was a counter-offer that destroyed the original offer. Butler had accepted Ex-Cell-O's offer, therefore the contract was governed by Ex-Cell-O's terms and they were not liable for the price increase.

Communication

If an acceptance is not communicated to the offeror then it will normally not be valid. However, in a unilateral contract the actual nature of the offer may make communication of the acceptance unnecessary. This was the case in *Carlill*, where the purchase and use of the Smoke Ball constituted acceptance. This is also the rule with reward cases. If Amy places an advert offering a £50 reward for the return of her dog and the advert is seen by Sally, who then finds and returns the dog, communication of her acceptance would be inferred from her actions.

► For a definition of unilateral contract see page 130 above.

► Don't forget the postal rules explained earlier in this chapter (see pp. 138–40), whereby the act of posting the letter makes the acceptance operative.

Silence does not constitute acceptance

Where two sides are in negotiation over the sale of a car, it would not be satisfactory for one side to write to the other offering £500 and saying, 'If I don't hear from you then I will take it that you accept my offer.' The following case illustrates that acceptance involves some positive action, mere mental acceptance being insufficient.

Felthouse v. Bindley (1862) 11 CBNS 869

This concerned the negotiations between a man and his uncle over the sale of a horse. It appears that the nephew thought that the uncle had bought the horse for 30 guineas, while the uncle thought that he had bought it for £30. Negotiations between the two continued and the uncle wrote stating, 'If I hear no more then the horse shall be mine for £30, 15 shillings'. Unfortunately, during the negotiations an auctioneer had mistakenly included the horse in an auction and had sold it elsewhere. This was contrary to the instructions of the nephew, who wished to sell the horse to his uncle. The uncle then sued the auctioneer in the tort of conversion, arguing that he was the owner of the horse at the time of the sale and that the auctioneer had no right to sell it.

► The Unsolicited Goods and Services Act 1971 (as amended) created law to deal with the unscrupulous practice of sending non-ordered goods and then demanding payment for them. Any goods, so received, merely have to be made available by a person for collection by the senders and do not have to be returned. If they are not collected within six months they become the person's property. Where a person gives written notice to a sender that goods must be collected within thirty days, if they are not collected within that period, they then become his or her property. This relates to business and private transactions.

COURT HELD
The nephew had failed to communicate his acceptance.
There was no contract between the nephew and the uncle for the sale of the horse. The action failed against the auctioneer.

Unauthorized acceptance

Acceptance can only be made by a person authorized to make that acceptance. It cannot be made by a third party without specific authorization. For example, if Nigel offers to sell his rabbit to Wendy, and Richard accepts for Wendy without speaking to Wendy, there wouldn't be a valid contract. This can be seen from the following case.

Powell v. Lee **(1908) KBD 99 LT 284**

This concerned the appointment of a headmaster by the six managers of a school. The plaintiff was short-listed and interviewed by the panel. The panel voted by three votes to two to appoint the plaintiff. No instruction was given to communicate this to the plaintiff. However, Dismore (honorary secretary of the group) decided to telegraph the plaintiff to inform him of the decision. At the next meeting the appointment was raised, the previous decision was overturned and a Mr Parker was appointed. The plaintiff then sued for breach of contract, alleging loss of salary of £11, 5 shillings.

COURT HELD
There was no contract between the school and Powell because there had been no authorized acceptance.

Ignorance of acceptor

Where a person is ignorant of an offer but complies with the terms of it, that person will not be able to claim any benefit under it. If Alice advertises a reward for the return of her diamond necklace and June finds and returns it with no knowledge of the reward, June will not be able to claim the money.

Prescribed method of acceptance

If an offeror states that a particular method of acceptance must be used, then normally that method must be followed to conclude the contract. However, if a method is used that is as quick and efficient as the directed one, a court may find that acceptance satisfactory.

Yates Building Company v. R.J. Pulleyn and Sons (York) Ltd **(1975) 119 SJ 370**

Land was offered for sale by the defendant to the plaintiff, the method

> ▶ **Doctrine of privity of contract** – only the parties to a contract can either benefit or suffer from that contract. If Dave offers his computer to Julia for £50 and Julia refuses that offer, Alan can't accept the offer because he is not privy to the contract. Of course Dave can make a separate offer to Alan, which Alan could accept.

of acceptance to be by recorded delivery or registered post. The plaintiff's solicitor accepted the offer by first-class post, the letter arriving within the prescribed time for acceptance. The defendant argued that there was no contract because of the way that the acceptance had been made.

COURT HELD

The directed method of acceptance had been advisory, not compulsory. The letter had arrived in good time and was sufficient to accept the offer. There was a valid contract.

Where no method of acceptance is prescribed, any method may be used to acknowledge acceptance. This may include written, implied or oral acceptance.

Motive of the acceptor

The courts will not be interested in the motive of the person who seeks to accept an offer, provided that he or she can satisfy the terms and conclude a contract. This is shown in the following case.

Williams v. Carwardine (1833) 5 C & P 566

The plaintiff was living with a man who she knew had been involved in the murder of William Carwardine. The defendant had published a notice offering a £20 reward for information leading to the conviction of the murderer. The plaintiff was savagely beaten by her partner and, fearing death, she confessed that her partner was involved in the murder. She brought an action to claim the reward from the person offering the reward who was refusing to pay it.

COURT HELD

The motive of the plaintiff was irrelevant. The court was satisfied that the plaintiff had seen the reward notice, had supplied the information and therefore was entitled to the reward.

 List the five rules relating to acceptance. In what circumstances can a counter-offer lead to the formation of a valid contract?

In the following chapter we shall examine the second essential element of a simple contract: consideration.

 Now that you have completed this chapter, look back at the chapter objectives at the beginning. Can you do all the things that these suggest? If not, look again at the relevant sections of the chapter.

► See the marginal note on p. 140 above, on *Holwell Securities Ltd v. Hughes*.

► *Domb v. Isoz* (1980) 2 WLR 565 established that where a solicitor, acting for a buyer or seller, has in his or her possession a signed contract, the exchange of that contract may be effected in any way recognized by law. This illustrates that a telephone conversation can be sufficient to create a contract. This method is used daily by solicitors to exchange contracts.

WANTED FOR MURDER REWARD £20

CHAPTER SUMMARY

1 Contracts are subject to a series of rules and regulations. In order for a contract to be a legally binding agreement it must contain the following elements:
   - agreement;
   - consideration;
   - intention to create legal relations;
   - form;
   - capacity;
   - legal purpose;
   - reality of consent.

2 In the absence of one of the essential elements a contract may be:
   - void;
   - voidable;
   - unenforceable.

3 An offer is a statement of the terms by which the offeror is willing to be bound. If the offer is accepted, by a person capable of accepting it, a valid contract will exist. An offer may be made to one person, a group of persons or to the whole world.

4 An invitation to treat is a legal term that can best be described as an invitation for others to make offers. Examples of this are the display of goods in a shop, items in a catalogue and cars in a car showroom. It is the potential purchaser who makes the offer to purchase an item in a shop, not the shopkeeper who may accept or refuse the offer.

5 An offer must be absolutely certain, there must be no vagueness in the terms of the offer, otherwise a valid contract may not exist. A court may strike out certain of the terms in a vaguely worded contract in order to make the performance of the contract possible.

6 There are special rules relating to the acceptance of an offer by post. An acceptance becomes valid the moment that it is posted, notwithstanding that it may never arrive. A letter withdrawing an offer will only become valid upon its receipt.

7 An offer may lapse in any of the following three ways: (a) upon the death of either party; (b) where an offer is conditional and that condition is not satisfied; (c) upon the expiry of a time limit specified in the offer.

8 Acceptance represents an unequivocal assent to the terms of an offer.

9 Acceptance must be absolute and unqualified; it must be communicated; the acceptor must be aware of the offer; where there is a prescribed method of acceptance that must normally be followed.

10 Consideration and intention to create legal relations

Chapter objectives

By the end of this chapter you should be able to:

▮ understand the role and importance of consideration in the formation of a contract

▮ appreciate the two different types of consideration: executory and executed

▮ recognize and understand the following rules relating to consideration:

    (a) consideration must not be past;
    (b) consideration must move from the promisee;
    (c) consideration must be real;
    (d) consideration must have some value, though it need not be adequate

▮ understand the principle and application of promissory estoppel

▮ explain the attitude of the courts to agreements between families and friends, known as domestic arrangements

▮ appreciate that certain factors can turn a domestic arrangement into a binding contract

▮ understand that the courts presume all business transactions are intended to create legal relations, but they recognize that a commercial agreement can be written to exclude any legal intention

▮ know that where a person seeks to avoid any legal intention they must state fully and clearly that they intend to do so in the agreement.

CONSIDERATION

English contract law is not concerned with agreements; it is concerned with **bargains**. It is in the nature of a bargain that *both* parties gain something. In a contract, this 'something' may be the actual money paid, the goods supplied or the act performed, or a promise to pay money, supply goods or perform an act. The legal term for this is **consideration**. In the sale of a car, on one side the consideration would be the car and on the other the money paid for

▶ **Bargain** – an agreement or contract establishing what each party will give, receive, or perform in a transaction between them, or something acquired or received in such an agreement.

it. In general, for an agreement to become legally enforceable there must be consideration on both sides. If either side fails to provide consideration then there exists no valid contract.

The one main exception to this is an agreement made under deed. A deed is a formal, written document that states that it is intended to be a deed and that the person signing it recognizes that he or she will be bound by the document. For example, a contract to make a gift of an item is invalid unless it is made in writing, in the form of a deed, because there is no consideration provided by the person receiving the gift.

> **Offer + Acceptance = Agreement**
>
> **Agreement + Consideration = Contract**

Executed or executory?

There are two types of consideration: executed and executory. Executed consideration involves one party promising to do something in return for the act of another: for example, the farmer promises to give a reward to any person who returns his cow.

The second type of consideration is called executory consideration. This exists in most business contracts. It is the promise of one party to do something for the promise of another party to do something else. Williams promises to pay £4,500 for a Zenex computer, while Zenex promises to deliver the computer and install it.

Validity of consideration

As we have discovered in the formation of an agreement, there are many rules and laws to be followed. The same exists for consideration. The following are the rules that cover the validity of consideration:

1 consideration must not be past;
2 consideration must move from the promisee;
3 consideration must be real;
4 consideration must have some value, though it need not be adequate;
5 consideration must be legal, clear and distinct, and possible.

Past consideration

Where two parties are in a post-contractual position, any promise made by either party will be of no value unless it is 'bought' by a corresponding promise or act by the other party. A post contractual promise that is made without any corresponding promise is known as past consideration and is not valid. Past consideration is exemplified in the following case.

Roscorla v. Thomas (1842) 3 QB 234

Thomas sold a horse to Roscorla for £30. After the sale Thomas promised that 'the horse was sound and free from vice'. The horse turned out to be vicious. Roscorla sued for breach of the promise.

COURT HELD
The promise was made after the contract had been concluded. It was therefore past consideration and had no value.

Past consideration can be more easily explained in a 'modern' example. Rachel and Mary are next-door neighbours and each has a child at the same school. Rachel's car was in the garage for three weeks awaiting a part from Poland. During that period Mary took the children to school and picked them up every day in her car. After Rachel got her car back she promised to give Mary £20 petrol money. If Rachel then fails to give that money to Mary, the agreement would not be enforceable in a court, because the promise was made after the act had been performed, i.e. past consideration. If Rachel had promised the money before the lifts were given, there would have been a valid contract.

The situation is different where an implied promise is made to pay for a future act. For example, if the washing machine breaks down and floods the kitchen, in blind panic you might call out an emergency plumber to stem the flow. Obviously there is an implied promise that you will pay the plumber for any work that the plumber performs. The implied promise is that you will pay a reasonable sum, not a £1,500 call-out charge. The following case shows how this rule was established.

▶ In *Eastwood v. Kenyon* (1835–42) All ER Rep 133, the plaintiff was guardian to the defendant and borrowed money to spend on her upbringing. The defendant later promised to repay the money when she was able to do so. The plaintiff sued to enforce the promise. The court held that it was past consideration, despite there being a moral obligation to repay the money.

Stewart v. Casey (1892) 1 Ch 104

Stewart was the joint holder of a **patent** granted in relation to storage containers. Stewart asked Casey to introduce and market the containers, which he did for two years. Stewart and the other patent holder then wrote to Casey agreeing to give him one-third of the patent's profits. Casey was also awarded the **letters patent**. Subsequently Stewart died and his executors demanded the letters patent from Casey, stating that he had no right to them as any promise made to him was, in effect, past consideration.

▶ **Patent** – the right granted to a person who has invented something new or different to produce and sell the invention exclusively. A patent will normally be granted for twenty years, after which time any one will be able to produce or manufacture the product.

▶ **Letters patent** – an official document that shows that the owner of the letters has the right to enjoy any benefits that derive from the patent.

COURT HELD
The original request made by Stewart carried an implied promise of future payment. The letter and award of the letters patent were merely quantifying the amount of payment. It was not past consideration and there was a valid contract between Stewart and his partner and Casey.

The rule in *Casey* was restated by the Privy Council in *Pao On v. Lau Yiu Long* (1980) AC 614, which stressed the need for a request for services by the plaintiff and the implication that they would be paid for.

 Define consideration. Outline the two different types of consideration, making up two distinct examples of each to illustrate the differences.

Consideration must move from the promisee

Consideration follows the same rules as the doctrine of privity of contract. If two parties contract to do something for the benefit of a third party and one of them breaches the contract, the third party would not be able to sue because that party was not privy to the contract. Further and, some argue, even more importantly, the third party has supplied no consideration and therefore is not in a valid contractual position. For example, if Mira promises to give Cleo £1,000 in return for Cleo's promise to give a job to Max, Max cannot enforce Cleo's promise, because he has not supplied consideration for it. This rule is illustrated in the following case.

Tweddle v. Atkinson (1861) 4 LT 468

The plaintiff had been made the beneficiary of an agreement between William Guy and John Tweddle, who were his father and prospective father-in-law, in which they had contracted to give £300 to the plaintiff upon his marriage. Payment was not made and William Guy died. The plaintiff sued Atkinson, who was Guy's executor, to enforce the contract.

 COURT HELD
The plaintiff could not succeed because he had not supplied any consideration for the promise that had been made for him.

Consideration takes privity of contract one step further, namely, whereas in privity a party cannot sue unless he or she is party to the contract, consideration rules that even where a person is party to a contract, that party cannot sue unless he or she has supplied consideration. The following case shows how this works in practice.

▶ Remember that consideration is not required where a contract is made by deed.

Dunlop v. Selfridges (1915) AC 847

Dunlop supplied tyres to a dealer, who in turn supplied them to Selfridges. The dealer had signed an agreement with Dunlop not to sell the tyres below the list price of £4.05 and also to sign, as agents, a similar contract with anyone that they supplied. In return they would be allowed discounts, which they could, if they so wished, pass on to retailers. Selfridges signed such an agreement, which also contained a **liquidated damages** clause, and then supplied a tyre at £3.65. Dunlop sued Selfridges for breach of the agreement.

COURT HELD

There was no contract between Dunlop and Selfridges for lack of consideration. Even though the dealers were agents of Dunlop, any discount given to Selfridges by the dealer represented consideration between the dealer and Selfridges. Consideration could not be interpreted to have passed from Dunlop to Selfridges

► **Liquidated damages** – an amount fixed in advance by the parties to a contract, in agreement as to what damages will be payable in case of breach of contract. (See Chapter 13, p. 232.)

Resale Prices Act 1976, s. 26, now gives the manufacturer a right of action against a person who breaches a resale price agreement made under the Act. There need not be any contractual· relationship between the retailer and the manufacturer. A good example of a valid resale price agreement is the net book agreement, whereby all retailers sell books at the same price. This is, of course, against the laws of free competition and some of the large booksellers have been prepared to breach this agreement. It is likely that in the future this legislation will be amended to end this type of agreement, thereby allowing the bigger retailers to sell books much cheaper.

Real consideration

There are three principles to be taken into account in determining whether a consideration is real.

1 If a party performs an act that he or she is already contractually obliged to do, that act is not a real consideration.
2 If a party has an existing public duty to perform an act, that act is not a real consideration.
3 If a party has an existing duty under a contract to a third party, the performance of that duty may constitute sufficient consideration for any further benefits relating to that performance.

Contractual obligation

If a person performs an act that he or she is already contractually obliged to do, then that act will not constitute consideration. The following two 'ship' cases show how this works.

Stilk v. Myrick (1809) 2 Camp 317

 The plaintiff was a seaman employed on a voyage to the Baltic and back. During the voyage, two of the crew deserted. The captain attempted to recruit replacements at Cronstadt but was unable to do so. He therefore entered into an agreement with the remaining crew, to divide the deserters' wages among them if they would 'work the ship home'. The crew agreed and the voyage was completed. The captain then refused to pay the promised amount. The plaintiff sued to enforce the agreement.

COURT HELD

The promise was not enforceable. The sailors had merely performed their contractual duties in working the ship home and had not supplied any consideration for the promise.

Hartley v. Ponsonby **(1857) 7 EL & BL 872**

This case is similar to the Stilk case. Hartley enlisted on the ship *Mobile*, which had a full complement of thirty-six. At Port Philip the crew had decreased to nineteen, the others having deserted. The defendant promised the plaintiff an extra £40, if he would sail the ship to Bombay with the remaining members of the crew. The plaintiff accepted and the voyage was completed. The defendant then refused to pay the £40. Hartley sued to enforce the contract.

COURT HELD

There was a binding contract. To sail the ship with half the crew missing was beyond existing contractual duties. The vast number of desertions had the effect of terminating the remaining crews' contracts, leaving them able to negotiate new contracts.

(ACT) What principles did the two ship cases establish? If Stilk or Ponsonby had declined the offers and refused to 'work the ship home', would either have been in breach of contract?

The principle outlined in these two cases has been more recently applied in the following case.

Williams v. Roffey Bros and Nicholls (Contractors) Ltd **(1990) 1 All ER 512**

(VC) Williams was a carpenter who was subcontracted to work on a block of flats by the defendants. He met financial difficulty and was promised an extra £575 per completed flat if he completed his contract on time, thus enabling the defendants to avoid a penalty clause in their main contract. Williams continued and completed eight further flats (he had previously completed nine of the twenty-seven flats). The defendants then paid a further £1,500, which did not fully honour their promise of £575 per flat. Williams stopped work and sued to recover the outstanding amount. The defendants argued that Williams had merely fulfilled existing contractual obligations, and that therefore he had supplied no consideration for the extra payment.

COURT HELD
There was a valid contract. The offer to make an extra payment to enable a contract to be completed on schedule, thus enabling the promisor to avoid a penalty clause, where the offer is made without economic duress or fraud, could constitute sufficient consideration. The Court of Appeal found that this case upheld the principle established in Stilk.

In the recent case of *Re Selectmove Ltd*, CA *The Times*, 13 January 1994, the Court of Appeal refused to apply the rule established in Roffey. The case concerned a company who had, according to them, entered into an agreement with the Inland Revenue to pay outstanding debts by instalments and other payments as they fell due. The company suggested that the agreement constituted consideration, i.e. the Inland Revenue would gain some practical benefit from it. The Court rejected the view, preferring to apply the rule established in *Foakes v. Beer* (see below, page 159), that the payment of an existing debt by instalments does not constitute consideration.

Existing public duty
If a person has an existing public duty to perform an act, the performance of that act will not constitute consideration. If the act performed is in excess of the public duty, then that might constitute consideration. The difference can be seen in the following two cases.

Collins v. Godefroy (1831) 1 B & AD 950

Godefroy promised Collins 6 guineas for his attendance as a witness in Godefroy's case. After the case he refused to pay the money, and Collins sued to enforce the agreement.

COURT HELD
The contract was not enforceable. Collins had been subpoenaed to appear at court and therefore had not supplied any consideration for the promise.

Glasbrook Bros v. Glamorgan County Council (1925) AC 270

This case concerned the supply of police cover to a coal mine during a strike. The police felt that a mobile watch on the mine would be sufficient, but the colliery manager, fearing an attack, insisted on a permanent guard. The latter option was agreed on at a cost of £2,200. The payment was then refused, the defendant arguing that the police

had supplied no consideration, as they had merely performed their duty. The council sued to enforce the payment.

COURT HELD

There was a valid contract. The police were bound to protect the premises but it was a matter for them to decide the level of protection. Where they supplied protection in excess of what they thought fit, then that could be sufficient consideration.

► In *Harris v. Sheffield United Football Club* (1987) 2 All ER 838, the principle established in *Glasbrook* was applied to the supply of police officers inside football grounds.

Existing duty to a third party

If a party has an existing duty under a contract to a third party, the performance of that duty may constitute sufficient consideration to warrant any further benefits relating to that performance. In such circumstances it will not be past consideration. The following case illustrates this complicated rule.

Shadwell v. Shadwell (1860) 9 CB NS 159

The plaintiff and defendant were nephew and uncle. Upon hearing of the engagement of his nephew, the uncle wrote offering to give the nephew £150 per annum until the nephew attained a certain salary, or until his own death, in return for the marriage. The nephew never attained the set salary and the money was paid for thirteen of the uncle's remaining eighteen years. The nephew then sued the executors to recover the outstanding five payments. The defendant suggested that no consideration had been given for the promise, because the plaintiff had been contractually obliged to marry before the promise was made.

► Don't worry! Engagement is no longer an enforceable contract, thanks to the Law Reform (Miscellaneous Provisions) Act 1970, s. 1(1).

COURT HELD

There was a valid contract. The plaintiff could recover the outstanding payments. The marriage was found to be adequate consideration to support the uncle's promise, for it had involved the plaintiff changing his position in life and incurring further responsibilities.

Value of consideration

The law is concerned that you have freely entered into a valid contract. It is not concerned whether or not you have got a good deal. In other words, the consideration does not have to be 'adequate'. The law maintains that as you freely entered into the contract you could agree to sell or buy anything at all, for any price. If Martin agrees to sell his Ferrari to Alison for £25, and Alison accepts the offer, that would be a valid contract. The courts would not be interested that the 'market value' of the car was £30,000.

As long as the consideration has some value, then the courts will be satisfied. This is shown in the following case.

Thomas v. Thomas (1842) 2 QB 851

A surviving wife was allowed to remain in occupation of her deceased husband's house, by his executors, provided that she kept the premises in good repair and paid £1 rent, per annum. On the death of one of the executors, the other threw her out. The widow sued, alleging breach of contract. The defendant argued that there was no contract for lack of consideration.

COURT HELD

There was a binding contract: the £1 per annum rent and the maintenance of the premises represented consideration, and the court was not concerned with its adequacy.

Consideration: the minor issues

Consideration must not be illegal: the services of a prostitute would not constitute valid consideration. The Latin maxim *ex turpi causa non oritur actio* illustrates the view of the law on illegal or immoral contracts.

Consideration must be clear and distinct. A promise to behave well in the future would not satisfy the criteria because it is vague and immeasurable.

The consideration promised must be possible. A promise to fly from the top of the Eiffel Tower to Big Ben, using a hang-glider, would not be valid because it would not be possible.

Consideration and the settlement of debt

It is a long-established common-law rule that part payment of a debt, offered in full satisfaction of the debt, will not be valid unless it is supported by some fresh consideration.

Frank owes Irene £1,000 due for payment on 14 June. If Frank offers Irene £800 on 14 June, in full settlement of that debt, and Irene being short of cash accepts it, can Irene later sue for the outstanding £200?

The answer is yes. Frank has got a £200 reduction and Irene has been given nothing in return for losing £200. No consideration has been supplied by Frank.

There are occasions where a variation on the payment of a debt can be sufficient to add fresh consideration to the agreement.

(a) The payment of a lesser sum before the due date, at the request of the creditor, would discharge the debtor from the liability of the whole debt. Where £500 is paid on 1 January at the request of the creditor, in lieu of a £600 debt due on 1 February, the whole of the debt would be discharged. The consideration would be represented for the creditor by the early payment and for the debtor by the £100 discount.

▶ *Chappell and Co. Ltd v. Nestlé Co. Ltd* (1959) 2 All ER 701 concerned a promotional offer, whereby to obtain free pop records, chocolate bar wrappers had to be sent in to Nestlé. The case hinged upon whether the wrappers constituted consideration. The House of Lords found that chocolate bar wrappers could form consideration.

▶ *Ex turpi causa non oritur actio* – no action arises from a base cause.

▶ In *White v. Bluett* (1853) 23 LJ EX 36, a promise to stop complaining was not found to be good consideration.

(b) Similarly to (a), the payment at a different place, or by a different method, at the request of the creditor could also discharge the debt.

(c) Where a creditor accepts goods in place of a debt, that debt will be discharged, regardless of the value of the goods. If Bob accepts a car in payment of a £500 debt, the value of the car would not matter, as the debt would be fully discharged. This is known as substituted performance.

(d) If the debtor and creditor dispute the amount outstanding and the creditor then accepts a payment in full settlement of the disputed amount, that will be valid.

(e) If a composition agreement is reached, the debt can be discharged. Composition agreements normally arise where a company, or person, is facing liquidation, or bankruptcy. A meeting of all the creditors is called and the debtor tries to arrive at an agreement that is satisfactory to all parties. This will normally consist of offering all the creditors an amount for every £1 that is owed, for example, 60 pence. Where agreement is reached at such a meeting and the debtor honours the agreement, the debt will be fully discharged. A creditor could not then seek to recover the other 40 pence or the other 40 per cent of what the creditor had originally been owed.

(f) Where payment of a lesser sum is made in full settlement of a debt by a third party, on the condition that the debtor will be discharged from the payment of that debt, the creditor will be bound if he or she accepts the payment.

► In *D and C Builders v. Rees* (1966) 2 QB 617 (see p. 162 below), payment of a debt by cheque, in lieu of a larger amount, was held not to constitute substituted performance.

► Green Shield Stamps were popular in the 1970s. The major retailers gave a certain amount of stamps for every pound spent in their shops. The stamps were saved in books by the shoppers, who could then exchange completed books for goods at Green Shield Stamp shops, which were similar to the Argos type of store.

 Graham enters into a contract with Keith to buy a Mini Metro, valued at £750. Keith is a keen collector of Green Shield stamps and he agrees to accept 5,000 Green Shield stamps in full payment for the car. Quoting relevant cases, outline the probable results in the following circumstances.

1 Keith refuses to complete the contract, arguing that the stamps are not worth £750.
2 Keith refuses to complete the contract stating that Graham is not providing any consideration because the stamps have little value.
3 Graham decides not to pay in stamps but says that he will be fully completing his contractual obligations by paying £750. Keith refuses the cash payment.

The major cases that have developed these rules are as follows.

Pinnel's Case (1602)

 Pinnel sued Cole for a debt of £8, 10 shillings, due on 11 November. In his defence Cole stated that he had, at the request of Pinnel, paid £5, 2 shillings and sixpence, on 1 October in full settlement of the debt.

COURT HELD

On a technicality Pinnel won the case. However, the court ruled that (a) payment of a lesser sum on the due date could not fully discharge the debt and (b) payment of a lesser sum in advance of the due date, at the request of the creditor, could fully discharge the debt.

Foakes v. Beer (1884) 9 App Cas 605

Mrs Beer obtained judgment against Doctor Foakes for £2,077, 17 shillings and 2 pence, for debt and £13, 1 shilling and 10 pence costs. They entered into an agreement, whereby Foakes would pay £500 immediately and the rest by instalments until the debt was discharged. Mrs Beer agreed that if the arrangements were adhered to, she would take no further action in the matter. Foakes duly completed his side of the agreement. Mrs Beer then brought an action to recover the interest payable on the debt, applicable under the Judgments Act 1838. Foakes relied on the agreement as being in full settlement of the debt.

COURT HELD

The debt had not been fully discharged and Mrs Beer could recover the outstanding amount. The agreement amounted to part payment of the debt and Foakes had not supplied any consideration for Mrs Beer's promise not to take any further action.

List the circumstances under which part payment of a debt may fully discharge that debt. Quoting relevant cases discuss the following problems. Rob owes Terry £500, payment being due on 14 November.

1 On 10 November Terry asks Rob to pay the debt, Rob says that he has only £450, would that be OK?
2 Rob offers to pay £450 by cheque, in full settlement, on 12 November.
3 Rob offers a cheque for £495, in full settlement, on the due date.

CONSIDERATION, EQUITY AND THE DOCTRINE OF PROMISSORY ESTOPPEL

As we saw in Chapter 3, equity has grown to bring an element of fairness to the application of the law. The **doctrine of promissory estoppel** comes from equity and the basic rules are as follows:

(a) there has to have been an existing agreement between the two parties, in which the defendant has an obligation to the plaintiff;

▶ **Doctrine of promissory estoppel** – a party to a contract promises the other that he or she will not enforce his or her rights under a contract in whole or part.

(b) the plaintiff must have agreed to forgo that obligation, abandoning his or her legal right;

(c) the defendant cannot have supplied any consideration for the forgoing of the obligation;

(d) the defendant must have relied on the plaintiff's promise not to enforce the plaintiff's rights and acted upon it, altering his or her position.

When all the above factors are present, equity has determined that it would be unfair to allow a plaintiff to go on to enforce his or her legal right, although the plaintiff has received no consideration for the abandoning of his or her right.

The historical development of equitable (promissory) estoppel can be traced through the following cases.

Hughes v. Metropolitan Railway Company (1877) 2 App Cas 439

 This case saw the emergence of promissory estoppel. The plaintiff was a tenant who had been given six months to carry out repairs to his leased property. If he failed to complete the repairs, under the terms of the lease, he faced eviction from the property. During the six-month period, the landlord was negotiating for the sale of the lease to the plaintiff. The negotiations subsequently broke down. At the end of the six-month period, no sale had been agreed and the repairs had not been completed. The landlord sought to evict the tenant.

 COURT HELD

The act of negotiating with the defendant should be regarded as a promise that, so long as the negotiations continued, the defendant would not enforce his legal right to evict the plaintiff. The six-month period would be construed as starting from the date of the breakdown of the negotiations.

Central London Property Trust Ltd v. High Trees House Ltd (1947) KB 130

In 1937 the defendants entered into a 99-year lease on a block of flats in London, at a rent of £2,500 per annum. War broke out and they had problems letting the flats. The defendant and plaintiff companies were closely associated and they entered into an agreement to vary the original agreement for the duration of the war. The new agreement halved the rent to £1,250 per annum. No consideration was given by the defendants for the rent reduction. The arrangement functioned throughout the war. All the flats became occupied in early 1945. The receiver of the plaintiff company, which had gone into liquidation, brought the action in 1945 to recover £625, being the difference between rent at the rate of £2,500 and £1,250 per annum for the quarters ending 29 September and 25 December 1945.

COURT HELD
The plaintiffs could recover the £625 rent claimed. The special conditions that were in operation when the rent was reduced had ended, therefore it was proper that they should return to the terms of the original agreement. They could not have recovered the rent in full for the period of the war years, as they would have been equitably estopped from doing so. They had agreed to forgo their legal right of collecting the full rent. The defendants had believed the promise and had acted upon it, thus altering their position. It would have been unfair to allow the plaintiffs to return to the original agreement. Lord Denning went on to say that promissory estoppel could be used as a defence, where a debtor and creditor agree over the acceptance of a lesser amount, in full settlement for a larger amount. Provided that they had truly reached an agreement and that the debtor believed in the promise and acted upon it, then it would be unfair to allow the creditor to go back on the agreement.

Promissory estoppel can only be used as a defence, not as a cause of an action. It is not possible to sue anyone under promissory estoppel. In the following case, promissory estoppel was described as 'a shield and not a sword'.

Combe v. Combe (1951) 1 All ER 767

This was a husband and wife dispute. In 1943 the wife obtained a **decree nisi** divorce and her solicitors requested that the husband pay her an allowance of £100 per annum. The husband agreed but failed to make any payments. The wife sued to enforce the agreement.

COURT HELD
The court of first instance held that it was an enforceable agreement, the wife had acted upon the husband's promise and the case fitted the High Trees principle. The husband appealed, arguing that the High Trees rule had been wrongly applied.

COURT HELD
The Court of Appeal held that the High Trees decision did not enable promissory estoppel to be used as a cause of action. In this case there was no contract because there was an absence of consideration in the formation of the contract. Promissory estoppel is only applicable as a defence in a post-contractual situation. Mrs Combe could not succeed in her claim.

► **Decree nisi** – Under the provisions of the Matrimonial Causes Act 1973, every decree of divorce will commence with a decree nisi. A decree nisi is a stage on the way to a full decree of divorce. After a decree nisi has been granted, any person may, within a time specified by the court, give reasons why the decree should not be made absolute. In the absence of any such intervention, the person who has applied for the divorce may make a further application to the court for a decree absolute. When the decree absolute is granted, the parties officially become divorced.

The final case in this section concerns a further interpretation of the *High Trees* decision. It further illustrates that where a person seeks an equitable remedy they must have acted equitably themselves.

D and C Builders v. Rees (1966) 2 QB 617

 The first hearing of this case established that payment of a lesser sum by cheque could not be construed as substituted performance. It provided no consideration, the creditors received no benefit and therefore it was invalid. The plaintiffs were a small building firm who had carried out work for the defendant. They were owed £482, 13s 1d by the defendant, which the defendant declined to pay. Some four months after the original demand, the defendant's wife telephoned, complained about the standard of work and offered £300 in full settlement. The plaintiffs were short of money and offered to accept the £300 and give the defendants a year to pay the remainder. Rees then insisted that they would never pay any more and that they would have to accept the £300 in full settlement. The plaintiffs, having no option, accepted the £300, signing a receipt agreeing that it was to be in full settlement. The plaintiffs then brought an action to recover the outstanding amount. The defence alleged bad workmanship and that there existed a binding settlement.

 COURT HELD
The plaintiffs could recover the outstanding amount. The defendants had supplied no consideration for the reduction they had received. The High Trees decision did not apply because the plaintiffs had no choice, other than to accept. Their acceptance had been forced by the actions of the defendant and there had been no meaningful negotiation. This breached the rule that where a person seeks an equitable remedy, they must have behaved equitably themselves.

One final factor must be remembered about promissory estoppel. This is that it does not destroy the rights of the promisor, it merely suspends them for as long as the special circumstances that caused the promise to arise. This was the situation in the *High Trees* case. There may be circumstances when it is possible for a promisor to give reasonable notice that the promisor intends to resume his or her legal rights. There might also be circumstances when it would be difficult to withdraw from promissory estoppel, because it might be too late or it could cause a major injustice to the promisee. In the latter event, a promisee would probably be bound by this waiver.

▶ In *Brikom Investments v. Carr* (1979) 2 All ER 753, the landlords of a block of flats promised to certain of their leaseholders that they would repair the roof at their own expense, waiving the obligation of the leaseholders to pay. Because of this promise certain of the tenants signed new leases. The landlords then sought to recover the cost from the leaseholders. The court held that they would be equitably estopped from doing so.

(ACT) In a group of three or four, discuss the application of promissory estoppel in the following circumstances. Kate is a single parent who owes £250 to Max, a moneylender. Max tells her that if she sells her television and gives him the proceeds of the sale he will let her off the rest of the money. Kate, being in a desperate situation, accepts the offer and sells the television for £100, which she gives to Max. Max then says that he wants the rest of the money.

(a) What might the result be if Kate sues Max to enforce the agreement?

(b) What if Max sues Kate for the outstanding £150?

Would your answers have been different if (a) Kate was really quite wealthy and had received £300 for the television, but had still only given him £100 or (b) Max had accepted the television in full settlement of the debt.

We shall now examine the third essential element of a simple contract: intention to create legal relations.

INTENTION TO CREATE LEGAL RELATIONS

Not every agreement that we enter into is intended to be legally enforceable. If they were we would probably spend most of our time in the courts! 'I'll meet you outside the cinema at 8 o'clock' is clearly not meant to be a legally binding agreement. Similarly, saying 'Would you like a lift home tonight?' is not going to land you in court, should the person to whom you offered the lift end up walking home. Where these types of agreements are regularized and placed on a more formal footing, a court may infer contractual obligations. For example, an agreement to enter into a car-sharing arrangement might carry contractual obligations.

Courts tend to use the following rules when deciding if the parties to a contract intended their agreement to be legally enforceable.

(a) Domestic arrangements, such as those between family members, are presumed not to intend to create legal relations. However, this may be **rebutted** (i) where the family has split up or (ii) where there is an outside influence.

(b) Commercial arrangements, such as agreements between businesses, are presumed to be intended to create legal relations. However, this may be rebutted where either party states clearly that the agreement is not intended to be legally enforceable.

▶ **Rebutted** – disproved by the acceptance of evidence to the contrary. It is an **irrebuttable presumption** (it cannot be disproved) that a child under the age of ten years is incapable of committing a criminal offence.

Domestic arrangements

Domestic arrangements that are not legally enforceable may include, as the following cases illustrate, informal husband-and-wife agreements, and inter-family arrangements made when the families concerned were on good terms.

Balfour v. Balfour **(1919) 121 LT 346**

(VC) The defendant was a civil servant based in Ceylon (now Sri Lanka). He returned to England with his wife on leave, where she, because of health reasons, decided to stay. He entered into an agreement to pay her an allowance of £30 per month, until she was well enough to return. They then decided to make the separation permanent and a decree nisi was obtained. The defendant declined to make any further payments and the plaintiff sued to enforce the agreement. The first hearing found for the wife, and the husband appealed.

COURT HELD

There was no binding contract, as the parties did not, at the time of the creation of the agreement, intend that it should be legally enforceable.

Jones v. Padavatton (1969) 2 All ER 616

The plaintiff entered into an agreement with her daughter, to pay her a maintenance allowance if she would move to England and study for the Bar examinations. In 1962 the daughter left America for England, where she began to study for the Bar exams. Things did not go well, she was unhappy with the standard of accommodation and in 1964 the mother entered into a further agreement, whereby she bought a house. The daughter was to live in the house, sublet the other rooms and keep the rent in lieu of the maintenance payments. This arrangement functioned for a period, during which time the daughter married. The plaintiff became unhappy about the arrangement, because the daughter failed to supply any details of the subletting. In 1967 the plaintiff claimed possession of the house.

COURT HELD

There was not an enforceable contract, as the parties never intended that the agreement was to be legally enforceable. The arrangements were extremely vague and were clearly family agreements that could only function with the goodwill of the family members. The agreements were not constructed to be legally enforceable.

Non-enforceable domestic arrangements

Family splits

The following case will show that when an agreement is made, and at the time it is made the family members are already split up, the courts may find that the parties intended to create legal relations.

Merritt v. Merritt (1970) 2 All ER 760

A separated husband and wife met to discuss their financial arrangements. The husband agreed to pay maintenance of £40 per month. He further agreed, in a signed, written document, that if the wife continued to pay the mortgage he would transfer the house to her at the conclusion of the mortgage. The plaintiff paid off the mortgage but the defendant failed to transfer the house. The plaintiff sought to enforce the agreement. The defendant argued that it was purely a family arrangement, not meant to be legally enforceable.

COURT HELD

The parties intended at the outset that the agreement should be legally enforceable. The agreement was made when the parties were living apart. Consideration was supplied by both sides, as the plaintiff paid the mortgage, while the husband received the benefit of being relieved of the debt to the building society. The plaintiff succeeded in obtaining the house.

Outside influence

This case illustrates the effect an outsider can have on a domestic arrangement.

Simpkins v. Pays (1955) 3 All ER 10

The plaintiff was a lodger, sharing a house with the defendant and her granddaughter. All of them entered a weekly newspaper fashion competition, each filling in one line of the coupon, which was submitted in the defendant's name. On one occasion the granddaughter's line on the coupon won £750. The defendant refused to share the prize with the plaintiff, who sued for her share of the winnings. The defendant argued that there was no intention to create legal relations and the agreement was intended to be binding in honour only.

COURT HELD

The plaintiff could succeed in her claim. The court decided from the circumstances that there was an intention to create legal relations. Clearly the entry was meant to be a combined venture, implying that any winnings would be equally shared.

Commercial arrangements

The law presumes that all commercial arrangements are intended to be legally enforceable. A heavy emphasis is placed on a party who wishes to avoid creating legal relations, to state the party's intention fully and clearly before the formation of a contract. This may be achieved by the inclusion of a statement in the contractual agreement.

This case shows how a company was presumed to have intended to create legal relations, despite the company's view that they had no such intention.

Edwards v. Skyways Ltd **(1964) 1 WLR 349**

The defendants entered into an agreement with the British Airline Pilots Association to make *ex gratia* (free) payments to pilots who were made redundant. The plaintiff was a redundant pilot who sought to obtain a payment from the defendants. The defendants argued that the term '*ex gratia*' indicated that it was not meant to be a legally binding agreement.

COURT HELD
There was a binding contract and the plaintiff could obtain a payment. The term 'ex gratia' did not indicate that the defendants did not wish the agreement to be legally enforceable. It merely meant that they were not admitting any pre-existing liability.

Non-enforceable commercial arrangements
The following cases show how companies or individuals have managed to enter into agreements that have not been legally enforceable.

Rose and Frank Co. v. J.R. Crompton and Brothers Ltd **(1925) AC 445**

The plaintiffs were an American firm who entered into an agreement with the defendants to sell their products in America. The agreement contained a clause that stated, 'not to be subject to legal jurisdiction in the courts of the United States of America or England'. The agreement functioned happily for a period, until the defendants ended the agreement. The plaintiffs then sued to enforce the agreement, while the defendants relied on the clause to avoid a contract.

COURT HELD
There was no valid contract. The clause clearly stated that the agreement was not meant to create a legally enforceable relationship.

In the next case the defendants used an 'honour clause' to avoid the contract.

Jones v. Vernon's Pools Ltd **(1938) 2 All ER 626**

 The plaintiff thought that he had won the pools. The defendants claimed that they had never received his entry. The coupon contained a clause that stated, 'this agreement to be binding in honour only and shall not give rise to any legal relationship'.

COURT HELD

There was no valid contract. The clause prevented any legal action.

ACT Find an example of a clause in a contract that precludes the agreement from having any legal intention. Using the cases outlined above, particularly *Jones*, present the argument that all commercial agreements should be presumed to carry legal intention. Could this work with a football pools company? Would the act of posting the coupon constitute the acceptance?

CHAPTER SUMMARY

1 Consideration is vital to the formation of a contract. Without consideration a contract will only be an agreement unenforceable at law, unless it is a deed.

2 Consideration can be defined as an act performed, goods bought, monies paid, or services rendered by a party, or an agreement to forgo any of the aforementioned.

3 Courts are not concerned with the value of consideration, just that consideration has been supplied by both parties. It is theoretically legally possible to buy a Rolls-Royce for £1!

4 Consideration may be executory – a promise by one party to do something in return for the promise of another – or executed – where one party promises to do something in return for the act of another.

5 An agreement contained in a deed does not require consideration.

6 Promissory estoppel may provide a defence for a person who has been promised by another party to an agreement, that the other party has agreed to forgo their legal right, the first party believing that promise and acting upon it, no consideration having been supplied.

7 Domestic arrangements are presumed not to be intended to create legal relations. It is a rebuttable presumption, which may be disproved by the splitting up of the family, an outside influence or other intervening factor.

8 Commercial arrangements are presumed to be intended to create legal relations. It is possible for a party to enter a commercial agreement that has no such intention. To do so they must state clearly and unambiguously their intention prior to the contract.

Form, capacity and illegality

► Remember from Chapter 9 the seven essential elements of a simple contract:
1 agreement;
2 consideration;
3 intention to create legal relation;
4 form;
5 capacity;
6 legal purpose;
7 reality of consent.

FORM

In some cases, such as the sale of land, a contract must be written. The vast majority of everyday contracts can be made orally, while nearly all business contracts are written. It is much easier to bring or defend an action in court with the evidence of a written contract.

There are three main areas where contracts must be written:

1 sale or transfer of land;
2 marine insurance;
3 consumer credit agreements.

Sale or transfer of land

The Law of Property (Miscellaneous Provisions) Act 1989 (LOP89),

s. 2(1), states that a contract for the sale or other **disposition** of an interest in land can only be made in writing and only by incorporating all the terms that the parties have expressly agreed in one document or, where contracts are exchanged, in each document.

Section 2(1) of the LOP89 is really the basis of the modern house purchase rule. An offer subject to contract will not normally satisfy the full requirements of the LOP89, s. 2(1). However, a recent case has illustrated a way in which a potential house purchaser can obtain some protection against being **gazumped**.

► **Disposition** – the transfer of property by some act of its owner, for example, by gift, exchange, will or sale.

► **Gazumped** – if the seller of a house agrees to sell to a particular person, for a given price, subject to contract, and then breaks the agreement, selling the house to another party for a higher price or demanding more money from the original purchaser, then that original purchaser is described as having been gazumped.

Pitt v. PHH Asset Management Ltd (CA August 1993)

The plaintiff (Pitt) wished to purchase a property owned by the defendants. There was another potential purchaser for the property. Pitt made an offer that was accepted by the defendants subject to contract. The acceptance was withdrawn when the other party made a higher offer. Pitt then threatened to obtain an injunction to prevent the sale to the third party and to tell the third party that Pitt was intending to withdraw his offer. This might have led to the third party reducing his offer. In response to this the defendants entered into an agreement with Pitt that they would not sell to any other party, for a period of fourteen days. During this time, Pitt guaranteed to exchange contracts for the purchase of the property. The defendants breached the agreement and sold the property. Pitt claimed damages for breach of contract. The defence alleged that there was no contract because the agreement concerned the sale of an interest of land and the contract had not been drawn up in accordance with the provisions of the LOP89, s. 2(1). Further, no consideration had been supplied.

COURT HELD
Pitt could obtain damages for breach of contract. Section 2(1) of the LOP89 did not apply because the contract was not for the sale of a right of interest in land. The contract was not to sell to another party. It constituted a so-called 'lock out' agreement, whereby one party contracts not to perform a certain act. Consideration was supplied by Pitt removing the threat of an injunction and limiting himself to two weeks to exchange contracts.

There are three exceptions to the LOP89, s. 2(1): namely auction sales, leases of land for less than three years and contracts regulated by the Financial Services Act 1986. A sale by auction is concluded when the auctioneer signifies a sale by banging a hammer on his or her desk. A lease for less than three years may be agreed orally.

Marine insurance

Marine insurance is taken out to cover one or all of the following: the loss of a ship; the loss of cargo; freight costs; and liability to a third party arising out of a voyage. Under the provisions of the

Marine Insurance Act 1906 only a written marine insurance policy can be valid.

Consumer credit agreements

The Consumer Credit Act 1974 (CCA74) governs the majority of consumer credit agreements. Under its provisions, a hire purchase agreement made between a consumer and a business for an amount not exceeding £15,000 will be called a **regulated agreement**.

As well as being written the document must contain the following information: the rights and duties imposed by the agreement; the amount and rate of the total charge for credit (if applicable); the protection and remedies available under the Act; and any other matters that, in the opinion of the Secretary of State, it is desirable for him or her to know about in connection with the agreement. If the agreement is not properly constructed then it can be enforced only with a court order. Such an order will be made only where a court feels that it is proper and just to enforce the agreement.

▶ **Regulated agreement** – a written agreement for more than £15,000, or a non-consumer hire purchase agreement, will be subject to the common law. It will not be a regulated agreement for the purposes of the CCA74.

Contracts that must be evidenced in writing

Certain contracts need not be written, but if a dispute arises and the parties end up in court, then there must be written evidence of the contract to enable a court to enforce the contract. This is a long-standing principle in law and was established in statute by the Statute of Frauds 1677, which stated that:

> No action shall be brought whereby to charge the defendant upon any special promise to answer for the debt, default or miscarriage of another person unless the agreement upon which such action be brought, or some memorandum or note thereof, shall be in writing and signed by the party to be charged therewith or some other person thereunto by him lawfully authorized.

Put simply, a contract of guarantee must be in writing if a person seeks to enforce it in a court. It need not be in writing at the commencement of the contract, but it must be written by the time of the dispute, otherwise a court will not enforce it. The written contract or memorandum need not be in any special format, though it must contain the material terms of the agreement, such as the names of the parties and the nature of the agreement. Further, it must state that the agreement is contractual and describe the nature of the contract.

Contract of guarantee v. contract of indemnity

It is important to establish the difference between these two different types of contract. A contract of guarantee will contain a debtor, a creditor and a guarantor. Where Susan sells goods to Andrew, Mike could guarantee that Andrew will pay for the goods, thus making himself secondarily liable for the debt. If Andrew fails to pay for the goods, then Mike is contractually bound to pay Jane. A guarantor plays no other part in the contract. Only contracts of guarantee are covered by the Statute of Frauds.

A contract of indemnity is slightly different in that the indemnifier makes himself or herself primarily liable for the debt.

The following case illustrates the difference between a contract of guarantee and a contract of indemnity, and shows the effect an indemnity has on a contract.

Mountstephen v. Lakeman (1871) LR 7 QB 196

The plaintiff was a builder who had been contracted by the defendant, the chairman of the Brixham Local Board of Health, to construct some mains sewerage works. Certain of the townspeople were given twenty-one days' notice to construct sewerage pipes to join the new mains system. Prior to the expiry the town surveyor, Robert Adams, suggested to the plaintiff that he might carry out the work specified in the twenty-one-day notice. The plaintiff indicated that he would be happy to do so if he was paid to carry out the work. A conversation later took place between the defendant and the plaintiff at which the defendant stated 'Go on Mountstephen and do the work and I will see you paid'. The plaintiff subsequently completed the work and submitted a bill to the council. The council declined to settle the account because it had not agreed to the extra work, neither had it authorized any of its officers to sanction the work.

COURT HELD
The plaintiff's claim succeeded. The defendant had not made a contract of guarantee on behalf of the council, but he had made himself personally liable by his statement of indemnity to pay the debt.

(ACT) List the types of contract that must be written. Explain the difference between a contract of indemnity and a contract of guarantee. Making reference to relevant cases explain the effect of an indemnity on a contract.

CAPACITY

We looked at capacity in Chapter 9, p. 128. Remember that both parties to the contract must be legally capable of entering into a

► **Ratifies** – confirms an action.

► **Necessaries** – defined in the Sale of Goods Act 1979, s. 3(3), as goods suitable to the condition in life of the minor or other person concerned and to his or her actual requirements at the time of the sale and delivery.

contract. The law recognizes that some people may not have the mental ability to appreciate the consequences of their actions and so should not be held liable for their actions. These people include drunks, the mentally disordered and minors.

Drunkenness

Mere drunkenness at the time of the formation of a contract will not necessarily affect the contract's validity. Obviously, if a person is so drunk that the person has no idea of what he or she is agreeing to, then that person has not really consented to a contract. In such circumstances the contract will be voidable at the option of the drunk. Such an option must be exercised within a reasonably quick time. If a drunk, in a later sober moment, **ratifies** a contract, the drunk will be bound by that contract. Regardless of the state of drunkenness, a drunk will be liable to pay a reasonable price for any **necessaries** sold and delivered to him or her, under the Sale of Goods Act 1979, s. 3.

Mental disorder

The position with mental disorder is similar to that of those who are suffering from drunkenness. A contract will be valid unless the other party knew of the mental disorder and understood that the person was incapable of appreciating the consequences of the other person's actions. A contract so formed will be voidable at the option of the mentally disordered person. Mentally disordered persons must also pay a reasonable price for necessaries (see above).

Minors

A person under the age of 18 is considered to be a minor in English Law. The Family Law Reform Act 1969 reduced the age from 21 to 18. The common-law rules governing the contractual capacity of minors have recently been modified by the Minors' Contracts Act 1987.

Generally speaking, a contract with a minor will be enforceable by the minor but not against the minor. Contracts concerning minors can be categorized into those that are valid and enforceable and those that are voidable.

Valid and enforceable contracts with minors

The government and the courts have always tried to protect minors in their contractual dealings. However, they are prepared to recognize that at certain times it is in everyone's interest that a minor should be bound to a contract. This section illustrates the two areas to which this concept applies and the one area to which it doesn't apply.

Contracts for necessaries

Where such necessaries (defined above) are delivered to the minor he or she will be required to pay a reasonable price for them, which may or may not be the contracted price. It is difficult to state what a 'necessary' is, as in each case it will depend on the nature of the goods and the financial situation of the minor concerned. For example, if Ralph (a minor), who lives in a rural village, enters into a contract whereby he obtains a motorbike that, in the absence of any public transport, he uses to get to work, then that motorbike could be considered to be a 'necessary'. However, if the village is served by a good public transport system that Ralph can use to get to work, then the motorbike probably wouldn't be considered to be a 'necessary'. The following case illustrates that in certain circumstances even clothes may not be considered to be 'necessaries'.

Nash v. Inman (1908) 2 KB 1

The plaintiff was a tailor who had supplied clothes to the value of £150.00 to the defendant, a Cambridge undergraduate. Among the goods supplied were eleven fancy waistcoats. The plaintiff argued that the goods were suitable to the student's life and situation, as he came from a very wealthy background and the plaintiff sued to recover the price of the goods.

► In 1908 a minor was a person under the age of 21.

COURT HELD

The plaintiff failed: the goods were not 'necessaries' because the defendant was already adequately supplied with clothes.

► Under the Minors' Contracts Act 1987, the tailor might have been able to recover the goods from the defendant.

Beneficial contracts of service, employment and apprenticeship

Where minors enter into a contract under this section that a court considers is beneficial to them, the contract will be enforced against them. This could include a variety of employment areas such as sport, engineering, the armed forces, education or commerce. The following case illustrates where a contract of apprenticeship, which on the whole was seen to be beneficial to the minor, was enforced by the court.

Doyle v. White City Stadium (1935) 1 KB 110

Doyle, a minor, was a boxer who was under contract to the defendant. In his contract was a clause that allowed for the forfeiture of the prize money should Doyle be disqualified for 'foul play'. Doyle was disqualified and sought to recover the prize money.

COURT HELD

Doyle could not succeed, as the contract taken as a whole was for his benefit and was therefore an enforceable contract.

Trading contracts

Minors are never bound to a trading contract, even though such a contract may be beneficial to them. However, a minor may sue the other party to a trading contract. The next case illustrates that a minor cannot be bound to this type of contract.

Cowern v. Nield (1912) 2 KB 419

Nield was a minor who was in business as a hay and straw dealer. He received payment for goods from the plaintiff, for which he refused to deliver. The plaintiff sued to recover the price of the goods.

COURT HELD

The plaintiff could not succeed. The defendant had not acted fraudulently and the contract could not be enforced against him.

Voidable contracts with minors

In certain cases, minors' contracts may be enforceable by and against them, but they may avoid the contract either before becoming 18 or soon afterwards. Certain contracts, such as contracts for non-necessaries or for loans, will not be binding upon a minor unless he or she ratifies the contract after becoming 18. Tim (aged 17) bought a bike (a non-necessary in this case) from Alex, taking possession of it, paying a deposit and agreeing to pay the balance over the next four months. Tim could then decide not to pay for the bike, leaving Alex unable to take action against him. If Tim started to pay the instalments, continuing to do so after his eighteenth birthday, then he would become bound to the contract. His actions would constitute the ratification of the contract.

Notwithstanding that the contracts are not enforceable against the minor, a minor can obtain good title to any goods obtained under such a contract. Therefore, a minor can pass on good title to a third party who purchases the goods in good faith at a reasonable price. If Tim sold the bike on to Chi, who bought it in good faith, then Mark would not be able to claim the bike from Chi, where Tim had failed to ratify the original contract. A third party will be able to retain the goods against any action by any other party. Where a minor pays monies or transfers property under such a contract, he or she will be able to recover those items only where there has been a total failure of consideration in the contract, i.e. where the minor had received no benefit from the contract.

Other contracts – for example, partnership, leases of land, company shares and marriage settlements – will be binding upon a minor unless he or she avoids them, either before becoming 18 or within a reasonable time afterwards. The 'reasonable time' will be determined by the courts. The following case is a good illustration of the liability of a minor in both types of voidable contract.

Steinberg v. Scala (Leeds) Ltd (1923) 2 Ch 452

The plaintiff applied for shares in the defendant company. They were allotted to her and she paid certain amounts, on different occasions, to the defendant company. Prior to becoming 21 (then the age of majority) she fell on 'hard times', and sought to avoid the contract and to recover the monies that she had paid. The defendant company agreed to remove her name from the Register of Members, thus ending any future liability against her, but they refused to repay the previously paid monies.

COURT HELD
The plaintiff could not recover the monies paid because there had not been a total failure of consideration. While the plaintiff had not received any financial benefit from the shares, she had obtained certain rights from the shares and, therefore, some benefit.

The Minors' Contracts Act 1987

Prior to the Minors' Contracts Act 1987 a court could apply the equitable remedy of restitution, where a minor had fraudulently obtained goods or money, for example, where a minor had pretended to be an adult in order to obtain goods. However, only the actual property concerned could be recovered. Therefore, if the goods had been exchanged or sold on, then nothing could be recovered from the minor. While this remedy still exists, its value has been reduced by the Minors' Contracts Act 1987, s. 3, which gives the plaintiff a much better chance of recovering something from a defaulting minor.

Section 2 of the Minors' Contracts Act 1987 changed the rule that contracts of guarantee, made on behalf of a minor, were not enforceable against a guarantor in case of default by the minor. The rules are now the same as those outlined earlier in this chapter.

Section 3 of the Act has gone some way to giving relief to parties who enter into unenforceable contracts with minors. Now a court may, if it is just and equitable to do so, require the defendant to transfer to the plaintiff any property acquired by the defendant under the contract or any property representing it. Where a minor obtains property under an unenforceable contract or subsequently repudiates a contract and exchanges that property for other goods, a court can order that the substitute goods be surrendered to the plaintiff. For example, if Nicola obtains a piano from Diane on credit, and swaps it for Ken's drum, and then defaults on the contract, a court could order Nicola to transfer the drum to Diane.

If Nicola sells the piano to Ken and then spends the money from the sale on consumable items – such as alcohol or food – which she then consumes, then Diane will not be able to recover anything from Nicola under this section. However, if Nicola retains the money and it is readily distinguishable from her own money, then Diane should be able to recover the money from the sale. If Nicola mixes the money with her own then it is not likely that Diane would be able to recover it.

The above two paragraphs illustrate the provisions of s. 3 of the Minors' Contracts Act 1987. The legislation is relatively new and cases have yet to come before the courts to demonstrate how the provisions will be applied in practice.

 Making reference to the appropriate cases, solve the following problem. Liam (aged 17) is a keen mountain biker. He has a racing bike but has always wanted a 'Craggy Peak' mountain bike. He is successful in obtaining his first job, which is in Wigglesthorpe, five miles from his house. He enters into a contract to buy a 'Craggy Peak' cycle to use to get to work. Is the Craggy Peak a 'necessary'? Would the answer be different if there were no public transport or if he didn't already have a racing bike?

The contractual capacity of companies has been dealt with fully in Chapter 5.

ILLEGALITY

While everyone is free to enter into a contract, there are certain contracts that are illegal, either by statute or at common law, which a court will not enforce. The obvious example is a contract to murder.

Contracts illegal at common law

▶ **Public policy** – the interests of the community.

If a contract is, on common-law principles, against **public policy**, this will normally make it an illegal contract. It is not really the role of the courts to judge what is against public policy. That is the role of the government, legislating through Parliament. However, under common law the courts have tended to recognize the following categories as being those where a contract will be ruled to be illegal because it is contrary to public policy:

1 contracts that involve sexual immorality;
2 contracts to defraud the Inland Revenue;
3 contracts to commit a crime or tort;
4 contracts that are prejudicial to the administration of justice;
5 contracts that may corrupt public life;
6 contracts that are hostile to friendly nations;
7 contracts to trade with the enemy in times of war.

An illegal contract will generally be unenforceable by either party.

Contracts that involve sexual immorality
It is not permitted to enter into a contract with a prostitute, or with anyone else, for sexual purposes. The following case illustrates that a contract need not be directly related to the supply of sexual services to be immoral.

Pearce v. Brooks (1866) 14 WR 614

The plaintiff was a coach builder who hired a coach to the defendant, a prostitute, knowing that she was a prostitute and that she was going to use it to ply her trade. The coach was returned damaged and the plaintiff claimed 15 guineas.

COURT HELD

The contract was unenforceable because it had been made for an immoral purpose.

Contract to defraud the Inland Revenue

Napier v. National Business Agency Ltd (1951) 2 All ER 264

The plaintiff was employed by the defendant company, being paid a salary, plus £6 per week expenses. Both the plaintiff and the defendant knew that the plaintiff's real expenses never amounted to more than £1 per week. The expenses were really being used as a means of defrauding the Inland Revenue. The defendant was sacked and claimed his salary in lieu of notice.

COURT HELD

The contract was unenforceable. The part relating to the expenses was illegal and had the effect of 'tainting the whole contract with illegality'. This last important point has been used in many subsequent findings.

Contracts to commit a crime or tort
A contract to murder, or to commit any crime or tort, will be unenforceable.

Beresford v. Royal Insurance Co. Ltd (1938) AC 586

A man committed suicide just before his life insurance policy expired, to enable his representatives to obtain the benefits from the policy. The defendants refused to pay the premium.

COURT HELD

The claim was unenforceable. The commission of a crime (as suicide then was) could not be allowed to benefit a person's estate.

Contracts that are prejudicial to the administration of justice
Where a person enters into an agreement not to prosecute or not to give evidence in a case against another party, such an agreement is unenforceable.

▶ It has been alleged that donations made to a political party may, depending upon their size, lead to a title. There would appear to be some evidence to support this claim. In recent times there has been controversy because the Conservative party continues to refuse to give details of its donors. However, Asil Nadir, currently on the run from the British police in Cyprus, is known to have been a donor to the Conservative party. Indeed, a government minister, Michael Mates, sent Nadir a watch inscribed 'Do not let the buggers get you down', referring to the fact that the police were after Nadir but that he was not to worry about it.

▶ *Ex turpi causa non oritur actio* – no action arises from a base cause.

Contracts that may corrupt public life

A contract to corrupt public life might be, for example, a contract entered into by a person to use his or her influence, in return for money, to award a title or commission, or to extricate someone from criminal proceedings.

Contracts that are hostile to friendly nations

Foster v. Driscoll (1929) 1 KB 470

The two parties contracted to import whisky into America during the period of prohibition.

COURT HELD
The agreement was illegal and unenforceable.

Contracts to trade with the enemy in times of war

It is illegal to trade with an enemy in times of war. Such contracts will be unenforceable.

Remedies and consequences of illegality under common law

The overriding rule in this case is expressed in the Latin phrase *ex turpi causa non oritur actio*. This refers to the principle that the courts may refuse to enforce a claim arising out of a plaintiff's own illegal or immoral conduct or transactions. Parties who have knowingly entered into an illegal contract may not be able to enforce it.

However, relief may be available in four situations:

1 in actions not based on the contract;
2 where the parties are not in pari delicto;
3 where there is repentance;
4 where there are innocent parties.

Actions not based on the contract

In the first situation, despite the fact that an illegal contract will be unenforceable, a party may be able to recover money or goods transferred under the contract, if the party bases his or her action other than on the contract – for example, in tort.

Euro-Diam Ltd v. Bathurst (1990) 1 QB 1

This case involved a contract for the sale of diamonds. The contract was illegal because the plaintiffs supplied their customers with a false invoice, thus enabling them to minimize German customs duties. Certain of the diamonds were stolen in transit and the plaintiffs sought to claim on an insurance policy from the defendants.

COURT HELD
The plaintiffs could succeed because the contract of insurance was totally separate from the illegal contract. The premium had been paid and there had been no deception of the insurance company.

Where the parties are *not* in pari delicto

With most illegal contracts, both parties are equally at fault and, as explained above, one party cannot recover money or goods transferred under the contract. This situation is summed up by the Latin phrase, ***in pari delicto potior est conditio defendentis***. However, where the parties are not *in pari delicto*, the less guilty party may be able to recover goods or property transferred under an illegal contract.

▶ ***In pari delicto potior est conditio defendentis*** – where two parties are equally at fault, the defendant will be in the strongest position.

***Hughes v. Liverpool Victoria Legal Friendly Society* (1916) 2 KB 482**

The defendant was induced by a misrepresentation, made by an agent of the company, to enter into an illegal life assurance policy. The defendant later sued to recover the premiums paid.

COURT HELD
The plaintiff could recover the premiums paid. The parties were not in pari delicto, as the agent was much more guilty than the defendant.

Repentance

The third situation is where the law is keen to see people realizing the error of their ways. If, before the illegal contract is substantially performed, a party repents and wishes to withdraw from the contract, he or she may be allowed to recover goods or property transferred under the contract.

Innocent parties

The final situation is where a legal contract may be turned illegal by the actions or intentions of one of the parties to the contract, leaving the other party innocent of any illegal intention. For example, a straightforward hire of a boat could be intended by the hirer to be used for the landing of illegal immigrants. The person actually hiring out the boat would be innocent. The guilty party would obtain no enforceable rights under the contract, while the innocent party could protect his or her rights by repudiating the contract as soon as that party learned of the illegality.

Contracts void at common law

Certain contracts that are at common law contrary to public policy are void but not illegal. Such contracts include: (a) contracts in restraint of trade; (b) contracts to remove an agreement from the jurisdiction of the courts; and (c) contracts prejudicial to marriage.

Contracts in restraint of trade

A contract in restraint of trade is one in which a person is unreasonably restricted from carrying out his or her trade, calling or profession. Such a contract is presumed void unless proved otherwise. A case for a restraint of trade can be made, for example, where a solicitor leaves a local practice. Then it might be reasonable to restrict that solicitor from operating in the same area. He or she will have acquired a knowledge of the client base which it would be unfair to allow the solicitor to 'poach'.

Restraints are found in four main areas: (a) employment, (b) the sale or transfer of a business, (c) restrictive trade practices and (d) sole trading agreements.

Employment

A restraint of trade may be written into a contract of employment to restrict an employee in two areas only, namely trade secrets and the soliciting or influencing of existing clients. No other restrictions are possible. An employee is entitled to take any skills acquired during the course of employment with him or her, provided that the two possible restraints are not compromised, where a restraint is in operation.

The width of the restriction will depend upon the nature of the trade secrets known and the availability of other competition in the area. In all circumstances the employer must prove that the restriction is reasonable between the two parties and in the interest of the general community. An employer will want to ensure that an employee will not be able to set up in business near to the employer and that the employee will not be able to use any secret processes or manufacturing techniques that he or she may have learned. Normally an employer will seek both a geographical and a time restraint.

The following cases illustrate how the courts have dealt with restraints.

Home Counties Dairies v. Skilton (1970) 1 All ER 1227

The defendant was a milkman employed by the plaintiffs. His contract of employment included a restraint that prevented him, for a period of one year, from selling dairy produce to any person who had been a customer in the previous six months of the plaintiff company. The defendant joined another dairy and continued to work the same round.

COURT HELD
Not surprisingly, the defendant was held to be in breach of the restraint, which was held to be reasonable.

Herbert Morris Ltd v. Saxelby (1916) AC 688

The defendant was the subject of a restraint, which prevented him from being engaged in the manufacture or sale of pulley blocks, overhead runways or overhead travelling cranes, for a period of seven years commencing upon his leaving the company. The company subsequently brought an action to enforce the agreement.

COURT HELD

The restraint was not reasonable between the two parties and it was not made in the wider interests of the public. It was unenforceable.

It appears that if there are no restraints of trade in a contract of employment, then an employee is free to take any trade secrets with him or her, or set up in business anywhere. The situation may be different if the employee records any information that is later used for the employee's own purposes, but where knowledge and skills rest in the employee's mind he or she will probably not be liable to the former employer.

Sale or transfer of a business

When a person buys a business, he or she usually buys the goodwill of the business as well. This means being entitled to trade with the existing customers without interference from the original owner. Indeed the goodwill of the business appears as an asset on the balance sheet. The geographical restraint has been allowed to be applied to the whole world, where courts have felt that this has been reasonable. A restraint will only be valid if it is required to protect the existing business; it will be void if it is used in an attempt to prevent legitimate competition.

The following cases illustrate the practical application.

► Remember **goodwill**, defined in Chapter 2, p. 12.

Nordenfelt v. Maxim Nordenfelt Gun and Ammunition Co. (1894) AC 535

The plaintiff was a manufacturer of guns and ammunition who sold his business to a company. There was a **covenant** in the sale under which the plaintiff agreed not to manufacture guns or ammunition for twenty-five years in any part of the world and further that he wouldn't compete with the company in any way. The company later sued to enforce the agreement.

► **Covenant** – agreement.

COURT HELD

*The covenant was reasonable and valid because the business was international. The provisions were not too wide in the circumstances. The court applied the **doctrine of severance** to the part of the covenant that related to not competing in any way, cutting it out, thus leaving a valid agreement.*

► **Doctrine of severance** – where a court rules a contract void through contravention of public policy, it may sever the bad part of the agreement, leaving the lawful section enforceable. A court will not add or alter words, nor will it cut material if what is left makes no sense. It will also not delete where it would involve removing a large part of the restraining clause.

► A restrictive trade practice is an agreement between two or more persons either to control or fix the prices or supplies of certain goods. A contract in restraint of trade is a contract of employment that contains a clause either preventing an employee from using any trade secrets that he or she has learned in the course of their employment elsewhere, or preventing an employee from starting up in business in competition with the employer.

Restrictive trade practices

A restrictive trade practice is an agreement between business owners and traders to control or regulate prices or output. This area is strictly controlled by the Restrictive Trade Practices Acts 1976/7 and the Resale Prices Act 1976.

A restrictive trade agreement is considered to be void and contrary to public policy, unless it can be shown to be in the public interest. The agreement must be registered with the Director General of Fair Trading and it must then be proved, in the Restrictive Practices Court, to be in the public interest.

 Research in your library to find an example of a valid restrictive trade practice.

A restrictive trade agreement must also be presumed void unless it can be proved in the Restrictive Practices Court that the agreement is in the public interest. An example of this is the net book agreement (as we saw in Chapter 10), under which books are sold at the same price in all bookshops. This agreement has come under threat in recent times, because the big retailers wish to cut their prices. Small booksellers argue that without the agreement they would all be put out of business and this would not be in the public interest.

Sole trading agreements

This type of agreement has tended to be recognized by the courts as having some validity, particularly where it is standard practice in an industry. However, all of these agreements will be subjected to a reasonableness test. Where it appears that an agreement has been forced upon a party who was in an unequal bargaining position and who hasn't made any reasonable gains from the agreement, it will be voided.

The following cases illustrate these points.

Schroeder Music Publishing Co. Ltd v. Macaulay (1974) 1 WLR 1308

► George Michael recently lost a High Court action against his employers, the Sony Corporation. Michael had sought to avoid his contract of employment on the basis that the conditions of the contract were too onerous. He lost the action because the court felt that when he had entered into the contract he had been on equal terms with his employers: prior to signing he had received advice from professional advisers, and he had been paid a vast amount of money under the contract.

 This case concerned a contract between the defendant, a young musician, and the plaintiffs, a music publisher. Under the agreement the company tied the musician to a very tight contract, giving it, among other things, world copyright of all compositions; the right not to exploit all compositions; and the right to terminate the agreement at any time on one month's notice.

COURT HELD
The agreement was an unreasonable restraint of trade. The publisher derived great benefit and little obligation from the agreement, while the musician was heavily burdened for little reward. The parties had not been in an equal bargaining position and the court had taken this into consideration when reaching its decision.

Esso Petroleum Co. Ltd v. Harper's Garage (Stourport) Ltd (1968) AC 269

 The defendant company owned two garages, one at Mustow Green and one at Stourport. Both were subject to a **solus** agreement with the plaintiffs. The company had two such agreements, under which, among other things, the company would only buy petrol from Esso; keep the garages open for certain hours; and if they were to sell the garages they would persuade the purchasers to continue with Esso. The agreement at Mustow Green had four years and five months to run from 1 July 1963. The other agreement was for twenty-one years and included a tied mortgage agreement for £7,000, that could not be paid back before the end of the twenty-one-year period. The defendants then offered to pay back the mortgage in August 1964. Esso, however, declined to accept it. The defendants then started selling a different brand of petrol, first from Stourport and later from Mustow Green. Esso brought the action seeking an injunction to enforce the agreements.

COURT HELD
The House of Lords held that solus agreements and tied mortgage arrangements could be subject to the rule of public policy against unreasonable restraints of trade. The shorter agreement was reasonable and was valid, but the longer agreement was for too long a period and could not be enforced.

▶ **Solus** – an agreement between a manufacturer or a supplier of goods with a retailer whereby, in return for being supplied with a particular good, a retailer agrees not to sell competing similar goods from its premises. The best example of this is petrol. You cannot buy Esso petrol from a Shell garage!

▶ In *Kores Manufacturing Co. v. Kolok Manufacturing Co.* (1959) Ch 108, two companies entered an agreement not to employ any of each other's staff who had previously worked for the other company in the preceding five years. This was ruled to be void because it was unreasonable between the two parties.

Contracts to remove a case from the jurisdiction of the courts

A covenant to take an agreement out of the jurisdiction of the courts will be void and illegal on the grounds of public policy.

Baker v. Jones (1954) 1 WLR 1005

This case concerned the rules of the British Weight Lifters Association. Under rule 40(vii) it claimed that the council of the association should be the sole interpreter of its rules and under rule 40(viii) the council's decision in all cases should be final. A member of the association sought a declaration that funds had been misused under the rules of the association.

COURT HELD
The matter was within the jurisdiction of the court. The two above-mentioned rules of the association were contrary to public policy and were void.

▶ Don't forget that it is possible to exclude an agreement from having legal consequences. For clarification, look back at the intention to create legal relations (p. 163).

Contracts prejudicial to marriage

Generally speaking, any contract that relates to preventing or restraining a person from marrying will be void. A contract to marry another on the death of an existing spouse will be void, but a contract to marry after a decree nisi has been obtained may be valid. A contract for immediate separation may be valid, but a contract for future separation will be void. So-called marriage brokerage contracts, where someone arranges a marriage for a couple, will be void.

 John is employed by Sparkling Window Cleaners. In his contract of employment there are a number of restraints of trade that restrict him, should he leave the company. Making reference to relevant cases, state which of the following restraints may be allowed.

1 'You must not work for any other window cleaning company within 15 miles of your place of employ.'
2 'You must not work for any other glaziers, window manufacturers or plumbers within 10 miles of your place of employ.'
3 'You must never work for any other window cleaning company within a 10-mile radius.'

Effect on contracts that are void by public policy

The above-mentioned types of contract (contracts in restraint of trade, contracts to remove an agreement from the jurisdiction of the court and contracts prejudicial to marriage) remain binding apart from the clause(s) that contravene public policy. Money or goods transferred may be recovered and any **collateral agreements** remain unaffected. The doctrine of severance may be applied as described above.

► **Collateral agreement** – a subsidiary contract, dependent upon the main contract.

Contracts illegal by statute

Certain statutes expressly state that agreements to perform certain acts will be unlawful. The following is an example.

Resale Prices Act 1976, s. 1, Collective agreement by suppliers

1 It is unlawful for any two or more persons carrying on business in the United Kingdom as suppliers of any goods to make or carry out any agreement or arrangement by which they undertake:
(a) to withhold supplies of goods for delivery in the United Kingdom from dealers (whether party to the agreement or not) who resell or have resold goods in breach of any condition as to the price at which those goods may be resold;
(b) to refuse to supply goods for delivery in the United Kingdom to such dealers except on terms and conditions that are less favourable than those applicable in the case of other dealers carrying on business in similar circumstances; or

(c)   to supply goods only to persons who undertake or have undertaken

    (i)   to withhold supplies of goods as described in paragraph (a) above; or

    (ii) to refuse to supply goods as described in paragraph (b) above.

▶ I have included the whole of this subsection to give you an idea of how complex and detailed an Act of Parliament is.

 In which two areas will a restraint of trade be acceptable in a contract of employment?

The above section of the Resale Prices Act 1976 tells us clearly which types of agreement are illegal. Other statutes may not be as specific and the courts will be left to decide upon the illegality. For example, many statutes state that a person must be licensed to trade in a particular industry. However, it is not clear whether a contract that an unlicensed person enters into will automatically be illegal. It appears that where the licensing or other statutory requirement is merely for a minor purpose, then the contract will not be affected.

The following two cases illustrate how different approaches have been taken by the courts to contracts entered into by unlicensed people.

Smith v. Mawhood (1845) 14 M & W 452

In this case an unlicensed tobacconist sold tobacco in contravention of a statute. He then undertook court action to recover for non-payment.

 COURT HELD

The tobacconist could succeed. The purpose of the legislation was to raise revenue by penalizing offenders; it was not intended to affect normal business contracts.

Cope v. Rowlands (1836) 2 M & W 149

The plaintiff was an unlicensed broker, trading in the City of London. A dispute arose with the defendant, who refused to pay his fees. The plaintiff brought the action to obtain his fees.

 COURT HELD

The plaintiff could not recover his fees. The purpose of the legislation was to protect the public from unlicensed dealers.

 List, with examples, contracts that are illegal at common law. What effect will illegality have upon a contract?

Remedies and consequences of illegality by statute

The same rules apply as outlined under contracts illegal at common law (see page 176).

Contracts void by statute

There are certain contracts that are void but not illegal by statute. Such contracts fall into two main types:

(a) gaming and wagering contracts;
(b) restrictive trade practices.

Gaming and wagering contracts

A wagering contract is more commonly known as a betting contract. It occurs where one person places a bet on the outcome of an event, such as a horse race. If the other party to the contract accepts the bet on a particular horse, then if the horse wins the other party pays a given amount, depending upon the odds offered on the horse. If the horse loses then the party who accepted the bet keeps the amount of money wagered. The essence of a wagering contract is that both parties must stand to win or lose. A wagering contract may also be made on the facts of a past event: for example, I could bet you £5 that Brighton won the FA Cup in 1982.

A gaming contract involves a game of chance for winning in money or for money's worth. An example is the playing of cards for money. All players must have an equal chance of winning. Both gaming and wagering contracts were made void by the Gaming Act 1845.

Restrictive trade practices

A restrictive trade practice is an agreement between business people and traders to control or regulate prices or output. This area is strictly controlled by the Restrictive Trade Practices Acts 1976/7 and the Resale Prices Act 1976. A restrictive trade agreement will be presumed void unless it can be proved in the Restrictive Practices Court that the agreement is in the public interest (see page 182 above).

 Now that you have completed this chapter, look back at the chapter objectives at the beginning. Can you do all the things that these suggest? If not, look again at the relevant sections of the chapter.

CHAPTER SUMMARY

1 Contracts for the sale or disposition of land, marine insurance and consumer credit agreements must be in writing.
2 Certain other contracts, for example, contracts of guarantee, need not be in writing, although in cases of dispute, to be

valid, written evidence of the contract must be produced to the court.

3 Drunks, mentally disordered persons and minors are afforded, in certain circumstances, limited protection with regard to their contractual capacity.

4 Contracts for necessaries and beneficial contracts of service can be enforced against minors, while trading contracts are unenforceable.

5 The following types of contracts are illegal at common law because they are against public policy: contracts that involve sexual immorality; contracts to defraud the Inland Revenue; contracts to commit a crime or tort; contracts that are prejudicial to the administration of justice; contracts that corrupt public life; contracts that are hostile to friendly nations; contracts to trade with the enemy in times of war.

6 The following types of contract are void at common law for contravention of public policy: contracts in restraint of trade; contracts to remove an agreement from the jurisdiction of the courts; contracts prejudicial to marriage.

7 In relation to contracts of employment, restraints of trade will only be allowed to restrict (a) trade secrets and (b) the soliciting or influencing of existing customers. Other restraints are presumed to be void. It is for the person seeking to rely on the restraint to prove that they are reasonable.

8 Restraints of trade may be allowed in the sale or transfer of a business, in restrictive trade practices and in sole trading agreements.

Reality of consent

► Remember from Chapter 9 the
seven essential elements of a simple
contract:
1 agreement;
2 consideration;
3 intention to create legal relation;
4 form;
5 capacity;
6 legal purpose;
7 reality of consent.

Chapter objectives

By the end of this chapter you should be able to:

▌ recognize that the courts look for a *consensus ad idem* in a contract, and that where no real agreement is evident a contract may be void by mistake

▌ identify the areas where the courts have been prepared to recognize mistake, such as mistake as to the subject matter, mistake as to the nature of a signed document and mistake as to the identity of one of the parties

▌ appreciate the effect of mistake on a contract

▌ understand the role of equity in cases concerning mistake, including the remedies of rectification, rescission and specific performance.

▌ recognize the constituent elements of a misrepresentation

▌ appreciate the common-law rules relating to misrepresentation, especially the rule established in *Hedley Byrne*

▌ understand and recognize the effects on a contract of the three classifications of misrepresentation: innocent, negligent and fraudulent

▌ appreciate the role that Parliament has taken in controlling misrepresentations under the provisions of the Misrepresentation Act 1967

▌ recognize the circumstances in which duress, undue influence and unconscionable bargains may be found

▌ appreciate where the courts have been prepared to accept duress, in relation to threats to the person, economic threats and threats to property

▌ appreciate that the effect of duress on a contract may render the contract void or voidable

▌ recognize the equitable remedy of undue influence and the circumstances under which it may apply

▌ know the remedies available under undue influence

▌ recognize the concept of unconscionable bargain and the circumstances under which it might be applied.

We shall now look at the final essential element of a contract: consent. A contract is invalid unless both parties give their consent freely. A person must not be forced into entering a contract. Further, the law looks for a *consensus ad idem*, an agreement by both contracting parties to identical terms. Where a party consents to a contract that he or she thought was for one thing, while the other party consented to the same contract that he or she thought was for a different thing, that contract may be invalid.

If certain factors are present when a contract is made, it may mean that there has not been genuine consent to that contract. We shall examine these factors, which fall into five main areas:

1 mistake,
2 misrepresentation,
3 duress,
4 undue influence,
5 unconscionable bargains.

► *Consensus ad idem* – agreement on the same thing.

MISTAKE

In a straightforward contract – for example, the purchase of a painting – the common law offers no help to a potential purchaser. The basic rule here is *caveat emptor*. If you are prepared to pay £2,000 for a painting that you mistakenly believe to be by Renoir, provided you haven't been misled by the seller, you will have no redress in the courts if the painting turns out to be worthless. For a mistake to have an effect on a contract, it must be an **operative mistake** as to a material fact. It should also be noted that a **mistake of law** will not invalidate a contract because all citizens are presumed to know the law, even if in reality they do not.

The courts have tended to recognize an operative mistake in three main areas:

1 mistake as to the subject matter of the contract;
2 mistake as to the nature of a signed document;
3 mistake as to the identity of one of the parties.

Further, a mistake may be **bilateral** or **unilateral**. Where a court is prepared to accept that there has been an operative mistake the contract will become void. Under a void contract all goods supplied and monies paid can be recovered.

► *Caveat emptor* – let the buyer beware.

► **Operative mistake** – a mistake of fact that has prevented the formation of a contract and that has the effect of making the contract void.

► **Mistake of law** – this refers to a situation where someone is mistaken as to the law on a particular point. It is no defence to claim that you did not know that it was against the law to commit a particular act, such as driving your car the morning after you had been drinking, still having an illegal amount of alcohol in your body.

► **Bilateral mistake** (also known as common mistake) – where the same mistake is made by both parties – will normally be operative only in cases of *res sua* and *res extincta* (see p. 191), and the circumstances illustrated below.

► **Unilateral mistake** – a mistake made by one party as to a fundamental fact concerning a contract, when the other party knows, or should have known, that the other party has made such a mistake.

Mistake as to the subject matter of the contract

Where there is no real consensus

If two parties are discussing a contract, and one party is talking of one thing while the other party believes that they are discussing something totally different, then there is no *consensus ad idem*. This is known as a mutual mistake. It is simply illustrated in the following case.

Raffles v. Wichelhaus (1864) 2 H & C 906

 This was a trading contract concerning the purchase of 125 bales of Surat cotton. The parties had agreed a contract that involved the delivery of the goods by the ship *Peerless*, sailing from Bombay. The defendant was talking about the ship *Peerless* that sailed from Bombay in October. The plaintiff was talking about a second ship, also called *Peerless*, which didn't sail until December. The plaintiffs brought the action when the defendants refused to accept delivery and to pay for the goods.

 COURT HELD

The plaintiff could not succeed. There was no binding contract between the two parties. It was void by mistake.

William Sindall plc v. Cambridgeshire County Council (1994) 3 All ER 932

In this case the plaintiff sought to have a contract for the purchase of development land from the council, for £5,082,500, rescinded on the grounds of misrepresentation and common fundamental mistake. The contract incorporated the National Conditions of Sale (20th edition), which contained a clause stating that the property was sold subject to any easements, public rights and liabilities affecting it. A further special clause provided that the purchaser was deemed to purchase with full notice and subject to all easements, rights and privileges now affecting the property. The problems in the contract arose when, in 1990, it was discovered that the land had a foul sewer running through it. The market value of the property had almost halved by that time and the plaintiff sought to have the contract rescinded on the grounds of fundamental mistake and misrepresentation. The vendors had replied to the standard enquiries before contract about the land, stating that as far as they were aware there were no rights of easement or public rights affecting the property, other than those disclosed in the contract. The files that would have indicated the presence of the foul sewer had previously been destroyed in a fire. The court had to decide if there had been any misrepresentation or mistake.

 COURT HELD

The contract could not be rescinded for mistake or misrepresentation. The nature of the contract, in particular the clauses outlined above, clearly made it the responsibility of the purchaser to ensure that the land was free from any encumbrances that might affect its uses. Because of the nature of the clauses there could be no grounds for mistake. The vendors had made enquiries about the land and had replied according to the information that they had to hand; therefore, there was no misrepresentation. If there had

been an actionable misrepresentation, damages would have been awarded in place of rescission. The damages would have reflected the difference between the market price at the time of the sale and the value of the land at that time, with the knowledge of the presence of the sewer.

Res extincta

Where there is mistake as to the existence, or condition, of the subject matter, this is known as *res extincta*. If two parties contract for the sale of an item that, unbeknown to both of them, is no longer in existence, then the contract will be voided by mistake. If Laura contracted to sell her hamster to Chris and, unbeknown to both of them, the hamster had already been eaten by his cat, then the sale would be voided by mistake. They both thought that the hamster was in existence, but it wasn't, it was in the cat! The next case illustrates the commercial application of this rule.

▶ ***Res extincta*** – matter that has ceased to exist.

Couturier v. Hastie (1856) 5 HLC 673

The plaintiff company shipped corn from Salonica. They sent the relevant documents to their agents in London to enable them to sell the corn. The agents employed a ***del credere*** agent, Couturier, to sell the corn. Couturier agreed the sale of the corn with another party, who subsequently **repudiated** the contract. Unbeknown to all parties the corn had become damaged in transit, and had been landed and sold prior to arriving in London. The plaintiff company sued the defendant under the *del credere* agreement.

▶ ***Del credere*** **agent** (from the Italian, meaning 'of trust') – an agent who agrees to protect his or her principal (the person for whom he or she is acting) against the risk of a buyer failing to complete a contract that the agent has arranged. The liability for the settlement of the contract is undertaken by the agent.

 COURT HELD
The plaintiff could not succeed against the agent. The contract for the sale of the corn was made when both parties mistakenly believed that the corn was still in existence, therefore, the contract was voided by mistake

▶ **Repudiate** – to indicate, by words or deeds, that a contract will not be completed. (See **Anticipatory breach**, Chapter 13, p. 230.)

Res sua

If a person, or a company, contracts to purchase something that he, she or it already owns, the contract is voided by mistake. This rare event is known as *res sua,* and when it has happened the circumstances have been extremely complicated, as can be seen from the following case.

▶ ***Res sua*** – matter that is owned.

Cochrane v. Willis (1865) LR 1 Ch App 58

This involved case concerned the defendant entering into an agreement with the plaintiff, whereby the defendant agreed to pay the plaintiff not to cut timber on land that belonged to the defendant's brother, in order to maintain the existing forest on the land. The plaintiff was the

► **Trustee in bankruptcy** – a party who is entrusted with the property of a bankrupt in order to deal with the property for the benefit of the bankrupt's creditors. A trustee's main role is to try to maximize the revenue from a bankrupt's assets and to distribute it to the creditors in the manner laid down by statute.

brother's **trustee in bankruptcy**. Unbeknown to either of the parties the brother had died and ownership of the land had passed to the defendant. The trustee brought the action to enforce the agreement.

> **COURT HELD**
> *The action failed. The defendant had entered into a contract relating to making a payment with regard to property that he already owned. Therefore,* res sua *applied and the contract was voided by mistake.*

Mistake as to the nature of a signed document

The courts have traditionally been reluctant to allow a person to avoid a contract on the grounds of mistake, where they have signed a contractually binding agreement. This rule applies regardless of whether the document is different to what a person thought that he or she was signing, or notwithstanding the fact that a person has not read the document. The following applies to situations where the contract affects a third party, for it will be relatively simple where no third party is involved for a party to avoid the contract because it has been fraudulently induced (see below).

Non est factum

► **Non est factum** – it is not [my] deed.

If a person feels that he or she has signed a document by mistake and was not reckless when signing the document, the person may be able to plead *non est factum*. However, it is very difficult for an adult of sound mind to plead *non est factum* successfully. These facts are clearly illustrated in the following case.

Saunders v. Anglia Building Society (1970) 3 All ER 961

This unfortunate case concerned a Mrs Gallie who had a leasehold interest in her house. Her nephew was in business with a Mr Lee. Gallie knew that her nephew wished to raise money on her house and that Lee was to help him in doing so. Lee asked her to sign a document, but because she had broken her spectacles she was unable to read it. Gallie asked Lee what the document was, to which he said that it was a deed of gift of the house to the nephew. Gallie signed the document, which in fact was an assignment of the house to Lee. Lee mortgaged the property to the Anglia Building Society, who then sought possession of the property when Lee failed to keep up the mortgage payments. Gallie pleaded *non est factum* and sought to have the assignment to the building society voided.

> **COURT HELD**
> *The action failed. The document that Gallie signed was not fundamentally different from the document that she had set out to sign. Further, she had been careless in not reading the agreement and in not taking legal advice.*

The following rules apply to the plea of *non est factum*:

1   It will not be open to a person over the age of 18 of sound mind, who signs a legal document having failed to read the document.
2   Where there is a mistake as to the identity of a person affected by the document, *non est factum* will not operate unless the mistake is so radical and fundamental that it totally negates the original intent of the assignee.
3   Where the mistake is as to the nature of the document signed, the document must be fundamentally and radically different from that which the **assignee** intended to sign.
4   *Non est factum* will not be valid where a person signs a blank document that is then completed by a third party, unless the assignee is acting under the instruction of the third party. The above rules apply for both blank and completed documents.

▶ **Assignee** – the person making the assignment, i.e. by signing the document.

Mistake as to the identity of one of the parties

There are two rules to be remembered here.

1   Where the parties to a contract meet face to face then normally the contract will not be voided by mistake.
2   If a contract is agreed in circumstances other than (1), mistake may void the contract where the party suffering the mistake clearly thought that he or she was dealing with a different person, and the identity of that person was crucial to the contract.

The following cases illustrate these two points.

Older students may remember the actor Richard Greene, who used to play Robin Hood in the old television series.

Lewis v. Averay (1971) 3 All ER 907

 Lewis advertised his car for sale. The advert was answered by a rogue who pretended to be Richard Greene, producing a cheque book and an admission pass to Pinewood studios in verification. A price of £450 was agreed for the car, Lewis accepting a cheque in the name of R. Greene. The cheque bounced because it had been stolen by the rogue. The rogue then sold the car to Averay and Lewis brought this action to recover the car from Averay in the **tort of conversion**.

▶ The important question here is: was the contract void by mistake or voidable through fraud? If it was void by mistake then Averay could not obtain good title to the car and Lewis would be able to obtain it. If it was voidable through fraud then, provided Averay had paid a reasonable price and bought it in good faith, he would have acquired good title and would be able to retain the car.

▶ **Tort of conversion** – this important tort is linked to the tort of trespass to goods (see Chapter 2, p. 11). The tort of conversion deals with a person who has intentionally and unlawfully obtained possession of goods, which is totally inconsistent with the rights of the actual owner of the goods.

COURT HELD
The contract was not voided by mistake. Lewis intended to sell the car to the person that he was dealing with, irrespective of the false identity of the person. The contract was voidable because of fraudulent misrepresentation (see below, p. 205): Lewis had not taken steps to avoid the contract prior to Averay's obtaining the car, therefore Averay retained the car.

▶ The case of *Lewis* should be taken as the normal rule. However, in *Ingram v. Little* (1961) 1 QB 31, in similar circumstances a car was sold to a rogue pretending to be another person. The false identity was checked by the vendors, who looked up the name in the telephone directory, before parting with the car and accepting a cheque in payment. The cheque bounced and the car was sold on by the rogue. The plaintiffs were awarded the car in conversion, the court holding that the identity of the purchaser was vital to the contract, this being evidenced by the fact that verification had been sought from the telephone directory. This case should be thought of as being exceptional and the rule stated in *Lewis* will usually be followed.

Cundy v. Lindsay **(1878) 3 App Cas 459 (HL)**

 The plaintiffs (Cundy) were Irish linen manufacturers, who received an order from a Mr Blenkarn, who pretended to be Blenkiron and Co., a reputable English company. The plaintiffs knew of the reputation of Blenkiron and supplied the goods on credit to Blenkarn, believing that they were trading with Blenkiron. Blenkarn failed to pay for the goods which he then sold on to Lindsay, who purchased them in good faith. The action was brought in the tort of conversion to recover the goods.

 COURT HELD
The contract was void by mistake and Cundy could recover the goods. The identity of the party was crucial to the plaintiffs, who only intended to supply the goods to Blenkiron and Co.

(ACT) Karen advertised her car for sale in the local paper. James viewed the car and offered to pay the asking price by cheque. Karen initially refused to accept a cheque, but after James had shown her a passport and some letters with a local address, she accepted a cheque for the car. The cheque was stolen and it subsequently bounced. Karen sued Julian, who had bought the car from James, in the tort of conversion to recover the car. Making reference to relevant cases, state whether she would be successful. If Karen intended to sell her car to Tracy's uncle Bill, and James pretended to be the uncle, would that have had any affect on the above circumstances?

Mistake and equity

We have learned that equity has grown in order to alleviate the harshness of the common law. In mistake certain equitable remedies have been used by the courts in order to bring a measure of justice to the contract.

Rectification

Where two parties have made an oral agreement that has then been mistakenly written down, a court may rectify that agreement by amending it to reflect the original intention of the parties. If Anna agrees to let Polly sell her products under licence for five years and Polly agrees to this, but if, when the contract is written down, the figure of '50 years' was recorded in place of '5 years', Anna could ask the court for rectification should Polly refuse to correct the figure.

The following case illustrates the practical use of rectification.

Thomas Bates and Sons Ltd v. Wyndham's (Lingerie) Ltd **(1981) 1 All ER 1077**

 This case concerned the lease of premises. The plaintiff leased premises to the defendant in 1956 with an option for renewal. The lease contained a clause that stated that upon renewal the rent was to be agreed between the parties or by reference to arbitration. The agreement continued happily and in 1970 a fourteen-year lease was agreed, at a rent of £2,350 per annum. This lease stated that it would be subject to rent reviews at five-yearly intervals, however, it did not contain an arbitration clause. The defendants signed the lease knowing of the omission of the arbitration clause. The parties fell into dispute when the plaintiffs sought to agree a new rent at the end of the first five years, while the defendants argued that they intended to pay £2,350 for the whole of the fourteen years, in the absence of any agreement between the parties. The plaintiffs sought an order of rectification from the court.

COURT HELD
The order was granted; the court inserted an arbitration clause into the contract.

Before a court will grant rectification the following must apply.

1 The written record of the contract must not conform to what the parties had originally agreed. If it does then rectification cannot be granted.
2 The contract was fully agreed between the parties, and there was no dispute over any of the terms between the time it was agreed and the time it was mistakenly recorded.
3 There was agreement on terms that failed to be included in the contract.

Rescission on terms

In certain situations a voidable contract can be set aside, and treated as though it never existed. This is known as rescission. Rescission can only be exercised where *restituto in integrum* is possible, i.e. where the parties can return to a pre-contractual position. Any money or goods that have been exchanged must be returned. Rescission will not be granted:

(a) where any benefit has been enjoyed by the party requesting it;
(b) where the requesting party has in any way **affirmed** the contract or has delayed in seeking rescission;
(c) where goods are no longer in existence or where a third party has acquired an interest in the goods.

Where a court is asked to grant rescission it may, in order to be fair, offer the parties rescission with certain conditions attached. The following case illustrates this point.

► *Restituto in integrum* – restoration to the original position.

► A contract is **affirmed** if a person does anything to indicate that he or she has accepted it, including any misrepresentations or other breaches of the contract that are contained in it. For example, if a person accepts faults found in a second-hand car that had been described as 'in excellent condition', then that would be taken as indicating that he or she intends to continue with the contract, i.e. the contract would be affirmed.

Solle v. Butcher (1950) 1 KB 671

The plaintiff (Solle) agreed to lease a flat from the defendant (Butcher) at a rent of £250 per annum. Both parties agreed to the rent believing the flat to be not subject to the current statutory rent controls. However, the flat was subject to the current rent controls and the maximum legally chargeable rent would have been £140.

If Butcher had realized that the flat was subject to the current rent controls he would have been able to add 8 per cent of the cost of recent improvements that he had made on to the maximum £140 rent. This would have made the legally chargeable rent around the £250 mark. As he did not realize, he failed to serve the required statutory notice on Solle that would have allowed him to increase the rent. Solle later realized that he had agreed to pay £250 when the maximum legally chargeable rent was £140. Solle then brought an action to reduce the rent to £140 per annum, while the defendant counterclaimed rescission.

► In this case the two parties could, of course, be described as landlord and tenant.

COURT HELD

There had been a bilateral mistake that could not invalidate the contract. The order of rescission was granted and Solle was given the option of (a) surrendering the lease or (b) remaining in the property as a licensee, while the statutory notices were served on him to allow a rent of £250 to be established in a new lease.

Specific performance

A court may grant an equitable and, therefore, discretionary remedy, ordering the party in breach of a contract to complete the contract. This order is known as specific performance.

► Specific performance was discussed in Chapter 9, p. 132.

However, in certain cases the courts have exercised an option not to grant an order of specific performance, especially where it would be unfair to do so. The next case illustrates this point.

Grist v. Bailey (1966) 2 All ER 875

Two parties agreed a reduced price for a house believing it to have a tenant who was guaranteed the possession of the property, known as a sitting or a protected tenant. However, the tenant was not protected and he vacated the house. The agreed price was £850, while the market value with vacant possession was around £2,500. The plaintiff (Grist) sued for specific performance, seeking to enforce the sale at the price of £850, while the defendant counterclaimed rescission.

COURT HELD

The contract was not void by mistake. Specific performance would not be granted because it would be unfair to enforce the contract against the defendant (Bailey). Rescission would be granted on the condition that the defendant offered the plaintiff an opportunity to purchase the property at its proper market value.

 Outline the rules relating to rectification. What is the difference between rectification and rescission? What effect will *res extincta* have on a contract? When can *non est factum* be used as a defence?

MISREPRESENTATION

When parties are discussing forming a contract many things may be discussed and some of these may be incorporated into the contract as terms. Other statements may not be contractual, but nevertheless they may induce or encourage a party to enter into a contract. Where untrue statements are made with the intention of inducing a contract they are known as misrepresentations. The person making such a statement is known as the **representor**. The person to whom it is made is the **representee**. A misrepresentation may have a **vitiating** effect upon a contract. Depending upon the type of misrepresentation – innocent, fraudulent or negligent – a contract will be voidable or damages will be available, or both.

► **Vitiating** – affecting the validity of (a contract). Legal scholars differ on which elements may be termed as vitiating, though most would normally include misrepresentation, mistake, duress and undue influence.

Traders' puffs

A traders' puff is not a misrepresentation because a misrepresentation generally must be measurable and be a statement of verifiable fact, not of opinion. If a company advertises that its powder washes cleaner than any other powder, it would not be a misrepresentation because it is probably impossible to measure. 'We sell the best cars' is another example. What does 'best' mean? However, where the puff becomes more specific, for example, 'There are more nuts in our Choc 'n' Nut than in any other bar', that becomes measurable and, if untrue, could become a misrepresentation.

Having established what a misrepresentation is *not*, let us now consider the essential characteristics of a misrepresentation:

(a) it must be an untrue pre-contractual statement of a verifiable fact;
(b) the fact must be material to the contract;
(c) the statement must be made to the other party;
(d) the statement must induce the contract.

An untrue pre-contractual statement of a verifiable fact

Form of the statement

A statement doesn't have to be made by words. A person's conduct may constitute a misrepresentation. Failure to make a statement or the omission of certain material from a statement may also constitute a misrepresentation. Such non-verbal 'statements' may become actionable misrepresentation in the following circumstances:

- in contracts of *uberrimae fidei*;
- in fiduciary relationships;
- where there is a change of circumstances;
- where disclosure is required by statute;
- where a representation is only partly true;
- where a fraudulent act induces a contract.

Contracts of **uberrimae fidei**

Uberrimae fidei describes a class of contracts where all material facts must be disclosed. The best example is a contract of insurance. Imagine that a motor insurance policy was taken out and at a later time the circumstances changed – for example, the car was no longer garaged – but the insurance company was not informed of the change. Under these circumstances it would be possible for the insurance company to avoid the contract. How many of us have failed to update our insurance companies on changed circumstances?

Fiduciary relationships

▶ *Uberrimae fidei* (of utmost good faith) and fiduciary relationships were discussed in Chapter 7, p. 86, on partnership.

If a person is in a position of trust in relation to another there is said to be a fiduciary relationship. That person is under a duty to disclose all information to the other and to act in the other's best interests. There is a presumption of *uberrimae fidei*.

Change of circumstances

Where the parties are in a pre-contractual stage and a party makes a statement that was true at the time but that prior to the conclusion of the contract becomes untrue, he or she is under a duty to inform the other party of the change. Failure to do so may become an actionable misrepresentation. This can be seen from the following case.

With v. O'Flanagan (1936) 1 All ER 727

EQ This case concerned the negotiations for the sale of a medical practice. The defendant doctor (O'Flanagan), in January 1934, represented to the plaintiff (With) that the annual income of the practice was £2,000. Between January and the signing of the contract in May, the defendant had been ill and the income had dropped to around £5 per week. This fact was not disclosed to the plaintiff who subsequently sued for rescission.

COURT HELD

The order of rescission was granted. The defendant's silence in relation to a material fact that had induced the contract amounted to an actionable misrepresentation.

Statutory disclosure

Certain statutes demand that particular details are disclosed. The Financial Services Act 1986, s. 163, states:

> a prospectus shall contain all such information as investors and their professional advisors would reasonably require, and reasonably expect to find there, for the purpose of making an informed assessment of:
> (a) the assets and liabilities; financial position; profits and losses; and prospects of the issuer of the securities; and
> (b) the rights attaching to those securities

Half truths

If a party makes a representation that he or she knows to be only partly true, then that party is under a duty to disclose the full truth to the other party. If he or she fails to do so it may amount to an actionable misrepresentation. For example, if a man who was selling his car stated, when asked, that as far as he knew there had been only one other owner, when he could have examined the log book to establish the actual number, that could be construed as an actionable misrepresentation.

► In *Dimmock v. Hallett* (1866) LR 2 Ch App 21 (CA), a landowner stated that all the farms were let, knowing that some of the tenants had been given notice to quit. This was held to be an actionable misrepresentation.

Hidden fraud

Where a person fraudulently carries out an act in order to **induce** a contract, that may be interpreted as an actionable misrepresentation. The next case illustrates this point.

► **Induce** – to persuade or influence a person to enter into a contract.

Schneider v. Heath (1813)

This case concerned the sale of a boat. Prior to the plaintiff viewing the boat the defendant pushed the boat into the water to conceal its rotten hull. The contract was concluded and the plaintiff subsequently sued for rescission of the contract.

COURT HELD

The contract was rescinded. The defendant's actions amounted to a misrepresentation.

Nature of the statement

The statement must be a verifiable fact of some existing or past matter. It cannot relate to a legal principle, though a false statement that there was a legal right in existence might be considered to be a misrepresentation. A statement as to a future intention would not be a misrepresentation because it is not in existence, so it would probably become a term of the contract.

An important exception to the last point occurs when the intent in a person's mind turns the misrepresentation into a statement of fact. This is best illustrated by the following case.

Edgington v. Fitzmaurice (1885) 29 Ch D 459

The directors of the defendant company obtained an investment from the plaintiff, representing that the money would be used to expand the company. The directors had no such intention; the money was to be used to pay off creditors. The plaintiff subsequently discovered the truth and sued the defendant for damages. The defendants argued that the statement was not a statement of fact, merely a statement of future intention.

COURT HELD

The plaintiff could succeed. While it was difficult to ascertain the state of a person's mind, when it could be ascertained it should be treated as a fact.

Statements of opinion

A statement of an opinion is not normally considered to be a verifiable fact. Therefore, generally an opinion cannot be held to be a misrepresentation. Where a person gives an opinion that he or she knows to be untrue, that may be treated as in *Edgington*, and it may be considered to be a fact. If an opinion is freely given when requested, with no deception intended, then no misrepresentation will occur. The following two cases illustrate these two rules.

Bisset v. Wilkinson (1927) 42 TLR 727

 This was a New Zealand case that was heard by the Privy Council. It concerned the sale of farmland. The vendor gave the opinion that the land would support 2,000 sheep. The land had never been used for sheep farming, the purchaser knew this and he also knew that the vendor was merely offering an opinion. The plaintiff later brought an action for rescission of the contract.

COURT HELD

The contract could not be rescinded: 'an erroneous opinion stated by the party affirming the contract, though it may have been relied upon and have induced the contract on the part of the party who seeks rescission, gives no title to relief unless fraud is established'. To establish fraud it would have been necessary to prove an intention to mislead.

Smith v. Land and House Property Corporation (1884) 28 Ch D 7

 This case concerned the sale of a hotel. It was described by the plaintiffs as having a most desirable tenant, with twenty-seven years of the lease to run. The plaintiffs agreed a price of £4,700 with the defendant company. Prior to the completion of the contract the hotel tenant went bankrupt. It emerged that the rent had not been paid and that the tenant had a history of non-payment. The defendant company refused to complete the contract and the plaintiffs sued for specific performance.

COURT HELD

The plaintiffs' action failed. Specific performance was not granted. The statement of opinion amounted to a misrepresentation, because the previous dealings with the tenant implied that it was an informed opinion, i.e. that the plaintiffs knew nothing detrimental about the tenant.

The fact must be material to the contract

A misrepresentation will generally be material to the case if, in the mind of a reasonable person, it would have affected that person's decision to enter the contract. For example, if Gareth misrepresented that his car had triple-speed windscreen wipers, when in fact it only had two-speed, then that probably would not be an actionable representation. However, if he said that the car was an excellent runner, when he knew that one of the pistons was not working, that probably would be an actionable misrepresentation.

In certain cases all representations are made **warranties** of the contract. In insurance contracts there is invariably a clause that makes all the proposer's answers material to the contract. This is known as a 'basis of the contract clause'. Where a proposer provides false information the insurance company can avoid the contract. The nature of the information is irrelevant, as the following case illustrates.

▶ **Warranty** – a term or promise in a contract, breach of which will entitle the innocent party to damages but will not result in the discharging of contractual obligations.

Dawsons Ltd v. Bonnin (1922) 2 AC 413

The plaintiffs insured one of their vehicles with the defendants. On the proposal form it was stated that the vehicle would be garaged in central Glasgow, when it was actually garaged on the outskirts of the city. The contract contained a 'basis of the contract clause'. The lorry subsequently caught fire and the plaintiffs claimed on the policy, while the defendants sought to avoid the policy on the basis of the clause.

COURT HELD

The defendants could avoid the contract. The clause meant that any untrue statement would enable the contract to be avoided.

Define misrepresentation. Outline the differences between a misrepresentation and a traders' puff.

The statement must be made to the other party

Where a misrepresentation is made to one party it will not be valid for another party to claim relief from it. This rule doesn't apply where the representor intended that the misrepresentation should be passed on. The following two cases illustrate this.

Peek v. Gurney (1873) LR 6 HL 377

A shareholder, who had bought shares on the stock market relying on details from the company prospectus, sought to gain redress from the directors who had made false statements in the document.

 COURT HELD
The plaintiff could not succeed. The misrepresentation was only meant to induce people to invest at the time that the prospectus was published. After that time its use was spent.

► Now Peek could probably find statutory relief from the Financial Services Act 1986, s. 150(1): 'the person or persons responsible for any listing particulars or supplementary listing particulars shall be liable to pay compensation to any person who has acquired any of the securities in question and suffered loss in respect of them as a result of any untrue or misleading statement in the particulars.'

 Under what circumstances may a failure to make a statement become an actionable misrepresentation? Ivan wants to sell his car to Jane. It has scratches all down one side, so he parks it against the wall in order to hide the condition. Jane views the car and purchases it, no mention being made of the scratches. Is Ivan guilty of a misrepresentation or is it just a case of *caveat emptor*?

Andrews v. Mockford (1896)

A gold-mining company wished to sell shares that they had issued, which had not been very well received by the public. They dispatched an 'expert' to South Africa who then falsely reported a rash of gold strikes in that area. This was aimed at increasing the value of the company and consequently the value of the shares. The plaintiff bought the shares on the stock market, having been influenced by the misrepresentation. On discovering the truth he sued the defendants.

 COURT HELD
The plaintiff could succeed. The defendants had intended that the misrepresentation should influence the whole of the general public. Where the shares had been purchased was irrelevant.

The statement must induce the contract

This can be considered to be a question of fact. If there is any question as to whether a party was induced into a contract by the misrepresentation, then it must be proved that he or she was. Where a misrepresentation is made that has not induced a contract, a party will not be able to claim relief from it. If a party knows the misrepresentation to be untrue then he or she is not being induced, or where, although the representation was false the party was not deceived by it, then again he or she will not have been induced.

The following two cases illustrate these points.

Horsefall v. Thomas (1862)

This case concerned the sale of a gun. The defendant had inserted a metal pin into the barrel of the gun to disguise a weak point. The plaintiff bought the gun without examining it. When it was fired it exploded. The plaintiff sued the defendant.

COURT HELD

The plaintiff could not succeed. He had not been induced into the contract by the misrepresentation.

The next case shows that even where a misrepresentation has been made, and a party has been given the means of ascertaining the truth, the representor will not escape the consequences.

Redgrave v. Hurd (1881) 20 Ch D 1

(EQ) The plaintiff, a solicitor, wished to take a partner into his practice. He placed an advert in the *Law Times* which was answered by the defendant. At an interview between the two parties the plaintiff stated that the income from the practice was £300 per annum. He produced accounts for 1877, 1878 and 1879 that showed that annual income amounted to £200 per annum. When questioned about the difference in figures the plaintiff produced other papers that he said accounted for the difference. In reality the papers only showed a further small income, still leaving the total at around £200. The defendant didn't examine the papers in great detail and agreed to join the practice. A price of £1,600 was agreed and the defendant placed a deposit of £100. The defendant later found out the truth and refused to complete the contract. The plaintiff sued for specific performance, while the defendant counterclaimed for rescission.

COURT HELD

Specific performance would not be granted, but rescission would. The defendant had been induced by the
misrepresentation, *notwithstanding the fact that he had been given the means of discovering the truth.*

Get together with two or three other students. Discuss whether any of you has entered a contract suffering a misrepresentation. Try to identify the different elements of the misrepresentation. Were you very dissatisfied after the contract? Did you take any legal advice or action? What would have been your legal remedies?

Different types of misrepresentation

There are three different types of misrepresentation: innocent, negligent and fraudulent. It is important to establish the specific type because different remedies apply to each of them. The common-law and equitable remedies have been supplemented with statutory remedies, under the Misrepresentation Act 1967.

Innocent misrepresentation

An innocent misrepresentation is one made absolutely free from fraud or negligence. It is a statement made in the belief that it is true, the representor having some grounds for believing it to be true.

Remedies

The equitable remedy of rescission (see above) is available, subject to the restrictions placed on it.

Under the Misrepresentation Act 1967, s. 2(2), a plaintiff cannot request damages. However, a court at its discretion may award damages, instead of rescission, when it is just and equitable to do so. The option of rescission must still be available for the court to exercise this option.

Negligent misrepresentation

A negligent misrepresentation is one made free from any fraud. It is a statement made where the person making it believes it to be true but has no reasonable grounds for doing so.

Remedies

▶ Rescission is available in addition to damages, or instead of suing for damages.

The common-law remedy was that of rescission but after the following very important case it was established that damages could be obtained when a negligent misstatement had been made.

Hedley Byrne and Co. Ltd v. Heller and Partners Ltd (1963) 2 All ER 575

VC This case went to the House of Lords. The appellants were an advertising company and the respondents were merchant bankers. A company called Easipower had requested the appellants to advertise for them on television and this involved Easipower being given credit. The appellants requested a credit reference from the respondents, who were bankers to Easipower. The respondents gave a reference that indicated that their clients were 'respectfully constituted and considered good'. Easipower went into liquidation, causing the appellants to lose £17,000. The appellants sued the respondents to recover their losses.

COURT HELD

The appellants could not succeed because the respondents were protected by a disclaimer clause that enabled them to avoid any liability for their reference. However, this case established that, in the absence of the disclaimer, the appellants would have been able to succeed. The facts of this case gave rise to a 'duty of care' between the two parties, despite the fact that they were in a non-contractual and a non-fiduciary position.

Duty of care

For the 'duty of care' rule established in *Hedley* to be applicable, there must be a 'special relationship' that requires the party to take particular care. This will occur where one party has special knowledge, skills or expertise, and gives information to another party knowing that the other will act upon that information. Obvious examples include banks, architects, surveyors, building societies and credit reference agencies.

Alternatively, damages can be claimed under the Misrepresentation Act 1967, s. 2(1), where a statutory right to damages is established where a party has suffered loss caused by a negligent misrepresentation. The onus of proof lies with the defendant to prove that he or she was not negligent, to avoid having to pay damages. Rescission has also been granted under this section.

Fraudulent misrepresentation

A fraudulent misrepresentation is one made in the knowledge or belief that it is untrue, or where the person making it is reckless or uncaring as to the truth of the fact. It must be more than just being negligent as to the truth, since an element of dishonesty is required.

Remedies

The equitable remedy of rescission and/or damages may be available, the damages action being brought under the tort of deceit. Any loss resulting from the fraud can be claimed to place the injured party in a similar position to the pre-contractual state.

The following case is the major case on fraudulent misrepresentation, illustrating the necessity of an element of dishonesty.

Derry v. Peek (1889) 14 App Cas 337

The appellants were the directors of Plymouth, Devonport and District Tramways Company, who were statutorily empowered to run trams by animal power and by consent of the Board of Trade, by steam and mechanical power. The directors issued a prospectus inviting share applications, stating that they had the right to run steam trams and that this would result in considerable savings. The Board of Trade subsequently refused to allow them to use steam on the length of the tramway and the company was wound up. The directors were sued for fraud by the respondent.

COURT HELD

The representation was not fraudulent, since when it was made the directors honestly believed it to be true.

ACT Outline the main provisions of the Misrepresentation Act 1967. What remedies does it provide for innocent, negligent and fraudulent misrepresentation?

DURESS

▶ **Duress** – pressure, especially actual or threatened physical force, put on a person to act in a particular way.

We have seen that all contracts must be freely entered into and that there must be a *consensus ad idem*. It is possible for a contract to be void or voidable through **duress**. If one party procures a contract by threatening the other party, or their friends or relatives, with violence, then that would constitute duress. Such a contract will be void or voidable. Duress is an old common-law concept referring to threats of violence. In recent times the concept of duress has been extended by equity to include economic threats and threats to property.

Violence to a person to induce a contract

The threat of violence must be unlawful, i.e. a threat to do something contrary to the criminal or common law; this includes false imprisonment. The following case illustrates that a threat of violence to a person will enable a contract to be avoided.

Barton v. Armstrong (1975) 2 All ER 465

This case was heard by the Privy Council. Armstrong and Barton were the chairman and managing director of an Australian company. Armstrong threatened to kill Barton unless he bought out his shares at a premium price and paid him a large amount of cash. Barton did as he was bid and later sought to have the agreement voided.

COURT HELD

The agreement was signed under duress. Barton was able to avoid the contract.

Economic threats

The courts have been prepared to widen the definition of duress to include economic threats. This is allowed only where the parties concerned are in an unequal bargaining position, i.e. where one party makes economic threats that are unwarranted and would probably cause economic loss to the other party. This is best explained by the following case.

***North Ocean Shipping Co. Ltd v. Hyundai Construction Co. Ltd, The Atlantic Baron* (1979) 3 WLR 419**

The two parties had contracted for the building and supplying of a ship. The defendants were the builders and the plaintiffs were the future owners. A price of $30,950,000 was agreed, to be paid in five instalments. The first payment was made in April 1972. In February 1973, when the dollar was devalued by 10 per cent, the defendants claimed an increase of 10 per cent on all the remaining four instalments. The plaintiffs declined but offered to go to arbitration to set a new figure. The defendants insisted that the extra 10 per cent be paid or they would return the first instalment and cancel the agreement. Meanwhile the plaintiffs had entered into a lucrative contract to let the tanker, upon completion, for a period of three years. If they failed to agree to the demand they would lose this second contract. The plaintiffs replied to the defendants agreeing to the increase, stating that they were not obliged to make the payments and that any payment made would not be prejudicial to their rights. The defendants accepted this arrangement. The contract was completed and in July 1975 the plaintiffs sued to recover the extra payments that they had been forced to make. The court action was delayed because they were concerned that the yard might refuse to deliver another tanker, which was the subject of a separate contractual agreement between them.

COURT HELD

The agreement had been entered into under duress, therefore, the contract was voidable, but the plaintiffs could not recover the money paid because they had affirmed the contract by delaying their claim.

Threats to property

Courts have been slow to allow threats to property to render a contract void through duress. However, it would now seem likely that, should circumstances arise where a person entered into a contract because threats had been made to damage his or her car or other valuable property, then duress might make a contract void or voidable.

1 Define duress.
2 Carla wants Ben to enter into a contract to purchase supplies from her. Ben doesn't want to because he can get the supplies cheaper elsewhere. Carla tells Ben that if he doesn't take her supplies she will tell the trading standards department that some of Ben's goods contravene European safety standards. Does this constitute duress?

▶ We have recently seen a spate of blackmail crimes, where goods have been threatened or damaged and large sums of money have been demanded. A Metropolitan police officer inserted splinters of glass into baby-food jars and then demanded money to reveal which bottles had been tampered with. It was after this incident that companies started to seal glass jars with a cellophane seal. Could this sort of crime be fitted to a situation of duress?

UNDUE INFLUENCE

We have seen that there is no real consent to a contract if it has been entered into under duress. Another situation in which a contract can be said to have been not freely entered into is where there is undue influence. An equitable remedy has evolved to protect parties who have suffered from undue influence. Undue influence occurs when someone from a position of power has exercised influence over another, which has resulted in the other party's entering into a grossly unfair contract or making a gift to the first party. The following relationships are recognized as being more likely to be ones where influence is exercised by one over another: parent–child; solicitor–client; doctor–patient; trustee–beneficiary; religious sect–follower; agent–principal.

▶ **Presumption** – an assumption made by the law.

In these above-mentioned relationships there is a **presumption** that there has been undue influence. It is for the influencing party to prove that there was no undue influence, thus establishing that the contract was freely entered into. This might be proved, for example, by evidence that independent advice had been taken. It will be for the court to decide whether a special or confidential relationship exists. In one exceptional set of circumstances, for example, a court ruled that there was a presumption of influence in a landlord–lodger relationship.

Where there is no such special or confidential relationship, it will be for the person claiming to have been influenced to prove that undue influence has taken place. The onus of proof shifts. Where a party is influenced to enter a contract by a third party, a stranger to the contract, it will not be voidable through undue influence.

The following cases illustrate the practical application of undue influence.

Allcard v. Skinner (1887) 3 TLR 751

 The plaintiff, a spinster, became a member of a Church of England Sisterhood, on the advice of the spiritual director. While she was a member she made gifts of property and money, without receiving any independent advice. She left the Sisterhood in 1879 and in 1884 claimed the return of the property.

 COURT HELD
The gifts were voidable through undue influence, though the plaintiff could not recover the goods because she had delayed her claim.

Lancashire Loans Ltd v. Black (1934) 1 KB 380

 A daughter, who was married and living in her own home, was induced by her mother to enter into an agreement with a moneylender, whereby the mother obtained money. A further similar arrangement was entered into. The daughter received no independent advice and did not understand the nature of the contracts. The money-lender later sued for money due under the arrangement. The daughter asked for the agreement to be set aside, alleging that undue influence had been exercised.

COURT HELD
The daughter could avoid the contract. The presumption of undue influence still remained, despite the fact that the daughter had married and left home. The presumption had not been rebutted, therefore the contract should be set aside.

▶ **Rebutted** – disproved by the acceptance of evidence to the contrary.

Inche Noriah v. Shaik Alli Bin Omar (1929) AC 127

 This case concerned a nephew and his elderly aunt. The nephew was managing his relative's financial affairs and he arranged for the majority of her assets to be transferred to him, by deed of gift. She had only received advice from the nephew's solicitor, who advised her that the gift was irrevocable. The aunt sought to have the deed set aside because she had been induced by undue influence.

COURT HELD
The deed should be set aside because the nephew had failed to rebut the presumption of undue influence.

A recent case has demonstrated that the law is by no means clear on the question of undue influence. The case illustrates what appears to be an extension of the application of undue influence.

Barclays Bank plc v. O'Brien (1993) The Times 22 October

 In this case, Mrs O'Brien was induced by a misrepresentation made by her husband to stand surety for the debt of her husband's company. The surety involved her executing a legal charge over the matrimonial home, in favour of Barclays Bank. Mr O'Brien had told Mrs O'Brien that the charge was to last for three weeks and was only to the value of £60,000. Barclays prepared the documents and sent them to the branch with instructions to ensure that both the husband and wife were fully aware of the implications of the documents. They were to be advised that, if they were in any doubt, they should consult a solicitor before signing the document. The local branch of Barclays failed to advise the O'Briens as instructed. Mrs O'Brien signed the legal document without reading it, believing it to be limited to £60,000 and to be of three weeks' duration. When Mr O'Brien's company overdraft rose to £154,000 the bank brought proceedings to enforce the legal charge. Mrs O'Brien claimed that she had been induced to sign the legal charge by the misrepresentation and undue influence exercised by her husband.

COURT HELD

The court of first instance rejected both defences. The Court of Appeal reversed the decision, though it rejected undue influence, accepting the defence of misrepresentation. The court stated that Mrs O'Brien would be liable for £60,000, the amount that she thought she was executing the charge for. The House of Lords held that the charge would be set aside, where a wife or other cohabitee was induced by undue influence, misrepresentation or other legal wrong, to stand surety for a partner's debt. A creditor would be presumed to have been notified of the intention of the assignee to set aside the transaction. To avoid this a creditor would have to warn the assignee, at a meeting at which the other partner was not present, of the legal consequences of signing the legal charge. The creditor should also warn the assignee to seek legal advice before signing the document.

It would appear that the normal rule in relation to banks and their clients is that where a bank has properly advised a client about a course of action that the client wishes to take, then no fiduciary or special relationship exists. Therefore, a bank need not advise a client to seek independent advice. Where a bank's advice is erroneous, it would seem to be more suitable to seek redress for negligence, as established in the *Hedley Byrne* case.

Remedies

Undue influence will make a contract voidable, thus enabling rescission to take place subject to the rules governing that equitable remedy. For example, if a third party, in innocence of the undue influence, purchases property for a reasonable price, he or she will acquire good title to the property, i.e. will be able to retain the property against an action from the original owner. In such circumstances the injured party will have to recover any proceeds of the sale from the influencing party. If a third party purchases property in full knowledge of the facts, he or she will not obtain good title to the property and may be ordered to return it to the original owner.

UNCONSCIONABLE BARGAINS

There is one other situation where a court may decide that there has been no real consent to a contract, and that is where the contract is an unconscionable bargain. This is a difficult concept to understand and explain. Loosely, an unconscionable bargain could be described as a contract that is on very unfair terms, but, as we have previously learned, the law is not concerned with whether or not a party obtains a good deal from a contract. It is legally possible to buy a Rolls-Royce for £5, provided the contract satisfies the prerequisite criteria.

In certain exceptional circumstances, however, courts have been prepared to recognize an equitable remedy of unconscionable bargain. It is not possible to state the exact circumstances when this will happen, as each case must be taken on its own merits. The circumstances will be very similar to those of undue influence and duress: there is unequal bargaining power; no independent advice is given; and the contract appears to be grossly disadvantageous to the party. However, there need be no dishonest intent on behalf of the party gaining from the contract, who may simply be acting in his or her own best interests or those of his or her company, without considering the other party.

The following case is one where the concept of an unconscionable bargain was discussed.

Lloyds Bank v. Bundy (1974) 3 All ER 757

(EQ)
(VC)
The defendant was an elderly farmer, whose family had banked with Lloyds at the same branch for a number of years. His son started a plant hire company which ran into difficulties. In 1966 the father guaranteed the son's overdraft of £1,500, placing a charge on his farm to secure the sum. The son's business deteriorated and the farmer, on the advice of the branch manager, agreed to further charges being levied on the farm to the value of £11,000, this figure being more than the farm was worth. In 1970 the bank demanded repayment of the monies, which the farmer was unable to pay. The bank commenced the action for possession of the farm.

COURT HELD
The court set aside the contracts through undue influence.
The circumstances of the case amounted to a presumption of undue influence, which the bank had failed to rebut. However, the court appeared to recognize the existence of an unconscionable bargain, under which a party might be able to gain relief, as described above.

(ACT) Which rebuttable presumption exists in relation to undue influence? How can the presumption be rebutted and on whom does the onus of proof rest? Where there is no such presumption, who then has to prove their case?

(ACT) Now that you have completed this chapter, look back at the chapter objectives at the beginning. Can you do all the things that these suggest? If not, look again at the relevant sections of the chapter.

CHAPTER SUMMARY

1 Mistake will void a contract, where a court accepts that there has been an operative mistake, i.e. a mistake of fact that has prevented the formation of a contract.

2 Where there has been a mistake as to the subject matter of the contract – for example, where there is no real agreement, where the subject of the contract has been destroyed or where a person mistakenly agrees to buy his or her own property – then the contract will be void through mistake.

3 It will be very difficult for a person who has signed a contractual document to try and avoid it later by mistake. A person may plead *non est factum*, though an adult of sound mind is unlikely to be successful with this defence.

4 Where two parties meet face to face, it is unlikely that a contract for the sale of goods will be voided by mistake, where the identity of one of the parties proves to be false.

5 Equity can offer remedies to alleviate the harshness caused by mistake, namely rescission, rectification and the refusal to grant specific performance in cases where it would be unfair to do so.

6 When a contract has been induced by a misrepresentation it may, depending upon the type of misrepresentation, be voidable or damages may be available, or both.

7 A misrepresentation is a pre-contractual statement of a verifiable fact that is material to the contract, that is made to the other party, that induces the contract and that is untrue. Generally a statement of opinion cannot be held to be a misrepresentation.

8 In the following circumstances the failure to make a statement may amount to an actionable misrepresentation: *uberrimae fidei*; fiduciary relationships; changes of circumstances; statutory disclosure; half truths; hidden fraud.

9 A misrepresentation may be innocent, negligent or fraudulent.

10 For the 'duty of care' rule established in *Hedley* to be applicable, there must be a 'special relationship' that requires the party to take special care. This will occur where one party has special knowledge, skills or expertise, and gives information to another party knowing that the other will act upon that information.

11 The Misrepresentation Act 1967 provides a statutory right to damages where loss is caused by negligent misrepresentation.

12 Duress is the procuring of a contract by violence or threats of violence. The threats may be made directly to the other party, or to their friends or relatives.

13 In recent times courts have been prepared to accept duress in relation to economic threats and threats to property.

14 An equitable remedy has evolved to protect parties who have suffered from undue influence. Undue influence occurs when one party, from a position of power, has exercised influence

over another party resulting in the second party's entering into a grossly unfair contract or making a gift to the first party. In such cases there exists a rebuttable presumption that undue influence has been exercised.

15 An unconscionable bargain may occur in circumstances very similar to that of undue influence and duress: there is unequal bargaining power, no independent advice is given and the contract appears to be grossly disadvantageous to the party. There need be no dishonest intent on the part of the party gaining from the contract.

13 *Discharge of contracts*

Chapter objectives

By the end of this chapter you should be able to:

▊ recognize the four ways of discharging a contract: agreement, performance, frustration and breach

▊ understand the concept of frustration, and the reasons for its growth and historical development

▊ know the ways in which a contract may be breached

▊ appreciate the purpose and different types of awards of damages, including the important concept of remoteness of damage

▊ recognize the equitable remedies available for breach of contract: rescission, specific performance, injunction and *quantum meruit*.

The legal obligations placed on the parties to a contract will end when the contract is completed or performed. However, as we have seen, life is not as simple as that. We must examine what happens when there is a dispute about the method of performance, when there is no performance and when there is only part performance.

Broadly speaking, contractual obligations can be ended in one of four ways:

1 agreement;
2 performance;
3 frustration; and
4 breach.

DISCHARGE BY AGREEMENT

As a contract has been formed by agreement between the contracting parties, so may it be discharged. This may be achieved by one of the following:

(a) agreement by the operation of a term in the existing contract;
(b) agreement to a release under seal;
(c) agreement according to the doctrine of accord and satisfaction;
(d) agreement via a waiver or with a new contract.

► Remember from Chapter 9 the seven essential elements of a simple contract:
1 agreement;
2 consideration;
3 intention to create legal relation;
4 form;
5 capacity;
6 legal purpose;
7 reality of consent.

Operation of a term in the existing contract

There may be a term in the contract that specifies a time for the end of the contract. These terms are commonly found in contracts for the lease of premises and in contracts of employment. It is normal in commercial premises contracts, such as for the lease of a shop or an office, for the leasehold to be for a fixed period of time, such as five years. At the end of that period the premises return to the control of the owner and the leaseholder either leaves the premises, having no further rights under the contract, or negotiates a new contract.

Contracts of employment are subject to the terms and conditions specified in the Employment Protection (Consolidation) Act 1978 (EPA78). The Act lays down certain minimum periods for the giving of notice to terminate employment. These are dependent upon the length of time that a person has been employed with the company. For example, a contract of employment might have a clause for 'three months' notice' either way. This means that, providing no other laws are being broken (race relations, sex discrimination, redundancy, unfair dismissal, etc.), either the employer or the employee may give three months' notice to the other party to bring the contract to an end.

Other types of contract may contain **conditions** or clauses that may provide for the discharge of obligations between the parties. These fall into three main types: determination clauses; conditions precedent; conditions subsequent.

Determination clauses

This type of contract is mostly to be found in the civil engineering and building industries. It allows one of the parties to the contract, normally the party that has commissioned the contract, to **determine** the contract upon the serious default of the other party.

Conditions precedent

A condition precedent has the effect of not creating contractual obligations until the condition specified in the contract arises. When the specified precedent occurs, then the contract comes into existence. If the condition precedent does not occur, or does not occur within the time period specified in the contract, then the contract will be discharged. For example, Jenny was expecting to be promoted and to be given a company car. Jenny entered into a contract with Ray, to sell him her existing car for £555, which contained a condition precedent stating 'should Jenny not be promoted within one month of the date of this contract, the agreement will be discharged'.

Conditions subsequent

A condition subsequent has the opposite effect to that of a condition precedent. It allows for the discharging of contractual obligations upon the occurrence of a specified event. For example, a

► Normally there will be an option for the renewal of a commercial leasehold contract, which will also have specified times for a rent review (for review, read increase), for example, a fifteen-year lease, with five-yearly rent reviews, with an option for renewal for a further fifteen-year period.

► See Chapters 20 and 21 for more details of the EPA78.

► **Conditions** – the most important terms in a contract, going to the root of the contract and being vital to the main purpose of the contract.

► **Determine** – end (a contract).

catering company could have entered into a contract to supply the workers, engineers and administrative staff of Channel Tunnel plc, the contract containing a condition subsequent stating 'this agreement to end on the day of the first commercial opening of the Channel Tunnel' (2010!).

Release under seal

> ► **Executory contract** – a contract where parties promise to perform certain acts in the future.

This applies in the case of an **executory contract**, where one party to the contract has failed fully to complete his or her side of the agreement. The party who is owed the obligation may agree to forgo the completion of the contract by the other party. This agreement must be made in the form of a written deed, because the other party has supplied no consideration for this action. If such an agreement were not in the form of a written deed it would be invalid. The party that had forgone its rights could later commence an action to enforce the contract or seek damages.

> ► Under the provisions of the Limitation Act 1980, an action on a simple contract must be brought within six years from the date of the breach. After six years the action will become 'statute barred', i.e. prohibited, by the Limitation Act 1980.

Doctrine of accord and satisfaction

The doctrine of accord and satisfaction also applies to executory contracts, where one party has failed to complete his or her side of the bargain. The injured party may accept something else in place of what had originally been offered. However, for this to be contractually binding there must be real agreement between the parties, and the injured party must not be forced into accepting the alternative, being under the threat of 'it's this or nothing'. The agreement to accept the new offer becomes the accord and the offer becomes the new consideration for the agreement. There must be an element of consideration for the accord and satisfaction to be binding, and for the contractual obligations to be discharged. For example, Roger ordered and paid for a black three-door Range Rover, to be delivered by Wilson's Garage. If the garage then offered a black and grey Range Rover, fitted out to a higher specification, for the same price and Roger accepts that offer, then that would discharge all other contractual obligations. (He could reject it if they failed to complete the contract and sue for breach.) In effect a new agreement is substituted for the old contract.

> ► See Chapter 10, page 157, for more on consideration and the settlement of debt.

Waiver and new contracts

Where, in an executory contract, neither side has completed its undertakings under the agreement, each side may agree to waive the other's obligations. This really becomes a new contract, with the consideration being represented by the forgoing of the rights under the contract. The new contract may merely agree to waive the existing agreement totally or it may substitute different obligations and live on in the form of a new contract.

DISCHARGE BY PERFORMANCE

In order to discharge contractual obligations a party must perform his or her side of the contract exactly as agreed in the contract. If the party performs them differently, or less than completely, that party will not have discharged his or her contractual obligations. The injured party may commence an action for damages for breach of contract. In an executory contract concerning the delivery of goods followed by payment, the party delivering the goods will generally not be able to bring an action under the contract for non-payment, until that party has fully discharged his or her obligations.

Completeness of performance

In general, then, for a party to discharge a contract by performance, that performance must be as agreed in the contract. This rule is a good guideline but is only part of the story. In the first of the following situations the rule does apply; the others are qualifications or exceptions to it:

1 in entire contracts;
2 in divisible contracts;
3 where there is substantial performance;
4 where partial performance is accepted;
5 where performance is prevented by the other party.

Entire contracts

In an entire contract only complete performance will result in the cessation of contractual obligations. The case described below is a very good illustration of this principle, showing how this rule can be extremely harsh.

Cutter v. Powell (1795) 6 Term Rep 320

 This case concerned a seaman who was employed as a second mate on the ship *Governor Parry*, on a voyage from Jamaica to England. His contract contained the following term: 'I promise to pay Mr T. Cutter the sum of thirty guineas, provided he proceeds, continues and does his duty as second mate in the said ship from hence to the port of Liverpool.' Cutter performed his duties but unfortunately died before the ship reached Liverpool. His wife sued for his wages claiming a ***quantum meruit***.

 COURT HELD
The wife could not succeed. The term in the contract made the agreement an entire contract which Cutter had failed to perform fully.

This case has been overtaken by legislation, as there are now rules under various Merchant Shipping Acts that make provision for

▶ ***Quantum meruit*** – as much as he or she deserves; an equitable remedy granting a payment for goods or services received in partial fulfilment of a contract. In this case, Mrs Cutter was claiming that she should be paid for the services her husband performed up to his death.

circumstances such as those in this case. The Law Reform (Frustrated Contracts) Act 1943 would also enable the wife to recover for the services rendered by her husband. (See below, page 222, for information on frustration.)

The modern application of the rule relating to entire contracts can be seen in the following case.

Bolton v. Mahadeva (1972) 2 All ER 1322

 The plaintiff contracted to install a central heating system in the defendant's house, for a lump sum payment of £560. The system was poorly installed, gave off fumes and failed to work properly. It was estimated that it would cost £179 to make it work properly. The defendant refused to pay for the central heating system, and the plaintiff brought the action to recover lump sum payment.

> ### *COURT HELD*
> *The plaintiff could not succeed, as the central heating system was so defective that the plaintiff had not fully performed his contractual obligations. The nature of payment by lump sum, i.e. a price for the whole job, meant that it was an entire contract and the plaintiff could recover nothing.*

Divisible contracts

Where it is clear that the parties intended one contract to be a series of agreements – for example, in a contract for the delivery of goods where goods are to be delivered on the 4th, 11th and 21st of each month – then each agreement will be considered to be a separate contract. Unless the contract contains a clause that states otherwise, payment will be due and legally enforceable after each delivery. Thus the performance of each distinct part of the contract will discharge obligations for that part of the contract.

Substantial performance

In cases other than those of entire or divisible contracts, a contract may be judged by the courts as one that has been substantially performed. A party who has almost completed what he or she was contractually obliged to do should be able to recover, on a *quantum meruit*, payment for what has been done. However, the party seeking this remedy may face a counterclaim for breach of contract, covering the contractual obligations that he or she did not perform.

The following case shows how the courts have treated substantial performance.

Hoenig v. Isaacs (1952) 2 All ER 176

This case concerned the decoration of a flat. The defendant employed the plaintiff to decorate and furnish a one-bedroomed flat. Payment was to be made by instalments and the first two were paid in accordance with the contract. The plaintiff then claimed to have finished the work and asked for the balance of £450. The defendant moved into the flat but was unhappy with the work, refusing to pay the full amount, sending £100, leaving an outstanding balance of £350. The plaintiff sued to recover the outstanding amount. The defendant argued that there had not been complete performance or, alternatively, that the work had been completed negligently.

COURT HELD

The contract had been substantially performed, as all work agreed under the contract had been completed. The plaintiff could recover the £350, less an amount of £55 18s 2d, the cost of correcting the poorly completed work.

Partial performance

Where a contract is partially performed and that partial performance is accepted by the injured party, he or she will be bound to pay the contractual price for the partial performance. In a contract for the sale of goods where Ross has ordered 250 footballs from Jack and Jack delivers 230 footballs, the delivery being accepted, Ross will be bound to pay the contractual rate for those footballs. This is governed by the Sale of Goods Act 1979, s. 30(1), which states:

> Where the seller delivers to the buyer a quantity of goods less than he contracted to sell, the buyer may reject them, but if the buyer accepts the goods so delivered he must pay for them at the contract rate.

There must be a real option for the injured party. Where he or she is forced into accepting partial performance, the injured party will generally not be compelled to pay for any benefit that they have received.

The following case illustrates this last point.

Sumpter v. Hedges (1898) 46 WR 454

The plaintiff, a builder, contracted with the defendant to erect certain buildings upon the defendant's land for a price of £565. He partially completed the buildings to the value of £333 for which he received part payment. He then told the defendant that he would be unable to complete the contract because he had run out of money. The defendant then completed the buildings himself, using the materials left by the plaintiff. The plaintiff sued for payment of the agreed sum.

COURT HELD

The plaintiff could not succeed; the defendant had no choice as to whether to accept the partial performance. The plaintiff had merely abandoned the contract. The plaintiff was awarded the value of the material that the defendant used, but nothing on a quantum meruit claim.

Performance prevented

A party may be unable to perform his or side of the contract exactly as agreed in the contract because he or she is prevented from doing so by the other party. In such an event the party may sue for breach of contract, as illustrated in the following case.

Planché v. Colburn (1831) 8 Bing 14, 131, ER 305

The plaintiff, an author, was contracted to write a volume on costume and armour for the 'Juvenile Library', for a fee of £100. Before the author could complete the work the defendant company scrapped the series. The plaintiff sued for breach of contract.

COURT HELD
The plaintiff succeeded and was awarded £50.

(ACT) In what four ways may a contract be discharged? Where a contract is discharged by performance, outline the rules relating to entire contracts and substantial performance, making reference to relevant cases.

Performance and the time of performance

Where the time of performance of a contract is stated it will become an essential condition of that contract and failure to perform the contract by the given date will be a breach of contract. Where a date is not given then the contract must be performed within a reasonable time.

Sale of Goods Act 1979, s. 10

(1) Unless a different intention appears from the terms of the contract, stipulations as to time of payment are not of the essence of a contract of sale.
(2) Whether any other stipulation as to time is or is not of the essence of the contract depends on the terms of the contract.

Supply of Goods and Services Act 1982, s. 14

(1) Where, under a contract for the supply of a service by a supplier acting in the course of a business, the time for the service to be carried out is not fixed by the contract, left to be fixed in a manner agreed by the contract or determined by the course of dealing between the parties, there is an implied term that the supplier will carry out the service within a reasonable time.
(2) What is a reasonable time is a question of **fact**.

▶ What is a reasonable time is a question of **fact** – in law a fact is that which may be decided by the court as being a fact, according to the circumstances of the case. For example, a court might decide that thirty days was a reasonable time in one set of circumstances and in another case it might decide on three months. In each case the selected time span would be considered to be a fact.

Where there is a delay in the performance of a contractual obligation, the question will arise of whether time was 'of the essence' of the contract. In commercial transactions it is normally presumed that time is of the essence, thus the time of performance will become a condition of the contract. However, where no time is stated then time will not initially be of the essence, performance having to be completed in a reasonable time. It must be remembered that early performance may have the same effect as late performance. In a contract for the delivery of goods where time is of the essence, early delivery will allow the receiving party to reject the delivery. If the contract is not then fully completed they will also be able to sue for breach of contract.

Where time is not of the essence in a contract and one party is extremely slow in performing its contractual obligations, a notice can be served on the defaulting party requiring it to complete its contractual obligations.

The following case illustrates this principle in action.

Charles Rickards Ltd v. Oppenheim (1950) 1 KB 616

The defendant bought a Rolls-Royce chassis from the plaintiffs, who contracted with a coach builder to build a car for the defendant. The exact details of the car body were agreed in August 1947, the car to be completed within six to seven months. The car was not completed on time but the defendant still agreed to accept delivery upon completion. By March 1948 the defendant had run out of patience. He wrote to the coach builders giving them notice that after 25 July 1948 he would not accept delivery of the car. The coach builders failed to meet the deadline and the defendant bought another car. In October 1948 the car was ready for delivery but the defendant refused to accept it. The plaintiffs sued to enforce the contract while the defendant counterclaimed for the cost of the Rolls-Royce chassis.

   COURT HELD
   The plaintiff could not succeed, but the defendant could
   succeed in his counterclaim for the cost of the Rolls-Royce
chassis. Initially, time was of the essence, though this had been waived
by the defendant. He had then made time of the essence again by
serving notice. The contract had not been fully performed by the given
time, so he was acting within his rights in rejecting the delivery.

Tender of payment

Where one party is under a contractual obligation to pay a sum of money he or she can discharge that obligation by the tendering of notes and coins, which must by law be accepted by the other party. The law places limits upon the tendering of amounts of copper, cupro-nickel and silver, but generally speaking notes and coins tendered in payment of a debt will discharge that debt. A payment by cheque will be conditional upon clearance, while a credit card payment will immediately discharge a debt.

DISCHARGE BY FRUSTRATION

There are times when contracts cannot be completed due to the influence of outside factors, or in personal service contracts due to illness or death. When this occurs a contract may be said to be frustrated. In order for frustration to apply, the supervening event must render the performance of the contract totally impossible. Where the contract just becomes more expensive, less profitable or more difficult to perform, then the contract will not be frustrated.

Historical background to frustration

It is only in more recent times that the courts have recognized the concept of frustration. The rule was that contractual obligations were absolute, this concept being best explained in the next case. I have included some quotations from the case as an illustration of the language of the time.

Paradine v. Jane (1647) King's Bench 82 ER 897

VC This case dates back to the English Civil War, concerning the lease of a property during that period and the non-payment of rent.

> [T]he defendant pleads, that a certain German prince, by name, Prince Rupert, an alien born, enemy to the king and kingdom, had invaded the realm with an hostile army of men; and with the same force did enter upon the defendant's possession, and him expelled, and held out of possession from July 19, 18 Car., till the Feast of the Annunciation, 21 Car., whereby he or she could not take the profits; whereupon the plaintiff demurred, and the plea was resolved insufficient.

If you have managed to understand this pleading you will now know that Prince Rupert took possession of this property for the Royalists during the Civil War, evicting the tenant. The tenant was contractually obliged to pay rent during that period even though he could not live at the premises. The landlord brought this action to recover the rent for this period.

COURT HELD
The landlord could recover the rent. The fact that the tenant could not live at the premises did not discharge him from his contractual obligations.

The courts first recognized the concept of frustration in the following case.

Taylor v. Caldwell (1863) 122 ER 826

 This contract concerned the hire of a music hall. The plaintiff contracted to hire the Surrey Gardens and Music Hall to give concerts. Prior to the date of the concerts the music hall was destroyed by fire. The plaintiffs sued for damages because they had spent money on advertising and other matters in preparation for the contract.

 COURT HELD
The contract was frustrated. Both parties were relieved of their contractual obligations. The court found for the defendants.

Effect of frustration on a contract

The situation governing the rights and duties of parties when a contract has become frustrated is governed by the Law Reform (Frustrated Contracts) Act 1943. Under the Act the following provisions apply:

1 any money paid is recoverable;
2 any money due ceases to be payable;
3 expenses incurred prior to frustration may be recovered;
4 where there has been partial performance prior to frustration and one party has received a valuable benefit (not a monetary payment), a *quantum meruit* may be available to the other party.

Exceptions to the Law Reform (Frustrated Contracts) Act 1943

The Act does not apply to contracts of insurance or voyage charterparties. It is also excluded by the Sale of Goods Act 1979 under the following two sections:

Sale of Goods Act 1979, s. 6

Where there is a contract for the sale of specific goods, and the goods without the knowledge of the seller have perished at the time when the contract is made, the contract is void.

Sale of Goods Act 1979, s. 7

Where there is an agreement to sell specific goods and subsequently the goods, without any fault on the part of the seller or buyer, perish before the risk passes to the buyer, the agreement is avoided.

Where the parties to a contract do not wish the Act to apply, they may exclude it by expressly agreeing to do so.

 Form a group to discuss the following problems. Make reference to relevant cases. Pauline ordered a flat-packed kitchen from Magic Kitchens, paying in full, delivery to be made within six weeks. What are the effects on the contract of the following events?

1 Delivery is made outside the six-week period, but Pauline accepts the delivery.
2 The delivery is made but one of the cabinets is different from the one that had been ordered.
3 No set date is made for delivery. After two months Pauline tells Magic Kitchens that unless delivery is made within fourteen days she will reject the whole consignment. Delivery is made four weeks later.

Different areas of frustration

The courts have tended to recognize frustration as occurring in the following areas:

(a) personal service contracts;
(b) subsequent illegality;
(c) cancellation of an event;
(d) destruction of the subject matter;
(e) frustration of the common venture;
(f) governmental and national emergency.

Personal service contracts

A personal service contract is one in which a person or group of persons is contracted to perform a certain act, for example, a singer is booked to appear at a night club. The death or incapacity of the person will frustrate the contract.

The following case gives an example of this type of frustration.

Robinson v. Davison **(1871) LR 6 Ex. 269**

The plaintiff entered into a contract with the defendant for her to accompany him on the piano. Prior to the performance the defendant fell ill and notified the plaintiff by letter that she would be unable to perform. The plaintiff sued for damages.

 COURT HELD
There was no fault attributable to either party and the contract was discharged by frustration.

Where the frustration has been caused by the fault of one of the parties then frustration will not apply. Most of the cases that illus-

► Michael Jackson was forced to postpone three concerts on his world tour in August 1993, owing to illness. His personal service contracts for those appearances were frustrated.

trate this point tend to have occurred in contracts of employment. The following case illustrates the non-application of frustration in such a case.

Norris v. Southampton City Council (1982) IRCR 141

 The plaintiff, a cleaner, was imprisoned for various offences. The defendants, his employers, wrote and dismissed him. Norris claimed unfair dismissal. The case went to the Employment Appeal Tribunal.

 COURT HELD
The contract was not frustrated because frustration was dependent upon neither party being at fault. In this case Norris had rendered himself unable to perform the contract. His actions amounted to a repudiatory breach of contract.

Subsequent illegality

Where parties agree a perfectly legal contract, which is later made illegal by legislation, the contract will be frustrated. This has tended to occur in times of war, when it becomes illegal to trade with the enemy. The 1990 Gulf War with Iraq affected a number of export contracts in this way.

Cancellation of an event

Where a particular event is the sole purpose of the contract, the cancellation of that event will, in the absence of any term or condition stating otherwise, probably frustrate the contract. Where the main purpose of the contract can still be achieved, but is affected in some more minor part by a cancellation, then the contract will not be frustrated. The following are the leading two cases on these two aspects of frustration.

Krell v. Henry (1903) 2 KB 740

The plaintiff advertised in the window of his flat that rooms in the flat were available for let, to view the Coronation procession. The defendant entered into a contract to rent the rooms for 26 and 27 June, the two days of the processions. On 24 June the defendant paid £25, leaving a balance of £50 to be paid. The procession was cancelled owing to the illness of the King. The defendant refused to pay the outstanding £50. The plaintiff sued to obtain the £50 while the defendant counterclaimed for the previously paid £25.

COURT HELD
The plaintiff could not succeed. The Coronation was the sole purpose of the contract, and it had been cancelled, thus frustrating the contract. Therefore, the counterclaim was successful.

Herne Bay Steamboat Co. v. Hutton (1903) 2 KB 683

 This case also concerned the illness of King Edward VII. The defendant agreed to hire the steamboat *Cynthia* on 28 June 'for the purpose of viewing the naval review and for a day's cruise round the fleet; also on 29 June, for a similar purpose'. On 25 June the review was postponed owing to the King's illness. The defendants failed to show up to take control of the boat that had been made ready for them. The plaintiffs redeployed the boat and sued for the loss of the balance of the fee of £150, the defendant having already paid a £50 deposit.

 COURT HELD
There was no frustration. The main purpose of the contract had not been defeated. It would have been possible to use the boat to tour around the assembled naval fleet. The plaintiffs were awarded the difference between the fee that they had been paid for the redeployment and the £200.

Destruction of the subject matter

This aspect has already been explained above, in *Taylor v. Caldwell*, where the subject matter of the contract, a music hall, was destroyed (see page 223).

Frustration of the common venture

This concept is similar to destruction of the subject matter, though in this instance the subject matter is not destroyed, but the commercial purpose of the venture becomes defeated. The parties can no longer achieve under the contract what they set out to do. The following case illustrates the commercial application of this rule.

Jackson v. Union Marine Insurance Co. (1874) LR 10 CP 125

▶ **Charter party** – a contract to hire a vessel, normally from one port to another for the purposes of moving goods.

The plaintiff, a ship owner, entered into a **charter party**, by which the ship was to proceed as quickly as possible from Liverpool to Newport, where it was to load a cargo of iron rails for San Francisco. To cover the eventuality of the ship failing to carry out the charter, the plaintiff took out a policy of insurance with the defendants. The ship sailed from Liverpool on 2 January 1872 and on 3 January ran aground in Carnarvon (now Caernarfon) Bay. It was freed on 18 February and repairs continued until the end of August. On 15 February the charterers abandoned the charter and hired another ship. The plaintiffs brought this action to claim on the insurance policy, while the defendants (the insurance company) alleged that there was no insurable loss because the plaintiffs could claim against the charterers for breach of contract.

COURT HELD
The plaintiff could succeed in claiming from the defendants. The charterers were not in breach of contract; the delay in

the ship being ready to take the cargo was so long as to put an end to the real commercial purpose of the contract. The contract between the ship owner and the charterers was discharged by frustration.

Government and national emergency

In times of war or other national emergency a government may requisition all supplies of food or other materials. At those times any parties that have contracted to supply the requisitioned articles, and who are no longer able to do so, may have their contracts discharged by frustration.

When frustration will not apply

Frustration will not apply in the following circumstances:

(a) where the agreement was impossible from the outset;
(b) where a contract merely becomes more difficult or expensive to perform;
(c) where there is provision in the contract for frustration;
(d) where a party is responsible for the act that caused the frustration;
(e) in contracts for the sale of land and leases.

 Define the legal concept of frustration. Making reference to relevant cases, outline when, in a personal service contract, frustration will (a) apply and (b) not apply.

Where the agreement was impossible from the outset

As we saw in Chapter 12, in the section on mistake, where two parties contract to do something that is not possible, the contract will be void by mistake. The contract will not be frustrated. Section 6 of the Sale of Goods Act 1979 also makes provision for this eventuality (see page 223).

Where a contract merely becomes more difficult or expensive to perform

Where a party has entered into a contract and that contract subsequently becomes more difficult or expensive to perform, he or she will not to be able to avoid contractual obligations through frustration. This means that a party might enter into a contract that at first is financially rewarding, but that, through some event, makes the contract unprofitable. The next case is a good example of this.

Tsakiroglou and Co. Ltd v. Noblee and Thorl Gmbh **(1962) AC 93**

The defendants entered into a contract to sell and deliver groundnuts from Port Sudan to Hamburg, to be shipped between November and December 1956. The Suez crises broke out, with England invading

► Remember *Couturier v. Hastie* (1856) 5 HLC 673 (see Chapter 12, p. 191), a case on mistake? The case concerned a shipment of corn that had become damaged in transit and sold to another party. Court held that the contract for the sale of the corn was made when both parties mistakenly believed it was still in existence, so the contract was void by mistake.

Egypt upon the closure of the Suez Canal. The defendants refused to complete the contract, claiming frustration, because they had planned to use the Suez Canal.

COURT HELD
The contract was not frustrated because it would still have been possible to deliver the goods via the Cape of Good Hope. The defendants were held to be in breach of contract.

Where there is provision in the contract for frustration

Where a contract makes provision for frustration that provision will apply. The modern application for this is to be found in pop concerts. The ticket will contain a term that states, for example, that, in the case of the cancellation or postponement of the concert, admission money will be returned upon application to the concert promoters.

Where a party is responsible for the act that caused the frustration

Where someone carries out an act that prevents them from performing their contractual obligations, they will not then be able to claim frustration. For example, if Jill agreed to transport corn from Arizona to Dundee on the good ship *William*, and she then sold the ship prior to completing the contract, she would not be able to claim frustration.

The following case illustrates that the event that causes the frustration of the contract must be outside the control of the parties and must not be caused by one of them.

Lauritzen (J.) AS v. Wijsmuller BV, The Superservant Two (1990) 1 Lloyd's Rep. 1

 The plaintiffs entered into a contract with the defendants to transport a drilling rig, using either of the ships *Superservant One* or *Superservant Two*. Prior to the date of performance one of the ships was destroyed. The defendants then refused to perform their part of the contract stating that the contract had become frustrated by the shipwreck.

COURT HELD
The defendants were in breach of contract. The sinking of one of the two ships had not frustrated the contract, as the contract could have been completed using the other vessel.

Contracts for the sale of land and leases

It is difficult to be conclusive about whether or not contracts in this section can be frustrated. No court has actually ruled on this matter, though in several instances courts have indicated a willingness to apply frustration to land and leases. The following case is an illustration of where a judge, in the House of Lords, indicated in his *obiter dicta* that frustration could apply to leases.

▶ *Obiter dicta* is explained in Chapter 3, p. 27.

National Carriers Ltd v. Panalpina (Northern) Ltd (1981) AC 675

The plaintiffs leased a warehouse to the defendants for a term of ten years from 1 January 1974 at a rent of £6,500 per annum for the first five years and £13,300 for the second five years. In May 1979 Hull City Council closed the only access road to the site because of the dangerous condition of a listed building. The closure prevented the defendants from using the premises as a warehouse. The road was closed for some twenty months, during which time the defendants ceased paying rent, claiming that the contract had been frustrated.

COURT HELD
The plaintiffs could succeed. The defendants must pay the rent. The House of Lords thought that frustration could be applied to leases. However, in this case the contract was not frustrated because access had only been denied for twenty months out of a ten-year lease. The House of Lords stressed that frustration of a lease would be very rare. I think that its decision was somewhat harsh on the defendants!

 Under what circumstances will frustration not apply? Explain the rule established in *Lauritzen (J.) AS v. Wijsmuller BV*.

DISCHARGE BY BREACH

A breach of contract occurs where a party fails to fully perform his or her contractual obligations. One party might repudiate a contract, by informing the other party, prior to the date of completion, that he or she has no intention of performing his or her contractual obligations. A repudiation is known as an **anticipatory breach** of contract. A party might perform an act that renders the completion of the contract impossible, and this is also an anticipatory breach. Simply, they might just fail to perform the contract in the agreed manner. Depending upon whether the defaulting party has been in breach of a term or a condition of the contract, certain remedies will be available to the other party.

▶ **Anticipatory breach** – an indication, either expressed in words or implied from conduct, that a contract will not be completed.

Types of breach

Breach of contract
A breach of contract occurs where one party fails fully to perform his or her contractual obligations. For example, in a contract for the

sale of goods the seller might deliver the wrong type of goods or fail to deliver the goods on time. Remember that in order to discharge contractual obligations performance must be completed in the exact manner specified in the contract. This rule is subject to exceptions. Certain contracts, for example, may allow given tolerances within which the goods must comply.

To discover if a breach of contract results in the discharging of contractual obligations, it must be established if the term breached is a **condition** or a **warranty**. Where a condition is breached the injured party has the choice of continuing with the contract and claiming damages, or of discharging himself or herself from the contract and claiming damages. A breach of a warranty only allows the injured party to claim for damages.

▶ See above (p. 215) for an explanation of **condition**, and Chapter 12 (p. 201) for an explanation of **warranty**. Note, however, that although warranties are usually less important terms in a contract, they are the important terms in a contract of insurance. If the insured breaches a warranty, the insurer can treat the contract as discharged by breach.

Anticipatory breach

A party may give notice that he or she has no intention of performing or is unable fully to perform his or her contractual obligations. When this occurs the injured party has a choice. He or she can immediately sue for breach of contract to obtain damages or can wait for the date of performance to arrive and then sue for damages. If the party takes the second option, he or she has to run the risk that some supervening act may render the contract void, thus preventing the party from claiming damages.

If a party chooses, he or she can ignore the repudiation by the other side, complete his or her part of the contract and then sue for the full amount due under the contract. For example, Monica contracted to place a series of advertisements in *Vogue* over a period of three months. Before the first advertisement appeared she changed her mind and wrote to *Vogue* cancelling the advertisements. *Vogue* could ignore Monica's repudiation, continue to place the adverts and then seek the full contract price at the end of the contracted period.

Where Stuart enters into a contract with Barbara to sell her his car on 14 November, and on 3 November sells the car to Derek, then obviously he will not be able to complete the contract. As soon as Barbara becomes aware that Stuart is not going to be able to complete the contract, she can bring an action for damages or she can wait for the date of performance.

The following three cases concern anticipatory breaches.

Hochester v. De la Tour (1853) 2 E & B 678

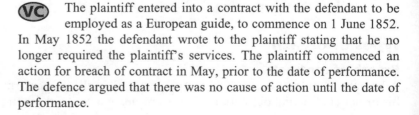 The plaintiff entered into a contract with the defendant to be employed as a European guide, to commence on 1 June 1852. In May 1852 the defendant wrote to the plaintiff stating that he no longer required the plaintiff's services. The plaintiff commenced an action for breach of contract in May, prior to the date of performance. The defence argued that there was no cause of action until the date of performance.

COURT HELD

The plaintiff could succeed. The defendant had repudiated the contract which constituted an actionable breach of contract.

Avery v. Bowden (1855) 5 E & B 714

The defendant chartered the ship *Lebanon*, which belonged to the plaintiff. Under the charter the ship was to be loaded with cargo at Odessa within 45 days. The ship went to Odessa where it awaited cargo. The defendant informed the captain of the ship that he was not going to be able to provide a cargo for the ship and that the ship should leave. However, the captain decided to wait until the expiry of the 45-day period, hoping that the defendant would be able to provide a cargo. Before the 45 days were up the Crimean war broke out and all contracts with the enemy were made illegal. The plaintiff sued for breach of contract.

COURT HELD

The plaintiff could not succeed. Had he treated the defendant's repudiation as an anticipatory breach of contract he could have succeeded. The supervening event had discharged all contractual obligations.

General Bill Posting Co. v. Atkinson (1909) AC 118

The defendant entered into a contract of employment with the plaintiff company, which contained terms allowing for twelve months' notice either way, and that within two years of the termination of employment the defendant would not work as a bill poster within 50 miles of the plaintiff company, without the permission of the company. The company then sacked the defendant, failing to give the required notice. The defendant then set up in business within 50 miles of the plaintiff company. The plaintiffs brought the action seeking an injunction and damages for breach of the contract.

COURT HELD

The House of Lords held that the plaintiffs could not succeed. By their act of disregarding the period of notice, they had repudiated the contract, leaving the defendant discharged from any of the other terms.

ACT Outline, using your own fabricated examples, circumstances that illustrate the three ways that a breach of contract may take place.

▶ In *Frost v. Knight* (1872) LR 7 Exch 111, a contract to marry upon the death of a parent was anticipatorily breached, the disappointed woman successfully obtaining damages under the principle in *Hochester*. Breach of promise to marry is no longer applicable, abolished by the Law Reform (Miscellaneous Provisions) Act 1970.

Damages

When a breach of contract occurs the injured party has various remedies available to him or her. A common-law right to recover damages is available for every breach of contract, flowing from the Latin maxim *ubi jus ibi remedium*. An award of damages, in the form of financial compensation, is aimed at placing a person in the position that he or she would have been in had the contract taken place.

There are three main forms of damages that can be awarded.

1 **Nominal damages** – these are awarded when a breach of contract has occurred, though the breach has been minor and no losses have been caused. For example, an award of a penny has been made.
2 **Substantial damages** – the aim of this award is to put the person in the financial position that he or she would have been in had the contract been performed.
3 **Exemplary damages** – these are awarded to give the plaintiff far more, in financial terms, than has been lost through the breach. They are only awarded in extremely rare cases and it is enough that you are aware of their existence.

Damages may be either **liquidated** or **unliquidated**.

Liquidated damages

When parties are agreeing the terms of a contract, they may make a provision as to what financial penalties should be paid in the event of a breach. This is known as a liquidated damages clause and it will normally be found in commercial contracts. To be valid, a liquidated damages clause must attempt to be a real pre-estimate of the anticipated effect of the breach. Where a court accepts a liquidated damages clause, it will enforce the clause regardless of the actual sustained loss. Therefore, where parties fix a small amount as liquidated damages, the figure will be valid, regardless of the fact that it is not a genuine pre-estimation of loss.

If the clause just allows for the payment of a large amount that has been randomly arrived at with no real attempt to pre-gauge the effect of a breach, it will be treated as a **penalty clause** and will not be enforced. A court will ignore the penalty clause, and follow the rules detailed in the unliquidated damages section, to establish the amount of damages.

The following two cases illustrate these points.

Dunlop Pneumatic Tyre Co. Ltd v. New Garage and Motor Co. Ltd **(1915) 30 TLR 625**

The plaintiffs supplied their goods to the defendants under an agreement whereby, in consideration of a trade discount, the defendants undertook not to tamper with marks on the goods; not to sell below list

---

► ***Ubi jus ibi remedium*** – where a right exists, a remedy exists.

► **Liquidated damages** – a specified amount of damages.

► **Unliquidated damages** – a non-specified amount of damages.

► **Penalty clause** – a clause put into a contract to penalize any breach of the contract. There will have been no real attempt to measure any loss that might be caused by a breach. The penalty clause will just set a financial sum to be paid, should a breach occur.

► British Rail has put liquidated damages clauses into the Citizens' Charter.

prices; not to supply certain persons named by the plaintiffs; not to exhibit or export any of the goods; and to pay £5 by way of liquidated damages for each breach. The £5 was stated not to represent a penalty. The defendants sold an item in breach of the agreement and were sued under it.

COURT HELD

The House of Lords decided that the plaintiffs could succeed. The £5 represented a pre-estimate of what the breach would cost the plaintiffs.

Cellulose Acetate Silk Co. Ltd v. Widnes Foundry (1925) Ltd (1933) **AC 20**

The parties entered a contract for the construction of a foundry. It contained a liquidated damages clause, which agreed that £20 would be payable for each week that the foundry was not erected, past the specified contractual date. The defendants were 30 weeks late in constructing the foundry. The plaintiffs sought to recover their actual losses, an amount of nearly £6,000.

COURT HELD

The plaintiffs could only recover the amount of £20 per week, as agreed in the contract.

Unliquidated damages

Where the parties have made no provision for the level of damages to be awarded, the court will decide the amount to be paid. The purpose of the court is not to punish the defaulter but to compensate the injured party. The aim of the 'measure of damages' is to put the injured party in the position that he or she would have been in had the contract been performed.

When establishing the amount of damages to be awarded, the courts will need to consider the following questions.

1 What loss has been suffered by the plaintiff?
2 What type of damage should the plaintiff be compensated for, e.g. economic loss, remoteness, mental anguish?
3 Has the plaintiff taken any steps to **mitigate** his or her losses?

▶ **Mitigate** – reduce or lessen.

Damages awarded may include amounts for financial loss, personal injuries, pain and suffering, and inconvenience and discomfort.

(ACT) What are the three different types of damages and in what circumstances may they each be awarded? What is the difference between liquidated and unliquidated damages?

Remoteness of damage

Before we examine these aspects in detail, we must consider

remoteness of damage. It would not be fair, equitable or practical to award damages for every loss that arises out of a breach. For example, if Peter agreed a contract with John to buy his Morris Minor for £250 and, unbeknown to John, Peter had arranged to sell the car on to a Morris Minor maniac for £25,000, it would not be fair to penalize John if he breaches the contract with an award of £24,750 damages against him. A reasonable person would not have envisaged such a loss arriving from a breach of the contract. However, in the unlikely event of John entering into the contract knowing of Peter's plans, and of the second contract, then it would be fair to award the £24,750 damages.

The rules governing remoteness of damage were established in the following celebrated case.

Hadley v. Baxendale (1854) 9 Exch 341

The plaintiff, a miller, hired the defendant to transport a broken mill shaft to be repaired at the manufacturers. The defendant promised to deliver the shaft on the following day. They failed to do so, however, and delayed the transportation for an unreasonable period of time. The plaintiff claimed damages for loss of production.

 COURT HELD
The plaintiff could not succeed. Damages were too remote to be awarded. Damages could only be awarded where they were reasonably and fairly considered to have arisen under the following circumstances:

1 *losses arising naturally, according to the normal course of things; or*

2 *losses that may reasonably be supposed to have been in the contemplation of the parties, at the time that they made the contract, and were the probable result of a breach of that contract.*

In *Hadley*, the loss did not arise from the normal course of events because normally a miller would be expected to have a spare shaft. The special circumstances, that the mill could not function without the part, were not considered to be contemplated by the parties when the contract was formed, i.e. the carrier did not know that the mill couldn't work without the shaft!

The principle was further refined in the next case.

Victoria Laundry v. Newman Industries (1949) 2 KB 528

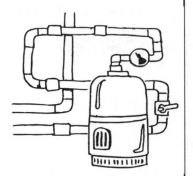

The plaintiffs ordered a boiler from the defendants, to be delivered on 5 June 1946. The defendants failed to deliver the boiler until 8 November, some five months late. The plaintiffs sued for loss of normal profits and loss of special profits of £262 per week, which they would have made from a special contract with the Ministry of Supply.

COURT HELD

The plaintiffs could recover for the normal profits, but they couldn't succeed in recovering the special profits. The special profits were not in the contemplation of both parties at the formation of the contract.

The court further refined the rules governing remoteness as follows.

1. The aggrieved party is only entitled to recover such part of the loss actually resulting, as was at the time of the contract reasonably foreseeable as liable to result from a breach of contract.
2. Reasonable foreseeability will depend upon imputed or actual knowledge. Imputed knowledge can be defined as that which every reasonable person is taken to know about the ordinary course of things. Actual knowledge occurs when a defendant is specifically told about a set of circumstances.
3. A plaintiff must show that if a reasonable defendant had considered the loss that a breach of contract would cause, he or she would have realized that the amount being claimed would have been likely to result from the breach.

The next case shows the modern, commercial application of remoteness.

Koufos v. Czarnikow Ltd (The Heron II) (1967) 3 All ER 686

The plaintiffs chartered the defendant's ship to carry a cargo of sugar from Constanza to Basrah. In breach of contract the defendant deviated on route, arriving nine days late at Basrah. The plaintiffs intended to sell the sugar upon arrival at Basrah. The defendant did not know this, but he did know that there was a sugar market at Basrah. Before the sugar could be sold the market price fell, partly owing to the arrival of another shipment. The plaintiff received £4,000 less than he would have done, had the contract been correctly performed. The plaintiff sued to recover the £4,000.

COURT HELD

The House of Lords allowed the plaintiffs to succeed. While the defendants did not know of the plaintiffs' intentions, it was held that it must have been in the contemplation of the parties that the sugar would be sold, as Basrah had a sugar market. Consequently it is reasonable to assume that during any delay in delivery the market price could fall, therefore causing the claimed losses. (The market price could have risen!)

In a contract for the sale of goods or services, if a party fails to pay the agreed price, then a plaintiff can only claim the agreed price. Remoteness and the measure of damages will not be applicable.

▶ Suing for the price of goods is covered in detail in Chapter 16.

► A recent case has seen an award given to a married couple who had a child after the husband had a vasectomy operation. The surgeon had failed to warn them that there was a possibility that the husband might later become fertile again.

Inconvenience and discomfort

Courts are now prepared to award damages where a person suffers inconvenience or discomfort as a result of a breach of contract. The following case illustrates this point.

Jarvis v. Swan Tours (1973) 1 All ER 71

The plaintiff booked a holiday from the brochure of the defendant, in which a holiday was described as a 'house party'. Among other things, candlelit dinners, afternoon tea, a yodeller and a hotel manager who spoke English were promised. The reality turned out to be somewhat different. The manager spoke no English, the food was poor and the defendant spent the second week as the sole resident of the hotel. He claimed damages.

> **COURT HELD**
> *The plaintiff was awarded £125 damages for his suffering and disappointment.*

Mitigation

An injured party must try to lessen his or her losses. For example, if someone was dismissed unfairly six months after the beginning of a two-year contract and did nothing towards gaining employment for the remaining eighteen months, that person would have failed to mitigate his or her losses. In such a case the injured party would not be able to recover the full contractual amount because he or she should have tried to get another job.

The following case illustrates this point.

Brace v. Calder (1895) 2 QB 253

VC The plaintiff was employed as a branch manager, on a two-year contract, by a four-man partnership. The partnership was dissolved on the retirement of two partners and the plaintiff was dismissed, in breach of contract, after five months. The remaining partners offered to re-employ the plaintiff under the same terms. The plaintiff refused the offer and sued for breach of contract.

> **COURT HELD**
> *The plaintiff could succeed because there had been a breach of contract, though he had failed to mitigate his losses and would only be awarded nominal damages.*

► The damages available under the Sale of Goods Act 1979 are discussed in Chapter 16.

 Explain the rule established in *Hadley* and refined in *Victoria Laundry*.

ACT Either alone or in a group apply remoteness to the following problems, making reference to relevant cases. Viki, a travel agent, sold Duncan a holiday that she described as a magical mystery tour of the Welsh valleys. Included in the tour description were the following: luxury accommodation; traditional Welsh cuisine; breathtaking sightseeing tours; and the full services of a tour guide. Duncan bought a super-duper camcorder in order to record the holiday. The tour turned out to be somewhat different from that described. The tour bus broke down on the first day in Pontypridd and Duncan was forced to spend the next three days waiting for it to be fixed. He was accommodated in the Kings Arms at Pontypridd where fish and chips were provided for his meals. Can Duncan claim damages for (a) the tour and/or (b) the camera?

Remedies from equity

All equitable remedies are discretionary, i.e. a court may choose not to grant an equitable remedy. The following equitable remedies may be available for a breach of contract:

(a) rescission;
(b) specific performance;
(c) injunction;
(d) *quantum meruit*.

Rescission
Rescission is the returning of the parties to a pre-contractual position. Any money or goods that have been exchanged must be returned. It will not be granted where: (a) any benefit has been enjoyed by the party requesting it; (b) where the requesting party has in any way **affirmed** the contract or has delayed in seeking rescission; (c) where rescission is no longer possible, i.e. where goods are no longer in existence, or where a third party has acquired an interest in the goods.

▶ See Chapter 12, p. 195, for an explanation of 'affirmed'.

Specific performance
A decree of specific performance is an order of the court, addressed to one of the parties to a contract, ordering them to complete their contractual obligations. It may be awarded at the discretion of the court, in cases where the award of damages may not be adequate to compensate the injured party. For example, the purchase of a unique object, or the sale of land, might not be satisfactorily compensated by the award of damages, in case of a breach of contract. A court might order the seller to complete the sale under an order of specific performance.

Specific performance will not be awarded where it is impractical to do so. It will not be awarded in cases of personal service or employment contracts, or where court supervision is required to enforce a contract, such as in the construction of a building. It may be granted to enforce an appointment, such as a teacher in a school, though only where the contract covers the appointment and not the duties, which might require supervision.

Equity demands equality, so specific performance is not available to minors or against minors. It would be unfair for minors to have specific performance available as a remedy, when it could not be enforced against them.

Injunction

An injunction is a court order, addressed to a named person, ordering that person not to break his or her contractual obligations. An injunction will only be granted to enforce a negative stipulation in a contract: for example, 'not to work for any other person in a similar capacity for the duration of the contract of employment'. The next case, which involves the film star Bette Davis, illustrates this.

Warner Bothers v. Nelson **(1937) 1 KB 209**

 The defendant, Bette Davis, entered into a contract with the plaintiffs. The contract contained a term under which she agreed 'not to render any services for or in any other phonographic, stage or motion picture production or productions or business of any other person ... or engage in any other occupation without the written consent of the producer being first had and obtained.' Davis decided to breach the contract, returning to London and entering into a contract with a third party to perform. The plaintiffs sought an injunction to prevent her from breaching the contract.

 COURT HELD
The injunction was granted, though it was confined to acting and to the jurisdiction of the English courts.

An injunction will not be granted if the terms of a contract amount to an order of specific performance, i.e. where a contract of employment amounts to a contract of slavery. The following case illustrates an instance where an injunction was refused.

Ehrman v. Bartholomew **(1898) 1 Ch 671**

The defendant had entered into a contract of employment with the plaintiff. The contract contained a clause under which the defendant agreed not to work for anyone else, for a period of ten years.

 COURT HELD
An injunction would not be granted. The longevity of the contract and the restrictiveness of the clause meant that the defendant would have to work for the plaintiff in order to live. The granting of an injunction would have amounted to an award of specific performance.

The following two types of injunction have become very popular since they were first awarded in the mid-1970s. Both take their names from the cases in which they were awarded. They have been described as the nuclear weapons of the law. It is more normal for them to be used in disputes between partners and in the commercial world.

A *Mareva* injunction prevents a person from removing assets outside the jurisdiction of the English courts or disposing of assets within the jurisdiction. Upon application by an injured party a *Mareva* injunction may be awarded where one party has breached a contract.

An *Anton Piller* order may be awarded to a plaintiff's solicitor, to be effected either alone or under the supervision of an independent solicitor. The order gives a solicitor the power to enter and search a defendant's premises, to seize any documents or other items that may be used in evidence against the defendant. The solicitor may retain the evidence for a limited period for the purposes of photographing or photocopying. The purpose of this order is to enable a plaintiff to preserve evidence when it is feared that the defendant might destroy it.

Quantum meruit

A party can claim on a *quantum meruit* in the following circumstances:

► See above (p. 217) for an explanation of **quantum meruit**.

(a) in a contract for services, when a contract fails to specify the remuneration to be paid;
(b) when there has been part performance in a divisible contract;
(c) where a breach of contract is treated by the injured party as discharging the contract;
(d) where one party is prevented by the other party from performing his part of the contract;
(e) where a new contract is implied by the conduct of the parties;
(f) where under a void contract a party has given benefit.

The following case shows the application of *quantum meruit*, where a new contract is implied by the conduct of the parties.

Steven and Co. v. Bromley and Son (1919) 2 KB 722

The defendant entered into a contract with the plaintiff, a ship owner, for the carriage of steel, at an agreed freight rate. When the defendant's shipment arrived, it contained half steel and half general merchandise. The shipment therefore attracted a higher freight charge. The plaintiff accepted the shipment and completed the contract. The defendant refused to pay the higher freight charges. The plaintiff sued on a *quantum meruit*.

COURT HELD
The plaintiff could claim the higher freight rate. It was possible to imply a new contract from the actions of the two parties. The quantum meruit represented a reasonable remuneration for the extra services provided.

 Outline the four equitable remedies listed above. In what circumstances will (a) rescission and (b) specific performance not be granted?

 Now that you have completed this chapter, look back at the chapter objectives at the beginning. Can you do all the things that these suggest? If not, look again at the relevant sections of the chapter.

CHAPTER SUMMARY

1 A contract may be discharged by agreement, performance, frustration and breach. Where a contract is ended by frustration the conditions stated by the Law Reform (Frustrated Contracts) Act 1943 must be considered.

2 Frustration may occur in the following areas: personal service contracts; subsequent illegality; cancellation of an event; destruction of the subject matter; frustration of the common venture; and governmental and national emergency.

3 Frustration will not apply where the agreement was impossible from the outset; where a contract merely becomes more difficult or expensive to perform; where there is provision in the contract for frustration; where the frustration is self-induced; and rarely in contracts or leases for the sale of land.

4 A breach of contract will occur when one party fails fully to perform his or her contractual obligations. A breach may take place anticipatorily, where a party states prior to the time of performance that he or she is not going to perform, or where a party carries out an act that makes performance impossible.

5 There are three main types of awards of damages: nominal, substantial and exemplary. The important rule, relating to remoteness of damage, was established in the case of *Hadley v. Baxendale*.

6 The equitable remedies of rescission, specific performance, injunction and *quantum meruit* may be available for a breach of contract.

Terms and exclusion clauses

TERMS OF CONTRACTS

In this chapter we shall examine the agreements that the parties to a contract have made, to discover the terms of the contract. The terms of a contract represent the undertakings and obligations of both parties to a contract. Terms may be **express terms** or **implied terms** and may be considered to be a condition or a warranty.

▶ **Express terms** – the actual details of the contract that have been arrived at by discussion between the parties.

▶ **Implied terms** – terms that are implied into the contract regardless of the agreement made between the parties. Terms may be implied by: (a) statute: e.g. Sale and Supply of Goods Act 1994, s. 14 (2), 'goods supplied under the contract must be of satisfactory quality'; (b) custom: the normal dealings in a particular industry; or (c) common law: a court may imply a term into the contract to make it a workable and sensible agreement where a contract is unclear or nonsensical.

Express terms

In the pre-contractual stage much discussion will take place on the different sections of the agreement. Some of these discussions will form the express terms of the contract, while others will be statements that the parties do not intend to form part of the contract. To distinguish between the two the courts use an intention test – see below. (Exclusion clauses are dealt with on page 246.)

Bannerman v. White (1861) 10 CB (NS) 844

In negotiations to purchase hops, the defendant asked the plaintiff if sulphur had been used in the cultivation of the hops, indicating that he would not be interested in the purchase if it had. The plaintiff replied that sulphur had not been used. A contract was agreed, though when the defendant discovered that sulphur had been used he refused to honour the contract. The plaintiff sued for the price of the goods.

COURT HELD

The plaintiff could not succeed. The promise that no sulphur had been used was a term of the contract as it was obviously very important to the defendant.

Where an agreement is written it may be easier to ascertain the intentions of the parties, but the agreement may not be clearly recorded. If the agreement is oral then it may be more difficult to ascertain the true intentions of the parties. If the agreement is a mixture of written and oral, then what is written may contradict what was agreed orally. When a court is attempting to ascertain what the parties have actually agreed to, in case of a dispute, the court will ask the simple question, 'What would a reasonable person think the intentions of the parties were, considering the circumstances at the time that the agreement was made?'

A court may consider any factor that it considers relevant in determining whether a statement is a term of the contract. Factors that it may consider include the following. Did either party have special knowledge? When was the statement made? (The nearer the statement was made to the actual formation of the contract, the more likely it is that it will be considered to be a term.) Was the statement made intending the other party to enter the contract in reliance upon it? If so, then it will be considered to be a term.

Uncertainty of terms

Where a court is unable to determine what it is that the two parties have agreed to, then the contract will not be valid through uncertainty of terms. An agreement to negotiate is not considered to be a binding contract. The following case illustrates these two points.

***Courtney and Fairbairn Ltd v. Tolani Bros. (Hotels) Ltd* (1975) 1 WLR 297**

The plaintiff entered into negotiation with the defendant, a developer, with regard to the construction of a motel, a hotel and a filling station. He wrote to the defendant saying, among other things, that if the defendant agreed he could instruct his surveyor to negotiate fair and reasonable contract sums in respect of each of the three projects, as they arose. The defendant then employed a different contractor to complete the projects. The plaintiff alleged a breach of contract.

COURT HELD

There was no binding contract. The terms of the contract were uncertain, there was no mechanism for determining the price of the contract and it merely amounted to an agreement to negotiate.

Court options

A court may be able to render an uncertain contract certain, using one of the following methods:

- by following trade or custom;
- by referring to previous dealings;
- by upholding an arbitration clause;
- by striking out irrelevant and meaningless terms;
- by referring to implied statutory terms;
- by implying sensible business terms

Trade or custom

Where, in a particular industry, there is a custom or trade, i.e. a particular way of doing things, a court may imply a term into the contract. The following case illustrates this point.

***Hutton v. Warren* (1836) 1 M and W 466**

The defendant, a landlord, gave his tenant farmer notice to quit, insisting that the land be cultivated during the period of notice (known as an **away-going crop**). The plaintiff cultivated the land and then sued to recover a fair return for the seeds and labour, because he received no benefit as he left the farm prior to the harvest.

COURT HELD

The plaintiff succeeded. The court implied that it was customary in these circumstances for payment to be made.

▶ **Away-going crop** – the Agricultural Holdings Act 1965, s. 65, Sch. 8, implies a term into a contract for the leasing of farmland that a farmer must be compensated for a crop that he or she has sown and tended, if the farmer leaves the farm prior to the harvesting of that crop.

Previous dealings

A court may make reference to the previous dealings of the parties to determine a contract. The following case illustrates this point.

Hillas and Co. Ltd v. Arcos Ltd (1932) 1 All ER Rep 494

The plaintiffs contracted with the defendants to purchase 22,000 standards of soft wood, of fair condition, during the season of 1930. There was an option to renew the contract for 100,000 standards, in the 1931 season. The contract operated successfully for the 1930 season, but the defendants refused to complete the 1931 section, stating that the agreement was too vague. The plaintiffs sued for breach of contract.

 COURT HELD
The House of Lords ruled that the agreement was binding. The contract was vague but it had operated without difficulty in 1930, therefore, it could be inferred that it was a workable agreement if the defendants had wished it to be.

Arbitration clause

Where reference is made in a contract to an arbitration clause, specifying that where the parties are in dispute they will refer to arbitration, the court will uphold the agreement.

Irrelevant and meaningless terms

Where an agreement contains terms that are irrelevant or meaningless, a court may strike out that term if it would leave a workable agreement that followed the original intentions of the parties.

Implied statutory terms

Certain terms are implied into most contracts regardless of the express agreements made between the parties. For example, Sale of Goods Act 1979, s. 14, states 'goods sold must be fit for the purpose for which they are sold'. This subject is covered in more detail in Chapter 15.

Sensible business terms

A court may imply a term into a contract to give effect to the express agreements made by the parties. The following, much-quoted case is the best example.

The Moorcock (1889) 14 PD 64

The owner of *The Moorcock*, a steamship, entered into an agreement with the owners of a wharf and jetty that was situated on the Thames, to off-load cargo at the wharf and, for that purpose, to berth at the jetty. When the tide was out, *The Moorcock* sustained damage when it settled on the river bed. The plaintiffs sued for the damage sustained.

► Remember the case of *Foley v. Classique Coaches* (see Chapter 9, p. 137), where the contract contained an arbitration clause? The court granted an injunction on the basis of the existence of this clause.

► Remember *Nicolene v. Simmonds* (see Chapter 9, p. 137), when the court struck out a meaningless term?

COURT HELD
*The plaintiffs could recover for the damage despite there
being no provision being made in the contract. The court
implied a warranty that it was safe for the ship to berth at the dock.*

ACT   What is the difference between an implied term and an
express term? How may an implied term be put into a
contract?

Condition, warranty or innominate term?

Having established that a statement is a term of a contract, it is then
important to decide whether the term is a condition, a warranty or
an innominate term. The following are definitions of the three
types:

> * **Condition** – a term fundamental to the performance of a
>   contract. A condition is a vital obligation under a
>   contract. When a breach of a condition occurs the injured
>   party may repudiate the contract, or may continue with it
>   and in either case claim damages.
>
> * **Warranty** – a term less vital to the performance of a
>   contract. The breach of a warranty will only allow the
>   injured party to seek damages and the performance of
>   the contract will not be affected.
>
> * **Innominate term** – a term that may be described as
>   either a condition or a warranty. The seriousness of a
>   breach of an innominate term will be dependent upon
>   the effect of the breach upon the contract. If the breach is
>   serious, i.e. the main purpose of the contract is defeated,
>   then the innominate term, whether described as a
>   warranty or a condition, will be treated as a breach of
>   condition. If the effect of the breach is minor, regardless
>   of the fact that the term has been called a condition, it
>   will be treated as a warranty.

The following three cases illustrate the interpretation of the different terms.

Bettini v. Gye (1876) 1 QBD 183

   The plaintiff, an opera singer, contracted with the defendant to
perform a series of concerts in England, commencing 30
March 1875, with rehearsals starting six days prior to that date. The
plaintiff's arrival was delayed to 28 March because of illness. The
defendant treated the contract as being discharged. The plaintiff sued
for breach of contract.

COURT HELD

The term governing the period of rehearsal was subsidiary to the main purpose of the contract, therefore it was a warranty. The defendant could not discharge the contract.

Poussard v. Spiers and Pond (1876) 1 QBD 410

The plaintiff contracted to perform in an opera, the first performance being on 28 November 1874. She was taken ill and did not recover fitness until 4 December. The defendants had hired a substitute performer, to whom they had given all of the plaintiff's performance dates. The plaintiff sued for breach of contract.

COURT HELD

The defendant was able to discharge the contract. The failure of the plaintiff to be able to perform on the first night amounted to a breach of a condition.

Cehave N V Bremer Handelsgesellschaft mbh (The Hansa Nord) (1975) 3 All ER 739

The buyers contracted to purchase a cargo of citrus pulp pellets which were to be used in the manufacture of pet food. Part of the consignment arrived damaged and the buyers rejected the whole consignment. The buyers then bought the cargo at auction, paying a much reduced price and proceeded to use the pulp for its original purpose. The sellers sued for breach of contract alleging that the buyers had no right to reject the goods.

COURT HELD

The buyers were in breach of contract as the effect of the breach on the contract was minimal. It was still fit for the original purpose. Therefore, it was a breach of a warranty, not a breach of a condition.

 Define condition, warranty and innominate term.

EXCLUSION CLAUSES

► Exclusion clauses are also known as exemption clauses.

When drawing up a contract, a party may seek to include an exclusion clause to limit or exempt liability for breach of contract or negligence. The courts have been prepared to accept such clauses where the parties are of equal bargaining power. However, where a stronger party has used its 'muscle' to impose an exclusion clause, courts have tended to scrutinize and, in some cases, overrule them. The consumer is also further protected by the Unfair Contract Terms Act 1977.

The common law and exclusion clauses

The courts have taken every possible opportunity to examine the validity of exclusion clauses. When assessing the validity of an exclusion clause, the courts will consider the following:

1 communication, relating to:
   (a) signed documents,
   (b) unsigned documents,
   (c) onerous clauses;
2 previous dealings;
3 privity of contract.

Communication

Where a party seeks to rely on an exclusion clause, he or she must show that the clause was an integral term of the contract, i.e. that the other person was aware of the existence of the term and that **entrance into** the contract was made with knowledge of the clause. Therefore, communication of the clause must have been made to the other party prior to the **formation** of the contract. Where the communication is post-contractual the clause will be invalid. This has the effect of making the time of the formation of the contract, i.e. offer and acceptance, of extreme importance.

Parties seeking to use exclusion clauses have communicated them in many ways: on the back of railway and other tickets; on posters; on signs; in small print; on receipts. The following cases illustrate how the courts have interpreted some of these different types of communication.

The first case illustrates that post-contractual communication will be invalid.

▶ **Entrance into** – the legal way of saying agreement to (a contract).

▶ **Formation** – the legal way of saying the time when the contract was actually entered into.

Olley v. Marlborough Court Ltd (1949) 1 All ER 127

The plaintiff, a guest at a hotel, paid for her room in advance upon arrival at the hotel reception desk. She then went to her room, which contained a notice excluding liability for the loss of customers' property. Subsequently, some fur coats were stolen from the room. The hotel sought to deny liability by relying on the exclusion clause contained in the notice.

 COURT HELD
The plaintiff could succeed. The contract had been concluded at the reception desk. Therefore communication of the exclusion clause had been post-contractual.

The next case shows an interesting interpretation of offer and acceptance.

▶ See Chapter 9 for a full discussion of offer and acceptance.

Thornton v. Shoe Lane Parking Ltd **(1971) 1 All ER 686**

 The plaintiff drove his car to the entrance of an automatic, multi-storey car park. At the entrance to the car park was a sign that stated: 'All cars parked at owners' risk'. An automatic machine issued a ticket to the plaintiff, the barrier rose, and he entered and parked the car. The defendant noticed that the ticket contained small print but he did not read it. It, in fact, stated that the ticket was issued subject to the conditions displayed on the premises. These conditions were on a number of notices that were situated around the car park. One of the conditions attempted to exempt the defendant from liability for damage to any property or for any personal injury, however caused. Upon returning to his vehicle some hours later, he was badly injured due to his own and Shoe Lane Parking's fault. He sued to obtain damages for his injuries. The defendants argued that the car park ticket contained an exclusion clause that enabled them to avoid any liability.

 COURT HELD
The defendants could not rely on the exclusion clause. The contract was concluded when the car was placed adjacent to the automatic entry machine. The 'offer' was represented by the sign 'Car Park' while 'acceptance' was achieved when a vehicle arrived at the entrance, adjacent to the automatic machine. Therefore, the exclusion clause was post-contractual and invalid.

Exclusion clauses in signed documents
Where a party signs a document that contains an exclusion clause it will be difficult for the party not to be bound. Only where there has been a misrepresentation, or ***non est factum***, will a party be able to avoid the clause.

The following case illustrates that a person who signs a document will be bound by it, whether or not he or she has read it.

L'Estrange v. Graucob Ltd **(1934) 2 KB 394**

The plaintiff bought a cigarette vending machine from the defendant. The contract contained a clause excluding liability for any express or implied condition, statement or warranty, statutory or otherwise. The plaintiff signed the contract without reading it. After a short period the vending machine failed to work and the plaintiff sued for breach of warranty.

COURT HELD
The defendant could escape liability by relying on the exclusion clause. Where a party signs a contractual document, in the absence of fraud or a misrepresentation, they will be bound by it.

▶ Remember from Chapter 11 that if a person has signed a document by mistake and was not reckless when signing the document, he or she may be able to plead *non est factum* (not my deed). However, it is very difficult for an adult of sound mind to plead *non est factum* successfully. See *Saunders v. Anglia Building Society* in Chapter 11, page 192.

The next case shows how a misrepresentation can affect an exclusion clause.

Curtis v. Chemical Cleaning and Dyeing Company (1951) 1 All ER 631

The plaintiff took her wedding dress to the defendant's dry-cleaning shop to have it cleaned. She was asked to sign a receipt containing a clause that stated: 'this article is accepted on the condition that the company is not liable for any damage howsoever arising'. The plaintiff asked why she had to sign the receipt and was assured by the shop worker that the clause would only cover the beads and sequins on the dress, so she signed it. Upon collection the dress was found to be stained and the plaintiff sued for damages.

 COURT HELD

The defendant could not rely on the exclusion clause because its nature had been misrepresented.

Exclusion clauses in unsigned documents

Where a document is unsigned it will need to be proved that the document containing the clause was integral to the contract and could be expected to contain contractual terms. The following two 'ticket' cases illustrate two different interpretations.

Parker v. South Eastern Railway Co. (1877) 2 CPD 416

The plaintiff deposited a bag at the station, receiving a ticket with the words 'see back' on the front. The back of the ticket gave notice that liability was not accepted for any item whose value was greater than £10. The plaintiff failed to read the ticket. The bag was lost and the plaintiff sued for damages of £24 10s, the value of the luggage.

 COURT HELD

The plaintiff could not succeed. The ticket gave notice of the terms and conditions of acceptance. It was reasonable to expect that such a ticket would contain contractual terms. The ticket amounted to a counter-offer that had been accepted by the plaintiff.

Chapleton v. Barry Urban District Council (1940) 1 All ER 356

The plaintiff was having a day out in Barry. He wished to hire two deck chairs, so he approached an attendant who was issuing them from a pile. Behind the pile was a sign that just gave the price of hiring the chairs, 2d per session. The plaintiff hired two chairs, receiving two tickets in receipt. On the back of the tickets was a clause that exempted the council from any liability from any accident or damage arising from the hire of the chairs. The plaintiff was injured when one of the chairs collapsed and he sued for damages. The defendants sought to rely on the exclusion clause.

COURT HELD
The plaintiff could succeed. No notice was given by the defendant of the clause prior to the issue of the ticket and in these circumstances it was unreasonable to expect the ticket to be considered as a contractual document. On many occasions a deck chair could be used prior to obtaining a ticket, so a ticket was normally used just as proof of having paid.

Onerous exclusion clauses

► **Onerous** – (of a contract, lease, etc.) having or involving burdens or obligations that counterbalance or outweigh the advantages.

Where a clause is extremely **onerous**, the party seeking to rely on it must prove that the clause was brought to the notice of the other party. It may not be enough just to include the clause in a written document, notwithstanding that the document is considered to be contractual. This rule was confirmed in the following case.

Interfoto Picture Library Ltd v. Stiletto Visual Programmes Ltd **(1988) 1 All ER 348**

These two companies had not previously worked together. The plaintiffs, at the request of the defendants, supplied transparencies to the defendants on 5 March 1984. The delivery note had a clearly marked return date of 19 March printed on the top of the form. On the bottom of the form were a number of conditions, one of which stated the following: 'All transparencies must be returned to us within 14 days from the date of delivery. A holding fee of £5.00 plus VAT per day will be charged for each transparency which is retained by you longer than the said period of 14 days.' The defendants did not use any of the photographs, forgot that they had them and did not return them until 2 April. The plaintiffs calculated their charges according to the clause, arriving at a figure of £3,783.50, for which they sued.

COURT HELD
The plaintiffs could not succeed in full. The clause was extortionate and unreasonable. It had not been brought adequately to the notice of the defendants and, therefore, did not become part of the contract. It was not sufficient to incorporate the term into the standard printed conditions. It should at least have been printed in bold type or a covering note should have been sent drawing specific attention to it. The plaintiffs were awarded a reasonable sum based on a quantum meruit *formula.*

Previous dealings

Where parties have contracted together on a regular basis, an exclusion clause may be construed as being part of the contract, notwithstanding that it was not included in the contract in dispute. The previous dealings of the parties may be examined to establish that it was normal for the clause in question to be considered as part of the contract. The following case illustrates this point.

J. Spurling Ltd v. Bradshaw (1956) 1 WLR 461

The defendants stored barrels of orange juice with the plaintiffs, who were warehousemen. The parties had contracted together over a number of years. A few days after depositing the barrels the defendant received a note in acknowledgement of the deposit. It also contained a clause exempting the plaintiffs from any liability for loss or damage to the property, caused by negligence, wrongful act or default by any of their employees. When the defendant collected the barrels several were damaged, some were empty and certain of them contained dirty water. The plaintiff sued the defendant to recover the charges that the defendant declined to pay.

   COURT HELD
The plaintiff could succeed. The clause was incorporated into the contract on the basis of the previous dealings between the parties. Similar circumstances had occurred on many previous occasions, with the document being supplied after the deposit had been made. The defendant could therefore be implied to have accepted the clause.

Previous dealings will more normally be implied in commercial dealings – that is, dealings between business persons. They will not necessarily be implied in private dealings. For example, the fact that a privately owned car had been serviced in a garage over a period of years would not allow the garage owner to imply a clause on the basis of previous dealings.

Privity of contract

Under this doctrine, because they are strangers to the contract, the servants or agents of the party seeking to rely on the exclusion clause will not be able to avoid liability. Only where the contract specifically includes other parties, and the other parties are aware of and agree to be party to the contract and supply consideration, will they be able to rely on an exclusion clause in the contract between the principals.

The following case illustrates where a third party could not rely on an exclusion clause.

Scruttons Ltd v. Midland Silicones Ltd (1962) 1 All ER 1

VC   This case concerned the shipment of a drum of chemicals from New York to London. The plaintiffs were the consignees while the defendants were the stevedores responsible for the discharging of the goods in London. The contract of carriage limited the liability of the carriers for damage to $500 and stated that the defendant could also benefit from this clause. The drum was negligently damaged and the plaintiffs sued in tort to recover the full cost of the damage of £593 from the stevedores. The defendants sought to rely on the exclusion-clause contained in the contract of carriage.

COURT HELD
The House of Lords ruled that the defendants could not rely on the exclusion clause because they were not party to the contract and could not derive any rights under it.

Rules of interpretation

Even when it has been established that an exclusion clause is part of the contract, a court, in seeking to interpret an exclusion clause, will adopt the following four rules:

1 the applicability rule;
2 the *contra proferentum* rule;
3 the repugnancy rule;
4 the rule of absolute performance.

Applicability

By the applicability rule, it must be proved that the exclusion clause covers the type of liability that the party is seeking to avoid. A court will strictly interpret the wording of the clause and will not extend the meaning to cover anything not mentioned. It is possible, in certain cases, to limit or exclude liability for negligence. However, if the term makes no specific reference to negligence it will not be enforced. The following case shows an interpretation of this last point.

White v. John Warwick and Co. Ltd **(1953) 1 WLR 1285 (CA)**

The plaintiff hired a cycle from the defendants. Under the contract the defendants were exempted from liability for any personal injuries to the hirer. The saddle tipped up and deposited the plaintiff on the road, causing him injury. The plaintiff sued in negligence.

COURT HELD
The plaintiff could succeed. The wording of the clause was interpreted to cover contractual liabilities only. No mention was made of negligence, therefore the plaintiff could succeed in negligence.

The following recent case also concerned whether or not an exclusion/indemnifying clause could cover negligence.

EE Caledonia Ltd v. Orbit Valve Co. plc (1995) 1 AU ER 174

The contract involved an engineer carrying out works on the plaintiffs' oil rig. The rig caught fire, through the negligent acts of the plaintiffs' servants, no fault being attributable to the engineer, and he was killed. The plaintiffs paid £642,627 in damages to the representatives of the deceased, which they sought to claim from the defendants, under an indemnifying clause in the contract. The clause stated:

> Each party hereto shall indemnify ... the other, provided that the other party has acted in good faith, from and against any claim, demand cause of action, loss expense or liability ... arising by reason of any injury to or death of any employee ... of the indemnifying party, resulting from or in any way connected with the performance of this [contract].

The court had to decide whether the clause covered the negligent acts of the plaintiffs or their employees. The test established in *Canada Steamship Lines v. R (PC)* (1952), I Lloyd's Rep. 1, was applied. First, was there an express reference to negligence and, second, were the words of the clause wide enough in their ordinary sense to cover negligence?

> **COURT HELD**
> *The clause did not encompass negligent acts, therefore the plaintiffs could not obtain an indemnity from the defendants.*

If a clause can only be construed to relate to negligence then it will be enforceable. This is shown in the next case.

▶ Remember which three factors have to be present to prove negligence? They are duty of care, breach of that duty and subsequent damage caused by the breach. In this case the court found that the hirers had been negligent in hiring out a cycle that was clearly not fit for the road. See Chapter 19.

Alderslade v. Hendon Laundry Ltd (1945) KB 189

The plaintiff sent handkerchiefs to the laundry to be laundered. The contract contained a clause limiting the damage to twenty times the contract charge for loss or damage. The handkerchiefs were lost and the plaintiffs sued for damages.

> **COURT HELD**
> *The defendant could rely on the exclusion clause since it could only be through negligence that they could lose items. The plaintiff could only recover the amount allowed in the limitation clause.*

In the next case the exclusion clause in the contract was constructed well enough to encompass both contractual and tortious obligations.

▶ If you need to remind yourself about tortious liability, refer back to Chapter 2.

Ailsa Craig Fishing Co. Ltd v. Malvern Fishing Co. Ltd (1983) 1 All ER 101

This case concerned the terms of a contract between Securicor and the Aberdeen Fishing Vessels Owners' Association. The basic circumstances were that Securicor had been employed to keep a constant watch on Aberdeen harbour. They had been negligent in failing to do so and, as a result, one ship became caught under the quay by the pressure of tidal waters. The ship sank, taking another vessel with it. Securicor's contract contained the following clause: 'If … any liability on the part of the company shall arise (whether under the express or implied terms of this contract or at common law, or in any other way) to the customer for any loss or damage of whatever nature arising out of or connected with the provision of the services covered by this contract, such liability shall be limited to the payment by the company of the sum of … (b) a maximum of £1,000 … in respect of all and any incidents during any consecutive period of 12 months.'

COURT HELD

The exclusion clause was sufficiently clear and lucid to encompass claims for the negligence of Securicor's employees. Liability was therefore limited to £1,000.

Contra proferentem

> **Contra proferentem** – in case of doubt or ambiguity the clause will be interpreted against the person seeking to rely on it.

Where the meaning of an exclusion clause is unclear it will be held to be *contra proferentem*. The next case is an example of this.

Alexander v. Railway Executive (1951) 2 All ER 442

The plaintiff, a touring magician, deposited trunks at Launceston railway station, paying 5d per trunk and receiving a ticket for each trunk. He told the porter that he would forward instructions for the delivery of the trunks. The ticket contained a clause that exempted the liability of the railway for loss, misdelivery or damage to any articles where the value was in excess of £5, unless at the time of the deposit the true value and nature of the goods was declared by the depositor and an extra charge paid. The plaintiff did not make any declaration as to the value of the deposited goods. The plaintiff's assistant returned to the station, gained access to the trunks without the tickets and stole items from them. The plaintiff sued for damages for breach of contract and the defendants tried to rely upon the exclusion clause.

COURT HELD

The plaintiff could succeed. The exclusion clause had been constructively communicated to the plaintiff but the defendants had fundamentally breached their contractual obligations by allowing unauthorized access to the trunks, so they could not rely upon it. The clause exempting liability from misdelivery did not cover deliberate delivery to the wrong person.

Repugnancy

The repugnancy rule is also known as the 'total non-performance rule'. Where the exclusion clause purports to exclude liability for the actual performance of the contract, the court will dismiss it. For example, if Shirley agrees to supply tulips to George, but includes in the contract a term that allows her to supply any variety of flowers, that would be repugnant to the main purpose of the contract.

Absolute performance

The rule of absolute performance is also known as the four corners rule. Under this rule a party will only be able to rely on an exclusion clause where the party has performed his or her contractual obligations absolutely, i.e. sticking to the letter of the four corners of every page of the contract. Any deviation from the contract will render the clause invalid. The following case shows the application of this rule.

***Thomas National Transport (Melbourne) Pty Ltd and Pay v. May and Baker (Australia) Pty Ltd* (1966) 2 Lloyd's Rep 347**

This Australian case concerned the transportation of goods by a sub-contracted carrier, who was contracted to take goods to a Melbourne depot. On this occasion the depot was closed and the subcontractor, in accordance with his instructions from the carriers, stored the goods in his garage overnight. During the night certain of the goods were damaged by fire. The plaintiffs sued while the defendants sought to rely on an exclusion clause in the contract.

COURT HELD
The exclusion clause was not valid. The carriers had not absolutely performed their contractual obligations. The storing of goods in a private garage when the depot was closed was normal procedure for them, but it represented a departure from their contract, which was to deliver the goods to the depot.

The current approach to exclusion clauses

The following very important case illustrates the modern approach of the courts to exclusion clauses.

***Mitchell (George) (Chesterhall) Ltd v. Finney Lock Seeds Ltd* (1983) 1 All ER 108**

 The plaintiff, a farmer, ordered 30 lb. of Dutch winter cabbage seeds from the defendant company, which was delivered and planted in 63 acres of land. The accompanying invoice limited the liability of the suppliers to replacing defective seed or repaying the cost of the seed. The resulting crop was useless and had to be ploughed into the field. The plaintiff sued for the commercial loss of the crop, £63,000.

► This case may be considered to have been decided in line with the provisions of the Unfair Contract Terms Act 1977 (UCTA77) and should be considered to be in line with current views on the allowance of exclusion clauses.

COURT HELD

The House of Lords ruled that the plaintiff could succeed. The contract had been made prior to the implementation of the Unfair Contract Terms Act 1977 and was, therefore, subject to the Sale of Goods Act 1893, s. 55. This required that it was fair and reasonable to allow reliance on the term. The court held that it was not fair or reasonable to allow the defendants to rely on the contractual limitation of their liability. The defendants had often made ex gratia payments when complaints had previously been made and the breach was as a result of gross negligence. Further, it would have been possible, and quite economic, to insure against such a situation.

(ACT)

1 How may an exclusion clause be communicated?
2 What was unusual about the circumstances and judgment in *Thornton v. Shoe Lane*?

Fundamental breach

For some time it was considered a rule of law that where a party fundamentally breached a contract, by performing some act totally different to what was agreed, the party would not be able to rely on an exclusion clause. However, in the following case it was ruled that it was possible to rely on an exclusion or limitation clause. The case would depend upon the **construction** of the contract.

► **Construction** – the wording of the clause or contract.

Photo Production Ltd v. Securicor Transport Ltd **(1980) 1 All ER 556**

(VC)   Securicor was employed by the plaintiffs to guard their premises for a fee of £8 15s per week. One evening a Securicor guard deliberately lit a fire, to keep himself warm. The fire got out of hand and burned the factory down, causing losses of £615,000. The plaintiffs sued for damages while the defendants sought to rely on the following exclusion clause:

> Under no circumstances shall the company [Securicor] be responsible for any injurious act or default by any employee of the company unless such act or default could have been foreseen and avoided by the exercise of due diligence on the part of the company as his employer, nor, in any event, shall the company be held responsible for (a) any loss suffered by the customer through burglary, theft, fire or any other cause, except insofar as such loss is solely attributable to the negligence of the company's employees acting within the course of their employment … .

► The contract was made before the coming into force of the UCTA77, but the decision was entirely in line with s. 9(1) of that Act.

COURT HELD

The House of Lords ruled that the exemption clause was valid. There was no evidence that Securicor had been negligent in employing the guard. References had been obtained prior to his being employed and it was impossible for them to have foreseen the circumstances that led to the burning down of the factory.

1 Explain the common-law rules relating to the interpretation of exclusion clauses.
2 Rabbit Products sent goods with Fetchit Carriers. The contract contained an exclusion cause excluding liability for loss or damage to the goods howsoever caused. The van carrying the goods ran out of petrol and was left overnight by the side of the road. During the night the goods were stolen from the van. How might the courts view this clause under these circumstances? Which rule of interpretation might they apply?

The Unfair Contract Terms Act 1977

Parliament has long been aware of the need for statutory control of exclusion and limitation clauses. Contracts for the sale of goods have been afforded protection under the Sale of Goods Act 1893, the Sale of Goods Act 1979, the Sale and Supply of Goods Act 1994, the Supply of Goods (Implied Terms) Act 1973 and the Unfair Contract Terms Act 1977. The UCTA77 has spread statutory control to other types of contract. We shall first examine the main provisions of the UCTA77, and then look at Directive 93/13/EC relating to unfair contract terms, which has recently been implemented in this country.

The UCTA77 does not apply to the following types of contract:

1 contracts of international trade;
2 contracts of insurance;
3 contracts relating to land;
4 intellectual property;
5 creation, dissolution or constitution of a company;
6 creation or transfer of securities.

The purpose of the Act is to protect consumers when they enter into contracts with businesses. Business-to-business contracts remain subject to the previously outlined rules, though where a business is considered to have acted as a consumer, i.e. has bought something outside its normal scope of business, it may be able to rely on the Act. The Act deals only with the fairness of exclusion clauses relating to contractual and tortious liability, and is not concerned with the other terms in a contract.

Under the UCTA77, s. 1, the Act applies (with exceptions) to liability arising out of the course of business dealings and liabilities arising out of the occupation of business premises.

Negligence liability

> **UCTA77, s. 2(1)**
>
> A person cannot by reference to any contract term or to a notice given to persons generally or to particular persons exclude or restrict his liability for death or personal injury resulting from negligence.

It is not possible to exclude liability for death or personal injury, caused by negligence, by the use of an exclusion clause.

> **UCTA77, s. 2(2)**
>
> In the case of other loss or damage, a person cannot so exclude or restrict his liability for negligence except in so far as the term or notice satisfies the requirement of reasonableness.

An exclusion clause may be used to limit liability other than under s. 2(1), provided that the clause is found to be reasonable.

Liability arising in contract

> **UCTA77, s. 3(2)**
>
> (a) Where one party deals as a consumer, or on the other party's written standard terms of business, then the other party cannot exclude or restrict his liability for breach of contract, unless the clause is found to be reasonable.
> (b) A term that purports to enable a party to tender (a) performance substantially different from that which was reasonably expected of him, or (b) in respect of the whole of any part of his contractual obligation, to render no performance at all: must also satisfy the test of reasonableness.

Dealing as a consumer

The Act has been designed to afford the greatest protection to consumers, who are defined in the UCTA77, s. 12.

> **UCTA77, s. 12(1)**
>
> A party to a contract deals as a consumer in relation to another party if:
>
> (a) he neither makes the contract in the course of a business nor holds himself out as doing so; and
> (b) the other party does make the contract in the course of a business; and
> (c) in the case of a contract governed by the law of sale of goods or hire-purchase, or by section 7 of this Act, the goods passing under or in pursuance of the contract are of a type ordinarily supplied for private use or consumption.

The following outlines consumer and non-consumer transactions under the Act.

1 C ↔ B = Consumer transaction
2 B ↔ B = Non-consumer transaction
3 C ↔ C = Non-consumer transaction
4 B* ↔ B = Consumer transaction

Here, B represents a business, while C represents a consumer. B*
represents a business making a transaction outside its normal business.

1   Where a person acting in his or her own individual capacity
    deals with another person acting in his or her normal business,
    then that will be a consumer transaction.
2   A businessperson dealing with a businessperson, within his or
    her normal scope of business, will be a non-consumer
    transaction.
3   A consumer dealing with a consumer will be a non-consumer
    transaction.
4   A businessperson acting in an irregular transaction, outside his
    or her normal scope of business, dealing with another
    businessperson will be a consumer transaction.

The following case illustrates the application of type 4.

***R and B Customs Brokers Co. Ltd v. United Dominions Trust Ltd
(1988) 1 All ER 847***

The plaintiffs purchased a car for one of their directors. The contract
included a clause excluding Sale of Goods Act 1979, s. 14(3), which
states that goods sold must be fit for the purpose for which they are
sold. Under the UCTA77 it is not possible to exclude s. 14(3), when it
is a consumer transaction. The vehicle was totally unsatisfactory and
the plaintiffs sued the defendant finance company.

COURT HELD

*The exclusion clause could not apply. The plaintiffs were
considered to be dealing as consumers and could, therefore,
succeed.*

Sale and hire purchase

Certain exclusion clauses will be void under any circumstances in a
consumer transaction. The following section of the Act gives
details.

UCTA77, s. 6(1)

(1)   Liability for breach of the obligations arising from:
      (a)   section 12 Sale of Goods Act 1979 [seller's implied under-
            takings as to title, etc.]
      (b)   section 8 of the Supply of Goods (Implied Terms) Act 1973
            cannot be excluded or restricted by reference to any con-
            tract term.

This means that it is not possible to exclude the implied condition,
that the person selling, or selling by hire purchase, has the right
(good title) to do so. This applies to consumer and non-consumer
transactions. For example, in a contract for the sale of goods, an

exclusion clause worded to exclude the fact that the seller of the goods had the right to sell the goods would not be valid.

UCTA77, s. 6(2)

(2) As against a person dealing as a consumer, liability for breach of the obligations arising from:
   (a) sections 13, 14 or 15 of the Sale of Goods Act 1979;
   (b) sections 9, 10 or 11 of the Supply of Goods (Implied Terms) Act 1973

cannot be excluded or restricted by reference to any contract term.

This means that any exclusion clause that purports to exclude the above-mentioned implied terms, which relate to description, quality and sale by sample, in contracts of both sale and hire, will be void in a consumer transaction. In a non-consumer transaction they will be subject to the test of reasonableness.

Business

Under the UCTA77, s. 14, a business includes the professions, government departments, local authorities and public authorities. Indeed, it has been held to include any person who works on a regular basis in any particular business. Only one-off contracts, performed on a casual basis outside a person's normal business, would seem to be able to avoid the Act.

Guarantee of consumer goods

UCTA77, s. 5

In the case of goods of a type ordinarily supplied for private use or consumption, where loss or damage:
(a) arises from the goods proving defective while in consumer use; and
(b) results from the negligence of a person concerned in the manufacture or distribution of the goods,

liability for the loss or damage cannot be excluded or restricted by reference to any contract term or notice contained or operating by reference to a guarantee of the goods.

A manufacturer or distributor cannot exclude liability in negligence for defective goods that they have supplied.

Miscellaneous contracts under which goods pass

Section 7 of the UCTA77 includes other types of contract – contracts for the supply of goods by hire, contracts of exchange, or contracts of work and materials – and excludes the Trading Stamps Act 1964. Implied terms as to fitness for purpose, title, merchantability and sample cannot be excluded under the Act.

UCTA77, s. 7

(2) As against a person dealing as consumer, liability in respect of the goods' correspondence with description or sample, or their quality or fitness for any particular purpose, cannot be excluded or restricted by reference to any such term.

(3) As against a person dealing otherwise than as a consumer, that liability can be excluded or restricted by reference to such a term, but only in so far as the term satisfies the requirement of reasonableness.

The following table gives a clear illustration of the use of exemption clauses under the UCTA77.

Exemption of statutory terms in contracts for the supply of goods

Exemption clauses in contracts for the supply of goods by way of –

	Sale, HP, exchange and work + materials		Hire	
	Consumer transaction	**Non-consumer transaction**	**Consumer transaction**	**Non-consumer transaction**
Title	Void	Void	Subject to reasonableness test	Subject to reasonableness test
Description	Void	Subject to reasonableness test	Void	Subject to reasonableness test
Quality and suitability	Void	Subject to reasonableness test	Void	Subject to reasonabless test
Sample	Void	Subject to reasonableness test	Void	Subject to reasonableness test

Source: D. Keenan and S. Riches, *Business Law*, 2nd edn, London: Pitman, 1990.

The reasonableness test in s. 11

This section refers to Sch. 2 of the Act to determine what a court should consider when deciding whether an exclusion clause is reasonable. The person seeking to rely on the exclusion clause must prove that it is reasonable by the UCTA77, s. 11(5). It is not for the consumer or other businessperson to prove that the clause was unreasonable. This section gives guidelines for determining reasonableness, though the final decision will rest with the court.

UCTA77, s. 11

(1) The term should have been fair and reasonable to be included having regard to the circumstances that were, or ought reasonably to have been, known to or in the contemplation of the parties when the contract was made.

---

(2) A court will still have the power, in appropriate circumstances, to rule that an exclusion clause is not part of the contract.

(3) Where a non-contractual notice is being used for the purposes of excluding liability, it should be fair and reasonable to allow reliance on it, having regard to all the circumstances obtaining when the liability arose or (but for the notice) would have arisen.

(4) Where a term purports to limit liability to a sum of money and the question of reasonableness arises the court ought to consider:

(a) the resources that he could expect to be available to him for the purpose of meeting the liability should it arise;

(b) how far it was open to him to cover himself by insurance.

The following extracts from Sch. 2 of the UCTA77 define the factors a court may consider when determining the reasonableness of an exclusion clause.

UCTA77, Sch. 2

(a) the strength of the bargaining positions of the parties relative to each other, taking into account (among other things) alternative means by which the customer's requirements could have been met;

(b) whether the customer received an inducement to agree to the term, or in accepting it had an opportunity of entering into a similar contract with other persons, but without having to accept a similar term;

(c) whether the customer knew or ought reasonably to have known of the existence and extent of the term (having regard, among other things, to any custom of the trade and any previous course of dealings between the parties);

(d) where the term excludes or restricts any relevant liability if some condition is not complied with, whether it was reasonable at the time of the contract to expect that compliance with that condition would be practicable;

(e) whether the goods were manufactured, processed or adapted to the special order of the customer.

 Deepak is the director of a lorry-leasing company. The company, on his behalf, bought a second-hand car for him to use in the course of the business. In the contract was a clause exempting the sellers from liability in respect of the Sale of Goods Act 1979, s. 14(3). The car engine blew up after completing 27 miles. Could Deepak's company successfully sue the car sellers? Would the answer be different if Deepak's company were motor dealers? Use relevant Acts, sections and cases to answer the questions.

The following case gives an illustration of how the courts have used the above guidelines to interpret reasonableness.

Woodman v. Photo Trade Processing Ltd **(1981) 131 NLJ 933**

The plaintiff took photographs at a friend's wedding, which he entrusted to Dixon's for developing and printing. He had been the only photographer at the wedding and had promised them to the happy couple as a wedding present. Dixon's lost the film. The plaintiff sued for damages. Dixon's sought to rely upon a standard industry exclusion clause that limited liability to the replacement cost of the film.

COURT HELD

The exclusion clause was unreasonable. The plaintiff had no alternative option available to him, as the clause was used across the whole industry. The defendants could have foreseen that some films were more irreplaceable than others, therefore the plaintiff was awarded damages of £75.00.

EUROPEAN DIRECTIVE 93/13 ON UNFAIR CONTRACT TERMS

The EC Directive on Unfair Contract Terms was implemented by Statutory Instrument (SI) 1994, Number 3159. The SI states that the new Regulations are to be known as the Unfair Terms in Consumer Contracts Regulations 1994 (UTCCR94). The authority for the SI comes from the European Communities Act 1972, Section 2(2). The Regulations were fully in force from 1 July 1995.

The UTCCR94 have been implemented to stand alongside the provisions of the UCTA77. They are part of the Commission's attempts to spread the single market across the breadth of consumer law. Prior to the Regulations, different European states had diverse provisions relating to contract terms in consumer contracts. The Regulations have standardized these provisions. They apply only to consumer contracts for the supply of goods and services, where contracts have not been individually negotiated.

In Regulation 2, the UTCCR94 gives definitions of some of the important terms in the Regulations. A consumer is defined as: 'a natural person who, in making a contract to which these Regulations apply, is acting for purposes which are outside his business.' A business includes 'a trade or profession and the activities of any government department or local or public authority'.

These definitions would appear to confine the Regulations solely to consumers, whereas under the UCTA77 it is possible for a business to act outside its normal scope to become a consumer. However, the Regulations, unlike the UCTA77, do not exclude sale by auction or competitive tendering from their scope.

Regulation 3 defines the terms to which the Regulations apply:

► See *R and B Customs Brokers*, above (p. 259)

(1) Subject to the provisions of Schedule 1, these Regulations apply to any term in a contract concluded between a seller or supplier and a consumer where the said term has not been individually negotiated.

(2) In so far as it is in plain, intelligible language, no assessment shall be made of the fairness of any term which
    (a) defines the main subject matter of the contract, or
    (b) concerns the adequacy of the price or remuneration, as against the goods or services sold or supplied.

(3) For the purposes of these Regulations, a term shall always be regarded as not having been individually negotiated where it has been drafted in advance and the consumer has not been able to influence the substance of the term.

(4) Notwithstanding that a specific term or certain aspects of it in a contract has been individually negotiated, these Regulations shall apply to the rest of a contract if an overall assessment of the contract indicates that it is a pre-formulated standard contract.

(5) It shall be for any seller or supplier who claims that a term was individually negotiated to show that it was.

Regulation 3(3) is really aimed at standard form contracts, where the consumer has not had any influence upon the contract. Even where the consumer has individually negotiated a term, 3(4) states that if an overall assessment of the contract still proves it to be a pre-formulated standard contract, the Regulations will apply. Regulation 3(5) lays the onus of proving a term to have been individually negotiated upon the seller or supplier.

Regulation 4 introduces to British law the concept of good faith, which is discussed in Schedule 2 of the Regulations.

(1) In these Regulations, subject to paragraphs (2) and (3) below, 'unfair term' means any term which contrary to the requirement of good faith causes a significant imbalance in the parties' rights and obligations under the contract to the detriment of the consumer.

(2) An assessment of the unfair nature of a term shall be made taking into account the nature of the goods or services for which the contract was concluded and referring, as at the time of the conclusion of the contract, to all circumstances attending the conclusion of the contract and to all the other terms of the contract or of another contract on which it is dependent.

Schedule 2 provides that when making an assessment of good faith, regard shall be had in particular to:

(a) the strength of the bargaining positions of the parties;
(b) whether the consumer had an inducement to agree to the term;
(c) whether the goods or services were sold or supplied to the special order of the consumer, and
(d) the extent to which the seller or supplier has dealt fairly and equitably with the consumer.

The provisions of this schedule are very similar to the guidelines for reasonableness found in the UCTA77. Clearly, there are going to be problems of interpretation and applicability with the different tests of reasonableness and good faith. The Department of Trade and Industry has taken the view that the two terms are distinct and should not be encompassed into each other. It may well be possible to have terms that are reasonable but are contrary to good faith. Equally it may still be possible to have a term that is unreasonable but has been set in good faith. Only time and the interpretation of the courts will tell.

Schedule 3 provides a list of terms that may be considered to be unfair. It is included as Appendix 1 (page 407).

Regulation 5 details the effects that the inclusion of an unfair contract term will have upon a contract.

> (1) An unfair term in a contract concluded with a consumer by a seller or supplier shall not be binding on the consumer.
> (2) The contract shall continue to bind the parties if it is capable of continuing in existence without the unfair term.

This Regulation has the affect of making a contract containing an unfair contract term voidable, in favour of the consumer. If it is possible for the offending term to be struck out, leaving the contract sensible and with the original intention intact, then a court may well remove the unfair term.

Regulation 6 states that a supplier or seller must use plain and sensible language, when constructing terms. If the term is unclear, it will be interpreted in favour of the consumer.

Regulation 8 gives the power to the Director General of Fair Trading to obtain an injunction to prevent the further use of a contract that contains an unfair contract term. The injunction may be spread to apply to any similar unfair contract terms.

The advent of the Regulations may be considered to be a movement forward in the harmonization of consumer law across the European Union. However, there will inevitably be problems with the interpretation of the Regulations, particularly as some of the provisions are similar to our UCTA77. Other aspects are also less than clear; their applicability has not been fully established by the Regulations.

(ACT) Now that you have completed this chapter, look back at the chapter objectives at the beginning. Can you do all the things that these suggest? If not, look again at the relevant sections of the chapter.

CHAPTER SUMMARY

1 The agreements that parties include in a contract are called terms. Terms may be expressly stated by parties or implied into a contract by trade or custom, previous dealings,

statutorily or by a court to give the contract a sensible meaning.

2 A term may be a condition, a warranty or an innominate term.

   (a) A condition is a term fundamental to the contract. When a condition is breached the injured party may repudiate the contract and seek damages, or continue and seek damages.

   (b) A warranty is a term less vital to the contract. Breach of a warranty will not end contractual obligations. The injured party will only be able to seek damages.

   (c) An innominate term may be described as a condition or a warranty. The seriousness of a breach of an innominate term will be dependent upon the effect of the breach upon the contract. If the breach is serious, i.e. the main purpose of the contract is defeated, then the innominate term, whether described as a warranty or a condition, will be treated as a breach of condition. If the effect of the breach is minor, regardless of the fact that the term has been called a condition, it will be treated as a warranty.

3 Common law may allow the use of exclusion clauses to limit liability for breach of contract or negligence.

4 When a party seeks to rely on an exclusion clause he or she must prove that the clause was an integral part of the contract, that the other party was aware of the existence of the clause and that the contract was entered into in the knowledge that the clause would apply.

5 Exclusion clauses may be communicated in a number of ways: on contractual documents; on receipts; on tickets; on bill boards; on signs or in many other ways. It will be very difficult to avoid an exclusion clause contained in a contractual document that is signed by both parties.

6 Where an exclusion clause is correctly worded it will be possible to exclude liability, even when one party fundamentally breaches a contract.

7 The Unfair Contract Terms Act 1977 aims to protect consumers, and in certain circumstances businesses, from unreasonable exclusion clauses.

8 The UCTA77 makes certain exclusion clauses void in any consumer transaction.

9 The Unfair Terms in Consumer Contracts Regulations 1994 implemented the EC Directive 93/13 on Unfair Terms in Consumer Contracts.

10 The UTCCR94 introduced the concept of good faith into British law and provided further protection for consumers against unfair contract terms.

15

The Sale of Goods Act 1979 (Part A)

Chapter objectives

By the end of this chapter you should be able to:

∎ recognize the elements of a contract for a sale of goods

∎ identify the four different types of good classified under the Sale of Goods Act 1979: specific, unascertained, future and existing

∎ recognize the terms implied by the Act

∎ understand the rules relating to the transfer of the property in the goods

∎ recognize the ways in which a seller may be able to prevent the passing of the property in the goods to a buyer, before full payment has been received

∎ understand the rules relating to the transfer of the risk in the goods.

∎ recognize the effects of recent legislation upon this area of law.

In the following five chapters we shall examine the statutes and case law relating to transactions concerning the consumer in both contract and tort. In this chapter and the next we shall look at the Sale of Goods Act 1979 (SOGA79). SOGA79 has recently had some of its most important sections amended by the Sale and Supply of Goods Act 1994 (SSGA94). A further, minor piece of legislation, the Sale of Goods (Amendment) Act 1994 (SOGA94), has also made some further amendments. We shall consider the effects of the two new Acts as we progress through this part of the book. In Chapter 16 we shall also study the Supply of Goods and Services Act 1982, and in Chapter 17 we shall examine the Consumer Credit Act 1974. Chapters 18 and 19 will look at various other legislation relating to the supply of goods and services, including the Consumer Protection Act 1987, the Fair Trading Act 1973 and the Trades Description Act 1968.

SOGA79, SS. 2 TO 20

The SOGA79 is an extremely important piece of legislation, so I will work through the main sections, quoting the wording of the Act

▶ Be aware that the SOGA79 is a consolidating Act, bringing together several previous Acts. Many of the cases in this chapter date from before 1979, yet contain references to sections of the 1979 Act. This is because many of the sections of the Sale of Goods Act 1893 were the same as the current 1979 Act. Therefore, it is simpler to quote the sections as being from the 1979 Act, though prior to 1979 they were from the 1893 Act.

▶ **Chattels** – the legal term used to describe property other than freehold land. We would more readily understand the term personal property in place of **chattels personal**. **Chattels real** are simply leaseholds, i.e. land or property held under a lease. A lease is a contract by which land or property is conveyed to a person for a specified period, usually for rent, although leases can also be owned.

▶ **Emblements** are an annual crop produced by agricultural labour (*fructus industriales*), not naturally growing things (*fructus naturales*).

▶ **Industrial growing crops** are similar to emblements but they take longer than a year to grow.

▶ **Tangible** – describes assets that can be touched.

▶ **Intangible** – describes assets that can't be touched.

and explaining the effects of the section by making reference to relevant cases. As there is so much to cover in relation to the SOGA79, I have, for the purposes of this book, divided the material into two parts: in this chapter we shall look at Sections 2 to 20; the following chapter will cover Sections 21 to 57.

Section 2: Contract of sale

SOGA79, s. 2

(1) A contract of sale of goods is a contract by which the seller transfers or agrees to transfer the property in goods to the buyer for a money consideration, called the price.

(2) There may be a contract of sale between one part owner and another.

(3) A contract of sale may be absolute or conditional.

(4) Where under a contract of sale the property in the goods is transferred from the seller to the buyer the contract is called a sale.

(5) Where under a contract of sale the transfer of the property in the goods is to take place at a future time or subject to some condition later to be fulfilled the contract is called an agreement to sell.

(6) An agreement to sell becomes a sale when the time elapses or the conditions are fulfilled subject to which the property in the goods is to be transferred.

Section 2 supplies the definition of a sale of goods. However, to understand the definition we need to further define 'goods' and 'transfer'.

Goods

SOGA79, s. 61 (as amended by the SSGA94), which is an explanatory section giving definitions and explanations of many terms found in the Act, describes goods as being:

> … all personal **chattels** other than things in action and money.

Section 61 then further defines what goods might be. **Emblements**, **industrial growing crops** and anything that is attached to the land that will be severed from the land prior to sale can be classified as goods. So where a forest is bought for the timber and the wood is to be severed from the land as a part of the contract, that would constitute goods. If the forest had been sold as a nature walk the contract would not come under the classification of goods. Mineral and other mining rights would not be goods either, though if the minerals or coal had been extracted, they would.

There is a simple 'rule of thumb' for determining whether something is 'goods'. If you can touch it – if it is **tangible** – it probably is, if you can't it isn't. Therefore, debts, patents, trademarks, rights or other interests in property and other **intangible** assets are not included under the SOGA79.

Money is not considered to be a good under the SOGA79, unless it is traded as a commodity on the exchange markets, or when money is antique, such as a Roman coin. Contracts of exchange or barter are also not covered by the Act. However, where an article is taken in part exchange, it might constitute a sale under the SOGA79. If it is not a sale then it would now be covered by the Supply of Goods and Services Act 1982 (SOGAS82), which would imply similar terms into the contract.

Goods are further classified under various sections of the Act into four types:

1 **specific goods** – goods identified at the time of the sale: for example, a specific chair in a furniture shop;
2 **unascertained goods** – goods that are only generally identified at the time of the agreed sale: for example, 2 tonnes of coal from a coal merchants;
3 **future goods** – goods that are yet to be grown or manufactured: for example, crops;
4 **existing goods** – goods that exist at the time of the contract, though at that time they may not be specific, i.e. they may not yet have been appropriated to the contract.

These four classifications will become more important later on when we consider buyers' and sellers' duties and remedies under the SOGA79.

Transfer

Certain types of contract of sale will be regulated by both the SOGA79 and the Consumer Credit Act 1974 (CCA74). In a straight-forward sale where the goods pass at the time of the sale, the transfer of the property in the goods will take place at the time of sale. In a contract where there are staged payments, the date that the final staged payment is fixed to occur will generally be the time that the transfer of the property in the goods takes place. This latter type of agreement is a conditional sale agreement and is subject to regulation by both the SOGA79 and the CCA74.

Credit sale agreements differ from conditional sale agreements, the transfer of property rights generally taking place immediately, no reservation being made until all monies have been paid. Credit agreements are subject to both the SOGA79 and the CCA74. Rental agreements are not concerned with the transference of ownership, therefore the vast majority will fall outside the provisions of the SOGA79.

Hire purchase agreements are not contracts of sale. A hirer merely has the right to **bailment** of the goods and the option to purchase at the end of the agreement. (Leasing contracts can be considered to be the same as hire purchase contracts.) These types of agreement are covered by the SOGAS82.

▶ **Bailment** – where goods are given to a person, called a bailee, under a contract of hire purchase by a bailor.

(ACT)
1 List the four types of goods classified under the SOGA79.
2 Which types of contract will not be covered under the SOGA79?

Section 3: Capacity to buy and sell

This section states that the normal rules apply relating to capacity to contract, and outlines that persons of limited capacity must pay a fair price for goods, which they have contracted to purchase.

> **SOGA79, s. 3**
>
> (2) Where necessaries are sold and delivered to a minor or to a person who by reason of mental incapacity or drunkenness is incompetent to contract, he must pay a reasonable price for them.
>
> (3) … necessaries means goods suitable to the condition in life of the person concerned and to his actual requirements at the time of sale and delivery.

► Remember how this was discussed in Chapter 11 in relation to the contractual capacity of minors?

Section 4: How a contract for the sale of goods is made

Contracts may be oral or written, or a mixture of both, or they may be implied by the conduct of the parties.

> **SOGA79, s. 4**
>
> (1) … a contract of sale may be made in writing (either with or without seal), or by word of mouth, or partly in writing and partly by word of mouth, or may be implied from the conduct of the parties.

Section 6: Goods that have perished

> **SOGA79, s. 6**
>
> Where there is a contract for the sale of specific goods, and the goods without the knowledge of the seller have perished at the time when a contract is made, the contract is void.

Section 7: Goods perishing before sale but after agreement to sell

► Examples of the application of SOGA79, ss. 6 and 7, may be found in Chapter 11, in the section on mistake.

> **SOGA79, s. 7**
>
> Where there is an agreement to sell specific goods and subsequently the goods, without any fault on the part of the seller or buyer, perish before the risk passes to the buyer, the agreement is avoided.

Section 8: Ascertainment of price

SOGA79, s. 8

(1) The price in a contract of sale may be fixed by the contract, or may be left to be fixed in a manner agreed by the contract, or may be determined by the course of dealing between the parties.

(2) Where the price is not determined as mentioned in subsection (1) above the buyer must pay a reasonable price.

(3) What is a reasonable price is a question of fact dependent on the circumstances of each particular case.

A contract need not generally be considered to be incomplete because the parties have failed to agree a price for the goods. Under s. 8(3) a court may determine a reasonable price.

Section 9: Agreement to sell at valuation

SOGA79, s. 9

(1) Where there is an agreement to sell goods on the terms that the price is to be fixed by the valuation of a third party, and he cannot or does not make the valuation, the agreement is avoided; but if the goods or any part of them have been delivered to and appropriated by the buyer he must pay a reasonable price for them.

(2) Where the third party is prevented from making the valuation by the fault of the seller or buyer, the party not at fault may maintain an action for damages against the party at fault.

Section 10, relating to stipulations about time being the essence of a contract, and s. 11, concerning when a term can be considered to be a condition or a warranty, have been dealt with in Chapter 14, under terms of a contract. However, to recap, late delivery or late payment will normally represent a breach of a warranty, not a breach of a condition.

Section 12: Implied terms about title

SOGA79, s. 12(1) (as amended by the SSGA94)

(1) In a contract of sale, other than one to which subsection (3) below applies, there is an implied term on the part of the seller that in the case of a sale he has a right to sell the goods, and in the case of an agreement to sell he will have such a right at the time when the property is to pass.

The following case shows an unusual application of this section to circumstances involving a stolen car.

Rowland v. Divall **(1923) 2 KB 500**

 This case concerned a stolen 'Albert' car. The defendant bought the car in April 1922 from the thief. The defendant later sold the car to the plaintiff, a car dealer, for £334. The plaintiff then sold the car on to a Colonel Railsdon for £400. The car was later seized by the police because it was a stolen car. The plaintiff repaid Colonel Railsdon his money and brought this action to recover the £334 from the defendant.

COURT HELD

The plaintiff could succeed. There had been a breach of the SOGA79, s. 12(1); the plaintiff had not received what he had contracted for, i.e. the property in the goods. The whole amount of £334 was awarded to the plaintiff.

SOGA79, s. 12(2) (as amended by the SSGA94)

(2) In a contract of sale, other than one to which subsection (3) applies, there is an implied term that:
   (a) the goods are free, and will remain free until the time when the property is to pass, from any charge or encumbrance not disclosed or known to the buyer before the contract is made; and
   (b) the buyer will enjoy quiet possession of the goods except so far as it may be disturbed by the owner or other person entitled to the benefit of any charge or encumbrance so disclosed or known.

SOGA79, s. 12(3, 4 and 5) (as amended by the SSGA94)

(3) This subsection applies to a contract of sale in the case of which there appears from the contract or is to be inferred from its circumstances an intention that the seller should transfer only such title as he or a third person may have.
(4) In a contract to which (3) applies there is an implied term that all charges or encumbrances known to the seller and not known to the buyer have been disclosed to the buyer before the contract is made.
(5) In a contract to which (3) applies there is also an implied term that none of the following will disturb the buyer's quiet possession of the goods, namely:
   (a) the seller;
   (b) in a case where the parties to the contract intend that the seller should transfer only such title as a third person may have, that person;
   (c) anyone claiming through or under the seller or that third person otherwise than under a charge or encumbrance disclosed or known to the buyer before the contract is made.
(5A) As regards England, Wales and Northern Ireland, the term implied by subsection (1) above is a condition and the terms implied by subsections (2), (4) and (5) above are warranties.

▶ In the case of *Mason v. Birmingham* (see Chapter 16, p. 308), the buyer of a stolen typewriter brought an action under s. 12(2). The court awarded her the purchase price plus the cost of a repair that she had carried out to the typewriter, for breach of warranty under s. 12(2).

Subsection 5A was added by the SSGA94 to clarify the position where any of the newly described terms in this section were breached.

Subsection 12(5) – (a), (b) and (c) – allows for the sale of limited title to goods, while maintaining terms relating to quiet possession, and knowledge of encumbrances and charges. It is difficult at first to think of circumstances in which these sections would apply, but there are, unfortunately, many examples. The most common one is the sale of goods by a bailiff when the goods have been seized after a judgment. If any of these subections is breached the purchaser will have a right of action against the seller of the goods.

Section 13: Sale by description

SOGA79, s. 13 (as amended by the SSGA94)

(1)   Where there is a contract for the sale of goods by description, there is an implied term that the goods will correspond with the description.

(2)   If the sale is by sample as well as by description it is not sufficient that the bulk of the goods corresponds with the sample if the goods do not also correspond with the description.

(3)   A sale of goods is not prevented from being a sale by description by reason only that, being exposed for sale or hire, they are selected by the buyer.

The vast majority of contracts for the sale of goods could fall into s. 13. This is because most goods are packaged when bought and there is no real opportunity to examine them at the time of sale, therefore they are generally sold by description. Mail-order goods are another example. The following classic case illustrates that, even when the purchaser has an opportunity to examine goods, it could still be a sale by description.

Beale v. Taylor (1967) 3 All ER 253

This case concerned the sale of a car that was advertised as a Triumph Herald 1200, a description that the advertiser believed to be correct. The plaintiff answered the advert and visited the defendant (who had advertised the car) to view the car. The plaintiff inspected the car, noticing a 1200 disc on the rear of it. He then bought the car. Subsequently he discovered that the car was in fact made up of two cars welded together. The front was a Triumph 948, the rear a Triumph 1200. The car was unroadworthy because the two half-bodies had not been properly welded together. The plaintiff brought the action under s. 13 for breach of condition, claiming damages.

COURT HELD

The plaintiff succeeded. The car was not what it was described to be, notwithstanding that the plaintiff had viewed the car before buying it. The defendant was in breach of s. 13.

▶ In *Smith v. Lazarus* (1981) (unreported) 23 June, Court of Appeal (Lexis), Smith bought a car from Lazarus, after first viewing it in near darkness at Lazarus's house. It had been advertised as having a full MOT. The morning after the sale he checked the car over to find that it was unroadworthy. He brought the action under s. 14, arguing that there was an implied warranty as to the fitness of the vehicle. The court held (unwillingly) that it was a case of *caveat emptor*. Smith had bought what he had seen, the warranty that the car had an MOT was valid. An MOT only meant that on one particular day the car was in a certain condition.

► Remember *caveat emptor* (let the buyer beware) from Chapter 12 (p. 189). A court will expect you to take care when you enter into a contract to purchase an item. They will not allow you to avoid a contract merely because you change your mind or decide that what you have bought is no good for you. If you get what you paid for a court will not help you.

► See the next chapter, p. 311, for the new provisions introduced by the SSGA94 relating to this area of law.

It may be possible to avoid the terms of s. 13 by including words in the contract such as 'bought as seen' or 'sold as seen', which have been held to remove the provisions of sale by description. It is always a good idea to include 'sold as seen' in the contract when selling a second-hand motor vehicle.

The courts have been prepared rigorously to endorse the conditions in s. 13. Where one party has failed to match the description in a minor and trivial way, and this has caused no loss to the injured party, they have been allowed to treat the variation as a breach of a condition. This is clearly shown in the next case.

Moore and Co. v. Landauer and Co. (1921) 2 KB 519

This case concerned the purchase of canned fruit to be delivered in cases containing thirty tins. Delivery was delayed and some of the tins were packed in cases of twenty-four, though the correct amount was delivered. The buyer rejected the whole consignment. The plaintiffs brought the action for damages.

COURT HELD
The plaintiffs could not succeed. The contract was a sale by description and the goods did not correspond with the description, therefore the buyer was entitled to reject the goods.

ACT Louise agrees to buy a stereo for £80 from Doxelows. She has the option to pay by the following methods:

(a) a hire purchase agreement over two years;
(b) a conditional sale agreement;
(c) a leasing agreement.

Which, if any, are subject to the Sale of Goods Act 1979?

Section 14: Implied terms about quality or fitness (as amended by the SSGA94)

> **SOGA79, s. 14(1) and (2) (as amended by the SSGA94)**
>
> (1) Except as provided by this section and section 15 below and subject to any other enactment, there is no implied term about the quality or fitness for any particular purpose of goods supplied under a contract of sale.
> (2) Where the seller sells goods in the course of a business, there is an implied term that the goods supplied under the contract are of satisfactory quality.
> (a) For the purposes of this Act, goods are of satisfactory quality if they meet the standard that a reasonable person would regard as satisfactory, taking account of any description of the goods, the price (if relevant) and all the other relevant circumstances.

(b) For the purposes of this Act, the quality of goods includes their state and condition and the following (among others) are in appropriate cases aspects of the quality of goods:

    (a) fitness for all the purposes for which goods of the kind in question are commonly supplied,

    (b) appearance and finish,

    (c) freedom from minor defects,

    (d) safety, and

    (e) durability.

(2C) The term implied by subsection (2) above does not extend to any matter making the quality of goods unsatisfactory:

    (a) which is specifically drawn to the buyer's attention before the contract is made,

    (b) where the buyer examines the goods before the contract is made, which that examination ought to reveal, or

    (c) in the case of a contract for sale by sample, which would have been apparent on a reasonable examination of the sample.

Subsection 6 now states that the terms implied by subsections 2 and 3 are conditions.

Section 14 has been heavily amended by the SSGA94. Before the changes, the criterion used to ascertain the quality of any goods was whether they were of 'merchantable' quality? Merchantable quality has now been replaced with satisfactory quality, which has been defined as 'the standard expected by a reasonable person'. This test is objective and, therefore, in certain circumstances, the goods may pass the test even when they are not to the standard required by the purchaser.

The new section continues by listing the factors that may be used to ascertain the satisfactory quality of goods. Depending upon the individual circumstances of each case, some or all of the factors may be applicable. The factors are not listed in any particular order of preference and none carries more weight than any other. Many of the provisions of the new section are similar to those they have replaced. However, it is considered that the law has been clarified and strengthened to enable the consumer to obtain redress more easily. While it will always be for the court to decide whether goods are of satisfactory quality, its task will be made easier by the inclusion of certain factors, such as appearance and finish, freedom from minor defects, safety and durability. For a new product, such as a brand new car, it is imagined that the appearance and finish would have to be immaculate. With time, and the progression of cases through the courts, the effects of the changes will become apparent. In the meantime, the following examples of the application of the old section may be considered to be a good guide to how future cases will be decided.

Subsection 14(2) tells us that when a person is in business and he or she normally supplies the goods in question they must be of 'satisfactory quality'. This applies, unless any defects have been pointed out to the buyer, or the seller has had a chance to examine the goods and ought to have noticed the defect. If the seller does not normally sell that type of goods then there is no implied condition of fitness or satisfactory quality. (Terms relating to description and satisfactory quality in sales by sample remain.) None of these provisions applies to private sales.

A buyer is not forced to examine goods. Where a buyer chooses to do so and fails to spot any obvious defects, he or she will lose the protection of the SOGA79, s. 14(2). Where any defects are pointed out they will also lose protection under this subsection.

There are many cases on the SOGA79, s. 14(2), because the definition of 'merchantable quality' was something that the courts interpreted according to the circumstances of each different case. Further guidance was given under the old subsection 14(6) of the 1979 Act.

SOGA79, s. 14(6)

(6) Goods of any kind are of merchantable quality within the meaning of subsection (2) if they are as fit for the purpose or purposes for which goods of that kind are commonly bought as it is reasonable to expect having regard to any description applied to them, the price (if relevant) and all other relevant circumstances.

The above subsection 14(6) has been replaced with the following new subsection 14(6) by the SSGA94:

As regards England and Wales and Northern Ireland, the terms implied by subsections 14(2) and 14(3) above are conditions.

You will remember that a breach of a condition of a contract gives the injured party more options than a breach of a warranty. Under the new subsection 14(1) the word 'condition' has been replaced by 'term'. When a dispute falls outside subsections 14(2) and 14(3), it will be for the courts to decide whether the term breached was a condition or a warranty. I have left in the old subsection 14(6) here to show how the Act sought to aid the courts in arriving at decisions under this section. The impact of the new sections will probably not be major and the following cases may still be considered to be a fair indication of how future cases will be decided.

The leading modern case under the old law concerned a motor vehicle.

Rogers v. Parish (Scarborough) Ltd **(1987) 2 WLR 353**

The plaintiff bought a new Range Rover from the defendants for £16,000 under a conditional sale agreement. It was defective in the engine, oil seals, body work and gearbox. Over a period of six months and 5,000 miles the garage attempted to fix the car. At the end of that period the plaintiff rejected the car and sued for the return of his pay-

ments, plus damages for the breach of contract under s. 14(2). The defence argued that because the car was roadworthy and worked it was of merchantable quality.

COURT HELD

The plaintiff could succeed. It was not enough that the car worked. In this case the court considered the type of car (top of the range), the reliability expected, the price paid, ease of handling, and the pride in the vehicle's interior and exterior appearance. If you pay top money you have a right to expect top performance.

Where the vehicle concerned is second-hand the buyer must not expect the same as would be expected from a new car. The following case illustrates this point.

Bartlett v. Sidney Marcus (1965) 1 WLR 1013

The plaintiff bought a second-hand Jaguar car. At the time of the sale it was pointed out that the car had a slightly defective clutch and the price was slightly reduced to £950. After a short period the car was taken to a garage where it was found that the clutch was seriously impaired, the repair costing £84. The plaintiff sued for the cost of the repairs.

COURT HELD

The plaintiff failed. The car was of merchantable quality: 'it is merchantable if it is in a usable condition, … [with] a second-hand car defects may appear sooner or later and, in the absence of an express warranty, he has no redress.'

The above result must be contrasted with the following case.

Crowther v. Shannon Motor Company (1975) 1 WLR 30

This case concerned the sale of a second-hand Jaguar, for which the plaintiff paid the defendants £390. The car was eight years old and had done 82,000 miles. The plaintiff drove the car for three weeks, covering 2,300 miles. The car then stopped going, and it was discovered that the engine was virtually useless and had been so when it was sold to the buyer. Expert advice stated that it was reasonable to expect a Jaguar engine to last for 100,000 miles. The previous owner of the car had sold it to the defendants on the understanding that the engine was finished. The plaintiff sued for the cost of a new engine.

COURT HELD

The plaintiff could succeed. The car was not of merchantable quality, neither was it fit for the purpose for which it had been sold (s. 14(3)).

► The courts have been prepared to use this case to achieve the same result in other similar cases concerning new cars, where the nature of the defects prevents the car from ever being restored to its new condition or where the defects have caused the vehicle to be dangerous to drive.

► Don't forget that merchantable quality has been replaced with satisfactory quality under the SSGA94.

▶ Law Commission Report No. 137 in 1987 recommended that subsection 14(2) be replaced by a section implying a term that goods be of 'acceptable quality', i.e. meet the standards of a reasonable person, considering the description, price, etc. The new SSGA94 has implemented many of the Commission's recommendations, substituting 'satisfactory quality' for 'acceptable quality'.

It would seem that where a defect occurs after the purchase of a second-hand car, the chances of succeeding against the seller are better when the event happens shortly after the purchase. Where any defect is pointed out that is subsequently found to be worse than at first thought, the buyer will have little chance of redress against the seller. The less that you pay for a vehicle the less your expectations of that vehicle will be, therefore the courts will offer you only limited protection.

Subection 14(3): Implied terms about fitness for purpose

SOGA79, s. 14(3) (as amended by the SSGA94)

(3) Where the seller sells goods in the course of a business and the buyer, expressly or by implication, makes known:
  (a) to the seller, or,
  (b) where the purchase price or part of it is payable by instalments and the goods were previously sold by a credit broker to the seller, to that credit broker,
any particular purpose for which the goods are being bought, there is an implied term that the goods supplied under the contract are reasonably fit for that purpose, whether or not that is a purpose for which such goods are commonly supplied, except where the circumstances show that the buyer does not rely, or that it is unreasonable for him to rely, on the skill or judgement of the seller or credit broker.

In this subsection the SSGA94 merely replaced the word 'condition' with 'term'. It has no effect since in subsection 14(6) (see above) it is stated that the term in subsection 14(3) is a condition.

Subsection 14(3) states that, where you purchase goods and you rely on the skill of the seller in advising you that the goods will do what you want to them to do, there is an implied term that the goods must perform as you have been advised. It does not matter if the goods are not normally used for the purpose that you want them for. A simple example might be the purchase of a television satellite dish, where you told the assistant that you wanted to be able to receive Canal Plus, a French channel, and you subsequently discovered that the dish only received programmes transmitted from Germany.

▶ Section 14(3) includes non-manufactured goods. A dairy was held liable under this section when a woman died of typhoid contracted from contaminated milk.

The skill and judgement of the seller are vital to this section, and it is considered that a seller has exercised skill and judgement in the selection of his or her stock. Where the seller has no say in the selection of his or her stock – for example, in a franchised business selling only one product – and the customer is aware of that fact, the seller will not be liable under this section. However, the seller would still be liable under the SOGA79, s. 14(2) (satisfactory quality).

If the goods normally have one use – for example, a washing machine to wash clothes, an umbrella to keep off the rain – then the purchaser makes the purpose of the goods known by implication.

The following unusual and painful Australian case illustrates this last point.

Grant v. Australian Knitting Mills Ltd (1936) AC 85

This case was heard by the Privy Council. It concerned a pair of woolly knickers. The plaintiff bought the knickers and wore them. Unfortunately after a couple of days he developed a skin rash which started at his ankles and spread to most parts of his body. It was discovered that the rash was caused by sulphite that had remained in the knickers after the manufacturing process. The rash forced him to spend a long period confined in hospital. Grant sued the manufacturers in negligence and the retailers under a section of the South Australian Sale of Goods Act 1895, which was the same as the SOGA79, s. 14.

COURT HELD
The plaintiff could succeed. The retailers were in breach of s. 14(2), as the goods were not of merchantable quality, and s. 14(3), as the goods were not fit for the purpose for which they were sold. The manufacturers were held to be liable in negligence.

► Don't forget that the House of Lords still acts as the final Court of Appeal for several of the Commonwealth countries. See Chapter 4. At the time of writing Australia still accepts the House of Lords as the final Court of Appeal, though it appears that Australia is going to reject its Commonwealth ties with Britain in the near future.

1 What is the implied term under the SOGA79, s. 14(2)?
2 What different views do the courts take with regard to new and second-hand motor vehicles?

> Under the Consumer Protection Act 1987 a **strict liability** offence has now been created to cater for situations like this, 'where any damage is caused wholly or partly by a defect in a product, every person to whom subsection (2) applies shall be liable for the damage ... (2) the producer of the product.' This will be considered in more detail in Chapter 19.

► **Strict liability** – an offence whereby the injured party does not need to prove any fault, negligence or intention on behalf of the other party. The injured party merely has to prove that the alleged incident caused the injury or loss.

Grant v. Australian Knitting Mills should be contrasted with the following case, which illustrates that, where a buyer has any special requirements or abnormal medical complaints that may affect a contract, they must make them known to the seller prior to the contract.

Griffiths v. Peter Conway Ltd (1939) 1 All ER 685

The plaintiff bought a made-to-measure tweed coat from the defendants. After wearing the coat she developed dermatitis and brought an action under s. 14(3) for damages. However, it was established that the defendant had sensitive skin and that the coat would not have affected a person with normal skin. She had not made her condition known to the defendants.

COURT HELD
The plaintiff could not succeed. Subsection 14(3) did not apply because the defendants had not been informed of the plaintiff's peculiar medical condition.

The following case strikingly demonstrates that the implied terms of fitness and merchantability (now satisfactory quality) apply to extra things supplied under a contract, such as packaging, containers, instructions and anything else supplied with the goods.

Wilson v. Rickett, Cockerell and Co. Ltd (1954) 1 QB 598

A housewife put some 'Coalite' coal on her fire, which had been delivered to her by the defendant coal merchants. Unknown to either party, the sacks of coal contained some explosives that had been used in the mining of the coal. The coal exploded, causing damage to the house. The plaintiff sued under SOGA79, s. 14, to recover damages.

COURT HELD
The court of first instance found for the defendant, stating that under s. 14(3) the Coalite was fit for the purpose and the explosion must have been caused by something delivered with the Coalite. The Court of Appeal ruled that there was a breach of s. 14(2). Clearly the goods had been supplied with the explosives, therefore they were not of merchantable quality. The plaintiff succeeded in obtaining damages.

The following case shows that where advice has been sought from a seller, the seller will be liable where his or her advice is acted upon.

Priest v. Last (1903) 2 KB 148

The plaintiff went into the defendant's chemist shop and asked for a hot-water bottle. The bottle was used by the plaintiff's wife who suffered from cramp. Soon after the purchase the bottle burst, causing her to be badly scalded. The bottle was examined and found to be unsuitable to be used as a hot-water bottle. The plaintiff sued under s. 14(3) for damages.

COURT HELD
The plaintiff could succeed. He had relied on the seller's skill and judgement. The hot-water bottle had been used for its obvious purpose, therefore, it didn't matter that he had not specifically informed the chemist what use he intended to make of the bottle.

It may transpire that goods are of a merchantable (now satisfactory) quality, but they are not fit for the purpose required. The following case illustrates this point.

► A solicitor who broke a tooth on a Bath bun that had a stone in it was able to obtain damages under s. 14(3). The bun was not fit for eating.

Baldry v. Marshall (1925) 1 KB 260

The plaintiff owned a Talbot racing car in which his wife refused to travel. He sought to change it for a car suitable for touring in, to keep his wife happy. The plaintiff's manager advised him that a Bugatti would be suitable. After inspecting the chassis of a Bugatti the defendant agreed to buy it, when the body had been put on it. When the Bugatti was delivered it was similar to the racing car and not suitable for touring. The plaintiff returned the car to the defendant and sued to recover the £1,000 deposit that he had paid.

COURT HELD

The plaintiff could succeed. The defendant was in breach of s. 14(3). The plaintiff had relied upon the skill and judgement of the seller in advising which car would be suitable.

Subsection 14(5): Sale by an agent

SOGA79, s. 14(5) (as amended by SSGA94)

The preceding provisions of this section apply to a sale by a person who in the course of a business is acting as agent for another as they apply to a sale by a principal in the course of a business, except where that other is not selling in the course of a business and either the buyer knows that fact or reasonable steps are taken to bring it to the notice of the buyer before the contract is made.

Subsection 14(5) allows a private seller to sell through an agent, and to be able to exclude the implied terms of satisfactory quality and fitness, provided that the buyer is made aware that it is a private sale, or reasonable steps are taken to bring it to his or her notice. Otherwise all the implied terms will apply when a sale is made by an agent, on behalf of a principal, when they are both acting in the normal course of their business.

 Making reference to relevant Acts and cases answer the following question.

Philip, who is allergic to leather, ordered a Morgan GT sports car, paying a deposit of £5,000. He advised the dealer, when making the order, that he wanted the top of the range model. When the car was delivered, it was the most expensive model that they produced. Philip accepted the car but after a short period the leather upholstery caused him to develop a skin rash. He then advised the dealer that he wished to reject the car because of the upholstery and refused to make any further payments. Can Philip do this?

Section 15: Sale by sample

SOGA79, s. 15 (as amended by SSGA94)

(1) A contract of sale is a contract for sale by sample where there is an express or implied term to that effect in the contract.

(2) In the case of a contract for sale by sample there is an implied term:

    (a) that the bulk will correspond with the sample in quality;

    (b) (repealed)

    (c) that the goods will be free from any defect, making their quality unsatisfactory, that would not be apparent on reasonable examination of the sample.

(3) As regards England and Wales and Northern Ireland, the term implied by subsection (2) above is a condition.

Prior to being amended, this section contained a clause, s. 15(2)(b), relating to the buyer having a reasonable chance to compare the bulk with the sample. This clause has now been included into the new subsections 34(2) and 35(2)(b) (see Chapter 16, pages 299 and 301).

The requirements of section 15 are that a contract will be a sale by sample only where there is clear evidence that the parties intended it to be so – for example, the contract would be worded to that effect. The mere provision of a sample would not turn a contract into a sale by sample. However, a court could interpret the circumstances of a contract to imply that it was a sale by sample. This section applies to both business and private sales. The following classic case illustrates the application of s. 15.

Godley v. Perry (Burton and Sons (Bermondsey) Ltd, Third Party, Graham, Fourth Party) **(1960) 1 All ER 36**

 This case concerned a small boy, a catapult, a newsagent and two wholesalers. The boy bought a catapult from the newsagent. Upon using it, it broke and caused him to lose an eye. When examined the catapult was found to be poorly made with material unsuitable for the purpose. The newsagent had bought the catapult on sample from a wholesaler, who had also bought it on sample from another wholesaler. The newsagent's wife had tested the sample catapult by pulling back the elastic a few times. The action was brought on behalf of the boy under s. 14(2 and 3) against the first defendant, who brought in his supplier under s. 15(2)(c), who also brought in his supplier under the same section.

COURT HELD

The boy could succeed. The catapult was unfit for the purpose (s. 14(3)) and not of merchantable quality (s. 14(2)). The two wholesalers were both found to be in breach of s. 15(2)(c). The catapult had a defect that was not readily apparent upon examination of the subject. The liability fed down the line from the newsagent to the first wholesaler and on to the second wholesaler.

Godley is an excellent example of the doctrine of privity of contract. Only the parties to a contract can benefit or suffer from that contract. Godley's contract is with the newsagent. He has no contract with either of the wholesalers. The newsagent has a contract with Godley and a contract with the first wholesaler, but they are two separate contracts. The same applies to the first wholesaler. He has two separate contracts: one with the newsagent and the other with the second wholesaler. It also illustrates that where a supplier or retailer is sued for a breach of condition the retailer can indemnify himself or herself against the supplier, who in turn can then claim an indemnity against his or her supplier or manufacturer.

► For more on the doctrine of privity of contract, see Chapter 14, p. 251.

The SSGA94 inserted a new section 15(A), which is detailed below.

> **SOGA79, s. 15(A) (as amended by SSGA94)**
>
> (1) Where in the case of a contract of sale –
>   (a) the buyer would, apart from this subsection, have the right to reject goods by reason of a breach on the part of the seller of a term implied by section 13, 14 or 15 above, but
>   (b) the breach is so slight that it would be unreasonable for him to reject them then, if the buyer does not deal as consumer, the breach is not to be treated as a breach of condition but may be treated as a breach of warranty.
> (2) This section applies unless a contrary intention appears in, or is to be implied from, the contract.
> (3) It is for the seller to show that a breach fell within subsection (1)(b) above.
> (4) This section does not apply to Scotland.

► Look back at the case of *Moore and Co. v. Landauer and Co.* (page 274). The court held that the buyer was entitled to reject the goods because, although the correct amount had been delivered, it had not been packaged in the way that was specified in the contract. This, however, would appear to fall outside the provisions of section 15(A).

The effect of this new section is to remove from a buyer who is other than a consumer (i.e. in a business transaction) the right to reject the goods for breach of condition, where the breach is so minimal or trivial that it would be unreasonable for him or her to reject them. The breach of condition must be treated as a breach of warranty unless the contract had indicated otherwise. For example, the exact details of delivery could have been made, by agreement, a condition of the contract. The new section 15(A) only applies to breaches of certain conditions; those under sections 13, 14 and 15 of the SOGA1979. This section will not apply to a consumer purchase.

Sections 16 to 20 of the SOGA79 are all concerned with the transfer of property between seller and buyer.

Section 16: Goods must be ascertained

> **SOGA79, s. 16**
>
> Where there is a contract for the sale of unascertained goods no property in the goods is transferred to the buyer unless and until the goods are ascertained.

If we recall the four different types of goods classified under the SOGA79 then this section will make sense.

1. **Specific goods** – goods identified at the time of the sale, for example, a specific chair in a furniture shop.
2. **Unascertained goods** – goods that are only generally identified at the time of the agreed sale, for example, 2 tonnes of coal from a coal merchant.
3. **Future goods** – goods that are yet to be grown or manufactured, for example, crops.
4. **Existing goods** – goods that exist at the time of the contract, though at that time they may not be specific, i.e. they may not yet have been appropriated to the contract.

Therefore, where a contract is for unascertained goods the property in the goods will rest with the seller until the goods become ascertained, i.e. until the particular goods are selected for delivery.

Section 17: Property passes when intended to pass

> **SOGA79, s. 17**
>
> (1) Where there is a contract for the sale of specific or ascertained goods the property in them is transferred to the buyer at such time as the parties to the contract intend it to be transferred.
> (2) For the purpose of ascertaining the intention of the parties regard shall be had to the terms of the contract, the conduct of the parties and the circumstances of the case.

It is extremely important to establish when the property in the goods passes between the buyer and the seller. This is because if the goods are destroyed it must be established who is the owner at that time and, therefore, who is to bear the loss. In the case of bankruptcy or liquidation it is also necessary to establish ownership of the goods. When considering the remedies of the buyer and seller, it again becomes vital to establish ownership in order to determine whether to claim for non-acceptance, non-delivery or the price of the goods.

Under this section the court will examine the intention of the parties to establish the time of transference of the goods. The following case is an illustration of this section.

Re Anchor Line (Henderson Brothers) Ltd **(1936) 2 All ER 941**

This case concerned the sale of a crane, with Anchor Line being the purchasers and Ocean SS Co. the sellers. The crane was to be sold under a deferred purchase agreement, under which Anchor was to pay annual payments in respect of interest and depreciation, the latter to be deducted from the purchase price at the completion of the sale. Under the contract, Anchor was given full charge and responsibility of the

crane. Anchor went into liquidation and the court had to establish who were the owners of the crane.

COURT HELD

The property in the crane had not passed to Anchor. The terms of the contract indicated an intention that the property would not pass until the completion of the contract.

 Tony bought an axe from the local blacksmith, who had bought a batch of fifty from a wholesaler, after being allowed to use a sample axe for a month to test the axe. The contract between the blacksmith and the wholesaler was one of sample. Tony was chopping some firewood when the axe head flew off and hit him on the foot, breaking his toe. Can Tony claim damages for breach of contract from (a) the blacksmith; (b) the wholesaler; (c) both? Use relevant Acts, cases and rules in your answer.

Section 18: Rules for ascertaining intention

SOGA79, s. 18

Unless a different intention appears, the following are rules for ascertaining the intention of the parties as to the time at which the property in the goods is to pass to the buyer.

Rule 1

Where there is an unconditional contract for the sale of specific goods in a deliverable state the property in the goods passes to the buyer when the contract is made, and it is immaterial whether the time of payment or the time of delivery, or both, be postponed.

Where the parties make no reference to the time of transference of ownership, s. 18 provides certain rules to be used in order to establish it. In a sale of specific goods, property passes at the time the contract is formed, irrespective of payment or delivery. The following case illustrates this point.

Tarling v. Baxter **(1827) 6 B and C 360**

This contract concerned the sale of a haystack. The deal was struck but before the haystack could be collected it burned down.

COURT HELD

The buyer was liable to pay for the goods despite the fact that he never received them.

Under s. 18(1) the goods must be in a deliverable state for this subsection to apply. The following case illustrates how the law may decide that goods are not in a deliverable state.

Underwood Ltd v. Burgh Castle Brick and Cement Syndicate (1922) 1 KB 343

This contract concerned the sale of an engine for £650. The engine was extremely heavy and was bolted to a concrete emplacement. It took two days to disconnect the engine, and a further week to dismantle it and load it on to the railway carriage. Unfortunately, the engine was damaged in the process of loading it. The buyers refused delivery of the engine because of the damage. The sellers brought the action, arguing that the property in the goods had passed at the time the contract had been made.

 COURT HELD
The plaintiffs could not succeed. The property in the goods had not passed to the buyers, the goods not being in a deliverable state.

> **SOGA79, s. 18**
> Rule 2
>
> Where there is a contract for the sale of specific goods and the seller is bound to do something to the goods for the purpose of putting them into a deliverable state, the property does not pass until the thing is done and the buyer has notice that it has been done.

This rule is fairly straightforward. Where specific goods have been contracted for, but something extra is to be done to them, the property in the goods will not pass until the extra work is completed. An example might be where a new car has yet to have a sun-roof fitted to it. The property in the goods would pass when the sun-roof was fitted.

> **SOGA79, s. 18**
> Rule 3
>
> Where there is a contract for the sale of specific goods in a deliverable state but the seller is bound to weigh, measure, test or do some other act or thing with reference to the goods for the purpose of ascertaining the price, the property does not pass until the act or thing is done and the buyer has notice that it has been done.

This rule is less rarely used than most of the others. It works in the following way. If you opted to purchase the champion marrow at a horticultural show, the price to be paid per pound, the property would not pass until the marrow had been weighed in order to arrive at the final price and that price had been notified to you.

SOGA79, s. 18
Rule 4

When goods are delivered to the buyer on approval or on sale or return or other similar terms, the property in the goods passes to the buyer:

(a) when he signifies his approval or acceptance to the seller or does any other act adopting the transaction;
(b) if he does not signify his approval or acceptance to the seller but retains the goods without giving notice of rejection, then, if a time has been fixed for the return of the goods, on the expiration of that time, and, if no time has been fixed, on the expiration of a reasonable time.

There have been many cases that have been subjected to this rule. For example, many disputes have arisen where property has been sold on to a third party or where property that has been given on a sale or return basis has not been returned. The basic ground rules under Rule 4(a) are as follows. If Amanda is given goods on sale or return and she does one of the following:

- pledges those goods to someone else,
- sells them to someone else,
- gives them on sale or return to another party,

she will be deemed to have accepted the goods.

Under Rule 4(b) the following ground rules apply:

- If Amanda is given goods on sale or return and she fails to notify the seller of her acceptance or rejection, and keeps the goods for more than a reasonable time, she will be deemed to have accepted the goods.
- If there is a time fixed for the notification of acceptance, then the goods will become accepted at the expiration of that time.

If the goods are seized by the purchaser's creditors, the property in the goods will not pass and acceptance will not be deemed to have taken place. A seller may exclude Rule 4 by stating in the contract that the ownership of the goods will not pass until payment has been made for them. It will still be possible, under certain circumstances, for a purchaser to get good title to the goods where the buyer sells them on. Equity may enable good title to be obtained by a third party. Where, by his or her conduct, the owner leads the purchaser to believe that the person selling the goods has the right to sell the goods, the true owner will be **estopped** from denying good title to the purchaser.

Where a mercantile agent, as described under the Factors Act 1889, s. 1, sells goods as detailed, the buyer will obtain good title to the goods.

► **Estopped** – where a person by words or conduct leads another person to believe that a certain state of circumstances existed, that person will be prevented from later acting as if a set of circumstances different from those that he or she had suggested existed. In other words, that person would not be able to sue successfully later for possession of the goods. See also doctrine of promissory estoppel, Chapter 10, p. 159.

Factors Act 1889, s. 2

(1) Where a mercantile agent is, with the consent of the owner, in possession of goods or of the documents of title to goods, any sale, pledge, or other disposition of the goods, made by him when acting in the ordinary course of business of a mercantile agent, shall, subject to the provisions of the Act, be as valid as if he were expressly authorised by the owner of the goods to make the same; provided that the person taking under the disposition acts in good faith, and has not at the time of the disposition notice that the person making the disposition has not authority to make the same.

The following cases illustrate the application of Rule 4.

Genn v. Winkel (1911) All ER 910

The plaintiff, a diamond dealer, delivered diamonds to the defendant on a sale or return basis. The diamonds were then passed on to a third party under the same terms, who then passed them on to a fourth party under the same terms. The fourth party lost the diamonds. The plaintiff sued for the price of the diamonds.

COURT HELD

The plaintiff could succeed. The defendant, by his actions, was deemed to have accepted the goods under Rule 4(a).

Poole v. Smith's Car Sales (Balham) Ltd (1962) 2 All ER 482

 This case concerned a dispute between two car dealers. The plaintiff in August 1960 transferred two cars, on a sale or return basis, to the defendants. One of the cars was sold and paid for, as agreed, in September. The plaintiff requested the return of the second car but the defendants failed to comply. The plaintiff then wrote to the defendant stating that if the car was not returned by 10 November it would be deemed to be sold to the defendants. The car was not returned until 24 November and it was in a much deteriorated condition, having been used as a 'runabout' by the defendant's staff. The plaintiff refused delivery of the car and sued for the agreed sale or return price of £325.

COURT HELD

The plaintiff could succeed. The defendants had failed to honour the sale or return agreement, and had failed to return the car within a reasonable time. Therefore, they must pay the agreed contractual price.

> **SOGA79, s. 18**
> **Rule 5**
>
> (1) Where there is a contract for the sale of unascertained or future goods by description, and goods of that description and in a deliverable state are unconditionally appropriated to the contract, either by the seller with the assent of the buyer or by the buyer with the assent of the seller, the property in the goods then passes to the buyer; and the assent may be express or implied and may be given either before or after the appropriation is made.
>
> (2) Where in pursuance of the contract, the seller delivers the goods to the buyer or to a carrier or other bailee or custodier (whether named by the buyer or not) for the purpose of transmission to the buyer, and does not reserve the right of disposal, he is to be taken to have unconditionally appropriated the goods to the contract.

In order for Rule 5 to operate there must be a definite action to appropriate the goods to the contract: for example, where goods are selected for delivery the purchaser must be informed of the selection. Where a buyer orders goods that he or she knows are held in stock by the supplier, the buyer gives implied permission for the supplier to take the goods from his or her stock, thereby appropriating them to the contract.

Where goods are delivered to a buyer, or are given to a carrier to transport to the buyer, that will constitute an unconditional appropriation to the contract. However, if the seller reserves a right of disposal over the goods, or where the goods are only part of a larger amount of goods to be delivered and it is impossible to determine a particular set of goods, then property in the goods will not pass. The following case illustrates this point.

Healey v. Howlett and Sons **(1917) 1 KB 337**

This case concerned a contract for the purchase of twenty boxes of fish, the seller being based in Valencia, the purchaser in Ireland. The boxes were shipped as part of a consignment of 200, all of them being identically packed. None of them was marked for delivery to the buyers. Twenty boxes were selected by the shippers and delivered to the buyers, who rejected them because the fish was not of a merchantable condition. The sellers sued for the price of the goods, arguing that the goods had been appropriated to the contract under s. 18, Rule 5(1).

   COURT HELD

The plaintiff could not succeed. The goods had not been appropriated to the contract. None of the assignment had been marked for delivery to the defendants. The shippers had merely selected twenty boxes from the consignment.

When will the property in the goods pass in a sale of goods? Outline the rules of s. 18. When will they apply?

Section 19: Reservation of right of disposal

SOGA79, s. 19

(1) Where there is a contract for the sale of specific goods or where goods are subsequently appropriated to the contract, the seller may, by the terms of the contract or appropriation, reserve the right of disposal of the goods until certain conditions are fulfilled; and in such a case, notwithstanding the delivery of the goods to the buyer, or to a carrier or other bailee or custodier for the purpose of transmission to the buyer, the property in the goods does not pass to the buyer until the conditions imposed by the seller are fulfilled.

This section allows a seller to ensure, in some part, that the seller will be paid for his or her goods by the placing of a clause in the contract stating that the property in the goods will not pass to the buyer until the goods have been fully paid for. Should the buyer become bankrupt or go into liquidation, the seller will be able to recover the goods as the property in the goods would not have been passed to the buyer.

If the goods have been sold on, or have been used in the manufacture of other goods and they have then been sold on, it will not be as easy to reclaim the goods. However, it is possible to include a clause that will allow the goods to be traced to the next buyer, thus allowing the proceeds of any sale to be recovered. This type of clause has become known as a Romalpa clause, after a famous case that involved the use of a retention clause. The case is described below.

Aluminium Industrie Vaassen BV v. Romalpa Aluminium **(1976) 2 All ER 552**

 The plaintiffs sold aluminium foil to the defendants. The contract contained the following clauses:

1 property in the goods would not pass until all monies owing to the plaintiffs had been paid;
2 the foil transferred under the contract should be stored separately from any other goods;
3 if the foil was used in the manufacturing of any other products they should be stored separately from other goods;
4 goods made under 3 above could be sold by the defendants but the proceeds should be transferred to the plaintiffs to satisfy any outstanding debts.

The defendants went into liquidation owing the plaintiffs £120,000. The plaintiffs sought to recover previously supplied foil to the defendants, valued at £50,000, and the proceeds of sales made after the liquidation of goods made (as in 3 above), valued at £35,000.

COURT HELD

The plaintiffs could recover both amounts of money. The terms of the contract created a bailor–bailee relationship between the two parties. Property had not passed to the defendants, therefore the plaintiffs could recover their own goods plus the proceeds of the sale of their goods since they had not been paid for.

Section 20: Risk prima facie passes with the property

SOGA79, s. 20

(1) Unless otherwise agreed, the goods remain at the seller's risk until the property in them is transferred to the buyer, but when the property in them is transferred to the buyer the goods are at the buyer's risk whether delivery has been made or not.
(2) But where delivery has been delayed through the fault of either buyer or seller the goods are at the risk of the party at fault as regards any loss that might not have occurred but for such fault.
(3) Nothing in this section affects the duties or liabilities of either seller or buyer as a bailee or custodier of the goods of the other party.

This is one of the more straightforward sections. Risk will transfer with ownership. For example, in the sale of goods at auction, the risk passes at the fall of the hammer. If the goods are accidentally destroyed before they are collected the buyer will have to bear the loss.

 Now that you have completed this chapter, look back at the chapter objectives at the beginning. Can you do all the things that these suggest? If not, look again at the relevant sections of the chapter.

CHAPTER SUMMARY

1 The Sale of Goods Act 1979 (as amended by the Sale and Supply of Goods Act 1994) governs contracts for the sale of goods by which the seller transfers or agrees to transfer the property in the goods to the buyer.
2 Section 12(1) implies a term into a contract that a seller has the right to sell the goods.
3 Section 12(2) implies a term that the goods are free from any

charge or encumbrance, and that the buyer will enjoy quiet possession of the goods.

4 Section 13 implies a term that where goods are sold by description, the goods will correspond with the description.

5 Section 14 implies the terms that where a seller sells goods in the course of a business, the goods must be of a satisfactory quality (subsection 14(2)) and the goods must be fit for the purpose (subsection 14(3)).

6 Section 15 implies a term that in a sale by sample, the goods will correspond with the sample.

7 Sections 18 to 20 provide guidelines as to when the property in the goods passes.

16

The Sale of Goods Act 1979 (Part B) and the Supply of Goods and Services Act 1982 (as amended by the Sale and Supply of Goods Act 1994)

Chapter objectives

By the end of this chapter you should be able to:

▌ know the implications of, and the exceptions to, *nemo dat quod non habet*

▌ understand the duties of the seller and buyer

▌ know the rules relating to the delivery and acceptance of the goods

▌ recognize the different remedies available to the buyer and to the seller

▌ recognize the contracts that will be subject to the Supply of Goods and Services Act 1982

▌ understand the implied terms related to sample, satisfactory quality, transfer of property and description

▌ know the implied terms related to the provision of services.

This chapter continues from Chapter 15, to complete an in-depth study of the Sale of Goods Act 1979 (SOGA79), and then examines the provisions of the Supply of Goods and Services Act 1982, both of which have been amended by the Sale and Supply of Goods Act 1994 (SSGA94).

SOGA79, SS. 21 TO 57

Section 21: Sale by person not the owner

SOGA79, s. 21(1)

(1) Subject to this Act, where goods are sold by a person who is not their owner, and who does not sell them under the authority or with the consent of the owner, the buyer acquires no better title to the goods than the seller had, unless the owner of the goods is by his conduct precluded from denying the seller's authority to sell.

► *Nemo dat quod non habet* – no one can give what he or she does not have.

This section follows the Latin maxim *nemo dat quod non habet*, a seller cannot give something that the seller has not got himself or herself, namely good title to the goods.

Under this section, where an agent sells goods without actual or apparent authority, good title will not be obtained by the buyer. Where an agent sells with authority, or where the agent is a mercantile agent, as described in Chapter 15, good title will be obtained. Two exceptions to the *nemo dat* rule are detailed under this section: estoppel and sale under a common-law or statutory power.

Section 21(1): Estoppel

Note the last part of the extract from SOGA79, s. 21(1), above: '… unless the owner of the goods is by his conduct precluded from denying the seller's authority to sell'. Equity may enable good title to be obtained by a third party, where the owner, by his or her conduct, leads the purchaser to believe that the person selling the goods has the right to sell the goods. The owner will be estopped from denying good title to the purchaser.

Section 21(2): Sale under a common-law or statutory power

► Section 22 used to allow a purchaser to obtain good title to goods, where they were bought in good faith in a market overt (open), the sale taking place between sunrise and sunset. This section was repealed by the Sale of Goods (Amendment) Act 1994.

Certain persons have a common-law or statutory power to sell goods. For example, dry cleaners have the power to sell unpaid for, non-collected items. A purchaser of any such item will obtain good title. Other examples include pawnbrokers, bailiffs and hoteliers whose bills have not been paid.

Sections 23–5 detail the other exceptions under which a person who buys in good faith may obtain good title to goods, notwithstanding the *nemo dat* rule. They include sale under a voidable title, sale by a seller in possession after sale and sale by a buyer in possession.

Section 23: Sale under voidable title

► Remember *Lewis v. Averay* (Chapter 12, p. 193)? That is a good example of a voidable contract where good title was obtained by an innocent party.

Where a voidable contract is in existence and a party sells goods obtained under the contract before steps are taken to avoid the contract, a buyer may obtain good title to the goods if he or she buys them in good faith.

If the voidable contract is avoided before the second sale takes place, then good title will not be obtained. This is the rule, even where it is not possible to communicate to the other party the intention to avoid the contract. This set of circumstances is illustrated in the following unusual case.

Car and Universal Finance Co. Ltd v. Caldwell (1964) 1 All ER Rep 290

► **Dishonoured cheque** – a cheque that the bank refuses to pay (honour).

This case concerned the sale of a car that was paid for with a **dishonoured cheque**. The car was sold on 12 January. The following day the cheque was dishonoured. The seller, being unable to trace the fraudulent purchaser, informed the police and the AA asking them to trace the vehicle. The fraudster sold the car on 15 January, to a third party.

COURT HELD

Good title had not been obtained by the third party. The seller had shown by his actions his intention to rescind the contract. Therefore the contract had been avoided prior to the resale of the goods to the third party. The seller was able to regain possession of the car.

Section 24: Seller in possession after sale

Where a seller sells specific goods and keeps them in his or her possession prior to collection by the buyer, if the seller then resells those goods to a third party, good title will be obtained by the third party providing that they have been bought in good faith. This also applies to sales by a mercantile agent. The original purchaser would have a right of action against the seller. In the circumstances outlined above, where neither purchaser has taken delivery of the goods, the original purchaser will have the right to the goods and the second purchaser would have a right of action against the seller.

Section 25: Buyer in possession after sale

A buyer may be in possession after a sale, but the property in the goods remains with the owner: for example, the goods have been delivered and an invoice issued but payment has not yet been made. If the buyer then resells the goods to a third party who buys in good faith, that new purchaser will obtain good title. The sale will be as if the buyer in possession were acting as a mercantile agent. This will apply even where the original seller avoids the original voidable contract.

For this section to apply, the buyer in possession must have bought or agreed to buy the item in question. The following are not buyers in possession: a buyer under a conditional sale agreement; a buyer in possession of goods given on a sale or return basis; a person in possession of goods obtained under a hire purchase agreement (not a car, see below); a buyer with an option to buy the goods.

The vital part of this section is that the buyer in possession must hold the goods with the permission of the owner. It will not matter that the owner withdraws the consent prior to the sale to an innocent third person. Clearly, therefore, this section will not apply if the goods have been obtained without the permission of the owner – for example, by theft.

 Under what circumstances will the *nemo dat* rule not apply, thus allowing a purchaser to obtain good title?

Hire Purchase Act 1964

Section 27 of the Hire Purchase Act 1964 allows a private purchaser to obtain good title to a vehicle, where he or she buys from a seller who has obtained the vehicle under a hire purchase agreement, not having full title to the vehicle. The purchaser must be ignorant of the existence of the hire purchase agreement, thereby purchasing the vehicle in good faith. This protection will not be available to motor vehicle or trade dealers. The following case illustrates this point.

Stevenson v. Beverley Bentinck (1976) 2 All ER 606

The plaintiff innocently bought a car that was the subject of a hire purchase agreement. The defendant finance company repossessed the car from the plaintiff when the original seller failed to maintain the hire purchase payments. The plaintiff was employed as a tool inspector, though he dealt in cars as a hobby. He had bought this particular car for his own use. The plaintiff sued for damages or the return of the car.

 COURT HELD

The plaintiff could not succeed. His work and hobby brought him into the classification of being a trade purchaser, therefore he could not obtain good title to the vehicle under the Hire Purchase Act 1964, s. 27.

SOGA79, SS. 27–37:PERFORMANCE OF THE CONTRACT

Sections 27 to 37 deal with the actual performance of the contract: for example, what happens when the wrong amount of goods are delivered, or where goods are delivered late or not at all.

Section 27: Duties of seller and buyer

> **SOGA79, s. 27**
>
> It is the duty of the seller to deliver the goods, and of the buyer to accept and pay for them, in accordance with the terms of the contract of sale.

The two parties to the contract are free to make their own arrangements about delivery and payment. Where the two parties have failed to reach agreement, the Act lays down the rules to be followed.

Section 28: Payment and delivery are concurrent conditions

SOGA79, s. 28

Unless otherwise agreed, delivery of the goods and payment of the price are concurrent conditions, that is to say, the seller must be ready and willing to give possession of the goods to the buyer in exchange for the price and the buyer must be ready and willing to pay the price in exchange for possession of the goods.

If no alternative conditions for payment have been made then the seller is entitled to receive payment before delivery of the goods is made. As soon as the price is paid the seller must deliver the goods.

The following rules apply to the delivery of the goods.

Place of delivery

Delivery will normally take place at the seller's place of business (SOGA79, s. 29(2)), the buyer collecting the goods, unless the contract allows for delivery by the seller. Where the seller is to deliver the goods by carrier, the delivery of the goods to the carrier will constitute delivery to the buyer (SOGA79, s. 32). The seller must make reasonable arrangements with the carrier for the delivery of the goods and, where the goods are to be sent by sea, the buyer must be given notice to enable him or her to insure the goods. The buyer will be liable for any deterioration suffered by the goods in transit.

Method of delivery

Delivery is the voluntary transfer of possession from one person to another (SOGA79, s. 61, as amended by the SSGA94). It may be made in any of the following ways:

1 the actual physical transfer of the property;
2 the transfer of the document of title to the goods;
3 the acknowledgement by a third party who is holding the goods, to the buyer, that the third party is holding the goods on the buyer's behalf;
4 the transferring of the means of control of the goods: for example, where the goods are held in a depot or warehouse, handing over the keys to that property.

Time of delivery

Where the time of delivery is fixed in the contract, failure to deliver by that time will constitute a breach of condition, the buyer being able to refuse late delivery and sue for breach of contract. Should the buyer refuse a reasonable request by the seller to deliver the goods the buyer will be liable for any resulting loss and charges, for care and storage of the goods (SOGA79, s. 37).

If no time is agreed, delivery must be made within a reasonable time and at a reasonable hour. The costs of putting the goods into a deliverable state – for example, putting goods into bags – will be borne by the seller.

Section 30: Delivery of wrong quantity

This section has been greatly amended by the SSGA94.

SOGA79, s. 30 (as amended by the SSGA94)

(1) Where the seller delivers to the buyer a quantity of goods less than he contracted to sell, the buyer may reject them, but if the buyer accepts the goods so delivered he must pay for them at the contract rate.

(2) Where the seller delivers to the buyer a quantity of goods larger than he contracted to sell, the buyer may accept the goods included in the contract and reject the rest, or he may reject the whole.

(2A) A buyer who does not deal as a consumer may not –
    (a) where the seller delivers a quantity of goods less than he contracted to sell, reject the goods under subsection (1) above, or
    (b) where the seller delivers a quantity of goods larger than he contracted to sell, reject the whole under subsection (2) above,
if the shortfall or, as the case may be, excess is so slight that it would be unreasonable for him to do so.

(2B) It is for the seller to show that a shortfall or excess fell within subsection (2A) above. . . .

(2D) Where the seller delivers a quantity of goods –
    (a) less than he contracted to sell, the buyer shall not be entitled to reject the goods under subsection (1) above,
    (b) larger than he contracted to sell, the buyer shall not be entitled to reject the whole under subsection (2) above,
unless the shortfall or excess is material.

(3) Where the seller delivers to the buyer a quantity of goods larger than he contracted to sell and the buyer accepts the whole of the goods so delivered he must pay for them at the contract rate.

(4) (repealed)

(5) This section is subject to any usage of trade, special agreement, or course of dealing between the parties.

This amended section has altered the law in favour of the supplier. Prior to the amendment, the rule to be followed was one of complete performance. If there was any slight deviation the purchaser could reject the whole consignment. Now, where a transaction between two non-consumers, i.e. a business contract, is completed with only a slight deviation from the terms of the contract, the purchaser will not be able to reject the whole consignment. It will be for the seller to show that the deviation was so slight as to fall within the new section 2A. We shall have to wait to see how the courts interpret this new section.

The courts still maintain the option of the *de minimis* rule. Where the variance in the performance of a contract was slight then the courts would not allow the injured party to reject the contract. In one case, 55 lb. of wheat that was delivered extra to the contracted amount of 4,950 tons was held to be too trifling to allow rejection of the consignment.

► In full: *de minimis non curat lex* – the law is not concerned with trifles. See the case of *Moore and Co. v. Landauer and Co.* (Chapter 15, p. 274), which was at odds with the *de minimis rule* and should be considered to be an exception.

Section 31: Instalment deliveries

Unless otherwise agreed, a buyer will not be bound to accept delivery by instalments.

Where the contract is **severable** or **divisible**, the terms of the contract will determine the outcome.

In a severable contract the remedies available to an injured party will depend upon the terms of the contract and the particular circumstances in each case. The injured party may be able to repudiate the whole contract or may have to settle for continuing with the contract and treating the variation as a breach of warranty. Where the parties make no reference to how to act in case of such a dispute, the court will apply the following tests.

1 What is the size and the effect of the breach upon the whole of the contract?
2 What is the likelihood of there being a further breach?

The following case illustrates the courts' application of the tests.

> **▶ Severable** – capable of being split. This normally refers to a contract where delivery is made by instalments.
>
> **▶ Divisible** – a contract where the obligations of the two parties are independent of each other. For example, a landlord may breach a covenant of a contract, such as failing to repair a property, but that will not prevent the landlord from bringing an action for the non-payment of rent; the two actions being independent of each other.

Maple Flock Co. Ltd v. Universal Furniture Products Ltd (1934) 1 KB 148

The case concerned a contract for the supply of 100 tons of flock, to be delivered by instalments. The first fifteen instalments were satisfactory but a check on the sixteenth discovered that the delivery contained more chlorine than was allowed under the contract. A further four instalments were made that were satisfactory. The buyers then refused further deliveries, seeking to repudiate the contract.

COURT HELD

The buyers could not repudiate the contract. One defective instalment could not allow them to reject the whole contract because there was no evidence of any likelihood of a further breach taking place.

In a divisible contract the rules are different. A breach on the first instalment will enable the injured party to repudiate the whole contract. Any later breach will be treatable only as a breach of warranty. Therefore the contract will continue and damages may be sought.

Section 34: Buyers' right of examining the goods

> **SOGA79, s. 34 (as amended by the SSGA94)**
>
> (1) (repealed)
> (2) Unless otherwise agreed, when the seller tenders delivery of goods to the buyer, he is bound on request to afford the buyer a reasonable opportunity of examining the goods for the purpose

> of ascertaining whether they are in conformity with the contract and, in the case of a contract for sale by sample, of comparing the bulk with the sample.

The SSGA94 repealed section 34(1), which stated that a buyer was not deemed to have accepted goods where they had been delivered and he or she had not been given the chance to examine them. Clearer guidelines relating to acceptance have been included in the amended section 35 (see below).

A buyer must be given a reasonable chance to examine the goods prior to accepting them to establish that the goods conform to the contract (SOGA79, s. 34). The examination will normally take place at the place of delivery. If the buyer is denied the opportunity, he or she will not be deemed to have accepted the goods. The following case is relevant to this section.

Bragg v. Villanova (1923) 40 TLR 154

This case concerned an international contract for the purchase of walnuts from Spain. The plaintiff received the shipping documents and paid the price for the goods prior to their arriving in England. Upon arrival the walnuts were found to be unsatisfactory. The plaintiff argued that he could reject the goods because he had not had a reasonable chance to examine them and he sued to recover the price paid. The defendant argued that the plaintiff could not reject the goods because he should have examined them at the port of departure.

 COURT HELD
The plaintiff could succeed. He had not had a reasonable chance to examine the goods, therefore the right of rejection had not been lost.

(ACT) Outline the rules relating to the delivery of goods. When will the placing of goods with a carrier constitute delivery?

Section 35: Acceptance

The SSGA94 amended section 35 to provide detailed examples of when the buyer is deemed to have accepted the goods. The fully amended section 35 appears below.

SOGA79, s.35 (as amended by the SSGA94)

(1) The buyer is deemed to have accepted the goods subject to sub-section (2) below –
  (a) when he intimates to the seller that he has accepted them, or
  (b) when the goods have been delivered to him and he does any act in relation to them which is inconsistent with the ownership of the seller.

(2) Where goods are delivered to the buyer, and he has not previously examined them, he is not deemed to have accepted them under subsection (1) above until he has had a reasonable opportunity of examining them for the purpose –
  (a) of ascertaining whether they are in conformity with the contract, and
  (b) in the case of a contract for sale by sample, of comparing the bulk with the sample.

(3) Where the buyer deals as consumer or (in Scotland) the contract of sale is a consumer contract, the buyer cannot lose his right to rely on subsection (2) above by agreement, waiver or otherwise.

(4) The buyer is also deemed to have accepted the goods when after the lapse of a reasonable time he retains the goods without intimating to the seller that he has rejected them.

(5) The questions that are material in determining for the purposes of subsection (4) above whether a reasonable time has elapsed include whether the buyer has had a reasonable opportunity of examining the goods for the purpose mentioned in subsection (2) above.

(6) The buyer is not by virtue of this section deemed to have accepted the goods merely because –
  (a) he asks for, or agrees to, their repair by or under an arrangement with the seller, or
  (b) the goods are delivered to another under a sub-sale or other disposition.

(7) Where the contract is for the sale of goods making one or more commercial units, a buyer accepting any goods included in a unit is deemed to have accepted all the goods making the unit; and in this subsection 'commercial unit' means a unit division of which would materially impair the value of the goods or the character of the unit.

The amended section 35 goes into great detail to indicate the circumstances under which a buyer will not be deemed to have accepted goods unless he or she has had a reasonable opportunity to examine them, to ensure that they are in conformity with the contract and, if relevant, with any sample. The amendments appear to strengthen the hand of the buyer. Under the new subsection (6), a buyer will not be deemed to have accepted the goods merely because he or she asks for, or agrees to, their repair by or under an arrangement with the seller, or the goods are delivered to another (the sub-purchaser) under a sub-sale or other disposition. So where goods are sold on to a third party directly from the seller, the buyer having no chance to examine the goods before the second sale, and the goods are found to be defective, he or she will not be deemed to have accepted the goods. For example, if Joanne buys bunk beds from Harry's store, and the beds are delivered direct from Beddington's (the manufacturer) to Joanne, then if the beds turn out to be defective, Harry would not be deemed to have accepted the goods. (Of course, Joanne would still have a right of action against Harry.) However, should the goods be retained by the sub-purchaser, the purchaser may be considered to have accepted the goods, via the sub-purchaser. So if Joanne hangs on to the defective beds, Harry may be considered to have accepted the goods via Joanne.

The new section 35 also introduces the concept of the 'commercial unit'. Where a buyer accepts any goods in a 'commercial unit', he or she will be deemed to have accepted any further goods due in the 'commercial unit'. The Act defines a commercial unit in subsection (7) above. An example of a commercial unit might be a set of encyclopaedias, whereby the acceptance by the buyer of the first volume would be deemed as acceptance of the whole collection. This section overrides the new section on partial rejection (35(a)). Should any of the subsequent volumes prove to be of unsatisfactory quality, the buyer will not be able reject it.

The buyer is deemed to have accepted the goods when he intimates to the seller that he has accepted them, or (except where section 34 provides) when the goods have been delivered to him and he does any action in relation to them that is inconsistent with the ownership of the seller, or when after the lapse of a reasonable time he retains the goods without intimating to the seller that he has rejected them.

The buyer must accept goods delivered in accordance with the contract. When acceptance, as described in this section, takes place, the buyer loses his or her right to repudiate the contract for breach of condition, though the right of action for damages for any breach will remain.

A buyer will also lose the right to reject goods under the following circumstances:

1 where a breach of condition is treated as a breach of warranty;
2 where a breach of condition is waived;
3 where goods have been sold by the first buyer, the second buyer wishing to retain the goods, therefore the original buyer would not be able to return them to the seller.

Where the goods are rejected upon examination the buyer must inform the seller, though the buyer is not bound to return them. It is the duty of the seller to collect them (SOGA79, s. 36).

REMEDIES

The SOGA79 deals separately with the remedies available to the buyer and to the seller, starting with the seller. An unpaid seller is defined in s. 38 as being someone to whom the whole of the price has not been paid or tendered, or to whom a conditional payment has been tendered and the condition fails to be met. An example would be where a cheque that had been given in payment was dishonoured (bounced).

A seller can take action on two fronts, against the buyer (personal remedies) and against the goods (real remedies). Invariably, the more productive action will be taken against goods, especially where the buyer has become insolvent. An unpaid seller may still have possession of the goods, notwithstanding that the property in the goods may have passed to the buyer.

UNPAID SELLERS' REAL REMEDIES

Under the SOGA79, s. 39, where the property in the goods has passed to the buyer, the unpaid seller is given three rights:

1 a lien on the goods;
2 where a buyer has become insolvent a right to stop the goods in transit;
3 a right of resale.

Further, where the property in the goods has not passed to the buyer, the unpaid seller has the right to withhold delivery.

► Remember from Chapter 7, p. 102, that a lien is the right of a seller to retain property until his or her claim on it is satisfied: for example, in the case of an unpaid seller, until the goods have been

SOGA79, ss. 41–3: Lien

Under ss. 41–3 the unpaid seller's right to a lien is detailed. The unpaid seller will be entitled to a lien in the following cases (s. 41):

(a) where the goods have been sold without any stipulation as to credit, i.e. where payment must be made before collection;
(b) where the goods have been sold on credit but the term of credit has expired;
(c) where the buyer becomes insolvent.

If part delivery has been made, then an unpaid seller may take a lien on the goods that remain to be delivered (s. 42). A lien will only give a right of retention, not a right of resale of the goods.

An unpaid seller will lose the right of retention or lien in the following circumstances:

(a) when he or she delivers the goods to a carrier or other bailee for delivery to the buyer without reserving a right of disposal over the goods;
(b) when the buyer or his or her agent lawfully obtains possession of the goods;
(c) if the lien or right of retention is waived (s. 43).

SOGA79, ss. 44–6: Stoppage in transit

Where a buyer has become insolvent, an unpaid seller has the right to stop any goods that are in transit to the buyer. The goods may be recovered and retained until payment has been received for them. The goods are considered to be in transit unless:

(a) they are delivered to the buyer or the buyer's agent;
(b) the carrier had previously acknowledged to the buyer that the carrier was holding goods on behalf of the buyer;
(c) the carrier wrongfully refuses to make delivery of the goods to the buyer.

If the buyer refuses the goods from a carrier they will be considered to be in transit.

SOGA79, ss. 47 and 48: Rescission and resale by seller

An unpaid seller has the right of resale under the following circumstances:

(a) where the goods are perishable;
(b) where the seller has reserved a right of resale under the contract;
(c) where the seller has notified the buyer of his or her intention to resell and the buyer does not within a reasonable time pay or tender the price.

The unpaid seller will still be able to bring an action for damages against the buyer where the seller has not recovered the full amount of his or her loss. In such a case the original contract of sale is rescinded and the unpaid seller will only be able to recover any loss suffered, not the original purchase price. Any buyer of goods sold under this section will obtain good title to the goods. The following cases illustrate two of the above sections.

The Bineta (1966) 2 Lloyd's Rep. 419

This case concerned the sale of a yacht called *The Bineta*. The purchaser defaulted on the payments and the seller retained the yacht on an unpaid seller's lien. The yacht was then resold some two years later to a different purchaser, who sought a declaration from the Admiralty Court that the yacht could be registered in his name, under the terms of the Merchant Shipping Act 1894.

COURT HELD
The declaration could be made. The purchaser had obtained good title to the yacht under s. 48(2).

R.V. Ward Ltd v. Bignall (1967) 2 All ER 449

This case concerned the sale of two cars, a Vauxhall Vanguard and a Ford Zephyr. The defendant paid a deposit of £25 against the purchase price of £850 for the two vehicles, the cars resting with the plaintiffs until the balance had been paid. The defendant then declined to pay the balance. The plaintiffs sold the Vauxhall for £350, and brought an action against the defendant for damages to recover the balance between the £850 purchase price, less the £350 for the Vanguard and the £25 deposit, plus £22 10s for advertising: a total of £497 10s.

COURT HELD
The plaintiffs could only partly succeed. Under s. 48(3), where a seller had exercised his or her right to sell goods, the contract was treated as being rescinded. Therefore the damages

applicable were measured as being those awarded for non-acceptance. The damages in this case were the difference in the selling price for the Vanguard plus the advertising costs, a total of £47 10s.

UNPAID SELLERS' PERSONAL REMEDIES

The unpaid seller may bring an action for the contract price (s. 49) or for non-acceptance of the goods (s. 50).

Section 49: Action for the price

> **SOGA79, s. 49**
>
> (1) Where, under a contract of sale, the property in the goods has passed to the buyer and he wrongfully neglects or refuses to pay for the goods according to the terms of the contract, the seller may maintain an action against him for the price of the goods.
> (2) Where, under a contract of sale, the price is payable on a certain day irrespective of delivery and the buyer wrongfully neglects or refuses to pay such price, the seller may maintain an action for the price, although the property in goods has not passed and the goods have not been appropriated to the contract.

This section allows an unpaid seller to bring an action in two different situations: first, where the property in the goods has passed to the buyer (s. 49(1)); second, where the buyer has neglected or has failed to pay by a specified date, regardless of whether the property has passed or not.

 What options are available to a buyer when a seller delivers a wrong quantity of goods?

Section 50: Damages for non-acceptance

> **SOGA79, s. 50**
>
> (1) Where the buyer wrongfully neglects or refuses to accept and pay for the goods, the seller may maintain an action against him for damages for non-acceptance.
> (2) The measure of damages is the estimated loss directly and naturally resulting in the ordinary course of events, from the buyer's breach of contract.
> (3) Where there is an available market for the goods in question the measure of damages is prima facie to be ascertained by the difference between the contract price and the market or current price at the time or the times when the goods ought to have been accepted or (if no time was fixed for acceptance) at the time of the refusal to accept.

The interesting application of this rule can be seen in the following classic cases.

Charter v. Sullivan (1957) 1 All ER 809

This case concerned the sale of a Hillman Minx car for the agreed purchase price of £773 15s. The defendant declined to pay for the car so the plaintiff resold it to a third party. He then sued the plaintiff for the lost profit on the sale of a car, asking for £97 15s. At the time this particular car was in very short supply and the plaintiff could sell every car that he could obtain.

COURT HELD

The plaintiff could only recover nominal damages. Under s. 50(2) the seller could only recover loss directly and naturally arising from the breach of contract. The seller could sell all of the Minxes that he could obtain, therefore he had not lost any profit.

Campbell Mostyn Ltd v. Barnett Trading Co. (1954) 1 Lloyd's Rep 65

This case concerned a contract for the sale of tinned ham that was wrongly rejected by the defendants. The plaintiffs sued to recover damages for lost profit at the time of the breach, i.e. the difference between the contract price and the market price. They subsequently resold the ham at a higher market price.

COURT HELD

The plaintiffs could succeed in obtaining nominal damages, despite the fact that they had later resold the goods and made a profit on the sale. Section 50(3) states that it is irrelevant that the market price of the goods has risen since the date of the breach.

BUYERS' REMEDIES

Under the SOGA79, ss. 51, 52 and 53, the buyer has a right of action for:

1 non-delivery;
2 specific performance;
3 breach of warranty; and
4 right of rejection.

Section 51: Non-delivery

Where a seller refuses or fails to deliver goods, the buyer will have a right of action for damages for non-delivery. The damages will be measured by the estimated loss directly and naturally resulting in the ordinary course of events from the seller's breach of contract.

Should there be an available market for the goods, the damages will be measured by the cost of replacing the goods by buying them elsewhere. Where replacement goods are readily available at the same or at a lesser price, the award of damages will normally be nominal.

Anticipatory breach

Anticipatory breach means where, for example, the buyer is informed by the seller prior to the date of performance of the contract, that the seller will not be performing his or her contractual obligations. Where this happens the buyer will be under a duty to mitigate his or her losses. Practically speaking, mitigation in this sense means that the buyer should obtain the goods from elsewhere as soon as possible. If the buyer fails to do so and the market price rises the buyer will be unlikely to obtain full damages to cover his or her losses.

The following case is an illustration of the measurement of damages under this section.

Williams v. Agius (1914)

This case concerned a contract for the sale of coal at 16s 3d per ton. The sellers failed to deliver the coal. The buyers intended to resell the coal at 19s 6d per ton. The market price at the date that the sellers failed to deliver the coal was 23s 6d. The defence argued that they should only have to pay the difference between the delivery and resale prices.

COURT HELD
The plaintiffs could recover the difference between the delivery price and the market price on the day that the contract was breached, in accordance with s. 50(3), this being 7s 3d per ton.

Section 52: Specific performance

In a case concerning specific or ascertained goods a court may grant specific performance to a wronged buyer where it feels that an award of damages will not be sufficient, such as in the purchase of a unique good. The following case illustrates specific performance.

Behnke v. Bede Shipping Co. Ltd (1927) All ER Rep. 689

(EQ) This case concerned the sale of a ship called *The City*, which the seller refused to deliver to the buyer. *The City* was one of only two models of a particular type of ship remaining, being quite old and practically unique. The plaintiff sued for a decree of specific performance.

COURT HELD
The plaintiff could succeed. A decree of specific performance would be awarded. The unique nature of The City meant that the loss of it would not be satisfactorily compensated for by an award of damages.

Section 53: Breach of warranty (as amended by the SSGA94)

The amended version of this section does not allow a buyer to reject goods for a breach of warranty. However, where a breach of warranty has occurred, a buyer will have a right of action for the price or for damages.

SOGA79, s. 53(2) (as amended by the SSGA94)

The measure of damages for breach of warranty is the estimated loss directly and naturally resulting, in the ordinary course of events, from the breach of warranty.

SOGA79, s. 53(3) (as amended by the SSGA94)

In the case of breach of warranty of quality such loss is prima facie the difference between the value of the goods at the time of the delivery to the buyer and the value they would have had if they had fulfilled the warranty.

This subsection is self-explanatory.

Mason v. Birmingham **(1949) 2 KB 545**

In this case the buyer of a stolen typewriter, who became the subject of enquiries regarding the purchase, brought an action, under the SOGA79, s. 12(2), for breach of warranty of quiet possession.

COURT HELD
The court awarded the buyer the purchase price plus the cost of a repair that she had carried out to the typewriter, which was a loss arising naturally from the breach.

Buyer's right of rejection

Where a seller is in breach of a condition, express or implied, a buyer will have the right to reject the goods and sue for damages. The right of rejection will be lost if the buyer is deemed to have accepted the goods. The buyer will then have to proceed as outlined above for breach of warranty (SOGA79, s. 11).

 When may a court grant specific performance?

Section 57: Auction sales

This section details the rules relating to sales by auction. They are quite straightforward and are as follows.

(a) Each lot is considered to be a separate contract.
(b) A sale is completed when the auctioneer ends that sale, normally by the fall of the hammer. Until that time a bidder may withdraw his or her bid.
(c) A sale may be subject to a reserve price. Where that price is not reached the auctioneer may withdraw that item. An auctioneer is not obliged to accept the highest bid in such circumstances.
(d) A seller may reserve the right to bid at an auction. Should a seller fail to do so, it will be unlawful for the seller to bid or for the seller to employ anyone else to bid on his or her behalf. It will also be unlawful for an auctioneer knowingly to take a bid from either a seller or a seller's representative, unless the seller has reserved the right to bid.
(e) An auctioneer is entitled to refuse any bid at an auction, notwithstanding that a reserve price has not been set.

 Adrian agreed to sell his Astra to Sandra, under a conditional sale agreement. Sandra paid £300, but prior to collecting the car she decided that she no longer wanted it. Adrian refused to give her back the £300 first payment.

1   What would be the likely result of any court action between the two parties and who has a right of action?

Some three months later and prior to the result of any court action between the two parties, Adrian sold the car to Geoff.

2   Under what circumstances can Geoff obtain good title to the goods? Illustrate your answer with relevant cases and sections of the SOGA79.

THE SUPPLY OF GOODS AND SERVICES ACT 1982

The protection afforded to consumers and others under the SOGA79 is only available for contracts that involve the exchange of goods for a monetary consideration. The Supply of Goods and Services Act 1982 (SOGAS82), as amended by the SSGA94, extends similar protection to other transactions that fall outside the SOGA79. The SOGAS82 is split into two parts: the first part dealing with any goods or materials supplied; the second part dealing with the work, labour or services provided.

> **SOGAS82, s. 1: The contracts concerned**
>
> (1) In this Act a 'contract for the transfer of goods' means a contract under which one person transfers or agrees to transfer to another the property in goods, other than an excepted contract.

The contracts that are 'excepted' and not subject to the SOGAS82 are:

(a) contracts for the sale of goods;
(b) hire purchase agreements;
(c) contracts where goods are exchanged for trading stamps;
(d) contracts made by deed that lack consideration;
(e) a contract intended to operate by means of mortgage, pledge, charge or other security.

Section 12 of SOGAS82 excludes contracts of employment and apprenticeship. The main types of contract that will fall into the jurisdiction of the act are as follows:

SOGAS82, ss. 2–5: Contracts for the transfer of property in goods

In this type of contract, materials may be supplied, such as spare parts in a contract for repair of a car. But the major part of the contract is the provision of the services or labour. Another example could be a contract to build an extension to a house where the builder provides both materials and the skills to construct the project.

Under ss. 2–5, similar terms to those implied under the SOGA79, ss. 12–15 (as amended by the SSGA94), are implied in contracts for work and materials, and **contracts for exchange or barter**, whereby a person obtains ownership of goods. The terms are applied in the same way as in the SOGA79. Section 2 of SOGAS82 may not be excluded whether the transferee is a consumer or a businessperson. Where a transferee is a consumer, ss. 3–5 may not be excluded. If the transferee is not a consumer, i.e. it is a business transaction, then ss. 3–5 may be excluded subject to the 'reasonableness' test contained in the Unfair Contract Terms Act 1977. (See Chapter 14, page 258.)

► **Contracts for exchange and barter** – The medieval version of these contracts could have involved the swapping of a sheep for a calf. Now we tend to use money that would turn the contract into a contract for the sale of goods. However, where goods are obtained by the giving of vouchers for them – for example, a soap powder promotion offering a free pack in exchange for vouchers – the implied conditions in ss. 2–5 will apply. An example of a contract of exchange could be where a faulty toaster is returned to a retailer, who exchanges it for a new toaster. The new goods will be subject the implied terms of ss. 2–5.

Guidelines for the reasonableness test from the Unfair Contract Terms Act 1977, Sch. 2:

(a) the strength of the bargaining positions of the parties relative to each other, taking into account (among other things) alternative means by which the customer's requirements could have been met;
(b) whether the customer received an inducement to agree to the term, or in accepting it had an opportunity of entering into a similar contract with other persons, but without having to accept a similar term;
(c) whether the customer knew or ought reasonably to have known of the existence and extent of the term (having regard, among other things, to any custom of the trade and any previous course of dealings between the parties);
(d) where the term excludes or restricts any relevant liability if some condition is not complied with, whether it was

> reasonable at the time of the contract to expect that compliance with that condition would be practicable;
>
> (e) whether the goods were manufactured, processed or adapted to the special order of the customer.

The following terms are **implied** by the SOGAS82 (as amended by the SSGA94) into a contract covered by the Act.

- **Section 2**: Implied term that the transferor has the right to transfer the property. Implied terms that the buyer will enjoy quiet possession of the goods and that the goods are free from any undisclosed third party claims or rights.
- **Section 3**: Implied term that in a transfer of goods by description, the goods will correspond with the description.
- **Section 4**: Implied condition that where goods are transferred in the course of a business they will be of satisfactory quality. The SSGA94 adds a new subsection 4(2)(a), which defines satisfactory quality as being: goods that meet the standard that a reasonable person would regard as satisfactory. The price (if relevant), description and all other relevant factors are to be considered in determining whether the goods are of satisfactory quality.
- **Section 5**: Implied terms that where goods have been transferred after reference being made to a sample, the bulk will correspond with the sample; that the transferee will have a reasonable opportunity to compare the bulk with the sample; that the goods will be free from any defect not immediately apparent.

▶ Remember what an **implied** term is in a contract? It is a term that is put into the contract whether the parties want it or not. In this case the terms are implied by statute. Refer to Chapter 14, p. 241, to refresh your memory.

Remedies

Where a supplier breaches an implied condition, the injured party may treat his or her contractual obligations as being discharged and, therefore, any monies due should cease to be payable. The injured party may then commence an action for damages. A breach of an implied warranty will not discharge an injured party's contractual obligations. The contract will continue, though a right of action for damages will exist.

SOGAS82, ss. 7–10: Contracts for the hire of goods

Section 6 describes a contract for the hire of goods as follows.

> **SOGAS82, s. 6**
>
> (1) ... a contract under which one person bails or agrees to bail goods to another by way of hire, other than an excepted contract.
> (2) ... an excepted contract means any of the following:
>   (a) a hire purchase agreement;
>   (b) a contract under which goods are (or are to be) bailed in exchange for trading stamps on their redemption.

Sections 7–10 imply terms into contracts for hire that closely mirror the terms implied by the SOGA79, ss. 12–15.

- **Section 7**: implied condition that the bailor has a right to transfer possession of the goods to the bailee. Implied warranty that the bailee will enjoy quiet possession of the goods for the duration of the hire.
- **Section 8**: implied condition that where a contract of hire is made by description, the goods will correspond with the description.
- **Section 9**: implied conditions that where goods are supplied for hire in the course of a business, the goods shall be of merchantable quality and be reasonably fit for the purpose.
- **Section 10**: implied conditions that where goods have been transferred after reference being made to a sample, the bulk will correspond with the sample; that the transferee will have a reasonable opportunity to compare the bulk with the sample; that the goods will be free from any defect not immediately apparent.

In a consumer transaction, ss. 8, 9 and 10 may not be excluded. In a non-consumer transaction the exclusion will be subject to the above-mentioned reasonableness test. In any transaction, s. 7 may be excluded, provided that it satisfies the reasonableness test.

SOGAS82, ss. 12–15: Contracts for the supply of services

Section 12 describes a contract for the supply of services as follows.

SOGAS82, s. 12

(1) [A contract for the supply of a service is] … a contract under which a person (the supplier) agrees to carry out a service.
(2) … a contract of service or apprenticeship is not a contract for the supply of a service.
(3) [A contract] … is a contract for the supply of a service for the purposes of this Act whether or not goods are also:
(a) transferred or to be transferred
(b) bailed or to be bailed by way of hire under the contract, and whatever is the nature of the consideration for which the service is to be carried out.

The Secretary of State may declare that one or more of ss. 13–15 will not apply to a particular provider of services. An example would be a contract for the services of a solicitor in a magistrates' court.

Contracts in this section will include those where the provider is responsible for providing a service only, such as a window cleaner, and contracts where goods are transferred and services are provided, such as the repair of a television set.

Sections 13–15 imply terms into contracts for the supply of services, and whether the terms are conditions or warranties will depend upon the circumstances of each case. If the term breached goes to the root of the contract, then it will be a breach of condition, otherwise it will be treated as a breach of a warranty.

- **Section 13**: implies the term that where a service is being supplied in the course of a business, the supplier will perform that service with reasonable care and skill. If you put your car into the garage to have the brakes adjusted, and when you retrieve the car the brakes fail to work, the supplier cannot have exercised reasonable care and skill.

- **Section 14**: implies the term that where a supplier is acting in the course of a business and time is not specified in the contract for performance, nor can it be ascertained by a course of dealing between the parties, the provider will perform the service in a reasonable time. The reasonableness will be a question of fact dependent upon the circumstances of each case. A television repairer might be expected to complete any repairs within a few days, while a repairer of antique clocks might be allowed three months to repair a clock.

- **Section 15**: implies the term that where consideration cannot be determined by the contract, or from a course of dealing between the parties, the customer will pay a reasonable price for the service rendered. In an emergency you might call out an emergency plumber to stop the water coming through your ceiling, giving no thought to the price, and being given no estimate for the work. In such circumstances the implied term would mean that you would be bound to pay a reasonable price for the service, not a £1,500 call-out charge.

(ACT) Norman is an avid fan of Lady Thatcher. He has heard that the BBC is planning to show a series of documentaries about her. Norman is particularly keen to record the programmes so he obtained a video recorder from a shop. Unfortunately for him the video failed to work. Norman missed the first episode. Making reference to relevant Acts and sections, outline what conditions or warranties may have been breached under the following different circumstances.

1 He hired the video.
2 He obtained the video by supplying vouchers in a special washing powder promotion.
3 He acquired the video in exchange for a faulty toaster, bought at an electrical retailer.
4 The video had just been repaired by an electrical repairer.
5 He had bought the video.

SOGAS82, s. 16: Exclusion clauses

Sections 13–15 of SOGAS82 may be excluded by express agreement as long as the exclusion term complies with the reasonableness test under the Unfair Contract Terms Act 1977 (see above, page 310 and Chapter 14, page 258).

 Now that you have completed this chapter, look back at the chapter objectives at the beginning. Can you do all the things that these suggest? If not, look again at the relevant sections of the chapter.

CHAPTER SUMMARY

1 Sections 21–5 of the SOGA79 detail the exceptions under which a person who buys in good faith may obtain good title to goods. Notwithstanding the *nemo dat* rule, they include: sale in a market overt; sale under a voidable title; sale by a seller in possession after sale; sale by a buyer in possession.

2 Sections 28–9 of the SOGA79 outline the rules relating to the payment for, and the delivery of, the goods. Unless stated otherwise, payment and delivery are concurrent conditions, i.e. a buyer must pay for the goods before, or as soon as, delivery has been made.

3 Section 30 of the SOGA79 gives the options available to a buyer, where a seller delivers a wrong quantity of goods. They include the right to reject the goods and the right to accept part or all of the goods.

4 Section 34 of the SOGA79 gives a buyer the right to examine the goods.

5 The remedies available to the buyer and seller include lien, stoppage in transit, rescission, resale, action for the price, damages and specific performance.

6 SOGAS82 applies to three main types of contract: contracts for the transfer of property in the goods; contracts for the hire of goods; contracts for the supply of services.

7 Sections 2–5 of SOGAS82 imply conditions into contracts for the transfer of property in the goods, where the transferor acts in the course of a business; relating to the transfer of the goods; goods bought by sample and description; and the merchantability and fitness of the goods.

8 Sections 7–10 of SOGAS82 imply conditions into contracts for the hire of goods, relating to fitness and merchantability, the transfer of the goods, and description and sample.

9 Sections 12–15 of SOGAS82 imply terms into contracts for the provision of services, relating to the level of service provided, the time of performance and the payment for services.

17 *Consumer credit*

Chapter objectives

By the end of this chapter you should be able to:

■ recognize the main provisions of the Consumer Credit Act 1974

■ identify the criteria necessary for an agreement to be regulated under the Act

■ know the agreements that are exempted from the provisions of the Act

■ understand the provisions of the Act which seek to protect a consumer before, at the time of, and after the signing of a regulated agreement

■ recognize the remedies available to debtors and creditors under the Act.

CREDIT

Credit is now available everywhere and it is accepted that the norm is to live in debt. One of the flagship policies of the Conservative government was the selling of council properties to tenants, thereby increasing the amount of home ownership and the amount of debt as a governmental policy. Home ownership is considered to be a 'good thing', though many who bought their council houses have found, to their cost, that they would have been better off continuing to pay rent, some having lost both their houses and their money.

Living in debt is a comparatively modern phenomenon. Many people born since the 1950s, however, tend to take credit for granted. People use credit to buy many goods and services – such as a new car or repairs to a house – and pay for them later, instead of saving up the money to buy them outright. Even the normal weekly food shopping can be paid for by credit card. For a large section of society, living with a mortgage is considered to be the norm.

Previous generations, those born before the 1950s, are often less happy about using credit as a means of purchase. For example, my parents, now both in their sixties, are extremely unhappy about buying anything on credit. They come from a time when to be behind with the rent was considered to be a terrible crime. Credit did exist for them in a minor way and I can remember the 'tally man' making his weekly call, bringing goods that would be paid for by making a weekly payment. Many people who lived in my road used to fail to answer the door to him when they were short of money!

Governments have been concerned about the growth of credit and at times they have sought to control the terms of credit agreements to regulate the amount of money in circulation. In this chapter we shall be examining the Consumer Credit Act 1974 (CCA74) and the Hire Purchase Act 1964 (HPA64).

CONSUMER CREDIT AGREEMENTS

Regulated agreements

The CCA74 creates regulated agreements that are defined as being credit agreements between a supplier and a consumer, not a registered company, though it may be a sole trader or a partnership. Regulated agreements are those that do not exceed £15,000. If the cost of the goods is more than £15,000 but the deposit leaves the balance resting at below £15,000, then it will be a regulated agreement. For agreements above £15,000, or those where the purchaser is not a consumer, then the common law will apply.

▶ For example, if the goods cost £16,500, and the deposit was 10%, i.e. £1,650, then the balance would be £14,850, and it would be a regulated agreement.

Hire purchase agreements

A modern hire purchase agreement entails a customer hiring goods, generally by paying a deposit followed by a series of instalments, the length of hire being determined by the agreement. At the termination of the agreement the hirer has the option to purchase the goods, normally by paying a nominal payment. The ownership of the goods rests with the supplier of the goods until the final payment is made. Therefore, if the hirer fails to meet any of the instalments, the owner can repossess the goods. Where goods subject to a hire purchase agreement have been sold on by a hirer, the owner can recover them from a third party.

▶ Under the Hire Purchase Act 1964, Part III, s. 27, good title may be obtained by the private purchaser of a car, which has been sold by a hirer when it has been subject to a hire purchase agreement, provided that the purchaser buys it in good faith having no knowledge of the outstanding hire purchase arrangement.

Modern hire purchase agreements normally operate in the following way. The sellers of goods rarely supply the credit themselves. This role is undertaken by a finance company. The average purchaser is probably not aware of this when buying from a retailer. However, for many goods – for example, domestic appliances such as washing machines – the seller displays the goods in his or her shop, and the purchaser selects the goods and agrees to buy them under a hire purchase agreement. The seller then sells the goods to a finance company, which immediately pays for the goods, while the purchaser signs an agreement with the finance company to buy the goods on credit.

In the above example the retailer will have a contract with the finance company for the sale of the goods and the retailer will also be considered to be in a relationship of agency with it.

The finance company will have a contract with the hirer that will be subject to the implied terms of the Supply of Goods (Implied Terms) Act 1973 (as amended by the SSGA94), similar to the Sale of Goods Act 1979, ss. 12–15. The following case illustrates how a seller was held to have a contract with a purchaser under a hire purchase agreement.

Andrews v. Hopkinson (1956) 3 All ER 422

This case concerned a car sold by the defendant, a second-hand car dealer. In order to induce the sale he said, 'It's a good little bus, I would stake my life on it; you will have no trouble with it.' The plaintiff bought the car, entering into a hire purchase contract with a finance company, who bought the car from the car dealer. One week later the plaintiff was injured when the car, which was later found to have faulty steering, was in collision with a lorry. The plaintiff was excluded from suing the finance company by a clause in the hire purchase agreement, therefore he sued the defendant.

► See Chapter 14, page 259, for the validity of exclusion clauses in hire purchase contracts.

COURT HELD
There was an implied contract between the plaintiff and the defendant containing the misrepresentation made by the defendant. The defendant was in breach of the agreement, therefore he was liable for damages. This case illustrates the application of the CCA74, s. 75, though it was decided before the creation of the Act.

Conditional sale agreements

Conditional sale agreements are almost identical to hire purchase agreements except that there is no option to purchase at the end of the contract. The agreement *is* to purchase. Otherwise the constituent elements are the same. Ownership rests with the supplier, whether it be a finance company or the actual supplier, until the final instalment is paid. The purchaser is not a buyer or a person who has agreed to buy, as defined in the SOGA79, therefore they will not be able to pass good title until all instalments have been paid. The implied terms of the SOGA79 (as amended by the SSGA94) will apply to this type of agreement.

Credit sale agreements

Under a credit sale agreement, possession and ownership of the goods passes immediately to the buyer, while the buyer is given a period of credit to pay for the goods. The buyer may resell the goods and pass good title to them, therefore the original seller will not be able to recover the goods from a third party if the buyer defaults on the payments for the goods.

▶ The CCA74, s. 75, makes the supplier and the creditor jointly responsible for any misrepresentations or breaches of contract. For example, if Deborah purchases a stereo system from Toxo, using a credit card supplied by Midwest Bank, and Toxo fails to supply the stereo system, Deborah will have a right of action against both Toxo and Midwest Bank. This is useful where the supplier becomes insolvent. Section 75 only applies to regulated agreements valued between £100 and £30,000.

▶ Certain major retailers and petrol companies offer their own credit cards for purchases made on their premises. These cards operate in the same way as an ordinary credit card.

Credit cards

Credit cards are issued to a named person (or company) after an agreement has been signed between the credit card company and the holder, relating to the terms and conditions of the use of the card. An annual charge may be made for the use of the card. The card may then be used to purchase goods from retailers who accept that particular credit card. The retailers will then be paid for the goods by the credit card company, who will deduct a percentage, around 2 per cent, for their services. The holder of the card will then be in debt to the credit card company for the full amount of the goods purchased. If the card holder settles the account in full on receipt of his or her statement, the card holder will incur no further charges. If there is an outstanding balance then interest will be charged on that amount in accordance with the agreement. A holder will be limited to the amount that can be spent on his or her card.

Charge cards

Charge cards function in the same way as credit cards, except that there is a joining fee payable, there is normally no credit limit and all accounts must be settled in full monthly.

Other sources of credit

The banks and building societies are major sources of credit, lending money for various different purchases, and providing overdrafts and mortgages.

CCA74, S. 16: EXEMPTED AGREEMENTS

The following are not regulated agreements for the purposes of the CCA74:

(a) credit sale agreements for less than £50 (these are only partially regulated);

(b) mortgages for the purchase of land, or for the purchase of land or buildings where the instalments are to be repaid in four or fewer instalments;

(c) agreements involving running credit – as in the case of a charge card – where the account is settled in full;

(d) credit agreements made where the creditor or owner is not acting in the course of his or her business (these are partially regulated);

(e) credit agreements where the annual percentage rate (APR) is less than 13 per cent or 1 per cent over **base rate**;

(f) fixed sum Debtor–Creditor–Supplier Agreement (DCSA), where there are to be four or fewer instalments;

(g) finance of foreign trade.

▶ **Base rate** – the rate at which the Bank of England lends money to the clearing banks, i.e. Barclays, Midland, Lloyds and National Westminster.

Section 16 also states the two consumer hire agreements that are exempted. They are the hire of meters for the measurement of gas, water or electricity and the hire of telecommunications equipment supplied by British Telecom.

(ACT)

1 Outline the definition of a regulated consumer credit agreement.
2 Which credit agreements are specifically excluded by the Act?
3 What is the major difference between a credit sale and a hire purchase agreement?

CONSUMER CREDIT ACT 1974 TERMINOLOGY

In order to understand which provisions of the Act relate to which type of agreement it is necessary to be able to understand the terminology used in the Act.

Section 10: Running account credit (RAC) and fixed sum credit (FSC)

Running account credit is where a person is allowed to pay for goods or services on a credit account up to a limited amount. The limited amount will remain and will immediately be available again when money spent has been paid off the account: for example, when someone has paid off what they owe a retailer on credit account. A fixed sum credit is where an agreement is made for a fixed amount, such as a bank loan for £2,000.

Section 11: Restricted use credit (RUC) and unrestricted use credit (UUC)

An RUC is where the credit allowed is tied to the purchase of a particular item or items. The majority of credit would fall into this classification, including hire purchase and credit card purchases. An UUC is where there exists no limit to the use of the credit, the best example being an overdraft.

Section 12: Debtor–Creditor–Supplier Agreement (DCSA)

A DCSA will exist where there is a connection between the person supplying the credit and the supplier of the goods. They may be one and the same person or they may have an existing business arrangement. A credit card transaction is a DCSA because the credit card company and the supplier have a business arrangement. A further example could be a car showroom that has an agreement with a finance company, whereby customers could obtain finance for vehicles purchased at the premises.

Section 13: Debtor–Creditor Agreement (DCA)

Where there is no connection between the supplier and the creditor the agreement will be a DCA. A bank loan taken out for no particular purchase would be a DCA.

Section 14: Credit tokens

> **CCA74, s. 14**
>
> (1) A credit token is a card, check, voucher, coupon, stamp, form, booklet or other document or thing given to an individual by a person carrying on a consumer credit business, who undertakes:
>   (a) that on production of it he will supply cash, goods, and services (or any of them) on credit, or
>   (b) that where, on the production of it to a third party, the third party supplies cash, goods and services (or any of them), he will pay the third party for them, in return for payment to him by the individual.
> (2) A credit token agreement is a regulated agreement for the provision of credit in connection with the use of a credit token.

▶ A check is a form of obtaining credit that has all but disappeared. A person seeking credit can approach a specialized company, who will issue a check, which is really a voucher with a value stamped upon it – for example, £30. The person could then take the check to any shop that accepted that particular company's checks, and obtain goods up to the value printed on it. Repayment of the loan would be made to the issuing company, normally on a weekly basis.

Most methods of payment for credit will come under the definition of this section, including credit cards, checks, vouchers and coupons.

Section 15: Consumer hire agreements

> **CCA74, s. 15**
>
> (1) A consumer hire agreement is an agreement made by a person with an individual (the hirer) for the bailment or the hiring of goods to the hirer, being an agreement which:
>   (a) is not a hire purchase agreement, and
>   (b) is capable of subsisting for more than three months, and
>   (c) does not require the hirer to make payments exceeding £15,000.
> (2) A consumer hire agreement is a regulated agreement if it is not an exempt agreement.

Section 20: Total charge for credit

Under this section the rules for establishing the exact cost of a credit transaction are specified. This is to ensure that a consumer will be able to establish and compare the true cost of any credit charge being made. The cost is called the annual percentage rate (APR) and this must be shown on any written agreement, as must the total credit charge (TCC).

Sections 21–43: Licensing of credit and hire businesses

The third part of the Act deals with the licensing and registration of consumer credit agencies. Certain agencies are exempt, namely local authorities and a corporate body empowered by an Act of Parliament. All other agencies that supply consumer credit or consumer hire schemes must be licensed, the licensing being controlled by the Director General of Fair Trading (s. 21).

CCA74, s. 25

(1) A standard licence shall be granted on the application of any person if he satisfies the Director that:
   (a) he is a fit person to engage in activities covered by the licence, and
   (b) the name or names under which he applies to be licensed is or are not misleading or otherwise undesirable.

This section continues by detailing the persons who may not be considered to be fit to hold a licence. Anyone who has:

- committed any offence involving fraud, dishonesty or violence;
- contravened any of the provisions of the Act;
- practised discrimination on grounds of race, sex, nationality or ethnic origin; or
- engaged in dubious or oppressive business practices.

These provisions will also apply to employees and business associates of the applicant.

Six types of consumer credit businesses are identified and licensed under the Act.

1 Consumer credit business – banks, building societies, finance companies and other lenders.
2 Consumer hire business – car hire, electrical equipment hire, etc.
3 Dealers who sell goods acting as agents for finance companies – electrical retailers, car dealers, etc.
4 Credit reference agencies – these are agencies that carry out credit checks against potential customers. They check to see if the potential customer has had a county court judgment made against him or her, has been credit blacklisted, or if the address at which he or she lives has a history of bad debt (ss. 157–9).
5 Debt collectors.
6 Counselling agencies – Citizens' Advice Bureaux.

If a non-licensed person conducts consumer credit business, he or she will be committing a criminal offence and the agreement will only be valid with the sanction of the Director General.

1 Define the following abbreviations: RAC; FSC; RUC; UUC; DCSA and DCA.
2 When does the property in the goods pass in the following agreements: (a) a hire purchase; (b) a conditional sale; (c) a credit sale?

Sections 43–7: Seeking business

These sections state the rules controlling advertising for business. The aim is to ensure the following.

CCA74, s. 44

(1) … an advertisement conveys a fair and reasonably comprehensive indication of the nature of the credit or hire facilities offered by the advertiser and of their true cost to persons using them.

The Act controls the advertising of consumer credit by creating regulations. The Consumer Credit (Advertisements) Regulations 1989 govern advertising published after 1 February 1990. Three different types of advertising are allowed:

1 simple advertisement – where neither a price nor an indication that credit or hire purchase is available appears;
2 intermediate advertisement – at the very least this must contain details of where full written credit details are available;
3 full advertisement – this must be very detailed, with a worked example of the credit being offered, including the APR.

Where loans are offered that are secured on houses or property, a warning must be included in the advertisement that states, 'Your home may be at risk if you do not keep up repayments on a mortgage or other loan secured on it.'

It is an offence to advertise goods or services on credit, where the advertiser does not state that he or she is prepared to sell the goods or provide the services for cash (CCA74, s. 45). It is a criminal offence to fail to comply with the advertising regulations, or to advertise misleading or false information (CCA74, s. 46).

Several offences may be committed by any person failing to comply with these sections of the CCA74.

- **Section 45**: where a person advertises offering an RUC but fails to state that the goods are also available for cash, that person will commit an offence.
- **Section 46**: where an advertisement contains false or misleading information, an offence will be committed.
- **Section 47**: where an offence is committed under s. 45 or 46, the following persons will also be guilty of an offence: the publisher of the advertisement; the person who created or devised the advertisement; and where the advertiser did not procure the publication of the advertisement, the person who did procure it.

Sections 48–54: Canvassing

These sections contain further offences relating to the canvassing of regulated agreements. It is an offence to canvass a regulated agreement off premises without a licence (s. 48). This is aimed at stopping traders from pestering people in the street or at their homes to take out credit that they don't want or to buy something that they don't need.

Section 50: Canvassing a minor

(1) A person commits an offence who, with a view to financial gain, sends to a minor any document inviting him to:
   (a) borrow money, or
   (b) obtain goods on credit or hire, or
   (c) obtain services on credit, or
   (d) apply for information or advice on borrowing money or otherwise obtaining credit, or hiring goods.

Section 51: Unsolicited credit tokens

This section makes it an offence to give a person a credit token if he or she has not asked for it. This does not apply to the renewal of a credit card or where an agreement has previously been made.

Sections 52–4: Quotations

These sections govern the provision of quotations. Failure to comply with these sections is a criminal offence.

GENERAL WORKINGS OF THE CONSUMER CREDIT ACT 1974

The aim of the CCA74 is to ensure that provision of credit is regulated and, therefore, that it is fair to people who take out credit, known as debtors. Protection is provided for debtors prior to their taking out the agreement, at the time that they take out the agreement and after the agreement has been taken out.

Prior to the agreement

- **Section 55**: Under this section full details must be given to a prospective hirer or debtor before he or she signs an agreement.
- **Section 56**: Where a person buys a good under a regulated agreement when the seller acts as a credit broker for the financier, or where payment is made for the goods by credit card, the 'negotiator' (i.e. the seller) will be considered to be an agent of the financier. This means that the creditor (the supplier of the finance) will be liable for any misrepresentations made by the agent, and that any payment made to the agent will be deemed to have been received by the creditor.

- **Section 57**: At any time prior to the completion of an agreement the prospective debtor may withdraw from the agreement, by giving notice to the negotiator, the creditor or his or her agent.
- **Section 59**: An agreement will be void if it purports to bind a person to enter as a debtor or hirer into a prospective regulated agreement. For example, an agreement to enter into a regulated agreement will be void.

Upon signing the agreement

The CCA74 lays down strict regulations governing the form that the agreement must take, the provision of copies of the agreement and the details that must be recorded on the agreement.

Under CCA74, s. 61, the agreement must be in writing, be legible, contain all terms of the agreement (other than implied terms), contain details of rights of cancellation (where applicable), be signed in person by the debtor and by or on behalf of the creditor in the signature box, all blank spaces must be filled in with the relevant details – for example, the APR and TCC – and a copy must be given to the debtor.

If the agreement fails to conform to the above, it will be an improperly executed agreement. It will be unenforceable by a creditor without a court order. A court may also enter the agreement and vary the conditions in favour of the debtor (CCA74, s. 127).

Under the CCA74, s. 62, the debtor must be given a copy of the agreement and any other document referred to in it, such as a copy of the conditions of sale. If the creditor signs the document at the same time, then the debtor will receive only one copy. Where, normally, the agreement has to be sent away to be signed by the creditor, such as a finance house, a second copy must be sent to the debtor within seven days of the document becoming fully executed (signed by all parties). If the agreement is cancellable (see below) then the second copy must be sent by post.

After the agreement has been made

Sections 67–74: Cancellation of agreement

The CCA74 further seeks to protect consumers by giving them, in certain circumstances, the right to reconsider their agreement and to cancel it. This right will be available in the following two sets of circumstances:

(a) where the agreement has been signed in off-trade premises: for example, in the consumer's home.
(b) where oral representations have been made by the creditor, or negotiator, to the debtor prior to the signing of the agreement, for example, statements about the quality or fitness of the goods.

In the above circumstances the debtor will have the right to receive

a second copy of the agreement, or notice of his or her right to terminate, within seven days of the full execution of the document.
Upon receiving the second copy or notice, the debtor has a five-day
'cooling off period', during which time the debtor can withdraw
from the agreement by sending written notice to the creditor.

► The postal rules will apply.
Acceptance will become valid upon
posting.

Where the right of cancellation has been exercised the parties
will be returned to the pre-contractual position. Any monies paid
must be returned and any goods received must be made available
for collection.

The Consumer Protection (Cancellation of Contracts Concluded
away from Business Premises) Regulations 1987 have given consumers further rights of cancellation, in addition to those outlined
above. The Regulations apply to a whole range of cash and credit
transactions (not regulated by the 1974 Act) under which goods
and services exceeding £35 are supplied. The Regulations apply
where a contract has been made as the result of an unsolicited visit
by a trader to the home or workplace of a consumer.

The Timeshare Act 1992 gives a consumer who has entered into
a timeshare contract a minimum fourteen-day cooling-off period,
during which time the consumer may cancel the contract.

DEFAULT AND TERMINATION

Credit agreements may be ended by a debtor's paying off or
defaulting on the agreement.

Sections 87–9: Default

CCA74, s. 87: Notice of default

The service of a notice of default on the debtor or hirer is necessary
before the creditor or owner can become entitled, by reason of any
breach by the debtor or hirer of a regulated agreement:

(a) to terminate the agreement, or
(b) to demand earlier payment of any sum, or
(c) to recover possession of any goods or land, or
(d) to treat any right conferred on the debtor or hirer by the
    agreement as terminated, restricted or deferred, or
(e) to enforce any security.

A breach is normally committed by the debtor or hirer failing to
keep up the payment of instalments. A default notice must detail
the nature of the alleged breach. If the breach is capable of remedy,
the notice must contain details of how it may be remedied and by
what date. If it is not capable of remedy, then the notice must
contain details of the sum, if any, payable in compensation for the
breach and the date by which that sum is payable.

The debtor must be allowed at least seven days after the service
of the default notice to remedy the breach. If the debtor does so
then the breach will be disregarded. Where the debtor fails to do so

the creditor may seek repossession of the goods, as detailed below.

Once a default notice has been served on a debtor he or she may apply to a court for a 'time order' (CCA74, s. 129). A time order will give the debtor time to pay off any outstanding instalments or time to remedy any breach. A court may also, in a conditional sale or hire purchase agreement, change the dates for payment of any future instalments.

 How does the Consumer Credit Act 1974 protect a consumer prior to, at the time of and after the signing of a regulated agreement?

Section 90: Retaking of protected hire purchase goods etc.

The effects of this important section are not widely appreciated by the general public. It states that where a person is a debtor under a regulated hire purchase or conditional sale agreement, a creditor will not be able to enter any premises to repossess goods without a court order.

Where a debtor is in breach of a hire purchase or conditional sale agreement and has paid one-third of the price of the goods under the agreement, plus all installation costs, the goods will become 'protected goods'. A creditor may repossess protected goods only with a court order (s. 90).

Section 91: Repossession without court order

> **CCA74, s. 91**
>
> If goods are recovered by the creditor in contravention of section 90:
> (a) the regulated agreement, if not previously terminated, shall terminate, and
> (b) the debtor shall be released from all liability under the agreement, and shall be entitled to recover from the creditor all sums paid by the debtor under the agreement.

This section is essentially punitive. Where a creditor repossesses goods in contravention of s. 90, i.e. without a court order, the agreement will be cancelled and the debtor will be able to recover all monies previously paid.

Sections 94–7: Early payment by debtor

In any consumer credit agreement a debtor may terminate the agreement by making early payment of it. The debtor may either inform the creditor of his or her intention to cancel, or merely pay off the balance. Where applicable, the debtor will be entitled to a rebate of interest for the early payment.

Sections 98–101: Termination

Section 98: Termination by creditor

A creditor may terminate an agreement for reasons other than non-payment: for example, where the debtor has become insolvent or where there has been no default and the agreement allows for termination by the creditor. Seven days' notice must be given of the termination and the debtor may be liable to pay up to half the purchase price of the goods, which can normally be repossessed by the creditor.

Section 99: Termination by debtor

> **CCA74, s. 99**
>
> (1) At any time before the final payment by a debtor under a regulated HP or regulated conditional sales agreement falls due, the debtor shall be entitled to terminate the agreement by giving notice to any person entitled or authorized to receive the sums payable under the agreement.

The good(s) must be returned to the creditor and any arrears paid off. The debtor will also be liable to pay the creditor the smallest one of the following.

1 Half of the purchase price. For example, if the goods cost £500 and £200 had been paid under the instalment plan, £50 would be due at the termination of the agreement. This is an aggregate payment and any **installation costs** must be discounted. Therefore, if the installation costs were £50, in the example above another £50 would have to be paid. If the debtor feels that the payment due under this section is too large, he or she may apply to the court for a reduction.

► **Installation costs** – costs incurred when delivering and fitting the good.

2 An amount specified in the agreement.
3 An amount decided by the court as suitable to compensate the creditor.

A court may also award damages to the creditor as compensation when the goods, which had been subject to the agreement, have been damaged (s. 100).

(ACT) Search among your family or friends to find someone who has recently entered into a credit agreement. Which type of credit agreement is it? Who were the lenders? Which Act(s) covered the agreement? Was it a regulated agreement? Does the agreement, as far as you can ascertain, comply with the legislation?

Sections 137–40: Extortionate credit bargains

An extortionate credit bargain is one in which the agreement has been made on grossly exorbitant terms, requiring that the debtor is subject to repayments at an extremely high rate of interest. It is against all the principles of fair trading.

When considering whether an agreement is extortionate the court will consider the following:

(a) interest rates at the time that the agreement was made;
(b) any relevant consideration;
(c) the age, experience, business capacity and state of health of the debtor;
(d) the financial pressure applied to the debtor;
(e) the relationship between the debtor and the creditor;
(f) the element of risk in the agreement for the creditor;
(g) whether or not a colourable cash price was quoted for any goods or services included in the credit bargain, i.e. the price of the goods was raised to hide the real credit charges (s. 138).

A court has the power to enter a credit agreement (not restricted to an upper limit of £15,000) and do any of the following:

(a) take direct accounts to establish what has been paid and what is due under the agreement;
(b) set aside the whole or any part of any obligation imposed on the debtor, or a **surety** by the credit bargain or any related agreement;
(c) require the creditor to repay the whole or part of any sum paid under the credit bargain or any related agreement by the debtor or a surety;
(d) direct the return of any property provided as security;
(e) alter the terms of the credit agreement or any security instrument (s. 139).

A debtor may make an application to a court to reopen an extortionate agreement or the debtor may request such action when enforcement proceedings, under the agreement, are being taken against him or her.

It does not necessarily follow that an agreement with a high rate of interest will be held by the court to be extortionate. If the creditor is taking a risk in lending the money – for example, if little or no security is supplied, and the creditor has little knowledge of the debtor – then the court may uphold the agreement. The following case is an illustration of this point.

► A **surety** is a person who agrees to be liable for the contractual debts of another, should the other person fail to honour their contractual obligations. For example, Patricia borrowed £5,000 from the bank, getting her father to stand surety for the loan. If Patricia failed to pay back the money, her father would become liable to repay the debt.

Ketley v. Scott (1981) ICR 241

A moneylender lent £20,500, at short notice, to a prospective house purchaser at an interest rate of 48 per cent. The money was used to complete a house purchase. The borrower's own bank had refused to lend him the money and the moneylender had received little security for the loan. The borrower later brought an action claiming that the terms of the agreement made it extortionate.

COURT HELD
The agreement was not extortionate: the lack of security, the fact that the borrower's own bank had refused him and the immediate need of the money meant that the 48 per cent interest rate was not excessive.

 Sean entered into a hire purchase agreement to rent a television to watch the football World Cup. The agreement was due to last for two years. After watching the World Cup, Sean decided to terminate the agreement. Would all the following be regulated agreements? What would Sean be liable to pay under the following circumstances?

(a) Sean had paid £250 in five instalments, the television being valued at £570.
(b) The agreement contained a clause stating that in case of termination a fee of £300 would be payable by the hirer.
(c) The agreement was a DCSA and Sean had paid two of the three instalments.
(d) Sean had paid six of the ten instalments, amounting to £300, the television being valued at £570. However, the set had been badly damaged.
(e) Sean failed to pay any of the instalments due under the agreement.

 Now that you have completed this chapter, look back at the chapter objectives at the beginning. Can you do all the things that these suggest? If not, look again at the relevant sections of the chapter.

CHAPTER SUMMARY

1 The CCA74 governs the provision of credit under regulated agreements.
2 A regulated agreement is defined as being a credit agreement between a supplier and a consumer, for a sum of less than £15,000.
3 The following are not regulated agreements under the Act: credit sale agreements for less than £50; land mortgages; running credit agreements; non-commercial credit agreements; credit agreements where the APR is less than 13 per cent; a credit agreement for the finance of international trade; a fixed sum DCSA with four or fewer instalments.
4 Sections 10–13 of the CCA74 define the following types of regulated agreements: RAC; FSC; RUC; UUC; DCSA; DCA.
5 Sections 21–43 of the CCA74 control the licensing and regulation of consumer credit agencies.

6 Sections 43–7 of the CCA74 control the advertising of consumer credit by the creation of regulations. The Consumer Credit Advertisement Regulations 1989 govern advertising published after 1 February 1990.

7 Sections 87–101 of the CCA74 outline the procedures to be followed, and the remedies available to both parties, in the case of termination or default.

8 Sections 137–40 of the CCA74 give the courts the power to examine a credit agreement that has been made on grossly exorbitant terms. A court may, if the circumstances warrant it, set aside the obligation, alter the terms of the agreement or require the creditor to repay all monies received.

Supply of goods and services: consumer protection

Chapter objectives

By the end of this chapter you should be able to:

▌ appreciate the role of the Director General of Fair Trading

▌ understand the provisions of, and the criminal offences created by, the Trade Descriptions Act 1968

▌ recognize the definition of a trade description, and the ways in which it may be applied

▌ know the way in which a false trade description may be applied to the provision of services, accommodation and facilities

▌ recognize the provisions of Part III of the Consumer Protection Act 1987 and how it governs the making of misleading indications as to price

▌ know the provisions relating to the supplying of safe consumer goods, made under Part II of the Consumer Protection Act 1987

▌ appreciate the criminal offences created by other Acts relating to the supply of consumer goods.

▌ recognize the implications of the General Product Safety Regulations, 1994.

CONSUMER PROTECTION LEGISLATION

We have studied how a consumer is protected by civil law when entering into contracts and credit agreements, and have discovered when and under which circumstances he or she can make recourse to the courts. In Chapter 17 we found that there are also criminal offences that may be committed by suppliers, advertisers, or others who try to dupe or cheat consumers. The State has always been keen to protect consumers from dubious traders, manufacturers, and suppliers of goods and services.

A number of Acts have created criminal offences relating to the supply, pricing, safety and quality of consumer products. The two major pieces of legislation regarding trade descriptions are the Trade Descriptions Act 1968 (TDA68) and the Consumer Protection Act 1987 (CPA87), and they will be discussed in detail in this chapter. Criminal offences under the Consumer Credit Act 1974 have been discussed in Chapter 17. Other Acts that create criminal offences relating to consumer goods will be mentioned at the end of this chapter.

Before turning to look at the provisions of the TDA68, we shall first look at how the government seeks to take an overview of the whole consumer area, by examining the role of the Director General of Fair Trading (DGFT).

THE FAIR TRADING ACT 1973 (FTA73)

The FTA73 created the office of the DGFT, who is head of the Office of Fair Trading (OFT). The DGFT has responsibility for the overall supervision of consumer protection (FTA73, s. 2). The DGFT is responsible for the discovery and elimination of harmful practices; the promotion of codes of practice and the control of individual traders who persistently contravene the laws relating to consumer protection.

The DGFT issues codes of practice to assist traders in achieving and maintaining a high standard of trade practice, in order to protect consumers' interests. The codes are not normally backed by powers of statutory enforcement, though the DGFT does have the power to prosecute traders who consistently flout consumer law in the Restrictive Practices Court.

THE TRADE DESCRIPTIONS ACT 1968

This Act creates certain criminal offences relating to trade descriptions.

Section 1: Prohibition of false trade descriptions

TDA68, s. 1

(1) Any person who, in the course of a trade or business,
  (a) applies a false trade description to any goods; or
  (b) supplies or offers to supply any goods to which a false trade description is applied;
shall, subject to the provisions of this Act, be guilty of an offence.

Section 1 of the TDA68 creates an offence of strict liability that can only be committed by a person in the normal course of his or her business. If a person commits the offence when doing something peripheral to his or her business, then that person will probably not commit an offence under this section. The following case illustrates this point.

Davies v. Sumner (1984) 3 All ER 831

The defendant applied a false trade description to a vehicle that he had sold, the vehicle having been used almost exclusively in the course of the defendant's business as a courier.

COURT HELD

No offence was committed. The selling of cars was not the business of the defendant, therefore the Trade Descriptions Act 1968 did not apply.

Section 1(1)(b) of the TDA68 creates an offence whereby a person can commit an offence if he or she sells or offers to sell something that has previously had a false trade description applied to it. An example is a jeweller selling a set of cutlery that had been marked by the manufacturer as being 'finest Sheffield steel', when it had really been imported from China.

▶ We saw in the law of contract that it is impossible to offer anything for sale, all offers being invitations to treat (except for the exceptions). Section 6 of the TDA68 manages to overcome this problem by stating that 'a person exposing goods for supply or having goods in his possession for supply shall be deemed to offer to supply them'.

Section 2: Trade description of goods

TDA68, s. 2

A trade description is an indication, direct or indirect, and by whatever means given, of any of the following matters with respect to any goods or parts of goods, that is to say:
(a) quantity, size or gauge;
(b) method of manufacture, production, processing or reconditioning;
(c) composition;
(d) fitness for purpose, strength, performance, behaviour or accuracy;
(e) any physical characteristics not included in the preceding paragraphs;
(f) testing by any person and results thereof;
(g) approval by any person or conformity with a type approved by any person;
(h) place or date of manufacture, production, processing or reconditioning;
(i) person by whom manufactured, produced, processed or reconditioned;
(j) other history, including previous ownership or use.

This section has been drafted to be a 'catch all' section with most imaginable circumstances being catered for. An interesting example is illustrated by the next case.

Sherratt v. Geralds the American Jewellers Ltd (1970) 114 SJ 147

The defendants sold a watch to the plaintiff that was described by the makers as a 'divers' watch' and as being waterproof. When the watch

was put into water it quickly filled with water and stopped working. The defendants were charged under the TDA68, s. 1.

COURT HELD

The defendants were convicted of the offence under the TDA68, s. 1(1)(b).

 What is a false trade description? Who can be guilty of applying a false trade description to goods?

Section 3: False trade description

> **TDA68, s. 3**
>
> (1) A false trade description is a trade description that is false to a material degree.
> (2) A false trade description that, though not false, is misleading, … shall be deemed to be a false trade description.

This means that, where the false trade description is not material to the supplying of goods, an offence will not be committed. The courts have tended to find against the defendant in cases where there is some doubt. The following case is an example of this.

Robertson v. Dicicco (1972) Crim LR 592

A second-hand car dealer described a car as being 'beautiful'. While the upper body work was good, the car was unroadworthy. The defendant was charged under the TDA68, s. 1(1)(a). He argued that his statement was meant to refer only to the appearance of the car.

COURT HELD

The defendant was convicted. The statement was false to a material degree. It was reasonable to assume that the statement was meant to refer to the whole of the vehicle, not just its physical appearance.

Any person can make a false trade description. It need not necessarily be made by a seller. A buyer is equally capable of committing the offence. The following case, relating to the purchase of a car, is the best example of this.

Fletcher v. Budgen (1974) *Times* 12 June

The defendant, a car dealer, bought a car from a customer for £2, telling him that it was no good and fit only for scrap. The defendant then repaired the car and advertised it for sale for £135. He was accused of committing an offence under s. 1(1)(a).

COURT HELD

The defendant was guilty of applying a false trade description made in the course of his business.

Misleading statements

A statement that is scientifically correct may still be considered to be a false trade description if it misleads a buyer who is lacking in scientific knowledge. This is illustrated by the next case.

► A half truth will also be a false trade description. A car that was described as having had only one registered owner, but had in fact been leased to five different keepers under leasing agreements, would be a false trade description.

Dixons Ltd v. Barnett (1989) 2 TLR 37

A customer bought a telescope from the defendants that was described as being capable of up to ×455 magnification. However, at the maximum magnification the image obtained was a mere blur; the maximum useful magnification was × 120.

COURT HELD

The defendants were convicted: the statement was scientifically correct, but to an ordinary customer it was misleading. A customer would be interested in the useful magnification, not the maximum magnification that a blurred image could be seen at.

Hidden defects

Where a businessperson sells on goods that have been repaired or that have defects that have been concealed, and is not aware of the defect, nor is there any reason to be aware, then no offence will have been committed. The following case exemplifies this point.

Cottee v. Douglas Seaton Ltd (1972) 3 All ER 750

The defendant, a car dealer, sold on a car that had been repaired by the use of plastic body filler. The repairs had been expertly carried out and the defendant was not aware of the work having been done. The purchaser discovered the repairs and the defendant was charged with applying a false trade description to the goods.

COURT HELD

A false trade description had been applied to the goods. They were purporting to be something that they were not, i.e. a car in good condition. However, the defendant was not guilty of the offence because he was unaware of the defects.

Disclaimers

Yet again we have to thank a second-hand car dealer for the rule in this case. Where a dealer sells a car that was obtained with a false milometer reading, and the dealer then describes the car as having that recorded mileage, not knowing whether it is true or false, he or she may be guilty of an offence under the TDA68, s. 1(1)(b). The dealer may try to avoid the commission of the offence by using a disclaimer. The rule regarding the use of disclaimers was established in the following case.

Norman v. Bennett (1974) 3 All ER 351

The defendant, a car dealer, sold a vehicle with a recorded mileage of 23,000 miles. The contract contained a disclaimer that stated that the milometer reading could not be guaranteed. The car's actual mileage was later proved to be 68,000. The defendant was charged with the offence under the TDA68, s. 1(1)(b).

COURT HELD

The offence had been committed. The disclaimer was not enough to avoid the offence. The court stated that to be valid a disclaimer would have to be as 'bold, precise and compelling as the trade description itself'.

A disclaimer will be subject to the terms of the Unfair Contract Terms Act 1977. A supplier or trader who makes a false statement – for example, a car dealer who turns back the clock on a car – will not then be able to rely on a disclaimer. Like past consideration, a disclaimer made after an offence has been committed will have no value.

► The motor trade, under the Motor Trade Code of Practice, is advised to disclaim all recorded mileages unless there is a service history to support the claim. This means that a potential purchaser is now really no better off because, with all mileages being disclaimed, it becomes even more difficult to establish a true recorded mileage.

Remedies

Offences under the TDA68 are criminal offences and it is for the prosecution to prove the ineffectiveness of a disclaimer. Under the TDA68, s. 35, the commission of an offence under this Act will not, in itself, make a contract for the sale or supply of goods void or unenforceable. We must remember that the TDA68 is concerned with criminal offences, i.e. seeking to punish the offenders, not to compensate the injured party. A court has a limited power to compensate a victim of crime, though to find a civil remedy the injured party would have a right of action under the Misrepresentation Act 1967 or the Sale of Goods Act 1979.

 Ron, a second-hand car dealer, sells one of his cars to a customer, the car showing a recorded mileage of 20,000 miles. With reference to relevant cases and Acts, outline Ron's criminal liability, if any, in the following circumstances:

(a) the previous owner told Ron that the milometer was a bit 'dodgy';

(b) Ron had put the milometer back from 40,000 miles, but he then put a large disclaimer on the milometer stating that the mileage could not be guaranteed;

(c) the previous owner had done 60,000 miles in the car, but prior to selling it to Ron he put the milometer back, Ron having no knowledge of this fact;

(d) Ron sold the car with a disclaimer placed on the milometer stating that the mileage couldn't be guaranteed.

Section 14: False or misleading statements as to services, accommodation or facilities

> **TDA68, s. 14**
>
> (1) It shall be an offence for any person in the course of any trade or business:
>   (a) to make a statement that he knows to be false; or
>   (b) recklessly to make a statement that is false;
>   as to any of the following matters, that is to say,
>   (i)   the provision in the course of any trade or business of any services, accommodation or facilities;
>   (ii) the nature of any services, accommodation or facilities provided in the course of any trade or business;
>   (iii) the time at which, manner in which or persons by whom any services, accommodation or facilities are so provided;
>   (iv) the examination, approval or evaluation by any person of any services, accommodation or facilities so provided; or
>   (v)   the location or amenities of any accommodation so provided.

Offences under this section are not strict liability. *Mens rea* must therefore be proved, i.e. it must be proved that the trader knew that the statement was false or that the trader was reckless as to its truth. Reckless may be defined as not caring whether the statement is true or false. It does not require an element of dishonesty. A promise to do something in the future will not usually put someone at risk of committing an offence under this section, because this section is concerned with existing facts.

▶ ***Mens rea*** – guilty mind or guilty intent, normally one of the essential elements of a crime.

Offences under s. 14(1)(a)

To establish an offence under this section it must be proved that the person making the statement knew it to be false. It is never easy to establish a state of knowledge. While these are not strict liability offences, the courts seem to be prepared to interpret them as if there were an element of strict liability in them. The next case is one of many brought under this Act concerning the descriptions applied to holidays. We have all heard of nightmare holiday reports: unfinished hotels, five minutes to the nearest beach (by aeroplane!), traditional cuisine (cockroaches!) and many other horror stories.

Wings Ltd v. Ellis **(1984) 1 WLR 731**

VC   The defendants, tour operators, published a brochure that contained a false trade description stating that the rooms in a hotel were air-conditioned. It also contained a photograph of one of the rooms that was, in fact, a photograph of a room in a different hotel. At the time of publication the defendants did not know that the description was false. Upon discovering the inaccuracy of the statement the defendants took steps to bring the mistake to the notice of their agents, and to clients who had already booked the holiday, by writing to them. A new customer booked a holiday, having seen the original description in the brochure. He was not advised of the mistake. The defendants were charged with committing an offence under the TDA68, s. 14(1)(a).

 COURT HELD
The House of Lords held that the offence had been committed. The statement was made at the time that the customer saw the holiday in the brochure. At that time the defendants knew that the description was false.

Offences under s. 14(1)(b)

Section 14(2)(b) defines recklessness:

> **TDA68, s. 14(2)(b)**
>
> [A] statement made regardless of whether it is true or false shall be deemed to be made recklessly, whether or not the person making it had reasons for believing that it might be false.

Sunair Holidays Ltd v. Dodd **(1970) 2 All ER 410**

A holiday brochure described all the rooms in a hotel as having a terrace. The defendant contracted with the hotel owners to supply the rooms with a terrace, but he had failed to verify that all the rooms were so equipped. A customer booked a holiday and was given a room without a terrace. The defendant was charged with committing an offence under s. 14.

 COURT HELD
The statement was not false at the time that it was made, therefore no offence had been committed.

Defences under the TDA68

The TDA68 provides a number of statutory defences against the various offences that can be committed under the Act. These are contained in ss. 24–5.

> **TDA68, s. 24**
>
> (1) In any proceedings for an offence under this Act it shall, subject to subsection (2) of this section, be a defence for the person charged to prove:

► It would not be impossible in a case like *Sunair* for the company to be prosecuted more than once. If another customer had complained in similar circumstances, a second prosecution could have been brought. The Department of Trade and Industry has to be consulted prior to a prosecution to ensure that several are not being made at the same time. However, this will not prevent a double prosecution for the same offence.

(a) that the commission of the offence was due to a mistake or to reliance on information supplied to him or to the act or default of another person, an accident or some other cause beyond his control; *and*

(b) that he took all reasonable precautions and exercised all due diligence to avoid the commission of such an offence by himself or any person under his control.

To have a valid defence, the accused would have to prove one of the defences listed in s. 24(a) and (b). The following case illustrates a successful defence.

Tesco Supermarkets Ltd v. Natrass (1972) AC 153

 This case concerned a special offer made by the store on 'Radiant' washing powder. In the store was a poster offering specially marked 'Radiant' packets at a reduced price. When the store ran out of specially marked packets, ordinary packets were put in their place. The poster was left displaying the reduced price because the store manager failed to remove it. The store was prosecuted for committing an offence under the TDA68, s. 11.

COURT HELD
The House of Lords ruled that the store had not committed the offence. The manager was held to be 'another person' for the purposes of the defence under s. 24 and the store had in place reasonable precautions to prevent such an event happening. (Now misleading price indications are covered by the CPA87, Part III, see page 340 below).

The TDA68, s. 23, allows for the prosecution of 'another person' (as in the *Tesco* case), even where that person is not acting in the course of a business. The following case is an example of this.

Olgeirsson v. Kitching (1986) 1 WLR 304

The defendant had bought a Granada car from Humberside police. While in their possession, the milometer had been replaced when it was reading 64,000 miles. The defendant purchased the car from the police when the milometer read 10,500 miles, though he had been informed of the real mileage. The defendant then sold the car on to a garage, stating that the car had travelled 38,000 miles, the mileage that the milometer was showing at that time. The garage sold the car on the basis that it had completed 38,000 miles. Later the true mileage was discovered and the defendant was charged under the TDA68, s. 23.

COURT HELD
The defendant was guilty of the offence, notwithstanding that he was not acting in the course of a business.

The TDA68, s. 24(3), provides a specific defence to a supplier of goods, if the supplier can show that he or she did not know and could not reasonably have found out that the goods did not conform to the description or that the description had been applied to the goods.

Enforcement of the TDA68

The TDA68 is enforced by trading standards officers who are local authority employees. At the magistrates' court the penalty is limited to £5,000, while a Crown Court conviction could bring an unlimited fine and/or two years' imprisonment.

Misleading price indications (TDA68, s. 11, and CPA87, s. 20)

The CPA87, Part III, repealed the TDA68, s. 11, and the Price Marking (Bargain Offers) Order 1979. It created the offence of giving a misleading price indication under the CPA87, s. 20.

> **CPA87, s. 20**
>
> (1) … a person shall be guilty of an offence if, in the course of any business of his, he gives (by any means whatever) to any consumers an indication that is misleading as to the price at which any goods, services, accommodation or facilities are available (whether generally or from particular persons).

The CPA87, s. 21, gives a list of circumstances under which a misleading price indication may be made:

(a) that the price is in fact less than it is: for example, where a recommended price is quoted as being higher than it actually is;
(b) the price or method of determining the price depends on facts that are not the case (e.g. false facts are used to determine the price);
(c) that the price covers matters in respect of which an additional charge is made;
(d) that the price of the good(s) is due to fall, rise or remain the same, when in reality the trader has no such expectation.

The provisions of the CPA87, s. 20(2), also cover statements that, though not being misleading at the time that they are made, subsequently become misleading. Unless a trader has taken reasonable steps to prevent consumers from relying on the misrepresentation they are liable for prosecution under this section.

The following two cases illustrate the practical application of the law in this area. The first case was brought under the TDA68, s. 11, when the legislation was applicable to both consumer and business purchasers. Under the CPA87, s. 20, a consumer is defined as a person who wants the goods, services or accommodation, other than for business purposes.

Richards v. Westminster Motors Ltd (1975) Crim LR 528

This case concerned the sale of a commercial vehicle. The defendants offered the vehicle for sale at an advertised price of £1,350. When a purchaser came to pay the agreed price for the vehicle, VAT was added to the price. The defendant was charged with committing an offence under the TDA68, s. 11.

COURT HELD
The defendant was guilty of the offence. He had given a misleading indication as to the price.

Read Bros Cycles (Leyton) v. Waltham Forest LBC (1978) RTR 397

Read Bros advertised a Yamaha motorcycle for sale at £40 below the recommended retail price of £580. A customer offered his motorcycle in part exchange for a Yamaha and his offer was accepted, being allowed £90 part-exchange for his vehicle. That should have left a balance to pay of £350, being made up of £580 − £40 − £90 = £350. However, Read Bros charged him the full list price, stating that the £40 discount applied only to cash or hire purchase transactions. They were charged under the TDA68, s. 11.

COURT HELD
The defendants were guilty of an offence under the TDA68, s. 11(2) (now under the CPA87, s. 20.). They had offered goods at a price that was lower than the price at which the goods were actually sold.

Code of practice
The Secretary of State has issued a code of practice in order to help retailers understand and abide by the rules established in the CPA87, s. 20. The code provides rules that state how 'bargain offers' should be made. Generally, the goods should have been on offer at the higher price for twenty-eight consecutive days, within the preceding six months. Retailers get around this provision by offering the goods for sale at one of their smaller stores, before putting the goods in a 'sale' in all of their larger stores.

A breach of the code will not constitute a criminal or civil offence, though it would be considered as good evidence for a prosecution under the CPA87, s. 20.

 Sunny Tours Ltd placed the following holiday advertisement in their brochure.

Spain 14 days for £300
All accommodation and food included
No extras, every room with hot and cold water.

Barry, after seeing the ad in the Sunny Tours brochure, booked a holiday. Upon arrival in Spain, Barry was forced to pay £26 airport duties. At the hotel there was cold water in his room and hot water in the bathroom, which was situated in a room two doors away.

When Barry returned home he complained to Sunny Tours about the extra expense and the lack of hot water. Sunny Tours said that the airport taxes were not their fault and that the hot water was so near to Barry's room, he really didn't have anything to complain about. Have Sunny tours committed any offences?

Defences

The CPA87 provides several statutory defences to offences committed under s. 20, contained in s. 24. They are as follows:

CPA87, s. 24

(a) the acts or omissions were authorized by the Secretary of State under the power to make regulations provided in the CPA87, s. 26;

(b) the price indication was published in a book, newspaper, film or other publication but not in the form of an advertisement;

(c) an innocent publication of an advert made by a publisher;

(d) for an offence under s. 20(1):

   (i) that the indication did not relate to the availability from him [the supplier] of any goods, services, accommodation or facilities;

   (ii) a price had been recommended to every person from whom the goods, services, accommodation or facilities were indicated as being available;

   (iii) the indication related to that price and was misleading as to that price only by reason of a failure by any person to follow the recommendation; and

   (iv) it was reasonable for the person who gave the indication to assume that the recommendation was for the most part being followed.

The CPA87, s. 39, provides a defence for an offence under s. 20(1).

CPA87, s. 39

(1) … to show that he took all reasonable steps and exercised all due diligence to avoid committing the offence.

Enforcement

Conviction under the CPA87, s. 20, will be met with a fine. It is not an imprisonable offence. The Act is enforced by trading standards officers.

CONSUMER SAFETY UNDER PART II OF THE CONSUMER PROTECTION ACT 1987

Part II of the CPA87 provides legal rules relating to the safety of consumer goods. The CPA87 consolidates and amends the earlier legislation on this subject area, including the Consumer Safety Act 1978 and the Consumer Safety (Amendment) Act 1986.

The CPA87 creates a criminal offence of supplying consumer goods that are not reasonably safe, or offering, agreeing to supply, or exposing for supply such goods. We shall now look at the offence in detail.

Section 10: The general safety requirement

CPA87, s. 10

(1) A person shall be guilty of an offence if he:
    (a) supplies any consumer goods that fail to comply with the general safety requirement;
    (b) offers or agrees to supply any such goods; or
    (c) exposes or possesses any such goods for supply.

Section 10 continues to give definitions of many of the important aspects of this offence. Section 10(2) provides that consumer goods will be unsafe if they fail to comply with the general safety requirement or if they are not reasonably safe having regard to all the circumstances, including:

(a) the manner in which, and purposes for which, the goods are being or would be marketed;
(b) the get-up of the goods;
(c) the use of any mark in relation to the goods and any instructions or warnings that are given with respect to the keeping, use or consumption of the goods;
(d) any published safety standards for the goods;
(e) the existence of any means by which it would have been reasonable (taking into account the cost, likelihood and extent of any improvement) for the goods to have been made safer.

Section 10(3) provides that any safety requirement will be met if the product complies with any UK or EC product safety regulations.

The above-mentioned offence in s. 10 can only be committed in relation to consumer goods. Section 10(7) defines consumer goods as being any goods that are ordinarily intended for private use or consumption. Certain goods are excluded by this section:

(a) growing crops and things attached to the land;
(b) water, food (covered by the Food Safety Act 1990), feeding stuff or fertilizer;
(c) gas;
(d) aircraft or motor vehicles;
(e) controlled drugs or licensed medicinal products;
(f) tobacco.

Section 11: Safety regulations

Under this section the Secretary of State may make regulations for ensuring that certain types of goods are safe. These regulations may also ensure that appropriate information is supplied with the goods or that goods that would be unsafe in the hands of certain people are not available to them.

Section 11(2) of the CPA87 lists the areas that may be covered by safety regulations under this section:

(a) the composition or contents, design, construction, finish or packing of goods;
(b) approval of goods under this section;
(c) any requirements as to inspection or testing;
(d) any warnings, information or instructions to be provided with the goods;
(e) any requirement relating to the provision of information to officials;
(f) prohibitions on certain goods or materials.

Section 12: Offences under the CPA87

Failure to comply with any regulations made under s. 11 will constitute a criminal offence under s. 12. Section 12 creates different offences to cover all aspects of the regulations that may be made:

(a) supplying, offering to supply, etc., any goods in breach of a prohibition;
(b) where test procedures have been stipulated by a regulation, failing to comply with the stipulation;
(c) failing to give information as required by the regulations.

▶ Problems may arise when a new product falls into an area that is covered by a regulation, but its design is so different that it would fail the compulsory safety test. For example, the compulsory safety test relating to pushchairs and prams includes a four-wheel stability test, therefore anyone trying to introduce a three-wheeled pushchair would have to campaign to get the test amended before the good could be sold in the UK.

Section 12(5) provides that upon conviction under ss. 11–12 a person will be liable to a fine and/or imprisonment for up to six months.

Many goods are covered by regulations made under s. 11. They include toys, electrical goods, prams and pushchairs, and other goods that are mostly used by children. Where a producer wishes to bring a new product on to the market, the producer must ensure that, where regulations are in existence governing that type of good, his or her good will comply. This could relate to a number of factors, including the size, specification or testing of the goods.

Sections 13–16: Prohibition, seizure and forfeiture

▶ These types of notice often appear in the newspapers. Normally they relate to electrical goods or toys, and ask any purchaser to return the goods or to contact the retailer for a refund or replacement.

The Secretary of State has wide powers under these sections to deal with unsafe goods. He or she may issue two types of notice under s. 13: a prohibition notice, prohibiting a person from supplying a certain good; and a 'notice to warn', whereby a person is ordered to issue a notice, at his or her own expense, about a particular unsafe good that he or she has supplied.

Section 14 gives a local authority the power to issue a suspension notice, which will ban a supplier from supplying any goods in breach of a safety regulation. The notice may last for a period of up to six months. Contravention of any of these notices will result in the commission of a criminal offence.

Section 16 provides a magistrates' court, on application, with the power to order the forfeiture of any unsafe goods where there has been a breach of the Act. The goods may then be destroyed, released for repair, reconditioned or scrapped.

Section 41: Remedies under the CPA87

Section 41 provides a right of action for breach of statutory duty, for a person who has suffered injury or loss as a result of a breach of any of the safety provisions, against the trader who supplied the good. This is an important section because it allows a person who has been injured by a gift, which has been supplied in breach of the Act, to sue the supplier or manufacturer without having to prove negligence. This right cannot be excluded.

(ACT) Sheila has imported some pushchairs from Japan that she is selling in her shop. The pushchairs have not been subjected to any UK or EC tests. Sheila is selling the pushchairs really cheaply. She tells every purchaser that they are 'great little buggies and that they don't need to have passed any tests here because they were checked in Japan'. Has she committed any offence? What actions could be taken to stop any more of the pushchairs being sold?

THE GENERAL PRODUCT SAFETY REGULATIONS 1994

The General Product Safety Regulations 1994 implemented the General Product Safety Directive 92/59 and came into force in October 1994, empowered by SI 1994 No. 2328. The Regulations are applicable to producers of consumer goods only. Where goods are produced to be used solely in a commercial environment – for example, goods produced by one business to be used in another business – the Regulations will not apply. Products that are antiques or that are second-hand and in need of repair will not be covered by the Regulations, provided the supplier makes it clear, for example in the contract of sale, that the Regulations do not apply. However, other second-hand goods will be covered by the Regulations, and this represents a major change in consumer law.

The Regulations impose a further statutory duty on the producers of goods to ensure that they are safe. The duty will exist in tandem with the statutory duty imposed by the CPA87, s. 10 (see above), though certain minor subsections of s. 10 have been dis applied by Regulation 5. The remaining provisions of the Regulations and the Act are not exactly matched and, therefore, in certain circumstances it may be necessary to determine which of the two applies.

Safety of products

'Safe' is defined in Regulation 2, to refer to:

> ... any product which, under normal or reasonably foreseeable conditions of use, including duration, does not present any risk or only the minimum risks compatible with the product's use, considered as acceptable and consistent with a high level of protection for the safety and health of persons, taking into account in particular –
> (a) the characteristics of the product, including its composition, packaging, instructions for assembly and maintenance;
> (b) the effect on other products, where it is reasonably foreseeable that it will be used with other products;
> (c) the presentation of the product, the labelling, any instructions for its use and disposal and any other indication or information provided by the producer; and
> (d) the categories of consumers at serious risk when using the product, in particular children, ... and the fact that higher levels of safety may be obtained or other products presenting a lesser degree of risk may be available shall not of itself cause the product to be considered other than a safe product.

Where products are regulated by other Acts or Directives in relation to safety standards then the Regulations will not apply. Now there would appear to be a need for producers to label any product that may have a potential for being unsafe, particularly where children may be the consumers. This requirement may be considered to be applicable to everyday products, such as household cleaning products, that may end up in the hands of children. Where products have an inherent danger, such as explosives or cigarettes, then the existing labelling requirements will probably not be disturbed by the new Regulations.

The producer

The term producer is defined in Regulation 2, and covers others in the distribution chain when the producer cannot be identified or is from outside the European Union. Provision is made to cover 'own branders' and others who present themselves as the manufacturers. Regulation 2 defines 'producer' as:

> (a) the manufacturer of the product, when he is established in the Community, and includes any person presenting himself as the manufacturer by affixing to the product his name, trade mark or other distinctive mark, or the person who reconditions the product;
> (b) when the manufacturer is not established in the Community –

> (i) if the manufacturer does not have a representative established in the Community, the importer of the product;
> (ii) in all other cases, the manufacturer's representative; and
> (c) other professionals in the supply chain, insofar as their activities may affect the safety properties of a product placed on the market;

Information

Regulation 8 requires that producers have good systems in operation to ensure that consumers are supplied with the relevant information to make them aware of the potential risks of a product, and that where problems arise the producer is able quickly to inform any consumer of problems with the product. For example, we have previously talked about product recalls; it may be now that producers, under these provisions of Regulation 8, must keep substantive customer records in order to be able to comply with the requirements.

> (1) Within the limits of his activity, a producer shall –
> (a) provide consumers with the relevant information to enable them to assess the risks inherent in a product throughout the normal or reasonably foreseeable period of its use, where such risks are not immediately obvious without adequate warnings, and to take precautions against those risks; and
> (b) adopt measures commensurate with the characteristics of the products which he supplies, to enable him to be informed of the risks which these products might present and to take appropriate action, including, if necessary, withdrawing the product in question from the market to avoid those risks.
> (2) The measures referred to in sub-paragraph (b) of paragraph (1) above may include, whenever appropriate –
> (i) marking of the products or product batches in such a way that they can be identified;
> (ii) sample testing of marketed products;
> (iii) investigating complaints; and
> (iv) keeping distributors informed of such monitoring.

Regulation 9 involves distributors in ensuring that producers comply with the safety and information provisions, requiring them not to supply dangerous products, to assist in passing on any information and to take part in any monitoring exercises.

Offences and defences

Regulation 7 defines the offence of producing an unsafe product. No person shall place a product on the market unless the product is a safe product. Regulation 9 creates a similar offence for a distributor of a dangerous product. Further offences are detailed in Regulation 13:

> No producer or distributor shall –
> (a) offer or agree to place on the market any dangerous product or expose or possess any such product for placing on the market; or
> (b) offer or agree to supply any dangerous product or expose or possess any such product for supply …

Penalties

For breaching the Regulations a person is liable, upon conviction at a Magistrates' Court, to a term of three months imprisonment, or a fine not exceeding £5,000, or both.

Other provisions

Regulation 14 provides a defence that a person took all reasonable steps and exercised all due diligence to avoid committing an offence. Where a product is subject to laws relating to health and safety requirements, Regulation 10 creates the presumption that the product is safe. The Regulations maintain the powers created under the CPA87 in relation to enforcement by means of prohibition notices and notices to warn. Officers of a commercial corporation, such as the directors, may be penalized under the regulations for the actions of a company in breach of the Regulations.

OTHER CRIMINAL OFFENCES RELATING TO THE SUPPLY OF CONSUMER GOODS

Where a person is convicted of a criminal offence relating to the supply of consumer goods, the courts have the power to grant a compensation order. This power was granted under the Powers of the Criminal Courts Act 1973, s. 35 (amended by the Criminal Justice Act 1982). For each breach a defendant may be ordered to compensate a victim (the consumer) up to £1,000. A compensation order may be awarded in place of, or in addition to, a fine.

Several other Acts create criminal offences relating to the supply of consumer goods. I have already detailed the offences available under the Consumer Credit Act 1974. Below are listed some of the others.

The Weights and Measures Act 1985

This Act governs the use of weighing equipment and the supplying of short-weight or short-measure goods. Two main offences are created under the Act. Section 17 creates the offence of having for trade purposes any weighing or measuring equipment that is false; s. 28 creates the offence of supplying a short weight or short measure.

The Food Safety Act 1990

This Act creates a number of offences relating to the preparation, quality and supply of food, most of which are strict liability offences. The offences created relate to: the processing or treating of food intended for sale for human consumption that in any way makes it injurious to health (s. 7); the food must satisfy the food safety requirement (s. 8); selling food not of the nature, substance or quality demanded (s. 14); making a false description about food (s. 15).

The Road Traffic Act 1988

This Act creates a number of offences, the most notable being the offence of selling a motor vehicle that is unroadworthy (s. 75). The offence may be committed by a private individual as well as by a motor trader.

The Unsolicited Goods and Services Act 1971

This Act created the offence of demanding payment for unsolicited goods or services. It also provides that a recipient of such goods does not have to return them and will become the owner of them if they are not collected within a specified period.

 Now that you have completed this chapter, look back at the chapter objectives at the beginning. Can you do all the things that these suggest? If not, look again at the relevant sections of the chapter.

CHAPTER SUMMARY

1 The Trade Descriptions Act 1968 creates a criminal offence of applying a false trade description to any goods, by a person acting in the course of his or her business (s. 1).
2 The TDA68, s. 14, creates the criminal offence of applying a false trade description to any service, accommodation or other facilities, made by a person in the course of his or her business.
3 The Consumer Protection Act 1987, s. 24, provides the following statutory defences:
   (a) that the commission of the offence was due to a mistake or to reliance on information supplied to him or her, or to the act or default of another person, an accident or some other cause beyond his or her control; *and*
   (b) that the person took all reasonable precautions and exercised all due diligence to avoid the commission of such an offence by the person or anyone under his or her control.
4 The CPA87, s. 20, created the offence of giving a misleading

price indication. By s. 20(1) '... a person shall be guilty of an offence if, in the course of any business of his, he gives (by any means whatever) to any consumers an indication that is misleading as to the price at which any goods, services, accommodation or facilities are available'. Section 24 also provides statutory defences to the above offence.

5 The CPA87, s. 10, provides that a person shall be guilty of an offence if 'he: (a) supplies any consumer goods that fail to comply with the general safety requirement; (b) offers or agrees to supply any such goods; or (c) exposes or possesses any such goods for supply'.

6 The CPA87, s. 11, gives the Secretary of State powers to make regulations for ensuring that certain types of goods are safe. Section 12 creates a criminal offence of failing to comply, or breaching, any of the regulations made under s. 11.

7 The CPA87, ss. 13–16, empower a Secretary of State to prohibit, seize and apply for the forfeiture of unsafe goods.

8 The General Product Safety Regulations 1994 implemented the EU Directive on Product Safety, creating a statutory duty on those who produce goods to ensure that they are 'safe'.

Supply of goods and services: product safety

Chapter objectives

By the end of this chapter you should be able to:

▌ recognize the three elements of the tort of negligence: duty of care, breach of that duty and resulting damage

▌ appreciate the rule established in *Donoghue*, and how the courts have applied and extended the rule

▌ understand the view of the courts relating to the existence of a duty of care, recognizing the limitations imposed by the House of Lords in *Murphy*

▌ recognize the implications of *res ipsa loquitur*

▌ appreciate the rules relating to remoteness, causation and contributory negligence

▌ understand the provisions of the Consumer Protection Act 1987, Part I, relating to product liability, including the statutory defences to offences under the Act

▌ recognize the rules relating to the recovery of economic loss in cases of professional negligence, including the rule established in *Hedley Byrne*.

In this chapter we shall examine how a consumer may be able to seek redress for personal injury, damage to property, reputation or goodwill, when he or she is in a non-contractual relationship. We have already considered the provisions of the Consumer Protection Act 1987 (CPA87, Part II), relating to statutory duty, which provides an injured party with a right of action against the supplier or manufacturer of a good supplied in contravention of the Act. We must also consider Part I of the CPA87, which implemented the EC Directive on Product Liability. First, however, we shall consider the tort of negligence, which has been the major source of redress for persons who have been injured by defective products.

TORT OF NEGLIGENCE

The tort of negligence may apply where a person alleges that another party has acted carelessly, and as a result of that carelessness they have suffered injury or damage. The injury or damage

▶ Remember from Chapter 2, p. 2, where the term is described in more detail, that tort is a civil wrong that is actionable in law, examples being negligence, trespass, libel and private nuisance.

will more normally be physical, but in certain sets of circumstances economic loss may also be recoverable.

The tort of negligence has three elements, all of which must be proved in order to succeed in a claim:

1 duty of care
2 breach of duty
3 damage resulting from the breach

Duty of care

A duty of care will exist where a plaintiff is able to prove that a defendant should have had the plaintiff in the defendant's contemplation when he or she committed the act in question and should have realized that there was a possibility of harm being caused to the plaintiff. Prior to 1932 there was no leading case on this subject. However, we shall now re-examine a case that we looked at in Chapter 3 (p. 28), which established the rules to be followed.

The neighbour principle

Donoghue v. Stevenson (1932) AC 562

 In this case a woman was bought a glass of ginger beer in a café by a friend. The beer was in an opaque bottle. After drinking some of the beer she poured more into a glass and out fell the remains of a decomposed snail. The plaintiff sued the manufacturer of the ginger beer under the tort of negligence, under which it had to be proved that the manufacturer owed a duty of care to the plaintiff.

COURT HELD
A manufacturer of products, which he sells in such a form as to show that he intends them to reach the ultimate consumer in the form in which they left him, with no reasonable possibility of intermediate examination and with the knowledge that the absence of reasonable care in the preparation or putting up of the products will result in an injury to the consumer's life or property, owes a duty to the consumer to take that reasonable care.

The court further ruled that in law you must be careful not to injure your neighbour, that is to say not to carry out any acts or omissions that could foreseeably injure your neighbour. A neighbour could be any person likely to be affected by the act or omission, so that they should have been in the contemplation of the party when the act was being contemplated. This became known as the neighbour test.

The case further established that:

(a) duty of care in negligence is based on the foresight of a reasonable man (read person);
(b) categories of negligence are **never closed**;
(c) duty of care relates to things that are not dangerous in

▶ **Never closed** – the court was indicating that it felt this principle could be spread to many other different sets of circumstances.

themselves; for goods that are dangerous in themselves, such as explosives, the duty of care is much higher.

Since the establishment of the rule in *Donoghue*, the neighbour principle has been subject to much debate and criticism. At times certain cases have extended the tentacles of the duty of care. Now, however, a recent ruling has suggested a retraction of the areas in which a duty of care will apply. Before looking at this case, it will be useful to examine the recent developments. In the next case the neighbour principle was developed.

► The rule established in *Donoghue* formed a precedent for other cases, including *Stennet v. Hancock and Peters* (see Chapter 3, p. 28).

Dorset Yacht Co. Ltd v. Home Office (1969) 2 QB 412

 A party of borstal trainees from the Portland borstal was taken on a training exercise to Brownsea Island, in Poole harbour. One evening seven of the boys escaped when they were left unsupervised by their three borstal officers, in contravention of Home Office guidelines. The seven boys boarded a yacht, which they started and crashed into the plaintiff's yacht, the *Silver Mist*. The boys then boarded the *Silver Mist* and committed further damage. The owners of the *Silver Mist* sued the Home Office as being vicariously liable for the negligent acts of the three borstal officers.

COURT HELD

The plaintiff could succeed. The Home Office was held to be liable for the actions of the borstal officers. The plaintiffs were found to be owed a duty of care because it was reasonably foreseeable that, if the boys escaped, boats in the harbour could be damaged. It was a likely consequence of the negligent behaviour of the borstal officers that the plaintiff's yacht would be damaged.

► Remember from Chapter 8, p. 113, that a vicarious liability is a legal liability placed on one person for the torts or crimes of another. An employer will normally be vicariously liable for acts committed in the course of his or her work by an employee. But see *Photo Production Ltd v. Securicor*, Chapter 14, page 256, and *Tesco v. Natrass*, Chapter 18, page 339.

(ACT) Outline the rule established in *Donoghue*. What prevented the injured party in this case from bringing an action for breach of contract? (Refresh your memory about this aspect of contract by referring back to Chapter 10, page 152.)

The two-tier test

Dorset Yacht v. Home Office was an important case because it gave the courts the power to apply the tort of negligence in new areas and situations. The next case marked a further development in the application of negligence.

Anns v. London Borough of Merton (1978) AC 728

The plaintiffs were the lessees of flats that had been built under plans approved by the defendants. The flats suffered structural movements because, the plaintiffs alleged, the foundations had not been constructed according to the building plans. The defendants had supervised the con-

struction of the foundations and had approved them as being suitable. The defendants alleged that they had no duty of care to the plaintiffs.

COURT HELD
The House of Lords ruled that the council did owe a duty of care to the plaintiffs, therefore the plaintiffs could recover damages.

Out of the decision in *Anns* evolved a two-tier test to establish whether a duty of care existed. First, is there a sufficient relationship of proximity such that, in the reasonable contemplation of the defendant, carelessness on the defendant's part may be likely to cause damage to the plaintiff? If so, a duty of care will exist.

Second, if the answer to the first question is yes, it is necessary to consider whether there are any considerations that ought to negate the duty of care, or any circumstances that should reduce or limit the scope of the damages that may arise out of a breach.

This test was taken and used as a vehicle to justify the extension of the duty of care into new areas. The test came in for much criticism, and several cases decided after *Anns* adopted a more conservative approach, resulting in the following decision.

Caparo Industries v. Dickman (1990) 1 All ER 568

 The plaintiffs were shareholders in Fidelity plc. The 1984 accounts were published, after being audited by the defendants. After seeing the accounts the plaintiffs mounted a successful takeover bid. They then alleged that the 1984 accounts were incorrect, stating that they should have shown a loss of £465,000, not a profit of £1.3 million. They sued the defendants in negligence, for damages.

COURT HELD
The defendants owed no duty of care to the plaintiffs. The court felt that now a duty of care should exist where it is fair, just and reasonable that the law should impose a duty of a given scope on the one party, for the benefit of the other. This heralded a distinct move away from the two-tier test established in Anns and a move back to the neighbour principle as set out in Donoghue.

Establishing a duty of care
The current legal position on this point was established by the House of Lords in the following case. The Lords used their powers under a **1966 Practice Statement** to state that the precedent they established in *Anns* was no longer considered to be good law.

Murphy v. Brentwood District Council (1990) 2 All ER 908

 In 1970 the plaintiff purchased a semi-detached house from a construction company. The house had been built on poor land

▶ **Practice Statement 1966** – Since the House of Lords Practice Statement, made in 1966, the Lords is no longer bound by its previous decisions, though it rarely overturns them (see Chapter 3).

that had required the construction of concrete rafts on which to build the houses. The design had been approved by the council after they had consulted independent engineers. In 1981 serious faults appeared in the house, in the form of cracks in the walls, and the fracture of the soil and gas pipes. Investigations showed that the raft design had been defective and that it had twisted, causing the damage to the property. The plaintiff sold the house, with defects, for £35,000 below the market value. He then sued the council for damages, alleging that they were liable for the negligence of the consultant engineers.

COURT HELD

The court of first instance and the Court of Appeal found for the plaintiff, based on the precedent of Anns. The defendants appealed to the House of Lords. The Lords ruled that the defendants were not liable because the council owed no duty of care to the plaintiff. The damage that had been caused to the house was, in fact, the result of a latent defect. It was not reasonably foreseeable. The plaintiff had not suffered any personal injury.

It would now seem that in order to establish a duty of care the courts will use the test of reasonableness, proximity and the neighbour principle. It will now be very unlikely that an injured party will be able to recover, through negligence, for pure economic loss. However, the Lords left open the question of whether the local authority would owe a duty of care for physical damage either to persons or to property other than the building.

 Summarize the results of *Donoghue*, *Dorset*, *Anns*, *Caparo* and *Murphy*, writing four or five sentences on the findings of the court in each case. In your opinion, why did the House of Lords see fit to overturn the other cases in *Murphy*?

Breach of duty

When the existence of a duty of care has been established, a plaintiff must prove that the duty of care was breached by the other party, i.e. that the party has failed to take reasonable care or has failed to act as a reasonable person would have done in the same circumstances. If the other party can prove that he or she has acted reasonably, given the circumstances of the case, then the other party will not be liable, notwithstanding that the plaintiff has suffered some injury or loss.

A court will take into account the following factors when considering whether a breach of a duty of care has taken place:

(a) the likelihood of any accident, injury or harm and the likely seriousness of such an incident;
(b) the cost and ease of prevention of the incident;
(c) the social need for the product;
(d) the particular circumstances applicable to that case, including,

where applicable, the level of skills of the defendant: for example, a doctor would be expected to exhibit a higher degree of skill and ability than a refuse collector.

The following case illustrates a set of circumstances where the courts were not prepared to find a breach.

Bolton v. Stone (1951) AC 850

 The plaintiff was struck by a cricket ball that had been hit out of a cricket ground. At the time of impact she had been standing outside her house on the highway, adjacent to the cricket ground. The cricket pitch was surrounded by a fence, whose top, owing to the slope of the ground, was 17 feet from the floor. The batsman had hit the ball 78 yards before it left the ground and it had travelled a further 22 yards before hitting the plaintiff. The plaintiff sued the club in negligence for damages.

COURT HELD

The plaintiff could not succeed. The cricket club had done all that was reasonable, given the circumstances, to prevent any injury. Only six times in thirty years had a ball been hit out of the ground and there was no record of any previous injury. The chances of any injury were so remote that a reasonable person would not have done more than the club to prevent any injury.

Res ipsa loquitur

In certain cases a person may suffer injury and not know, nor be able to prove, how it has happened or that someone else has been negligent. In such circumstances a person may be able to plead *res ipsa loquitur*. For example, if a man was walking along the road and a carpet fell out of the upper floor of a carpet showroom and hit him, he wouldn't know how the accident had happened. In circumstances like this the onus of proof shifts from the plaintiff to the defendant, who must prove that he or she was not negligent and had taken all reasonable care to prevent the incident. Where goods are supplied, the manufacturer or supplier will be presumed to have been negligent unless he or she can prove otherwise.

► *Res ipsa loquitur* – the facts speak for themselves.

The following two cases illustrate the application of *res ipsa loquitur*.

Steer v. Durable Rubber Manufacturing Co. Ltd (1958) *The Times* **20 November**

This case concerned a small girl and her water bottle. The bottle burst when it was only three months old, causing the girl to be scalded. The plaintiff was not in a position to prove how the bottle had burst. However, she did establish that the normal life of such a hot-water bottle was three years.

COURT HELD

The court accepted the plaintiff's plea of res ipsa
loquitur. *The manufacturers could not prove that they had not
been negligent, therefore they were held to be liable.*

Daniels v. R. White and Sons (1938) 4 All ER 258

The plaintiffs purchased a bottle of lemonade, manufactured
by the defendants, from a pub. The lemonade contained carbolic acid and the plaintiffs sued the manufacturers in negligence,
successfully pleading *res ipsa loquitur*.

COURT HELD

*The defendants were able to prove that they had not been
negligent. They had excellent control systems in place to
ensure the quality of the final product, which should have eliminated
the risk of any carbolic acid getting into the lemonade. The plaintiffs
were able to recover damages from the landlord of the public house
under the SOGA79, s. 14(2), the goods not being of merchantable
quality.*

The result of this case has been considered to be unusual, because it
would appear that it could only have been through negligence that
the acid got into the lemonade. The defendants should therefore
have been found liable. Later cases have not strictly followed the
ruling in this case.

Damage resulting from the breach

After establishing a duty of care, plus a breach of that duty, a plaintiff must prove that he or she has suffered loss or damage from the
breach. If the first two factors are present, but loss or injury is
caused by some other factor, then the defendant will not be liable.

Causation

A plaintiff must be able to prove that, if it were not for the negligence of the defendant, he or she would not have suffered the loss
or injury. In other words, he or she must prove **causation**. The following case illustrates where a breach of a duty was held not to
have caused the death of the plaintiff.

► **Causation** – the relationship
between an act and the
consequences it produces.

**Barnett v. Chelsea and Kensington Hospital Management Committee
(1969) 1 QB 428**

The plaintiff, William Barnett, and two others were employed as night-
watchmen at a college in Chelsea. On New Year's Day 1966, at 5 a.m.
they shared a pot of tea. Soon afterwards they all started vomiting. The
plaintiff attended the defendant hospital where the duty doctor failed to

examine him. He was sent away, and told to go to bed and call his own doctor. The plaintiff returned to work, where he died at 2 p.m. It was later established that he had been murdered by persons unknown putting arsenic in his tea. The plaintiff's wife sued the hospital in negligence.

COURT HELD

The defendants were not liable. They had been negligent in failing to treat the night-watchman. However, it was established that had he been treated when he attended the hospital he would still have died of arsenic poisoning.

ACT What factors will a court take into account when considering whether there has been a breach of a duty of care? Would there be a breach of a duty of care in the following set of circumstances?

Gary Gubbins, the Albion centre forward, has been playing for the Albion for twelve years. He is an excellent header of the ball, but his shooting ability has left a lot to be desired. At the 'sea' end of the ground he has regularly kicked the ball over the bar and out of the ground over a low fence; this has happened as many as fifteen times in a season. Betty Bicknell, a hot-dog seller with a stall at the sea end, has been hit twice by Gary's poor shots. When a third shot knocked over Betty's stall, causing her leg to be burned, Betty threatened to sue. Could she succeed? State cases and give reasons for your answer.

Remoteness of damage

Not everyone affected by the act of another person will be able to claim damages. Only persons who suffer damage that is reasonably foreseeable when the negligent act is committed will be able to recover. Non-foreseeable damage will be too remote to be recovered.

The present position appears to be that an act will be too remote if any damage resulting from it would not have been foreseen by a reasonable person. If the type of damage is foreseeable, then the guilty party will be liable for all of the consequences and losses arising from the act. The leading case on this issue is described below.

The Wagon Mound (No. 1) **(1961) AC 388 (Privy Council)**

VC The defendants were the charterers of the steam ship *The Wagon Mound*, which was moored in Sydney harbour. By their negligence a quantity of bunkering oil was spilled into the harbour, some of which drifted over to the wharf owned by the plaintiffs. At that time a ship was being repaired at the wharf, and welding equipment was being used. The repairers stopped welding and enquiries were made about the safety of welding in close proximity to the oil. They were advised that it was highly unlikely that bunkering oil would ignite when it had been mixed with water. The welding was recommenced and molten metal fell on to some debris, igniting it, which in turn ignited the oil. The oil fire caused widespread damage to the plaintiff's property, including the wharf.

COURT HELD
The defendants were not liable. Given all the circumstances it was not reasonably foreseeable that the oil would ignite and cause the damage, i.e. the damage was too remote.

Contributory negligence

Where the three elements of negligence have been proved, the defendant may allege the defence of contributory negligence, i.e. that the plaintiff contributed to the act that caused the injury or loss by his or her own negligence. The Law Reform (Contributory Negligence) Act 1945 governs contributory negligence. Where a person is considered to be partly to blame for an accident, or have made their injuries more severe than they would otherwise have been by being negligent, then their damages would be reduced according to their blameworthiness. For example, if a person were found to be 50 per cent blameworthy for an act, then that person's damages would be reduced by 50 per cent. The following case illustrates contributory negligence.

Sayers v. Harlow UDC (1958) 1 WLR 623

 The plaintiff went into a women's lavatory in Luton, just prior to catching a coach to London. When she went to leave the cubicle, the lock had jammed and she was locked in the loo. She shouted and banged on the door for fifteen minutes to no avail. She then tried to climb out of the cubicle but was unable to do so. In the process of returning to the ground she put her foot on the toilet roll holder, which rotated, and she fell on to the floor and was injured. She sued the council in negligence for damages.

COURT HELD
The plaintiff could succeed. However, she was considered to be 25 per cent to blame for her own injuries, therefore her damages were reduced by 25 per cent.

 A plaintiff is found to be 5 per cent blameworthy for his injuries, £10,000 being awarded in damages. What effect will a successful plea of contributory negligence have on the case?

PRODUCT LIABILITY UNDER THE CONSUMER PROTECTION ACT 1987, PART I

This part of the CPA87 came into force on 1 March 1988, implementing the EC Directive on Product Liability. It introduced a range of strict liability offences, covering injury and damage caused by defective products. This was an important step forward for any person who suffers such an injury or loss, because under the CPA87 a plaintiff no longer needs to prove negligence. Where an injury or damage occurs that is caused by a defective product, the manufacturer or producer of the product will be liable unless he or she can rely upon one of the statutory defences.

Who is liable?

The CPA87, s. 1(2), defines the producer of a product as being:

> **CPA87, s. 1(2)**
>
> (a) the person who manufactured it;
> (b) in the case of a substance that has not been manufactured but has been won or abstracted, the person who won or abstracted it;
> (c) in the case of a product that has not been manufactured, won or abstracted but essential characteristics of which are attributable to an industrial or other process having been carried out (for example, in relation to agricultural produce), the person who carried out that process.

The CPA87, s. 2(2), lists the persons who will be liable under the Act:

(a) the producer;
(b) anyone who suggests that he or she is the producer of the goods by putting a brand mark on them: for example, Tesco's own-branded goods.
(c) anyone who has imported the good into the EC in the course of his or her business;
(d) where the producer or manufacturer cannot be identified within a reasonable time, the supplier of the product.

This has the effect of ensuring that it should always be possible to find a defendant, when damage has been caused by a defective product.

Establishing liability

The CPA87, s. 2, establishes liability as being where any damage is caused wholly or partly by a defect in a product. In order to be successful a plaintiff will need to establish that:

1 damage has been caused;
2 the product was defective; and
3 the defective product caused the damage.

Is the product defective?

The CPA87, s. 1(2), defines a product as being any goods or electricity and includes a product comprised in another product, whether by virtue of being a component part or raw material or otherwise. The CPA87, s. 2(4), excludes game or agricultural produce that has not undergone any industrial process from being a product.

The CPA87, s. 3(1), defines defective as follows.

> **CPA87, s. 3(1)**
>
> (1) ... not such as persons generally are entitled to expect.

The CPA87, s. 3(2), gives a list of factors that persons generally are entitled to expect in relation to the safety of a product.

> **CPA87, s. 3(2)**
>
> (a) the manner in which, and purposes for which, the product has been marketed, its get up, the use of any mark in relation to the product and any instructions for, or warnings with respect to, doing or refraining from doing anything with or in relation to the product;
> (b) what might reasonably be expected to be done with or in relation to the product; and
> (c) the time when the product was supplied by its producer to another.

Section 4: Defences

The CPA87, s. 4, provides a series of statutory defences.

(a) The defect was caused by compliance with statutory or EC regulations.
(b) That the person proceeded against did not at any time supply the product to another, such as a stolen prototype. In such a case the person may have obtained the stolen prototype from the thief, the producer having no intention to supply the prototype to any person.
(c) That the product was not supplied in the course of a business, i.e. that it was a gift from the producer.
(d) That the defect did not exist in the product at the relevant time.
(e) That the state of scientific and technical knowledge at the relevant time was not such that a producer of products of the same description as the product in question might be expected to have discovered the defect if it had existed in the producer's products while they were under his or her control. This defence is known as the 'development risks' defence. Under the EC Directive a choice was given as to whether or not to incorporate this defence into domestic legislation. Britain chose to include it so as not to threaten the development of new products. This defence really takes the strict liability element

out of an offence, for a product that has been developed in a new area. Medicinal products are an illustration of this. When oral contraception was introduced, some of the side-effects were not revealed by the tests then in use, so a drugs company sued under this Act could have used this defence.

(f) Where a defect in a product is attributable to a component element, and the default is wholly caused by the design of the product, then the supplier of the component element will not be liable.

Sections 5–6: Damage

The CPA87, s. 5, details the types of damage or loss that will be recoverable under the Act.

> **CPA87, s. 5**
>
> (1) … damage means death or personal injury or any loss or damage to any property (including land).

This section then makes significant exceptions under which the Act will not allow damages to be recovered:

(a) damage to the product itself;
(b) damage to any property in respect of which the value of the claim would be under £275;
(c) damage to any commercial property.

The CPA87, s. 6(4), states that a defendant may be able to plead contributory negligence in order to reduce the amount of damages payable.

Section 7: Prohibition on exclusions from liability

> **CPA87, s. 7**
>
> The liability of a person by virtue of this Part to a person who has suffered damage caused wholly or partly by a defect in a product, or to a dependant or relative of such a person, shall not be limited or excluded by any contract term, by any notice or by any other provision.

Put simply, it is impossible to avoid liability under the CPA87 by the use of an exclusion clause.

Time limit for claims under the CPA87

The CPA87 provides an absolute maximum time bar on claims of ten years. After that time no new claims may be commenced, though any claims that have been started can be finished.

Normally, claims will be limited to three years from the date that the right of action arose or three years from the time that the plaintiff became aware:

(a) that he or she had suffered injury or damage;
(b) that the damage suffered could be ascribed to the supply of a defective product;
(c) of the identity of the defendant, for example, where there has been difficulty in identifying the producer of a product.

The three-year limit may be extended in certain circumstances, such as in cases of fraud, mistake or concealment.

 What is the major difference between claiming under the CPA87 and making a claim in negligence?

Helen bought her mother a toaster for Christmas. The instructions with the toaster advised that only sliced bread should be used in it. Helen's mum only liked uncut loaves so she used the toaster to toast bread she sliced herself. The toaster worked well for three months, but then it caught fire when a thick piece of bread kept it turned on when a fault developed in the ejection mechanism, thus causing £3,000 of damage to the kitchen. Could Helen's mum bring a claim under the CPA87? What would the defence be likely to plead? Would Helen's mum be able to bring a claim under the tort of negligence?

PROFESSIONAL NEGLIGENCE

We have discovered that in the tort of negligence damages are unlikely to be recoverable for anything other than injury or physical damage to property. Economic loss will not normally be recoverable. However, the area of professional negligence provides the exception, allowing pure financial loss to be recovered.

Professional negligence exists where the help or advice of a professional person has been given negligently and the person advised suffers loss as a result of the negligently given advice. Professionals who come into this category will include, among others, solicitors, barristers (both with restrictions), bankers, credit reference agencies, surveyors and accountants.

Prior to 1963, professional negligence was only recognized where a fiduciary relationship existed between the two parties. The case of *Hedley Byrne*, which we examined in Chapter 12, established that a party may be able to recover for professional negligence where a 'special relationship' existed.

The case concerned an advertising company who requested and received a credit reference for one of its clients from the client's bankers, and on this basis allowed the client credit. The credit reference included a disclaimer enabling the bankers to avoid any liability for their reference. The company's client then went into liquidation, and the company sued the bankers to recover its losses.

▶ See the marginal note in Chapter 7, p. 86, for an explanation of fiduciary relationships.

▶ Look back at Chapter 12, pp. 204–5, and reread the case of *Hedley Byrne v. Heller*, and the explanation of the rule it established.

It could not succeed, but the case established that it would have done so in the absence of the disclaimer. A duty of care existed because there was a 'special relationship' between the two parties. As we saw in Chapter 12, a 'special relationship' occurs where one party has special knowledge, skills or expertise, and gives information to another party knowing that the other will act upon that information. Examples of specialists are banks, architects, surveyors, building societies and credit reference agencies.

Accountants and financial advisers

We shall now examine the reaction of the courts to certain of the professions that have featured in this area of professional negligence. The courts have not interpreted the definition of a special relationship liberally. The case of *Caparo Industries v. Dickman*, which we looked at earlier in this chapter (p. 354), illustrates the restrictive approach that the courts have taken. The plaintiffs, shareholders of Fidelity plc, mounted a successful takeover bid for the company, having seen the 1984 accounts, which had been audited by the defendants and which showed a profit of £1.3 million. They then alleged that the accounts should have shown a loss of £465,000, and unsuccessfully sued the defendants in negligence, for damages.

The case showed that accountants owed no duty of care to investors who might invest in companies on the basis of published accounts. However, where accountants or directors know that a particular person will be relying on given figures, or statements as to the financial viability of a company, for the purpose of making a takeover bid, then a special relationship and a duty of care will exist between the two parties. This is illustrated in the next case.

Morgan Crucible Co. plc v. Hill Samuel Bank Ltd **(1991) 1 All ER 148**

The plaintiff announced a takeover bid for a company called First Castle Electronics plc. The bid was treated as being hostile by First Castle, who issued documents to their shareholders advising them to reject the bid. Contained in the documents was a profit forecast that predicted an increased profit of 38 per cent for the financial year. The document also contained a statement from the company that the profit forecast had been correctly calculated. The plaintiff then increased his bid and successfully completed the takeover of the company. The plaintiff later alleged that the accounting policies used in the calculation of the profit forecast were negligently misleading, leading to a massive overstatement of the profits.

 COURT HELD
The Court of Appeal held that in the circumstances it was possible for a special relationship to exist. The plaintiff was an identifiable bidder, to whom the financial directors of Castle had

made certain statements and representations, intending that the plaintiff would rely upon the statements. They therefore owed him a duty of care not to mislead him.

Surveyors and valuers

Surveyors will generally not be in a contractual relationship with a house purchaser, the contractual relationship being between the building society and the surveyor. Therefore, a purchaser will generally not be able to sue a surveyor in contract. However, the position appears to have been established that where a surveyor carries out work negligently, and provided that the negligence can be proved by the purchaser, a duty of care will exist. The case that established this principle is illustrated below.

Yianni v. Edwin Evans (1982) 2 QB 438

The plaintiffs sought to buy a house valued at £15,000 and they applied for a £12,000 mortgage from the Halifax Building Society. The Halifax instructed the defendants to value the property, though the plaintiffs paid the Halifax for the survey. The Halifax advised the potential purchasers to have an independent survey carried out, as they would not accept any responsibility or liability for the valuation being undertaken by the defendants. The defendants reported that the house was satisfactory as security for the £12,000 advance. The plaintiffs purchased the property but soon discovered that it had structural defects that would cost £18,000 to remedy. The plaintiffs sued the defendants in negligence.

COURT HELD
The plaintiffs could succeed. Given the circumstances it was reasonable to imagine that the valuers should have had the plaintiffs in their contemplation as persons who were likely to rely on their report and valuation, therefore a duty of care existed between the two parties.

▶ This decision was subsequently reaffirmed in the joint case of *Smith v. Eric S. Bush* and *Harris v. Wyre Forest District Council* (1989) 1 AC 829.

Solicitors and barristers

Neither solicitors nor barristers will be liable in negligence for the work that they carry out in court. This was established in the following case.

Rondel v. Worsley (1967) 1 AC 191

The plaintiff had been convicted of causing grievous bodily harm when being defended by the defendant barrister. He brought this action alleging that the defendant had conducted his case negligently, resulting in the plaintiff's being convicted.

COURT HELD

The House of Lords ruled that the defendant could not succeed. Barristers could never be liable in negligence for their conduct of a case in court.

This immunity will extend to immediate pre-litigation work (i.e. the preparation of work for a court case). Otherwise a barrister will be liable for professional negligence as established in *Hedley*, for example, where an opinion is given 'in chambers' on a point of law to a client.

Solicitors are also immune for work carried out in court. However, they owe a duty of care to their client, and perhaps to other parties, as established in the *Hedley* principle. The following case illustrates this point.

Ross v. Caunters (1980) Ch 105, (1979) 3 All ER 580

The plaintiff was an intended beneficiary of a will drawn up by the defendant firm of solicitors. The will was sent to the client with instructions for its completion, though the solicitor failed to advise his client that if the will was witnessed by a beneficiary, or by the spouse of a beneficiary, then a gift to that beneficiary would be invalidated. The plaintiff's husband witnessed the will, which prevented the plaintiff from receiving any benefit under the will. The mistake was not discovered until after the death of the client, causing the plaintiff to lose her legacy. The plaintiff sued the defendant, alleging negligence.

COURT HELD

The plaintiff could succeed. The defendant owed a duty of care to her and she had suffered as the result of his negligence.

 What was the important principle established in *Hedley Byrne*?

 Now that you have completed this chapter, look back at the chapter objectives at the beginning. Can you do all the things that these suggest? If not, look again at the relevant sections of the chapter.

CHAPTER SUMMARY

1 The tort of negligence exists to enable a person who has suffered damage or loss, as a result of the negligent act of another, to claim damages from that loss.

2   *Donoghue* established the principles that a duty of care is based on the foresight of a reasonable person; that negligence could be extended to cover many different areas; that a higher level of care would be required with dangerous substances.

3   The *Donoghue* principle was liberally interpreted for many years until, in the case of *Murphy* in 1990, the House of Lords chose to overrule itself and redefine the law in this area. The existence of a duty of care would now seem to be based on a test of reasonableness, proximity and the neighbour principle.

4   In certain circumstances, for example, *res ipsa loquitur*, a defendant will have to prove that he or she had not been negligent in causing the accident to happen, rather than the plaintiff having to prove negligence on the part of the defendant.

5   A defendant may be able to plead contributory negligence, where a plaintiff has been partly to blame for the incident that has caused the injury or loss. Under the Law Reform (Contributory Negligence) Act 1945, an award of damages will be reduced by the percentage level of blame attributed to the plaintiff.

6   The CPA87, Part I, introduced a range of strict liability offences relating to injury and damage caused by defective products.

7   The *Hedley Byrne* case established that in a special relationship, for example, where one party has sought professional advice from another, such as in making an application to a bank for a credit reference, then a duty of care may exist.

Employment law

SOURCES OF EMPLOYMENT LAW

Employment law stems from common and statute law. It is an area where British governments have become increasingly at odds with their European partners. The Prime Minister, John Major, managed to score a success, according to the Conservatives, in securing an opt-out for Great Britain over the issue of the European Social Chapter. The Social Chapter provided for, among other things, a basic minimum wage of around £3.52 per hour. The Conservatives argued that, if employers were obliged to pay such an amount, many would be forced out of business.

However, at the time of the opt-out it was considered that the European Court of Justice would rule for any UK citizen who brought an action under the European Social Chapter to enforce the minimum wage. We have seen other court rulings, some from the European Court of Justice and others from the House of Lords, that have greatly affected the law relating to employment. Most notable are the decisions relating to equal pay and, most recently, the decision from the House of Lords that part-time employees should have the same rights as full-time employees.

EMPLOYER AND EMPLOYEE

Before considering modern employment law it is necessary to establish that the relationship between two parties is that of employer and employee. In recent times the distinction between the two has become somewhat blurred, with the advent of sub-contracting and massive self-employment.

It is vital to establish the nature of the relationship between any two parties because the vast majority of protective employment law applies only to employees: for example, the Employment Protection (Consolidation) Act 1978 (EPA78). Where a person sub-contracts work to an independent contractor, that person will not be responsible for collecting tax from the contractor, paying National Insurance contributions, or paying holiday or redundancy pay. An employer will not be liable for any injury or loss caused by a negligent act or omission on the part of an independent contractor that he or she has employed.

An employer will be vicariously liable for any injury or loss caused by an employee, provided that the employee was acting in the course of the business of the employer.

▶ Remember from Chapter 8, p. 113, that a vicarious liability is a legal liability placed on one person for the torts or crimes of another. See also Chapter 19, p. 353.

In most cases the relationship will be that of employer–employee. The employer will have advertised the position, interviewed applicants and appointed the employee. Once in employment an employee will be expected to work the hours specified in the contract of employment, complete the work or tasks specified and generally be supervised by the employer. In return, the employer must pay money, usually known as either wages or salary, depending upon whether it is paid weekly (wages) or monthly (salary).

Historical development

In times past it was less easy to establish whether a person was employed or not. The courts evolved two tests with which to establish if a relationship of employer–employee was in existence.

Control test

This test asked the following question: is the employer in control of the person, instructing him or her not only in what to do but also in how it should be done? If the answer to the question was yes, then an employer–employee relationship existed. This relationship is known as a **contract of service**.

The control test became outdated and was found to be unsuit-

▶ **Contract of service** – A contract by which a person agrees to undertake certain duties under the direction and control of an employer in return for a specified wage or salary.

able with the advent of highly skilled workforces. For example, a local authority could employ a plastic surgeon, but it could not supervise or control the surgeon's work.

Organizational test

In the period after the Second World War the organizational test evolved. In this it was recognized that control had ceased to be the most influential factor. In its place the following question was asked: is the person fully integrated with others in the operation of the business? This was able to cover situations like that of the surgeon described above.

Multiple test

The courts now tend to use a multifunctional test to establish the relationship between two parties. A court will consider all the factors of the case, including payment of wages, method of appointment, collection of income tax, payment of holiday pay, National Insurance contributions, sickness pay and pensions, and the power to dismiss or suspend, to establish the relationship between two parties. The following questions may be asked. Is this person in business in his or her own right? Does the risk of financial success or failure fall on the employee? If the answer to either of these two questions is yes, then it will probably not be an employer–employee relationship, but will be a **contract for services**.

In certain circumstances it may be difficult to establish whether a person is employed or self-employed and, if employed, who the employer is. A modern trend in employment is for the employees of one company to be contracted out to complete a specific task for another company. For example, the Channel Tunnel workforce was composed of a consortium of construction firms. Other trends include using outworkers (people who work from home), casual labour and people on government training contracts (e.g. YTS). It is far from clear whether people working under these sorts of conditions are employees. It would appear that, following the interpretation in *Ready Mixed Concrete* (below), these three types of workers are not employees. Conversely, it is perfectly possible for the director of a company also to be an employee of the company.

The next two cases show the historical development of this area.

▶ **Contract for services** – whereby a person or company employs an independent person to perform a particular service.

Mersey Docks and Harbour Board v. Coggins and Griffiths (Liverpool) Ltd (1946)

The plaintiffs (Board) were the employers of a Mr Newell, who was a crane operator. On one occasion Mr Newell was hired, together with a crane from the plaintiffs, by the defendants' (Coggins) stevedore company. While working for the defendants, Mr Newell acted negligently and caused injury to a person. The issue before the court was who was liable for the injury together with Mr Newell, the Board or Coggins?

COURT HELD

At this time the control test was being used to establish the employment relationship. Mr Newell considered himself to be an employee of the Board and the court ruled that he was still under the general control of the Board, therefore the Board was liable. In this type of case it is presumed that the general employer will be liable. To avoid liability the general employer will have to prove that control of the employee has passed to the temporary employer. More often than not it will be the general employer who has to bear the liability.

Ready Mixed Concrete (South East) Ltd v. Minister of Pensions and National Insurance (1968) 2 QB 497, (1968) 1 All ER 433

The plaintiffs were in business as concrete manufacturers. They used drivers to deliver their concrete. The drivers were paid on a piecework basis, i.e. on how many deliveries they made. The plaintiffs provided lorries, which the drivers bought on hire purchase, painted in the company colours, maintained and could use only for company business. The drivers received no holiday pay, had no specified hours of employment and could employ substitutes to work on their behalf. The court had to decide whether the drivers were employees. If they were, the plaintiffs would be liable to pay National Insurance contributions, on their behalf, to the defendants.

COURT HELD

The drivers were not employees. The court identified three major elements to a contract of employment:

1   an employee provides skill in return for payment;
2   an employee agrees to be subject to a measure of control by the employer;
3   the other terms of the contract relating to, for example, holiday and sick pay, National Insurance contributions, and payment and collection of income tax are all consistent with a contract of employment.

(ACT) Explain the difference between a contract of service and a contract for services. What factors will a court or tribunal take into account when trying to establish whether or not a contract of service is in existence?

CONTRACT OF EMPLOYMENT

A contract of employment must conform to the normal rules for the formation of a valid contract. There must be offer and acceptance, consideration, intention to create legal relations, capacity and true consent, and the contract may not be for an illegal purpose. A contract of employment need not be written down, though the vast majority are. However, under the EPA78, s. 1(2) (as amended by the

► In a situation where an employee carries out a negligent act causing injury or damage to another party, an employer will be liable under vicarious liability, provided that the negligent act is carried out in the course of the employer's business. The employee will also be liable to the employer for the act, i.e. the employer could recover from the employee any money that he or she has to pay out. In reality this rarely, if ever, happens. First, the employee probably would not have the resources to meet the claim and, second, such an action would not be good for industrial relations.

▶ The TURERA93 amended the rules relating to the provision and the content of written particulars. Now all employees who have worked for more than one month, even those who normally work less than eight hours per week, are entitled to being provided with written particulars within two months of commencing employment. The statement of the written particulars may be given in instalments, provided that it is supplied in full within the prescribed time limit.

Trade Union Reform and Employment Rights Act 1993 (TURERA93), an employer must provide, within eight weeks of the commencement of an employment, written particulars to all employees who work for eight or more hours a week.

Written particulars

The written particulars must include the following information:

EPA78 (as amended by the TURERA93), s. 1(2)

(a) the names of the employer and employee,
(b) the date when the employment began, and
(c) the date on which the employee's period of continuous employment began (taking into account any employment with a previous employer which counts toward the period).

Names of employer and employee
Both parties to the contract must be clearly identified.

Date employment began
The date employment commenced becomes important when it comes to calculating the eligibility to, and the amount of, redundancy, holiday pay and required periods of notice. Further, to qualify for unfair dismissal (see below), a person must have been employed for two years continuously with an employer.

Date period of continuous employment began
Since certain of the rights available to employees are determined by length of service, it is important to determine when continuous employment began. In certain circumstances continuous service with consecutive employers may be counted as being continuous, for the purposes of claiming redundancy or unfair dismissal payments. This may be so in the following circumstances.

(a) Where, under the EPA78, there is a transfer of an employee between associated companies, employment is considered to be continuous. For example, if Stefan is employed by Goose Holding plc and he is transferred to a subsidiary company, Goose Legs plc, his period of continuous service would carry through after the transfer.

(b) Where a person is employed within the same company under a number of different contracts, perhaps performing different jobs, then all the contracts will be considered together as one for the purposes of determining the length of continuous service. For instance, Isobel was employed as a cashier, and she worked for nine months as a cashier before being promoted to supervisor, when she was given a new contract. After eighteen months as a supervisor, she was unfairly dismissed. Isobel can add together the two contracts to arrive at the two years' continuous service required to be able to claim unfair dismissal.

(c) Where a person is employed by a partnership, a change in the partnership – for example, a retiring partner being replaced by a new partner – will not affect the employee's continuous employment.

Sale of the business

This is another area where recent legislation, in the form of the TURERA93, has been used by the government to bring UK law in line with an EC Directive, under threat of enforcement from the EC Commission. The Directive on Acquired Rights (77/187) was implemented in part by the Transfer of Undertakings (Protection of Employment) Regulations 1981 (SI 1981/1794) (TUR81). However, the regulations were clearly at variance with the Directive in a number of areas, one such area being the restriction of the scope of the regulations to commercial ventures.

The most important aspect of TUR81 related to the protection of employees' rights when a business was sold or transferred. It ruled that:

- the terms and conditions of the employees must be maintained by the new owner of a business or enterprise that has been bought or transferred;
- the dismissal of any employee for a reason relating to the transfer of the business is automatically unfair, unless there is an economic, technical or organizational reason for the dismissal (see *Meikle v. McPhail*, Chapter 21, page 397);
- where there is to be a transfer or sale of a business, any recognized trade union in existence at the enterprise must be informed and advised as to how the transfer will affect employees.

As outlined above, the regulations applied only to commercial businesses. This had the effect of removing this aspect of protection from the thousands of public sector employees, such as health, education and council workers. Section 33 of the TURERA93 amended the EPA78 to include non-commercial organizations and to define further that a transfer of a business could take place whether or not any property is transferred.

The regulations apply only where there is a dismissal immediately before the transfer of the business. Therefore, in a sale by an administrative receiver of an insolvent company, all employees would normally be dismissed prior to the sale at the insistence of the purchaser. This would enable the new owner to avoid taking over the responsibility for the employment rights of the employees. The dismissed employees would have to make their claim against the insolvent company, with little chance of obtaining any money. This practice was effectively ended by the House of Lords in the following case.

Lister v. Forth Dry Dock and Engineering Co. Ltd (1989) 1 All ER
1134

The plaintiff was dismissed one hour before the transfer of the business
in order to avoid the provisions of the regulations. He claimed that he
had been unfairly dismissed by the original owners but could not claim
against them because they had gone out of business.

COURT HELD
*The House of Lords ruled that the plaintiff could claim
against the new owners of the business. The Lords agreed
that there had been a break in the employment but that the Regulations
had to be interpreted so as to cover situations where employees were
dismissed just prior to a transfer of the business.*

Further details required by the EPA78, as amended by TURERA93

The following must be set out in the details of the contract and be
included in the written particulars.

1. the amount of pay and the method by which pay is calculated,
   e.g. £5.50 an hour, overtime to be paid at double time;
2. when wages or salary will be paid, e.g. monthly or weekly;
3. how many hours will be worked each week, e.g. 40 hours;
4. terms and conditions relating to the following:
   (a) entitlement to holidays and holiday pay;
   (b) provision for sick pay and procedures to be followed in
       case of sickness;
   (c) pensions and pension schemes;
5. the length of notice an employee is obliged to give and entitled
   to receive to terminate his or her contract of employment.

The EPA78, Part IV, s. 49, provides the minimum periods of notice
required to be given:

Notice to be given	By an employer	By an employee
After 1 month's employment	1 week	1 week
After 2 years' employment	2 weeks	1 week
After 3 years' employment	3 weeks	1 week
For each extra full year	1 week extra/year	1 week
After 12 years' employment	12 weeks	1 week

ACT Stefan has been employed by an old family friend as a
double-glazing salesperson. The contract is agreed over the
telephone. The pay is to be £75 per week basic with 10 per
cent commission on all the double glazing that he sells. The
employment is to commence on 4 April 1995. If there were
no written contract would this agreement be valid? Under

the TURERA93, what written particulars would have to be given to Stefan, in what form and within what time scale?

Where an employer fails to adhere to the provisions of the EPA78, s. 49, a court will take into account the required provisions when assessing damages for a breach of the contract of employment, i.e. an employee's outstanding notice will be calculated financially. It is normal for pay to be taken in lieu of notice. For example, if, on 14 May, Toby gave one week's notice to quit his employment, his employer could pay him his due wages, including an extra week up to the 21 May to cover his notice, and Toby could finish work a week early.

Under the EPA78, s. 5, the above provisions do not apply where an employer has exercised his or her common-law right to dismiss an employee without notice for gross misconduct, such as violence, drunkenness or disobedience.

The following details were added to the written particulars by TURERA93:

1 the title of the job, or a brief description of it;
2 where the employment is not intended to be permanent, the period for which it is expected to continue, or, where it is a **fixed-term contract**, the date at which it is to end;
3 the place of work, including the employer's address – if the employee is required to work at various addresses, or in various areas, that must also be noted;
4 where there are collective agreements that affect the terms and conditions of employment – for example, an agreement with a trade union – this must also be noted;
5 where an employee is required to work outside the UK, any rules and regulations relating to that fact, including method and currency of payment, period to be spent abroad, any additional benefits payable, terms and conditions relating to a return to the UK.

Changes under the TURERA93

The following particulars must be given to an employee in one document:

- the amount of pay and the method by which pay is calculated, e.g. £5.50 an hour, overtime to be paid at double time;
- when wages or salary will be paid, e.g. monthly or weekly;
- how many hours will be worked each week, e.g. 40 hours per week;
- entitlement to holiday pay;
- job title or a brief description of the job;
- where the employment is for a fixed period, the length of the contract;
- the place of employment; where an employee is required to work at a number of different places, that fact should be noted together with the address of the employer.

► This section is important where a claim is made under the Equal Pay Act 1970, for equal payment for like work. It is also relevant in claims for unfair dismissal, where an employer declares that a position has become redundant.

► **Fixed-term contract** – a contract appointing a person for a fixed term, for example two years, at the end of which the employer will have no further obligations. They are increasingly found in the education sector, where some institutions are taking on staff only on fixed-term contracts.

► The TURERA93 allows for certain particulars to be given by reference being made to a document, such as a staff handbook or a collective agreement. The matters allowed to be referenced in this way are pension arrangements, entitlement to notice, grievance procedures and disciplinary matters.

(ACT) You are the personnel manager of a small company. Dominic has just been employed by your company as a catering assistant. He will work 42 hours a week on a shift system. His normal pay will be £4.20 per hour, overtime will be paid at time and a half. Using the above information, draw up a set of written particulars for Dominic. Make up any other required details.

RIGHTS AND DUTIES OF THE EMPLOYER

The contract of employment will generally make provision for hours of work, level of payment, holiday pay, etc. However, if any of these matters is not covered, a court may imply terms into a contract to cover these major points. Other terms will be implied by statute relating to the duties of an employer under a contract of employment.

The following are the major duties of the employer:

- payment of wages;
- fulfilment of statutory obligations, including a number concerning health and safety, and non-discrimination;
- duty of care;
- indemnity for expenses or liabilities incurred by employees in the course of their business.

Payment of wages

It is a fundamental duty of an employer to pay wages. If no provision is made in a contract of employment to pay wages, a term will be implied into the contract to pay 'reasonable wages'. (The amount of pay must be recorded in the written particulars.)

Holiday pay

There is no statutory duty to pay holiday pay. However, the contract should detail the entitlement. The amount of holiday pay may have been reached through a collective agreement. (The amount of holiday pay must be recorded in the written particulars.)

Sick pay

There is no obligation on an employer to pay sick pay. All employees have a right to statutory sick pay (SSP), for the first twenty-three weeks of absence through sickness. SSP is paid by the employer as a benefit on behalf of the government. The employer is then able to recoup the money from the government in a number of different ways, depending upon the size of the employer.

Pay slips

An employer must provide an employee who is employed for eight or more hours a week with an itemized pay statement detailing all deductions (EPA78, s. 8, as amended by the TURERA93).

Provision of work

Surprisingly there is no duty placed on an employer to provide work. The fact that you pay a gardener does not give him or her a right to work in your garden. However, certain types of employee may have the right to work. These include those who are highly skilled and need to practise their skill, those who need to be in the public eye and those who work on commission, such as plastic surgeons, actors and salespeople, or people who are on piecework.

Pay during lay-off

When an employer lays off an employee, the employee will have a common-law right of action for breach of contract, unless the power to lay off has been made an express term of the contract. An employee who has been laid off has a statutory right to receive pay under the EPA78, s. 12.

Obligations imposed by statute

Entrance into the EC has forced the UK to make various statutory changes to employment law. I shall consider the major statutory obligations under the headings of the different Acts.

Health and Safety at Work Act 1974

Employers must provide a statement of policy regarding the health and safety at work of their employees. Six new EC directives, effected in 1993, have harmonized and added new areas to health and safety at work, and all firms must fully comply with them before 1997.

The most important directive, relating to the management of health and safety, was implemented by the Management of Health and Safety at Work Regulations 1992 (SI 1992/2051). This regulation may be briefly examined under the major section headings.

Risk assessment
Employers (with five or more employees) must make a written assessment of the health and safety risks to their employees at the place of work and also the risks to other persons affected by the operation of the business.

Health and safety arrangements
Employers (with five or more employees) must make provision to implement procedures to deal with the identified risks.

Health and safety assistance
All employers must appoint a health and safety adviser to ensure that the arrangements are implemented.

Procedures for serious and imminent danger and for danger areas
Procedures must be established to deal with health and safety emergencies.

Information for employees

All employees, full-time and part-time, must be given training and information on health and safety at work.

Co-operation and co-ordination

Where two or more employers share a workplace they must co-operate to comply with the regulations.

Capabilities and training

Employers must ensure that all workers are competent to do their jobs. This must be effected by the implementation of a programme of training and, where necessary, for example, where new technology, machinery or new work practices have been introduced, retraining.

The other directives relate to matters concerning:

1 the cleanliness, safety and tidiness of the workplace, including the provision of separate toilet facilities;
2 the use of visual display units (computer screens);
3 the provision and use of protective equipment;
4 the use, safety and provision of machinery;
5 the methods of manually handling goods that may cause injury at work.

A breach of health and safety regulations may result in the employer or the directors of a company facing criminal prosecution. In a severe case, such as one where a flagrant breach of health and safety regulations has resulted in the death of an employee, the charge may be one of manslaughter.

Sex Discrimination Acts 1975 and 1986 and the Race Relations Act 1976

These Acts may be considered together, because the Race Relations Act 1976 (RRA76) was largely based on the Sexual Discrimination Act 1975 (SDA75). Compliance with the Acts is overseen by the Equal Opportunities Commission and the Commission for Racial Equality respectively.

Under these Acts it is unlawful for an employer (the discriminator) to discriminate against a person on the grounds of race, creed, sex, marital status, nationality or colour. A person will be discriminated against if he or she is afforded less than equal treatment relating to:

- training;
- promotion;
- appointment;
- provision of facilities;
- transfer; or
- the provision of any other benefit.

Equal Pay Act 1970

This Act implies a term into contracts of employment that, where men and women are employed in 'like' work, the pay should be the same, regardless of sex.

Employment Protection (Consolidation) Act 1978

Sections 29–31 of this Act provide that an employer must give paid time off work in the following circumstances:

- public duties, like Justice of the Peace;
- attendance at industrial tribunals;
- to look for work, where a person has been given notice of redundancy;
- ante-natal care.

Duty of care

Employers owe a duty of care to their employees to ensure that the workplace is a safe environment and that work practices are safe. In more recent times this duty has been widened to ensure that an employer does not impose working conditions upon an employee that are too harsh. In the case of junior hospital doctors, a 90-hour week was considered to be a breach of this duty.

An employer is basically responsible for ensuring that all employees are working in a safe environment, with established methods of work practices for ensuring safety, such as:

- where necessary, the provision and use of protective clothing and equipment;
- the provision of clear notices and procedures for dealing with dangerous equipment;
- the provision of training to all personnel using equipment;
- proper methods of supervision to ensure that employees do not become injured through overworking;
- a clean and tidy workplace with proper storage of goods etc.;
- the provision of emergency procedures.

Indemnity

An employer must indemnify an employee for any expenses or liabilities incurred by an employee, while he or she is acting in the course of the employee's business.

ACT Outline the situation of employees when a business is sold or has gone into liquidation. What effect did the decision in *Lister v. Forth Dry Dock* have on employees who are dismissed at the time of a liquidation or sale of a company? Include the changes made by the TURERA93 to the transfer of businesses.

RIGHTS AND DUTIES OF THE EMPLOYEE

The rights and duties of an employee will normally be spelled out in the express terms of the contract or in the written particulars. However, there are also implied terms, both statutory and otherwise, affecting the rights and duties of an employee.

Statutory duties

> **Management of Health and Safety at Work Regulations 1992 (SI 1992/2051), s. 12(1): Employees' duties**
>
> Every employee shall use any machinery, equipment, dangerous substance, transport equipment, means of production or safety device provided to him by his employer in accordance both with any training in the use of the equipment concerned which has been received by him and the instructions respecting that use which have been provided to him by the said employer in compliance with the requirements and prohibitions imposed upon that employer by or under the relevant statutory provisions.

Under this section an employer has a statutory duty to use machinery properly, i.e. as he or she has been trained to. Further, it must be used only for the purpose for which the employee has been trained to use it.

Section 12(2) continues by placing a statutory duty on an employee to inform an employer of any circumstance or situation at the workplace that the employee feels is a health and safety threat, provided it has not been previously reported.

Work

As previously mentioned, there is no duty imposed on an employer to provide work. However, an employee must work in accordance with his or her job. Should an employee refuse to work, an employer will have a common-law power to summarily dismiss the employee for breach of contract. Obviously, a strike is a breach of contract and an employer may, and some do, dismiss all strikers who are in breach of their contracts of employment. However, such an action is normally the last measure to be taken. During industrial problems in the further education sector, the employers responded to a one-day strike by deducting one day's pay from all striking employees.

Lawful orders

An employee must obey the lawful order of an employer. A lawful order must relate to the business activity and must not be for an unlawful purpose. Further, the order must not place the employee in a position of potential harm or danger, other than in those special occupations that are in themselves intrinsically dangerous, such as deep-sea diving.

▶ Notwithstanding the breach of contract, an industrial tribunal may still rule the dismissal of strikers to be unfair. If certain strikers are singled out to be sacked, i.e. they are treated less favourably than the other strikers, they would be able to claim for unfair dismissal. Similarly, if all the strikers were sacked, but only some were offered re-engagement, the strikers who were not offered re-engagement would also be able to claim for unfair dismissal.

Compulsory relocation is not covered by lawful order, but has to be included as an express term of the contract. For example, the employment contract with the Metropolitan Police states that an officer may be posted anywhere within the Metropolitan Police District. A failure to move to a new posting could result in the dismissal of an officer. Many modern employment contracts contain clauses stating that an employer retains the right to move an employee to a different area. A failure to comply would result in the employer having the power to dismiss an employee. If there were no such clause in the contract, it would not be a dismissable offence for an employee to refuse to move.

▶ The concept of the lawful order was clearly explained to me when I was in the Metropolitan Police Force. If the sergeant orders you to stand in the rain all night long directing traffic, that is a lawful order. If the sergeant tells you to go and get the fish and chips, that is not a lawful order, but you had better do it in any case!

Competence and skill

An employer will have a common-law power to dismiss an employee who is incompetent at his or her job, if the employee has claimed to have a particular skill for the purposes of gaining employment. An example could be where a person pretends to have certain skills as a computer programmer in order to obtain employment. Once in the position it would soon become fairly obvious that the person is not competent at the job.

▶ An employer could raise the defence of incompetence against a claim of unfair dismissal, see Chapter 21, page 395.

All employees must exercise a reasonable degree of care and skill in carrying out their employment. An unskilled employee will also be covered by this rule. However, if an unskilled employee breaches this duty, it is very unlikely that an employer would be able to dismiss him or her merely for one misdemeanour.

Work practices

Duty of fidelity

During the period of employment an employee must not use any secret knowledge, processes, information or formulas for his or her own gain outside the workplace. Equally, the poaching of the employer's customers for 'out of hours' work would also be considered to be a breach of the contract of employment.

An employee must not use information gained in the course of his or her employment, such as customer lists, in order to start up a rival business. Nor can an employee approach customers of his or her current employer with a view to soliciting the employer's business. An employer has a common-law power to dismiss an employee who was involved in such practices. An employer might be able to obtain an injunction to stop an employee from using such information for the benefit of the employee or another employer. The following case illustrates this point.

Wessex Dairies v. Smith (1935) 2 KB 80

The defendant, Smith, a milkman who was in the last week of his employ with the plaintiffs, asked his customers if they would switch their custom to a new round that he proposed to start himself.

COURT HELD

There was a breach of contract. Smith could not solicit customers for his new round.

However, an employee may take any skills or information that the employee learns in an employment, such as computer programming skills, when he or she leaves an employment. Unless there is a valid restraint of trade in the contract, he or she may probably also take any information relating to processes, customers, etc., that he or she is able to retain mentally. In the absence of a valid restraint of trade in the contract of employment, it will be very difficult for an employer to stop an ex-employee from approaching and soliciting his or her customers. (That is the nature of business life!) The following case is a good illustration of these points.

► For a fuller discussion on employment and restraints of trade, see Chapter 12.

Faccenda Chicken Ltd v. Fowler (1987) Ch 117

The plaintiffs sought an injunction to prevent two of their previous employees from using information relating to customers and prices, in their own business. The defendant had previously set up and run a successful sales operation for the plaintiff company. The defendant was using knowledge gained in his employ with Faccenda to solicit customers and undercut prices.

COURT HELD

*The plaintiffs could not succeed. The defendant had not made lists of the customers or the prices while in the employ of the plaintiff, nor had he approached customers prior to leaving the company. The information had been gained as part of the general work experience. It did not amount to a **trade secret**.*

► **Trade secret** – information about a particular employment that generally should not be disclosed after the employment has ended (for example, the recipe for Coca-Cola). In deciding whether information amounts to a trade secret, a court may consider the following:
1 the nature of the information;
2 the type of the employment;
3 whether the employee was aware that the employer thought that the information was a confidential trade secret;
4 whether the particular information could be separated from other information that the employee was free to use.

Second employment

Unless there is an express term in the contract of employment forbidding an employee to work at any other job at the same time as his or her full-time employment, then an employee may do so. However, if the second position is for a competitor, or it affects the employee's performance at the full-time position, then an employer may be able to summarily dismiss the employee.

Inventions

Where an invention is made by an employee in the course of the business of the employer, it will normally belong to the employer.

Patents Act 1977, s. 39

(1) ... an invention made by an employee shall, as between him and his employer, be taken to belong to his employer for the purposes of this Act and all other purposes if:
  (a) it was made in the course of the normal duties of the employee or in the course of duties falling outside his

> normal duties, but specifically assigned to him, and the circumstances in either case were such that an invention might reasonably be expected to result from the carrying out of his duties; or
> (b)   the invention was made in the course of the duties of the employee and, at the time of making the invention, because of the nature of his duties and the particular responsibilities arising from the nature of his duties he had a special obligation to further the interests of the employer's undertaking.

Notwithstanding this section, the Patents Act continues by stating that an employee may be entitled to a share of the profits from the invention, where it is just that he or she should do so: for example, where the tremendous benefit to the employer is not reflected in the amount of salary paid to the employee.

> **Patents Act 1977, s. 39**
>
> (2)   Any other invention made by an employee shall, as between him and his employer, be taken for those purposes to belong to the employee.

Employers are becoming much more jealous and covetous of their employees' efforts. In education, many new appointees are forced to sign contracts that give the ownership of the employee's works to the employer.

 What are the statutory duties of an employer to an employee in relation to matters of health and safety?

MUTUAL DUTIES

There are several areas where employers and employees owe each other a mutual duty of care. I will briefly examine them under the following headings.

Property

An employee must account for, and deal properly with, all property belonging to the employer. Failure to do so could result in summary dismissal for gross misconduct, i.e. where property is stolen by an employee. An employee must not take bribes or make secret profits from his or her employment.

An employer must indemnify an employee for any monies that are paid out during the course of employment. For example, any agreed expenses that are incurred by an employee in the normal course of his or her employ must be reimbursed by the employer.

Mutual trust and behaviour

Employers and employees are under a mutual duty to behave properly and courteously to each other. This includes not swearing at, abusing or mistreating each other. An employee will also be under the same duty with regard to other employees. An employer must not maliciously accuse an employee of any criminal offence, poor work practices or generally deride him or her. In recent times this duty has been extended to protect employees when employers have sought to act unfairly to prevent an employee from complying with his or her contractual duties. An example would be ordering an employee to move to another part of the country, for no operational reason, simply to force an employee to leave the company.

Vicarious liability

As mentioned above, an employer will be liable to a person who suffers harm or injury that has been caused by the negligent act of an employee. However, the employer will be liable only when the employee is acting in the course of his or her employment. If the employee has gone off on a 'jaunt' of his or her own unrelated to the employment, an employer may be able to avoid liability.

It is best to explain this point with the help of a modern example. Trevor was employed by British Gas as a fitter and was given a company van to use. One morning on the way from one appointment to another he drove recklessly and knocked Claire over, causing her serious injury. British Gas would be vicariously liable to compensate Claire. If Trevor had decided to take the company van to Dieppe to stock up on cheap French beer at the weekend outside company hours and had then knocked Claire over, British Gas would not be liable.

It is not always simple to establish whether an employee is acting in the course of business or not. On occasions, an employer may still be liable for the negligent act of an employee, even when an employee has carried out a forbidden act. A good guide is that if a negligent act is done in the normal course of the employment, while the employee is acting in the furtherance of the employer's business, then the employer will probably be liable. It has been held that the employer of a milkman who negligently caused injury to a boy who was helping him to deliver milk was vicariously liable, despite the fact that the milkman had been forbidden to allow anyone else to travel on the company milk float. The court felt that the boy and the milkman were acting in the furtherance of the company's business.

When an employee moves outside the scope of his or her employment, however, and commits a crime or a negligent act that results in a third party suffering injury, loss or damage, then an employer will probably not be vicariously liable. A lorry driver who gave someone a lift when he had been forbidden to allow other persons to travel in his company vehicle had, it was held, stepped outside the terms of his employment in disobeying the prohibition. In this case, the court felt that the driver was not acting in the furtherance of company business.

 Now that you have completed this chapter, look back at the chapter objectives at the beginning. Can you do all the things that these suggest? If not, look again at the relevant sections of the chapter.

CHAPTER SUMMARY

1 The vast majority of protective employment law applies only to contracts of service. Self-employed persons, employed under a contract for services, are less well protected.

2 To establish whether a contract of service is in existence, a court will consider the following matters: the payment of wages; the method of appointment; collection of income tax; the payment of holiday pay; the power to dismiss or suspend; and whether an employee bears any financial risk in the venture.

3 A contract of employment must conform to the normal rules for the formation of a valid contract. The EPA78, s. 1 (as amended), provides that an employer must, within two months, provide an employee with written particulars of his or her employment.

4 An employer has a duty, among other things, to pay wages; to provide itemized pay slips; to pay wages during a lay-off; to comply with legislation with regard to health and safety provision; and to give paid time off in certain circumstances.

5 The Race Relations Act 1976 and the Sexual Discrimination Act 1975 make it unlawful for an employee to discriminate against a person, or to treat a person less favourably, on the grounds of sex, race, creed, marital status, nationality or colour. The Equal Pay Act 1970 requires employers to pay the same wages to men and women employed to do 'like' work.

6 An employer owes a duty of care to his or her employees and has to indemnify them for any expenses incurred in the course of their employment. An employer will be vicariously liable for the negligent acts of employees that cause harm or injury to others, provided that the employee was acting in the course of his or her employ.

7 An employee's duties to an employer mainly derive from the common law. They include a duty to work, a duty to obey a lawful order, a duty to display a level of competence and skill in one's work, and a duty of fidelity.

21 Termination of a contract of employment

Chapter objectives

By the end of this chapter you should be able to:

▮ appreciate the make-up, role, scope and jurisdiction of industrial tribunals and the Employment Appeal Tribunal

▮ understand that in order to be able to make a claim for unfair dismissal or redundancy, a claimant must be qualified and entitled as specified in the Employment Protection (Consolidation) Act 1978 (EPA78) (as amended by the Trade Union Reform and Employment Rights Act 1993 (TURERA93))

▮ recognize the different types of dismissal: actual, constructive, dismissal after a fixed-term contract and dismissal after maternity leave

▮ appreciate the provisions relating to maternity provision: for example, the statutory right to fourteen weeks' maternity leave for all employees, regardless of length of service

▮ understand the circumstances in which a dismissal may be justified by an employer, under the EPA78 (as amended by TURERA93)

▮ recognize the circumstances in which a contract of employment may be frustrated

▮ know the remedies that may be available to an employee who has been made redundant or who has been unfairly dismissed.

In this chapter we shall examine the ways in which a contract of employment may be brought to an end. Parliament has taken a major role in the regulation of employment law, and, while the common law has some relevance in this area, we shall mostly be examining the statutory regulations. Before examining the rights and duties of the respective parties at the termination of the contract, let us remind ourselves of the structure of the courts in which most employment disputes are heard.

INDUSTRIAL TRIBUNALS

Industrial tribunals have become one of the busiest players within our legal system. TURERA93 gave the chairperson of an industrial tribunal the right, in certain circumstances, to preside alone. Normally, the legally qualified chairperson sits with two lay persons, one a representative from the employer, the other from the employee. Industrial tribunals hear cases brought mainly under the following Acts:

Equal Pay Act 1970
Sex Discrimination Acts 1975 and 1986
Employment Protection Act 1975
Race Relations Act 1976
Employment Protection (Consolidation) Act 1978
Trade Union Reform and Employment Rights Act 1993.

Procedure

A complainant must institute proceedings by submitting an application containing his or her details, the nature of the claim and the party being claimed against. The claim must be submitted within three months of the date of the termination of the contract. There are provisions for an extension to six months in certain extenuating circumstances. Where the termination was as a result of strike or other industrial action, the time limit is six months. The details of the case will be seen by a conciliation officer who will attempt to resolve the case by a process of consultation. If the conciliation officer fails to resolve the dispute, the case will be heard by a full tribunal. Nearly 35 per cent of all cases are resolved by conciliation.

The procedure of industrial tribunals has recently been amended by the Industrial Tribunal (Constitution and Rules of Procedure) Regulations 1993 (ITR93), which came into force in December 1993. The new regulations have both strengthened the powers of industrial tribunals and given them more investigative powers. Industrial tribunals have been given new powers to determine whether either party has the right to bring or defend an action and the right to hold a pre-hearing review (PHR) in all cases. Where, after a PHR, a tribunal thinks that either party has little or no chance of success, it can require either party to lodge a deposit of £150 in order to be able to continue either to defend or to bring the action.

EMPLOYMENT APPEAL TRIBUNAL

Although this court is called a tribunal, it is generally considered to be a court. It is staffed by judges from the High Court and the Court of Appeal and lay persons with appropriate specialist knowledge. The lay persons are representatives of employers and representatives of workers, normally trade unionists. The court's main jurisdiction lies in hearing appeals from industrial tribunals, brought on points of law.

Constitution

Normally one judge and either two or four lay persons preside, with an equal number of lay persons being drawn from employers' and workers' representatives. Procedure in the tribunal is relatively informal. Appeals can be made from this court to the Court of Appeal (Civil) on any question of law in England and Wales, to the Court of Session in Scotland or the Court of Appeal in Northern Ireland.

A contract of employment is the same as any other contract. It may be terminated by performance, breach, agreement or frustration. Employment contracts may also be terminated by the death of either party, the cessation of business by the employer, the appointment of a receiver or the sale or transfer of the enterprise. However, it is not quite as simple as this list suggests, and we shall now examine how and why the courts will determine that in a given set of circumstances there has been a redundancy, an unfair dismissal or a justifiable dismissal.

UNFAIR DISMISSAL AND REDUNDANCY

When a contract of employment is terminated either by the resignation of the employee or by dismissal by the employer, one or both parties may have a right of action against the other. Action is more commonly taken by employees, who may bring a case before an industrial tribunal if they feel that they have been unfairly dismissed.

Unfair dismissal

Where a person wishes to bring a case of unfair dismissal before an industrial tribunal, the person must establish that he or she was in a relationship of employment, as defined by the EPA78 (see Chapter 20), and that the following criteria are satisfied.

Age

A person who has reached the normal age for retirement in his or her particular employ – statutory age 65 for both men and women – may be dismissed. Therefore, a person who is dismissed on his or her sixty-fifth birthday could not bring an action for unfair dismissal.

Continuous employment

The EPA78 states that only full-time employees (those who work sixteen hours or more per week) who have been in that employ for two years or more, or part-time employees (those who work between eight and sixteen hours per week) who have been continuously employed for five years, qualify for the statutory unfair dismissal and redundancy payments. However, in the following

▶ Different occupations have different agreed ages for retirement. Judges and members of parliament, for example, are able to carry on into their dotage. Police officers are normally retired after serving thirty years in their particular force.

case the House of Lords ruled that the above-mentioned criteria were in breach of Article 119 of the EEC Treaty and the Council Directive on Equal Pay 75/117, and were also incompatible with the Council Directive on Equal Treatment 76/207.

Equal Opportunities Commission and another v. Secretary of State for Employment (1994) 1 All ER 910

This case concerned a Mrs Day who had been employed by a local authority for eleven hours a week, for just under five years, before she was made redundant. The Equal Opportunities Commission (EOC) became involved, through correspondence, with the Secretary of State who stated that the EPA78 provisions relating to qualification for unfair dismissal and redundancy payments were not in breach of any EC directives. The EOC sought a judicial review of this decision. The two lower courts refused the application and it was left to the House of Lords to hear the case on appeal. The House of Lords had first to decide if the EOC had the power to seek a judicial review, and second whether judicial review was applicable in this case.

The House of Lords decided that they would review the case and that the EOC had the right to bring it. The EOC argued that the provisions relating to part-time workers outlined above were discriminatory against women, because the vast majority of part-time workers are women. Further, part-time workers are generally less well paid than full-time workers, which constituted a breach of the EC Directive on Equal Pay.

 COURT HELD
The appeal by the EOC was allowed. The Lords ruled that the provisions of the EPA78, whereby part-time workers were treated differently from full-time workers in respect of redundancy pay, were incompatible with Article 119 of the EEC Treaty and the Directive on Equal Pay. The same provisions of the EPA78, whereby part-time workers are subject to different conditions from full-time workers in relation to claims for unfair dismissal, are incompatible with the Directive on Equal Treatment at Work.

It is not yet certain what the implications of this decision are. It would seem clear that now there can be no distinction between full-time and part-time employment for the purposes of making a claim for redundancy or for unfair dismissal. The qualifying limit for continuous employment must now be considered to be two years for all employees.

What is not clear, either from English or from EC law, is whether there is any necessary minimum hourly requirement to qualify for the statutory entitlements. The figure of eight hours has been proposed by the Social Affairs Commissioner of the EC, in a report made in 1990. At the moment it would seem difficult to imagine that employers will be able to treat workers differently, based merely on the amount of hours that they work.

► The two-year qualifying period of service will not be required where a dismissal is deemed to be automatically unfair (see below).

► These provisions will not apply where a dismissal is automatically unfair, for example, where an employee is dismissed for trade union activities, as defined by the Trade Union and Labour Relations (Consolidation) Act 1992 (TULRA92), s. 152.

▶ Female service personnel used to be exempt, under the EPA78, from being able to claim for unfair dismissal, when they were dismissed because they had become pregnant. At the time of writing, the government is in the process of repealing this section of the EPA78, following the 1990 House of Lords decision below.

Other criteria

- The provisions for unfair dismissal do not apply to persons employed fully or wholly outside the UK.
- A person who is dismissed while undertaking industrial action will not be able to commence proceedings for unfair dismissal.

 What criteria must be satisfied before a person is eligible to make a claim for unfair dismissal? Outline the changes made by the ruling in *EOC v. Secretary of State for Employment*.

Recent developments

We must, when considering the provisions of the EPA78, especially relating to the exemption of the armed forces, consider other relevant legislation. We have noted that it is unlawful to discriminate against a woman, where on the grounds of her sex she is treated less favourably than a man would be treated. This has interesting implications in the area of dismissal. The Ministry of Defence carried out a policy of forcing all female service personnel who became pregnant to resign. In 1990 the House of Lords ruled that this policy was contrary to EC Directive 76/207 outlawing sexual discrimination at the workplace. Therefore, all those personnel who had been forced to resign were deemed to have been discriminatorily dismissed.

There are currently hundreds of cases involving dismissed female service personnel waiting to be heard by industrial tribunals. It is estimated that the Ministry of Defence has so far paid out £10.3 million in compensation for these types of cases. It is estimated that there are around 4,000 potential claimants and the total compensation payments may exceed £50 million. Currently, there are 1,929 former service personnel who have lodged a complaint alleging sexual discrimination.

The case of *Marshall v. Southampton and SW Hampshire Area Health Authority (No. 2) 3* (1993) IRLR 445 established that the maximum statutory limit of £11,000 (from the EPA78) was no longer valid for persons employed by the State, being in contravention of the EC Directive on Equal Treatment. There is now no maximum to the amount that may be awarded. For private-sector employees, there will soon be regulations passed that will abolish the maximum statutory limit. The maximum limit on claims for racial discrimination, which currently stands at £11,000, will also be abolished by the issue of new regulations. In April 1994, a former army major was awarded £299,851, after resigning to comply with army policy when she became pregnant. This large award was drastically reduced when the Ministry of Defence appealed against it.

Dismissal

It is possible to distinguish four different types of dismissal:

1 actual;
2 constructive;
3 fixed-term contracts;
4 dismissal after maternity leave.

Actual dismissal

This occurs when an employer dispenses with the services of an employee, either by letter or face to face at the workplace. It is relatively simple to establish when an actual dismissal has taken place. It would be for an industrial tribunal to decide whether the dismissal was fair or not. An instant actual dismissal could be fair in a number of circumstances, for example, where an employee assaulted his or her employer.

Constructive dismissal

This is the reverse of actual dismissal because it is the employee who quits his or her job after the employer has done something that has affected the employee or the employee's position so fundamentally as to breach the contract. Examples of such conduct by an employer are: moving the employee to a different location; physically assaulting the employee; lowering the employee's wages; and verbal abuse of the employee. It will still be for an industrial tribunal to decide on the fairness of the dismissal, notwithstanding the above examples.

▶ In one set of circumstances, when an employer told an employee to 'f*** off' if he did not like the job, the tribunal held that this did not amount to an unfair dismissal. The language used was normal for that industry. In another case where the same language was used, the tribunal held that it did amount to unfair dismissal.

Fixed-term contracts

A failure to renew a fixed-term contract will result in a dismissal. It is possible for an employer to make it a term of the contract that there will be no right for an employee to claim for unfair dismissal, where a fixed-term contract is to run for one year or more.

Dismissal after maternity leave

A woman who has been on maternity leave and has satisfied the criteria for being eligible for maternity pay has a right under the EPA78, s. 39, to return to work. If her old position is no longer available because of some change or reorganization in the business, she must be offered suitable alternative employment. If an employer refuses to reinstate such an employee, a dismissal will be deemed to have taken place (EPA78, s. 56). If there is alternative employment which is not offered to her, she will be able to claim for unfair dismissal. If she refuses an offer of alternative employment, she will not be able to make any claim against the employer. If no alternative employment is available she will be considered to have been made redundant.

▶ For the new provisions relating to maternity in TURERA93, see p. 394 below.

 Make notes on the four different types of dismissal. What is the fundamental difference between actual and constructive dismissal?

Automatically unfair dismissal

The law dictates that in certain circumstances a dismissal will always be unfair. The law for this is contained mostly in the EPA78. Aspects relating to trade unions are contained in the TULRA92. The following are the major circumstances in which dismissal will automatically be unfair.

Pregnancy

EPA78, s. 56
Failure to reinstate after pregnancy constitutes automatically unfair dismissal.

TURERA93, s. 23
An employee will automatically be deemed to have been unfairly dismissed where the principal reason for her dismissal is that she was pregnant or where she was dismissed for any other reason connected with her pregnancy. There is no requirement for a person who has been so dismissed, or made redundant, to have been in continuous employment for two years.

The following case gives a recent illustration of how the European Court of Justice interprets sex discrimination relating to pregnancy.

Webb v. EMO Air Cargo (UK), The Times, 15 July 1994

Mrs Webb was recruited by EMO as a replacement for one of its staff, who was due to take maternity leave some six months later. The defendants employed Mrs Webb to work alongside their pregnant member of staff, prior to that member of staff taking maternity leave, so that she could be trained to perform her duties. EMO also envisaged keeping Mrs Webb employed after the return from maternity leave of the member of staff. Two weeks after commencing her employment, Mrs Webb became pregnant. Upon hearing of her pregnancy, the defendants dismissed her. Mrs Webb brought proceedings, claiming unfair dismissal on the grounds of direct sex discrimination. Mrs Webb was unsuccessful in the Industrial Tribunal, on appeal at the Employment Tribunal, and at the Court of Appeal. However, the Court of Appeal gave leave for an appeal to the House of Lords, who referred the matter to the European Court of Justice.

 COURT HELD
Mrs Webb had been the subject of direct discrimination on the grounds of sex. It was unjustifiable to dismiss a pregnant woman who had been employed on a contract for an indefinite period, merely on the basis of her future temporary absence from that position. The European Court of Justice was interpreting the Council Directive 76/207/EEC of 9 February 1976 relating to the equal treatment of men and women in employment. Mrs Webb can now pursue her claim for unfair dismissal.

Health and safety

EPA78, s. 57(a)

If an employee who has been designated as having responsibility for health and safety takes some action in relation to his or her duties, and is dismissed for that action, such a dismissal would be automatically unfair, regardless of age and length of continuous employment. An example might be where an employee felt that there was danger at the workplace and he or she felt that it was necessary to prevent employees from entering or returning to the workplace.

TURERA93, Sch. 5

Schedule 5 has made some important amendments to the EPA78 relating to health and safety. Employees now have a right not to be dismissed, and not to be treated less favourably, on the grounds that they were carrying out their function as a safety representative, or where they have left their workplace or taken appropriate steps to protect others in circumstances of serious and imminent danger. The dismissal of a person who is exercising a statutory right has also been made automatically unfair.

EPA78, s. 59: Redundancy

Dismissal on grounds of redundancy would be unfair where there has been some unfairness in the selection of a particular employee for redundancy.

EPA78, s. 60(a): Action taken by employee

If an employee brings an action against his or her employer to enforce a statutory right – for example, an action under the EPA78 – and is dismissed for that action, such a dismissal would be unfair.

EPA78, s. 63: Pressure to dismiss

The dismissal of an employee would be unfair if pressure has been put on the employer to dismiss the employee, perhaps by other employees. An example of such pressure might be a threatened strike by unionized workers who were seeking to get their employer to sack a non-union employee.

TULRA92, s. 152: Trade unions

If an employee proposes to become a member of a trade union, takes part in union activities or refuses to become a member of a trade union, and is dismissed for so doing, such a dismissal would be unfair. This section not only protects the right of a person to engage in trade union activities, it also, in effect, outlaws the **closed-shop** agreement.

Employment regulations

The Transfer of Undertakings (Protection of Employment) Regulations 1981 (TUR81) rule that where a business, or part of a business, is sold or transferred, then the employees are transferred with the

▶ **Closed shop** – the practice whereby only those people who belonged to a particular union could be employed at a particular workplace or in a particular industry.

▶ See *Meikle v. McPhail* on p. 397 below.

business. If they are dismissed then their dismissal will automatically be considered to be unfair. Where the old or new employer dismisses an employee just before or after the transfer, the employer will have a defence if he or she can show that the dismissal was for economic, technical or organizational reasons and that in the circumstances the dismissal was reasonable.

Maternity rights

TURERA93 has, it is hoped, gone some way to establishing a clear set of rules on maternity rights for the courts to interpret. The most important amendments are summarized below.

- The dismissal of an employee on any grounds related to her pregnancy is now an automatically unfair dismissal.
- All pregnant employees have a right to fourteen weeks' maternity leave.
- Where an employee is dismissed for a reason related to pregnancy, she may now claim for unfair dismissal, regardless of length of service.

(ACT) Without looking back at the last section, list the circumstances under which a dismissal will automatically be unfair. There are nine main sets of circumstances. If you did not get them all, refer back and then try again.

TURERA93, s. 25
Where, because of health and safety regulations, a woman cannot continue to work in an environment because of pregnancy, she must be offered suitable alternative employment or, where there is no suitable alternative, she may be suspended with pay.

Two-tier benefits
There is now a two-tier set of maternity benefits dependent upon an employee's length of service. All employees will have the right to fourteen weeks' maternity leave. Employees with two or more years' continuous service will have the right to return to work at any time up to twenty-nine weeks after the birth of the child, while those with less than two years' service will only have the right to return up to fourteen weeks. In both cases, employees must conform with the relevant provisions for notifying the employer of their intention to return to work.

Reasons for fair dismissal

An employer must give an employee written notice of the reasons for the dismissal (EPA78, s. 53). In order to defeat an action for unfair dismissal an employer must show that the facts of the case illustrate that they acted fairly and reasonably. The industrial tribunal will determine, on the basis of the given facts, whether the dismissal was unfair. The EPA78, s. 57, outlines reasons that may be used by an employer as fair and reasonable in justifying dismissal.

EPA78, s. 57(2A): Capability or qualifications

A reason for dismissal would be fair and reasonable if it is related to the capability or qualifications of the employee for performing work of the kind that he or she was employed by the employer to do. Clearly, an employee should be capable of performing the job that he or she has been employed to do. If the employee is not capable, then an employer will be justified in dismissing him or her. It is not that simple, however, because an employer has a duty to ensure that an employee is properly trained to be able to perform the tasks asked of them. An airline pilot who failed to land a plane properly, causing damage to the plane, was held to be justly dismissed under this section. The next case illustrates an instance where incompetence was not found to be a just reason for the dismissal.

Davison v. Kent Meters Ltd **(1975) IRLR 145**

An employee assembled around 500 parts in the wrong order. She claimed that the charge hand had shown her how to complete the tasks and that she had completed them as shown. The charge hand denied showing the employee how to work and stated that she should have known how to do it.

 COURT HELD

The dismissal was unfair. If the charge hand had not shown her how to perform the operations, he should have done. Further, if she had been more closely supervised then her work could have been corrected.

EPA78, s. 57(2B): Conduct

There are many types of conduct that will enable an employee to be justly dismissed. They include violence, theft, drunkenness, incompetence, dangerous behaviour, refusal or failure to obey a lawful order, failure to comply with safety regulations, abusive behaviour, sleeping at work and failing to observe the prescribed dress standard at work.

This last type of conduct is illustrated in the following famous case.

Boychuk v. HJ Symons (Holdings) Ltd **(1977) IRLR 395**

The plaintiff, a female accounts audit clerk, was employed by the defendants. Her duties involved her in meeting with the general public. She began to wear badges at work that stated both her support for lesbians and the fact that she was a lesbian. Her employers took no substantive action against her until she started to wear a white badge with the words 'Lesbians ignite' written in large letters upon it. She was asked to remove the badge, which she refused to do. The defendants advised her that she would be dismissed if she failed to remove the badge. The plaintiff was subsequently dismissed and she brought an action for unfair dismissal.

COURT HELD

The Employment Appeal Tribunal decided that the employer was acting reasonably and was, therefore, entitled to dismiss the plaintiff. An employer must have the discretion to decide which sort of dress conduct in the workplace might be offensive to work colleagues or customers.

ACT You are a personnel manager. Nancy, an employee, has just come to see you for advice. She is pregnant and wants to know what her maternity rights are. What benefits would she be entitled to if she had been continuously employed for (a) five weeks, (b) nineteen months or (c) fifteen years?

Where an employee is convicted of a criminal offence outside the workplace, an employer can normally justifiably dismiss the employee.

EPA78, s. 57(2C): Redundancy

An employee may justifiably be made redundant, i.e. dismissed because the job is no longer in existence. However, a redundancy may still be an unfair dismissal if the employer acts less fairly towards the redundant employee than towards other redundant employees. In *Williams v. Compair Maxam Ltd* (1982) ICR 156, the Employment Appeal Tribunal laid down five principles that an employer should follow to ensure correct and fair procedures for the selection of redundancies:

(a) the employer should give employees and trade unions as much notice as possible of forthcoming redundancies;
(b) the employer should consult with the trade unions to arrive at the best method of effecting the redundancies and the criteria for selection should be agreed;
(c) the criteria for selecting employees for redundancy should be objective and, therefore, be capable of being checked;
(d) the selection for redundancy should be made in accordance with the selection criteria;
(e) an employer should attempt to find alternative employment for an employee who is to be made redundant.

The above principles are only guidelines. Breach of any one of the guidelines will not automatically result in an unfair dismissal. The guidelines are more appropriate for a large company when a lot of redundancies are to be made.

A small enterprise may still be able to make a person redundant on economic grounds. The following case is a good example of the application of this point.

Meikle v. McPhail (Charleston Arms) (1983) IRLR 351

The plaintiff was a barmaid who was made redundant by the defendants, the new owners of the pub. She claimed that the dismissal was automatically unfair under the TUR81. The defendants claimed the defence of economic need for the redundancy, made available to them by the TUR81.

COURT HELD
The redundancy did not amount to an unfair dismissal. The new employer had made the decision for economic reasons and had not been unfair in selecting the plaintiff for redundancy.

EPA78, s. 57(2D): Contravention of a duty or restriction imposed by an enactment

A reason for dismissal would be fair and reasonable, according to the EPA78, s. 57(2D), if 'the employee could not continue to work in the position which he held without contravention (either on his part or on that of his employer) of a duty or restriction imposed by or under an enactment'.

It may not be immediately apparent what this section is getting at. Two examples may help, however. Where Parliament closes down an employer for running a dangerous business, then the employees who lose their jobs will not have been unfairly dismissed. If a driving licence is vital to the performance of an employee's job and he or she becomes banned from driving, the employer will be able to dismiss the employee.

The above legislation does not cover all the circumstances under which an employee may be fairly and reasonably dismissed. We shall now examine some of the other occasions when an employee may be reasonably and fairly dismissed.

► In one interesting case, it was held that a salesperson who lost his licence and hired a chauffeur to enable him to perform his duties was unfairly dismissed. His employers should have given him time to see if the arrangement could have worked.

Other substantial reason

Where an employer seeks to use some other substantial reason to justify dismissal the employer must have, at all times, acted reasonably and fairly. This means that any **grievance and disciplinary procedures** must normally have been followed.

There are many cases, other than those outlined above, in which employers could show to an industrial tribunal that they acted fairly and reasonably in the circumstances. For example, where the employee is under suspicion of a crime, especially theft from his or

► **Grievance and disciplinary procedures** – the contract of employment will normally contain the procedure to be followed in case of a complaint, a dispute or where disciplinary action is to be taken. In disciplinary action the standard provision is for one or two verbal warnings, to be followed by two written warnings and then dismissal.

her employer, then dismissal might be justified if the employer could produce some evidence to support his or her suspicions, such as money regularly missing from a till when the employee was working at that till. However, in such a case the suspension of the employee until any criminal court action has been completed is the more normal procedure to follow. In such a case the employer must make a fair and reasonable investigation, allowing the employee to make any comments or to suggest any innocent explanations in answer to any allegation.

Where commercial necessity dictates, an employer is allowed a certain leeway to change the terms of the contract of employment. Clearly, there is no legal obligation on an employee to accept a change in the terms or conditions of his or her employment. If an employee refuses any change then an employer might have reasonable grounds for dismissing him or her. If an employer changes the working hours of the business and certain of the employees refuse to accept the change, then those employees can be held to have been fairly dismissed. However, it must be commercially necessary for an employer to make changes for such a dismissal to be fair.

An employer may be able to dismiss an employee to protect the business. Examples of this have been found where two close family members have been employed in a business and one has either moved to a rival employer or set up a rival business, leaving the existing member of the family in the employer's business. An industrial tribunal has held that it is was fair and reasonable to dismiss the remaining family member. The people concerned would have to be close family, i.e. husband and wife or, perhaps, brothers and sisters.

FRUSTRATION AND THE CONTRACT OF EMPLOYMENT

The normal rules of frustration apply to a contract of employment. There must be some intervening event that, not being the fault of either party, renders the performance of the contract impossible. Where there is blame attached to either party, the contract will not be frustrated and the injured party may bring an action for repudiatory breach. Frustration will normally arise in three sets of circumstances: imprisonment, death and long-term absence, normally through sickness or injury.

Imprisonment

The more normal rule is that imprisonment will frustrate a contract. However, there is a view that the party who is imprisoned is to blame, and therefore the contract cannot be frustrated. This view is illustrated by the case of *Norris v. Southampton City Council* (see Chapter 13, p. 225), where the plaintiff, a cleaner, was imprisoned and his employers wrote and dismissed him. Norris claimed unfair dismissal. The case went to the Employment Appeal Tribunal, which held that Norris had rendered himself unable to perform the contract, and that his actions amounted to a repudiatory breach of contract.

Absence

The long-term sickness of an employee (or even an employer) may lead to the frustration of the contract. An employer would have to consider the following factors before treating the contract as being frustrated:

- the size and resources of the business organization;
- the nature of the illness and the prospects for recovery;
- the length of absence;
- the need to hire a replacement and the possible implications of that;
- the length of time that the employee has been employed;
- the level of skills of the employee;
- the terms of the contract.

The mere absence from work for a long period of time will not automatically frustrate a contract. Conversely, a relatively short absence may frustrate the contract where a person is highly skilled and a replacement is immediately needed.

Death

The death of an employee or employer will discharge a contract from the date of the death. An employee may make a claim for redundancy against the employer's estate. Where an employee is re-engaged, or an offer of re-engagement is made within eight weeks of the death, by the employer's personal representatives, the employee will not be considered to have been dismissed. If the employee unreasonably refuses such an offer, the employee will lose his or her right to a redundancy payment.

TERMINATION BY OTHER MEANS

A contract of service may also be ended by the methods examined below.

Notice

As discussed in Chapter 20, a contract of service may be brought to an end by either party giving the required notice. Where an employer breaches the required period of notice, an industrial tribunal will take that into account when calculating an award. The employer will not otherwise be penalized.

Termination by agreement

An employee and employer may mutually agree to end a contract. If this happens, the employee will not have the right to claim for unfair dismissal. A person who agrees to be made voluntarily redundant, however, will have the right to a redundancy payment. Where a person accepts a new contract of employment from his or her existing employer – for example, upon promotion – the existing contract is said to be terminated by agreement.

Discharge by performance

A contract may be terminated by performance, where a person has been employed to complete a specific task. For example, a computer systems designer would be employed to fit a new computer system. At the completion of the task no dismissal would be deemed to have taken place. Similarly a fixed-term contract will terminate upon the expiry of the fixed term: for example, a three-month contract will terminate at the end of three months.

Termination after pregnancy

Where an employee elects not to return to work after maternity leave, the contract becomes terminated and no dismissal is deemed to have taken place.

Partnership dissolution

Where a partnership is dissolved, through death, resignation or bankruptcy, an employee will be considered to have been made redundant.

Administration orders

► To refresh your minds on the different ways in which a company may be terminated, refer to Chapter 8, pp. 118–19.

When an administrator is appointed to take control of a company, the employees are not automatically deemed to be dismissed. If the administrator continues to trade with the company then the employees' contracts will normally be taken on. Indeed, if an administrator fails to notify employees otherwise, they will automatically be adopted within fourteen days of the administrator being appointed. If employees are adopted, they will be entitled to their wages before the administrator can claim his or her fees or expenses, out of the company's assets. If employees are dismissed, they will be entitled to a redundancy payment, the dismissed employee becoming an unsecured creditor for the value of the redundancy payment.

Administrative receiver

Where the administrative receiver is appointed by debenture holders, the provisions are similar to those that apply when an administrator is appointed. However, it is normal for the managing director of the company to be dismissed. Where a receiver is appointed by a court, all employees' contracts are terminated and they have a right to claim for redundancy. A receiver may offer to re-employ the employees, which is an offer to be employed by the receiver, not one to continue employment with their previous employer.

Bankruptcy

Where a person is made bankrupt the contracts of any employees will not automatically end, unless there is a term in the contract to that effect. In practice, the bankrupt will no longer have the means of paying any employees and they will be considered to be dismissed. Employees so dismissed will be able to make a claim for redundancy and will also be able to become preferential creditors for any wages or other monies owed to them.

Company liquidation

A company may be voluntarily wound up by a resolution being passed by its members or it may be compulsorily wound up by a court order. In the latter case the employees are dismissed and they may claim for unfair dismissal. Where a court places a receiver in charge to continue trading, instead of winding up the company, the employees may either be considered to be continuing in their employment or they may consider themselves to be dismissed, depending on whether the receiver is able to offer to continue their employment. Where a company is voluntarily wound up and ceases trading, the employees are deemed to be fairly dismissed, and they may make a claim for redundancy. If the company continues to trade then the position is the same as if the company had been compulsorily wound up and had continued to trade.

► Refer back to Chapter 8 to remind yourself of the procedures of liquidation that are discussed here.

 Outline the different effects that an administration order, bankruptcy and the voluntary winding up of a company will have upon employment contracts.

REMEDIES

An industrial tribunal may award one of three main remedies for unfair dismissal, though the vast majority of successful claimants, some 75 to 80 per cent, will receive an award of compensation. Originally, it was thought that the tribunals would make more use of their power to order the **reinstatement** or the **re-engagement** of a claimant.

The compensation order has evolved as the most practical remedy. Where an employee has been in dispute with his or her employer, bad feelings may have developed between them and it would not be sensible for the employee to return to the same employment. Further, it may not be practicable for an industrial tri-

► **Reinstatement** – where the employee is given his or her old job back, at the same level and on the same pay and conditions.

► **Re-engagement** – where the employee is given a different job or the same job back on different terms and conditions.

bunal to order one of the other remedies. For example, in the time that the action has taken to come before the tribunal, an employer may have recruited other staff, or the job may have changed or may no longer be in existence.

Compensation

The amount of compensation to be awarded, and the criteria for calculating the award, are contained in the EPA78, ss. 72–9. Compensation is made up of two elements: a basic award and a compensatory award. The basic award is calculated after account is taken of the employee's age, length of service and weekly wage at the time of his or her dismissal. In certain circumstances an industrial tribunal may also award an additional or a special award.

Basic award (EPA78, s. 73)

The following formula is used in calculating both the basic award and the redundancy payment.

(a) For each complete year of
employment when the employee
was aged 41 or more   1½ weeks' pay
(b) For each complete year of
employment when the employee
was aged between 22 and 41   1 week's pay
(c) For each complete year of
employment when the employee
was aged between 18 and 22   ½ week's pay

An employee may only claim for a maximum of twenty years' employment, at a maximum weekly wage that is currently set at £205. Therefore, the maximum award is 20 x 1½ x £205 = £6,150.

Compensatory award (EPA78, s. 74)

A compensatory award is meant to compensate the employee for all the other losses that he or she will incur because of the unfair dismissal. These may include:

• expenses in bringing the action;
• loss of earnings up to the date of the hearing;
• loss of future earnings;
• loss of any statutory right;
• loss of any other benefits, such as company car, pension benefits or health insurance.

The maximum amount for a compensatory award is currently set at £10,000.

Additional award (EPA78, s. 78)

This may be given where an employer refuses to comply with an order of reinstatement or re-engagement where the dismissal is not automatically unfair. Where the dismissal was contrary to the Race

▶ In an automatically unfair dismissal – for example, where a person has been sacked for taking part in union activities – the minimum award will be £2,700 (EPA78).

▶ An employee may be found to have contributed to his or her dismissal and, on the same basis as contributory negligence, may have his or her award reduced accordingly: for example, 20 per cent where the employee was 20 per cent to blame. An employee is also under a duty to mitigate his or her losses, i.e. get, or try to get, another job. An industrial tribunal will take a failure to attempt to mitigate losses into consideration when assessing an award.

Relations Act 1976 or the Sex Discrimination Act 1975, then the award will be calculated as follows.

(a) Between 26 and 52 weeks' pay, at a maximum weekly rate of £205, being a minimum of £5,350 and a maximum of £10,660. In other cases (i.e. not unfairly dismissed through sexual or racial discrimination) the award will be calculated as below.
(b) Between 13 and 26 weeks' pay, at a maximum weekly rate of £205, being a maximum of £5,350 and a minimum of £2,665.

Special award (EPA78, s. 75A)

When a person has been subject to a dismissal that is automatically unfair, this award may be paid when an industrial tribunal has not ordered the employer to reinstate or to re-engage the employee, though the employee has asked to be re-engaged or reinstated. The special award shall be paid at the following rate:

(a) one week's pay × 104, or
(b) £13,400, whichever is the greater, but not exceeding £26,800.

There is no limit on the amount paid per week to be used in the calculation.

Where an employer refuses to reinstate or re-engage an employee, or fails to show good reason why he or she will not implement an order to reinstate or to re-engage an employee, the award may be increased according to the following calculation:

(a) one week's pay × 156, or
(b) £20,100, whichever is the greater.

Again there is no limit on the amount paid per week to be used in the calculation and no upper limit on the amount that could be paid.

▶ Brian has been found to have been unfairly dismissed. He is now 35 and had worked for his employer for seventeen years. His salary was £185 per week when he was dismissed. Calculate his redundancy payment.

COMMON-LAW REMEDIES

Almost all claimants rely on the statutory remedies available to them, though there exists a right of action at common law for damages, for breach of contract. However, people in certain occupations, such as football managers and chief executives, who tend to be employed on fixed-term contracts for large salaries, often sue for breach of contract. This is because they are often able to obtain a larger amount for damages than they would under the statutory provisions.

At common law a claim may be made for the loss of salary that would have been earned under the contract and loss of other benefits. Clearly, a person who is on a five-year fixed-term contract, being paid £75,000 per year, is going to be better off suing for damages at common law. The duty to mitigate still applies, but even so the chances are that the amount that will be awarded at common law will be far in excess of a statutory payment.

▶ See Chapter 13, p. 238, for an example of how an injunction may still be used in a contract of service. Remember Bette Davis?

Other common-law remedies

The equitable remedies of specific performance and injunction may not be used to compel a person to work, nor to compel a person to attend a place of work.

Trade Unions and Labour Relations (Consolidation) Act 1992, s. 236

No court shall, either by way of:
(a) an order for specific performance or specific implement of a contract of employment, or
(b) an injunction or interdict restraining a breach or a threatened breach of such a contract,
compel an employee to do any work or attend any place for the doing of any work.

Therefore, apart from the use of an injunction as a negative stipulation, it would seem that a court is unlikely to be able to grant either of these common-law remedies. Indeed, courts are becoming increasingly less likely to allow the use of an injunction in contracts of employment, even as a negative stipulation.

REDUNDANCY

The Redundancy Payments Act 1965 established the right of an employee to a redundancy payment. The EPA78 gives a definition of when redundancy has occurred.

EPA78, s. 81

(2) For the purposes of this Act an employee who is dismissed shall be taken to be dismissed by reason of redundancy if the dismissal is attributable wholly or mainly to:
(a) the fact that his employer has ceased, or intends to cease, to carry on the business for the purposes of which the employer was employed by him, or has ceased, or intends to cease, to carry on that business in the place where the employee was so employed, or
(b) the fact that the requirements of that business for employees to carry out work of a particular kind in the place where he was so employed, have ceased or diminished or are expected to cease or diminish.

To qualify for a redundancy payment an employee must have been continuously employed in the position for two years since reaching the age of 18 and must be under the age of statutory retirement (65). Several types of employees are excluded from being able to make a claim for redundancy by the EPA78. They include domestic servants who are closely related to their employers, those employed fully or mostly outside the UK and those employees on a fixed-term contract of two years or more, who have agreed to forgo their right to make a claim for redundancy.

In some circumstances it is easy to recognize whether or not a redundancy has occurred. For example, if a local village store closes down because it cannot compete with a newly opened hypermarket, any shop worker who fits the eligibility criteria will be able to make a claim. However, on some occasions it will be less clear whether a redundancy has occurred or not.

We have learned that the management has the right to make commercial decisions to change work patterns, locations, etc., and that if staff refuse to change they will be dismissed, losing their right to a claim for redundancy. The definition of redundancy in the Act is not absolutely clear and the industrial tribunals will judge each case on its merits, normally examining the contract of employment to establish if a redundancy has taken place. Where an employee has a so-called 'mobility clause' in his or her contract, i.e. is contracted to work where the employer directs him or her, and the employee ceases to work in a particular area, he or she will not be able to refuse to move to work in a different area and make a claim for redundancy. In such a case he or she will be deemed to be dismissed for misconduct. Where there is no mobility clause in the contract, an employee would be able to make a claim for redundancy.

► Do not forget that in the previous chapter and earlier in this one we have stated that an employee could lose his or her right to redundancy in the following circumstances: where they are dismissed while on strike; where they are dismissed for misconduct; where they have accepted an alternative offer of employment from the employer; or where they have refused to accept a reasonable offer of alternative employment.

► To calculate the amount of a redundancy payment, refer back to the formula used to calculate a basic award for unfair dismissal.

 Now that you have completed this chapter, look back at the chapter objectives at the beginning. Can you do all the things that these suggest? If not, look again at the relevant sections of the chapter.

CHAPTER SUMMARY

1 Industrial tribunals deal with complaints made by employees who allege that they have been unfairly dismissed, made redundant or have been treated in contravention of any other Act relating to employment, or racial or sexual discrimination.
2 The ruling in the *EOC v. Secretary of State for Employment* (1994) changed the law relating to the amount of hours needed to be worked per week, to qualify under the EPA78 for unfair dismissal or redundancy payments.
3 An actual dismissal will occur when an employer dispenses with the services of an employee. Constructive dismissal is deemed to have happened when an employee leaves his or her employ because the employer has done something that fundamentally breaches the contract of employment.
4 A dismissal will always be unfair in the following circumstances:
   • failure to reinstate after pregnancy or for any reason related to a pregnancy;
   • dismissal of an employee for reasons relating to his or her activities as a health and safety officer.

- dismissal on grounds of redundancy, where there has been unfairness in the selection of a person for redundancy;
- dismissal of an employee who has brought an action against his or her employer to enforce a statutory right;
- dismissal of an employee where pressure has been put on an employer to dismiss him or her;
- dismissal of an employee for a reason relating to trade union activities;
- dismissal where a business has been sold or transferred.

5 A dismissal may be shown to be fair and justifiable by an employer under the EPA78:
- where an employee is found to be incapable of performing the task for which he or she has been employed;
- for a reason related to the conduct of an employee;
- where an employee has been made redundant;
- for a reason relating to a duty or restriction imposed by law;
- for another substantial reason.

6 Frustration of a contract of employment may be deemed to have occurred in cases of death, imprisonment and long-term absence, normally through sickness.

7 A contract of service may also be terminated:
- by the giving of the required period of notice;
- by agreement;
- by performance;
- after pregnancy, where a woman declines to return to work;
- upon the dissolution of a partnership;
- where a company is wound up or placed into liquidation;
- where an employer is made bankrupt.

8 An industrial tribunal may award one of three main remedies for unfair dismissal: compensation, reinstatement or re-engagement. Over 75 per cent of successful claimants receive an award of compensation.

9 An employee who has been made redundant has the right to receive a redundancy payment. To qualify for such a payment an employee must be aged 18 or over, and have been continuously employed for a period of two years, from that age.

Appendix 1: Unfair Terms in Consumer Contracts Regulations 1994
(Implemented by SI 1994 No 3159)

Schedule 3

1 **Terms which have the object or effect of –**

(a) excluding or limiting the legal liability of a seller or supplier in the event of the death of a consumer or personal injury to the latter resulting from an act or omission of that seller or supplier;

(b) inappropriately excluding or limiting the legal rights of the consumer vis-à-vis the seller or supplier or another party in the event of total or partial non-performance or inadequate performance by the seller or supplier of any of the contractual obligations, including the option of offsetting a debt owed to the seller or supplier against any claim which the consumer may have against him;

(c) making an agreement binding on the consumer whereas provision of services by the seller or supplier is subject to a condition whose realisation depends on his own will alone;

(d) permitting the seller or supplier to retain sums paid by the consumer where the latter decides not to conclude or perform the contract, without providing for the consumer to receive compensation of an equivalent amount from the seller or supplier where the latter is the party cancelling the contract;

(e) requiring any consumer who fails to fulfil his obligation to pay a disproportionately high sum in compensation;

(f) authorising the seller or supplier to dissolve the contract on a discretionary basis where the same facility is not granted to the consumer, or permitting the seller or supplier to retain the sums paid for services not yet supplied by him where it is the seller or supplier himself who dissolves the contract;

(g) enabling the seller or supplier to terminate a contract of indeterminate duration without reasonable notice except where there are serious grounds for doing so;

(h) automatically extending a contract of fixed duration where the consumer does not indicate otherwise, when the deadline fixed for the consumer to express this desire not to extend the contract is unreasonably early;

(i) irrevocably binding the consumer to terms with which he had no real opportunity of becoming acquainted before the conclusion of the contract;

(j) enabling the seller or supplier to alter the terms of the contract unilaterally without a valid reason which is specified in the contract;

(k) enabling the seller or supplier to alter unilaterally without a valid reason any characteristics of the product or service to be provided;

(l) providing for the price of goods to be determined at the time of delivery or allowing a seller of goods or supplier of services to increase their price without in both cases giving the consumer the corresponding right to cancel the contract if the final price is too high in relation to the price agreed when the contract was concluded;

(m) giving the seller or supplier the right to determine whether the goods or services supplied are in conformity with the contract, or giving him the exclusive right to interpret any term of the contract;

(n) limiting the seller's or supplier's obligation to respect commitments undertaken by his agents or making his commitments subject to compliance with a particular formality;

(o) obliging the consumer to fulfil all his obligations where the seller or supplier does not perform his;

(p) giving the seller or supplier the possibility of transferring his rights and obligations under the contract, where this may serve to reduce the guarantees for the consumer, without the latter's agreement;

(q) excluding or hindering the consumer's right to take legal action or exercise any other legal remedy, particularly by requiring the consumer to take disputes exclusively to arbitration not covered by legal provisions, unduly restricting the evidence available to him or imposing on him a burden of proof which, according to the applicable law, should lie with another party to the contract.

2 Scope of subparagraphs 1(g), (j) and (l)

(a) Subparagraph 1(g) is without hindrance to terms by which a supplier of financial services reserves the right to terminate unilaterally a contract of indeterminate duration without notice where there is a valid reason, provided that the supplier is required to inform the other contracting party or parties thereof immediately.

(b) Subparagraph 1(j) is without hindrance to terms under which a supplier of financial services reserves the right to alter the rate of interest payable by the consumer or due to the latter, or the amount of other charges for financial services without notice where there is a valid reason, provided that the supplier is required to inform the other contracting party or parties thereof at the earliest opportunity and that the latter are free to dissolve the contract immediately. Subparagraph 1(j) is also without hindrance to terms under which a seller or supplier reserves the right to alter unilaterally the conditions of a contract of indeterminate duration, provided that he is required to inform the consumer with reasonable notice and that the consumer is free to dissolve the contract.

(c) Subparagraphs 1(g), (j) and (l) do not apply to:
   – transactions in transferable securities, financial instruments and other products or services where the price is linked to fluctuations in a stock exchange quotation or index or a financial market rate that the seller or supplier does not control;
   – contracts for the purchase or sale of foreign currency, traveller's cheques or international money orders denominated in foreign currency;

(d) Subparagraph 1(l) is without hindrance to price indexation clauses, where lawful, provided that the method by which prices vary is explicitly described.

Appendix 2: Table of statutes

Appendix 3: Table of cases

Page numbers given in bold refer to cases given in detail; those in italic are passing references.

Index